OUR AWESOME LORD

FRANK G. TUNSTALL

CREATION
HOUSE

OUR AWESOME LORD by Frank G. Tunstall
Published by Creation House
A Charisma Media Company
600 Rinehart Road
Lake Mary, Florida 32746
www.charismamedia.com

Unless otherwise noted, all Scripture quotations are from the Holy Bible, New International Version of the Bible. Copyright © 1973, 1978, 1984, International Bible Society. Used by permission.

Scripture quotations marked GW are from *God's Word*, Grand Rapids, MI: World Publishing, 1995.

Scripture quotations marked NLT are from the Holy Bible, New Living Translation, copyright © 2007. Used by permission of Tyndale House Publishers, Inc., Wheaton, IL 60189. All rights reserved.

Scripture quotations marked KJV are from the King James Version of the Bible.

Scripture quotations marked TLB are from The Living Bible. Copyright © 1971. Used by permission of Tyndale House Publishers, Inc., Wheaton, IL 60189. All rights reserved.

Scripture quotations marked THE MESSAGE are from *The Message: The Bible in Contemporary English*, copyright © 1993, 1994, 1995, 1996, 2000, 2001, 2002. Used by permission of NavPress Publishing Group.

Scripture quotations marked NAS are from the New American Standard Bible. Copyright © 1960, 1962, 1963, 1968, 1971, 1972, 1973, 1975, 1977 by the Lockman Foundation. Used by permission. (www.Lockman.org)

Scripture quotations marked NKJV are from the New King James Version of the Bible. Copyright © 1979, 1980, 1982 by Thomas Nelson, Inc., publishers. Used by permission.

Unless otherwise noted, all Greek and Hebrew definitions are from *Strong's Exhaustive Concordance of the Bible*, ed. James Strong (New York: Abingdon Press, 1890).

Cover design by Amanda Potter

Library of Congress Control Number: 2008929193
International Standard Book Number: 978-1-59979-451-8 (hardcover version)
International Standard Book Number: 978-1-59979-609-3 (paperback version)

12 13 14 15 16 — 9 8 7 6 5 4 3 2
Printed in Canada

Our Awesome Lord is my tribute to the Savior who took my hands off a plow when I was a boy and put them on a Bible.

Who is like you—majestic in holiness, awesome in glory, working wonders?

—Exodus 15:11

The people you live among will see how awesome is the work that I, the Lord, will do for you.

—Exodus 34:10

For this reason I kneel before the Father.

—Ephesians 3:14

To Rev. John Swails and Dr. W. R. Corvin, and the late
Rev. H. P. Robinson and the late Dr. R. O. Corvin,
my early mentors in the Word of God

❧ ACKNOWLEDGMENTS

EXPRESS MY HEARTFELT appreciation to a number of dear brothers and sisters, whose advice and counsel have been of great value to me. They have hearts to serve, like our awesome Lord:

Dr. Danny Penny; Rev. Jimmy Whitfield; Dr. Terry Tramel; Dr. Harold Dalton; Dr. Aldon Preston; Rev. Bob Shafer; Chaplain, Lieutenant Colonel Hugh H. Morgan, USAF, Retired; Dr. John Tunstall; Dr. Chuck Chitwood; Rev. John Parker; Rev. L. D. Driggers; Rev. Elvio and June Canavesio; Nina Corvin; Rosa Baker; Jim Tunstall; Peggy Henderson; Rev. Greg Whitlow; and Phyllis Price.

~ CONTENTS

THE APOSTLE PAUL diligently searched the Old Testament through the bifocals of Jesus' cross and resurrection for insight into how Israel's Messiah made atonement for the sins of the whole world. When the Holy Spirit gave him the strategy, Paul admonished his readers, "Your attitude should be the same as that of Christ Jesus" (Phil. 2:5).

The mission of this volume is to explore this attitude, the strategy by which Jesus went about His monumental assignment. In that process, we will seek to discover how Jesus' mindset blesses and inspires all who make His way of thinking their own. Achieving this will also unveil why it is appropriate to describe Jesus Christ as our awesome Lord.

> Your attitude should be the same as that of Christ Jesus: Who, being in very nature God, did not consider equality with God something to be grasped, but made himself nothing, taking the very nature of a servant, being made in human likeness. And being found in appearance as a man, he humbled himself and became obedient to death—even death on a cross! Therefore God exalted him to the highest place and gave him the name that is above every name, that at the name of Jesus every knee should bow, in heaven and on earth and under the earth, and every tongue confess that Jesus Christ is Lord, to the glory of God the Father. Therefore, my dear friends, as you have always obeyed—not only in my presence, but now much more in my absence—continue to work out your salvation with fear and trembling, for it is God who works in you to will and to act according to his good purpose.
>
> —PHILIPPIANS 2:5–13

This study is possible because the Holy Spirit serves with perpetual commitment to unveil the Messiah from the pages of Holy Writ. He blossoms in our lives as the Rose of Sharon and the Lily of the valley (Song of Sol. 2:1; John 16:13–15.)

The Bible is written primarily in masculine language. That usage in this volume embraces feminine equality, too. Brackets "[ ]" are used from time to time to insert information and add emphasis.

Chapter One

THE INCARNATION STRATEGY

My lover is radiant and ruddy, outstanding among ten thousand.
—SONG OF SOLOMON 5:10

Your attitude should be the same as that of Christ Jesus.
—PHILIPPIANS 2:5

He became what we are that He might make us what He is.[1]
—SAINT ATHANASIUS

WHAT PEOPLE COULD not do for themselves in their efforts to reach up to God, Jehovah God did by extending His arm down. Jesus moved from eternity into time, taking into His loving hand the latch to man's heart. He came into the world knowing what it would cost Him, willing from eternity to bear man's sins in His own body on the cross (1 Pet. 2:24.) He who knew no sin became a "leper" like us (Matt. 8:2–3; 2 Cor. 5:21.)

~ My Fellow Lepers ~

Joseph Damien was a nineteenth-century missionary who ministered to lepers on the island of Molokai, Hawaii. The suffering lepers grew to love him, and revered the sacrificial life he lived before them.

One morning before Damien was to lead daily worship, he was pouring some hot water into a cup when the water swirled out and fell on his bare foot. It took him a moment to realize that he had not felt any sensation. Gripped by the sudden fear of what this could mean, he poured more hot water on the same spot. No feeling whatsoever.

Damien immediately knew. He walked tearfully to deliver his sermon. No one at first noticed the difference in his opening line. He normally began every sermon with, "My fellow believers." That morning he began with "My fellow lepers."[2]

I. The Method of the Incarnation

According to God's timeless strategy, His supreme effort to connect with humanity was the actual birth of a special baby, during the reign of Caesar Augustus. The Roman Empire was at its apex.

A. The Incarnation—Planned in Eternity

David understood that God desires worshipers with changed hearts. This was so true the king penned, "Sacrifice and offering [God] did not desire," neither did He want "burnt offerings and sin offerings" (Ps. 40:6). The writer of Hebrews applied the passage to the Messiah and summarized God's agenda for His Son in a single sentence: "A body you prepared for me" (Heb. 10:5). "He is the lamb who was known long ago before the world existed" (1 Pet. 1:20, GW).

God's Son volunteered in eternity to become the incarnate Messiah (John 17:24; Eph. 1:4; and 1 Pet. 1:19–21.) He was looking for people who would worship Him in spirit and in truth (John 4:23–24). The Holy Spirit inspired David to pen how the Son expressed Himself in the long-ago summit of the Godhead that framed the plan of salvation: "Then I said, 'Here I am, I have come—it is written about me in the scroll. I desire to do your will, O God'" (Ps. 40:7–8; see also Heb. 10:7–10). This very special infant's eternal home had been the ivory palaces of glory, yet He condescended to "the company of ordinary people" (Ps. 45:8; Rom. 12:16, NLT).

B. The Trinity and the Incarnation

The Gospel writers present the incarnation in the Trinitarian terms of the Father, the Son, and the Holy Spirit. "This is how the birth of *Jesus Christ* came about," wrote Matthew; after Mary was engaged to Joseph, but before they were married, "she was found to be with child through the *Holy Spirit*" (Matt. 1:18, emphasis added). *God* sent the angel Gabriel to Nazareth to make the announcement to Mary that her baby would be called "the Son of God" (Luke 1:26–28, 32, 35). The Virgin Mary miraculously conceived the child by the creative power of the Holy Spirit, without a sexual union. This Trinitarian focus foreshadows that the Father and the Holy Spirit would be His primary support system while growing up and throughout His earthly ministry (Acts 10:38).

C. The Incarnation Announced by Angels

The angel Gabriel also gave Mary the name for the baby, "Jesus," meaning "savior" (Luke 1:26–33; 2:8–15). His assignment was to "save His people from their sins" (Matt. 1:21).

When the time had fully come, God sent his Son, born of a woman, born under law, to redeem those under law...that we might receive the full rights of sons.

—GALATIANS 4:4–5

Jesus of Nazareth is God become flesh. "He made His dwelling among us" as the promised Messiah (John 1:1, 14, 41). This "rose of Sharon," who sets our hearts to pounding, "is radiant and ruddy, outstanding among ten thousand" (Song of Sol. 2:1; 5:4, 10).

D. A Sinless Incarnation

The holy birth of Jesus explains why the church has always taught He was born without an inherited sin nature. The Babe of Bethlehem's manger was fully human, like all other infants. He was also unlike any other in that Gabriel said He would be "the Holy One" and "the Son of God" (Luke 1:35). The very fact of His sinless birth to the virgin laid the foundation for Him to be the last Adam,1 the perfect sacrifice for sin, and the author of the new covenant (1 Cor. 15:45; Heb. 9:15; 10:12).

God spoke, and Mary conceived the Son of God (Gen. 1:1–3; John 1:1–3, 14). Isaiah prophesied His virgin birth would be one of the clearest indicators the baby really was the Messiah: "The Lord himself will give you a sign: the virgin will be with child, and will give birth to a son, and will call him Immanuel" (Isa. 7:14; Matt. 1:23). The Hebrew term *Immanuel* means "God with us;" hence, Isaiah prophesied both Jesus' virgin birth and His deity. The evidence is incontrovertible, yet no fact of the Christian message has been assailed by critics quite like the Biblical teaching of the Virgin Birth: that Jesus Christ became actual flesh and blood, spotlessly conceived by the Virgin Mary.

E. The Mystery of the Incarnation

While the story of God becoming truly human defies rational explanation, this divine miracle is without question the revelation of Holy Scripture. This redemptive achievement established Jesus as the firstfruits of the new covenant that redeems the sons of Adam and makes them "like God in true righteousness and holiness" (Eph. 4:24).

F. The Incarnation, a Revelation of God as Father

The portrait of God as a Father is implied in the Old Testament, but the Incarnation makes it explicit (Ps. 2:7; Luke 1:32, 35; John 3:16; 1 John 3:1).

---

1 The Greek word translated "last" in 1 Corinthians 15:45 is *eschatos*, which indicates finality. In other words, there will never be another.

The Father's love is deep, so as to be unfathomable; in fact, He is the ultimate model for all fathers. The heavenly Father yearns to pick up and hold in His strong arms each of His fallen children. The Father's Son and our Savior came to the earth to become His Father's arms extended to lost humanity. This is such a fact of the gospel that Jesus told Philip, "Anyone who has seen me has seen the Father" (John 14:9).

As heavenly Father, He is loving and benevolent, as well as tough and determined. However, He is neither arbitrary nor whimsical. Jesus taught that the Father loves everyone and maintains such a continuing knowledge about His own that He is aware of what they need before they ask Him (Matt. 6:8). All may become His children through Christ (John 3:3–5; Matt. 5:45; John 1:12). He delights to give good things to His offspring, including declaring them sons of God and co-heirs with Christ (Matt. 7:11; Rom. 8:17; 1 John 3:2; Ps. 84:11). The incarnation of Jesus unveiled, therefore, a portrait that shows love is the essence of His Father and assures that all humanity can rely on His love (1 John 4:16).

G. The Incarnation and Postmodern Strategy

The virgin birth of Jesus Christ boldly confronts contemporary postmodern thinking. Postmodernism denies the existence of God and of objective truth and asserts that all religious ideas are constructs of individual, fertile imagination. Everything spiritual, in fact, is said to be shaped by the cultural context of a particular time, place, and community. Since God does not exist, neither does objective right or wrong.

Yet, one needs go no further than the Virgin Birth to establish the fatherhood of God, the sonship of Jesus Christ, the reality of objective truth, and the certainty of both right and wrong. The message of the incarnate Christ to all people everywhere is that as a historical event, "God became flesh and dwelt among us" (John 1:14). When Jesus' story is told fully and completely, people worldwide, without fail, find it very attractive.

II. The "Self-Emptying" Strategy

Thomas Aquinas (1225–1274) grew up with all of the blessings of luxury, yet he made the decision as a young man to put aside his wealth and advantages to follow Jesus Christ. Aquinas's parents vigorously opposed his decision.[3]

When God's Son made the choice to empty Himself of His heavenly privileges and attributes and pay the price to redeem the world, it pleased His Father.

God so loved the world that he gave his only begotten Son.

—JOHN 3:16, KJV

⋙ Laying Aside Affluence ⋘

Born into great wealth and privilege, Thomas Aquinas owned his own residence in Naples, as well as his own attendants, and a host of servants. With plumes and flowing silks, he took up riding on horseback around the bay.

Aquinas visited the Blue Grotto and Capri. He had a taste for beauty and liked to repeat Augustine's saying: "If the work of His hands be so lovely, O how much more beautiful must be He who made them."

Then quite suddenly, saying nothing to his parents, Aquinas surrendered all of his privileges and wealth and embraced the Dominican Order of Preachers. He put on their white and black habit, and announced that his titles were henceforth in abeyance. He seemed hardly aware of the furor that inevitably arose from his action.

Aquinas had been a prince and was now vowed to a life of poverty as a wandering friar, and he welcomed the change. His mother complained to the pope and the archbishop of Naples. The pope offered to make him lord abbot of Montecassino with the privilege of wearing his Dominican habit. He refused and wandered alone to Rome. His mind was made up, and he surrendered it all.

Years afterwards, when he came to write the *Summa Theologica*, Aquinas penned Jesus' simple statement beneath the question "Whether duties toward parents are to be set aside for the sake of religion?"

"Whoever loves father or mother more than me," quoted Aquinas, "is not worthy to follow Me." He also cited from Jerome's famous letter to Heliodorus: "Though your father fling himself down on the doorstep, trample him underfoot, go your way and fly with dry eyes to the standard of the Cross."[4]

In his profound Christological statement to his readers in Philippi, the apostle Paul summarized the Godhead's plan of action and enjoined them to choose the Lord's mindset as their own.

Your attitude should be the same as that of Christ Jesus: Who, being in very nature God, did not consider equality with God something to be grasped, but made himself nothing, taking the very nature of a servant, being made in human likeness. And being found in appearance as a man, he humbled himself and became obedient to death—even death on a cross. Therefore God exalted him to the highest place and gave him the name that is above every name, that at the name of Jesus every knee should bow, in heaven and on earth and under the earth, and every tongue confess that Jesus Christ is Lord, to the glory of God the Father. Therefore, my dear friends, as you have always obeyed—not only in my presence, but now much more in my absence—continue to work out your salvation with fear and trembling, for it is God who works in you to will and to act according to his good purpose.

—PHILIPPIANS 2:5–13

Fundamental to understanding this blueprint is the fact that Jesus Christ was both divine and human, two natures in one person.

A. Two Natures—His Divinity

"Being in very nature God," is the way Paul described the Messiah (Phil. 2:6). The apostle wrote to the Colossians, "In [Christ] dwelleth all the fullness of the Godhead bodily. And ye are complete in him" (Col. 2:9–10, KJV). Jeremiah the 3 foretold His incarnation in these terms: "'The time is coming,' says the LORD [Jehovah], 'when I will place a righteous descendant from King David's line. He will be a King who rules with wisdom. He will do what is just and right throughout the land. And this will be his name: 'The LORD Is Our Righteousness'" [Jehovah Tsidkenu] (Jer. 23:5–6, NLT). In this statement, Jeremiah said the Messiah would be a descendant of David, but also announced He would carry the name Jehovah. The passage is another of the strong prophecies in the Old Testament of the deity of Jesus Christ.

The Nicene Creed of A.D. 325 gives a clear formulation of the divinity of Jesus:

> We believe…in one Lord Jesus Christ, the only-begotten Son of God, Begotten of the Father before all the ages, Light of Light, true God of true God, begotten not made, of one substance with the Father, through whom all things were made; who for us men and for our salvation came down from the heavens, and was made flesh of the Holy Spirit and the Virgin Mary, and became man…[5]

The Chalcedonian Creed of A.D. 451 says:

> Following the holy fathers, we all with one accord teach men to acknowledge…two natures, without confusion, without change, without division, without separation; the distinction of natures being in no way annulled by the union, but rather the characteristics of each nature being preserved and coming together to form

one person and subsistence, not as parted or separated into two persons, but one and the same Son and Only-begotten God the Word, Lord Jesus Christ; even as the prophets from earliest times spoke of him, and our Lord Jesus Christ himself taught us, and the creed of the fathers has handed down to us.[6]

Jesus was not half-God and half-man. He was fully divine and fully man. This means that the person Jesus Christ possessed both a human and a divine nature. He was not merely a man who had God in Him, nor was He a man who "manifested the God principle." He *is* God, the second person of the Trinity (John 1:1, 14): "The Son is the radiance of God's glory and the exact representation of his being, sustaining all things by his powerful word" (Heb. 1:3). Jesus' two natures were not mixed together, yet they functioned in unity in the one person of Jesus, the God-man. The following illustrate the sweeping extent to which the Scriptures portray Jesus' deity.

- He accepted worship (Matt. 2:2, 11; 14:33).
- Jesus is the essence of Deity bodily (Col. 2:9).
- He gives eternal life (John 10:28).
- He was called God (John 20:28; Heb. 1:8).
- Jesus was also called the Son of God (Mark 1:1).
- He knew all things (John 21:17).
- He was sinless (Heb. 4:15; 1 Pet. 2:22).
- Jesus destroyed the works of the devil (1 John 3:8).

The apostle John spoke of the divine nature of Jesus when he said, "The Word was God" (John 1:1). Jesus is the Word in His own person; therefore, He has always been greater than the written embodiment of His Word. "Jesus did many other things as well," wrote the apostle John. "If every one of them were written down, I suppose that even the whole world would not have room for the books that would be written" (John 21:25). This "Son of God has come and has given us understanding, so that we may know him who is true. And we are in him who is true—even in his Son Jesus Christ. He is the true God and eternal life" (1 John 5:20).

"No one has ever seen God.... because God is Spirit" (John 1:18; 4:24). As Spirit, He is not limited to time and space and is not visible to human eyes, yet the miracle of the Incarnation is that "God became flesh" (John 1:14).

Jesus in the flesh demonstrated the attributes of God in His ministry, like the following examples.

- He claimed omnipotence: "All authority in heaven and on earth has been given to me" (Matt. 28:18).
- Jesus was omniscient, knowing all things. He "would not entrust himself to them, for he knew all men. He did not need man's testimony about man, for he knew what was in a man" (John 2:24–25; 16:30; 21:17). He even knew the specific four-drachma coin in the mouth of a fish in the Sea of Galilee that Peter would catch (Matt. 17:27).
- Jesus demonstrated omnipresence, being everywhere at the same time. He "saw" Nathaniel from many miles away while he was sitting under a fig tree "before Phillip called [him]" (John 1:48). Jesus said to His disciples at the conclusion of His earthly ministry: "I am with you always, to the very end of the age" (Matt. 28:20).
- Jesus possessed immutability (unchangeableness): "Jesus Christ is the same yesterday and today and forever" (Heb. 13:8).
- The Scriptures ascribe eternality to Him: "He is before all things and by him all things consist" (Col. 1:17; see also John 8:58; Rev. 1:17).
- The Bible describes a special glory that belonged to Jesus Christ from eternity. The aura that surrounded the eternal throne of God manifested in many demonstrations recorded in the Old Testament. Moses, for example, wrote that the glory of the Lord settled over Mt. Sinai and hung there for seven days until Moses went up into the mountain to meet with God (Exod. 24:16–18; see also Exod. 33:22; 40:34–35; Num. 14:10; 1 Sam. 4:21; Ps. 19:1; John 1:14). Wise men from the East followed the star to the house in Bethlehem where baby Jesus was. When they found Him, they worshiped Him, presented their gifts of gold, frankincense, and myrrh to him, and departed with the feeling they had found their Messiah (Matt. 2:1–12).

There never was a time when Jesus Christ was not fully divine, the "living water" (John 4:10; 7:37; Col. 1:17). Even in His death He told the thief on the cross, "Today you will be with me in paradise," and it was a credible and authoritative promise (Luke 23:43). Jesus could offer the guarantee because He and "the Father are one" (John 10:30).

Jesus demonstrated complete knowledge of people. When the disciples were disputing who would be the greatest in the Lord's kingdom, "Knowing their thoughts," the Gospel writer says, Jesus "took a little child and had him stand beside him" (Luke 9:47). The Lord then went on to teach, "He who is least among you all—he is the greatest" (v. 48).

Jesus was divine from the moment of His conception by the Holy Spirit. He was Deity in the womb and in the manger (Luke 1:35). The Lord did not become God at His birth or at some point after His birth. As the child is fully the man, but without maturity, so Jesus Christ was truly God even in infancy, although He had to grow up and come to full human awareness of His person and mission (Luke 2:52).

B. Two Natures—His Humanity

"Being found in appearance as a man" is the way Paul described the Messiah's humanity (Phil. 2:8). The whole point of the incarnation was to bring God's Son into the world: "The Word became flesh and dwelt among us," to save "whosoever will" (Matt. 1:21; John 1:14; 3:16).

The Nicene Creed expressed it this way:

> Who, for us men and for our salvation, came down from heaven, and was made flesh of the Holy Spirit and the Virgin Mary, and was made man; and was crucified also for us under Pontius Pilate, and suffered and was buried, and rose again on the third day according to the Scriptures, and ascended into the heavens, and sitteth on the right hand of the Father, and cometh again with glory to judge living and dead, of whose kingdom there shall be no end...[7]

Jesus came to this earth in a body (Heb. 10:5; Luke 24:39). In that body, Jesus prayed to his Father (John 17). He was also tempted (Matt. 4:1). He actually experienced death while hanging on the cross (Rom. 5:8).

Neither an angel nor some other newly created being was born that day in the humble stable at Bethlehem. Mary's womb opened to give birth to a truly human baby. The infant immediately started crying, and was born hungry, like all babies. Yet, He was also very God of very God.

The human nature of Jesus experienced all of the sinless characteristics of the flesh. He needed sleep (Matt. 8:24); he experienced hunger (Matt. 4:2; 21:18); He became tired (John 4:6); He felt the pain of thirst (John 19:28); and there were times when He needed strength (Matt. 4:11; Luke 22:43). Jesus accepted the limitations of His own incarnation in a physical body. He moved in and out among people, going and coming. John recorded the Lord "had to go through Samaria" (John 4:4). "I am going there to wake him up," Jesus said regarding Lazarus (John 11:11). After He arrived, Martha went to get her sister, Mary, and said to her, "The Master is come and calleth for thee"

(John 11:28, KJV). He who was the Water of Life cried out on His cross, "I am thirsty" because He was thirsty (John 19:28).

Regarding His human nature, the angel Gabriel gave the baby the name *Jesus,* meaning "savior." This not-uncommon name is the Greek equivalent of the Hebrew word *Joshua* (Luke 1:31; Acts 7:45).

The very human terms people used to refer to Him demonstrate His humanity. He was a Jew (John 4:9). John the Baptist announced that "a man" had come after him, and said He was "preferred before me: for he was before me" (John 1:30, KJV). Jesus even called Himself a man (John 8:40). An indictment against Him for blasphemy included the charge that He claimed to be more than "a mere man" (John 10:33). Clearly, His critics perceived Him as being a man. Paul said He was "the man from heaven" (1 Cor. 15:49; see also Rom. 5:17; 8:3). Peter described Him as "a man accredited by God to you by miracles, wonders and signs, which God did among you through him" (Acts 2:22). Paul went so far as to tell Timothy that "the man Christ Jesus" is the "one mediator between God and men" (1 Tim. 2:5). "Since death came through a man," Paul taught, "the resurrection of the dead also [came] through a man" (1 Cor. 15:21). The Lord will return the second time as a glorified man to judge the world in righteousness (Acts 17:31).

Jesus often claimed the term *Son of man,* a reference to His humanity. The martyr Stephen used the expression when he was dying from a cruel stoning at the hands of evil religious leaders, including Israel's high priest: "Look," he said, "I see heaven open and the Son of Man standing at the right hand of God" (Acts 7:56). This was also the Messiah's name that was foretold by the prophet Daniel, who ascribed to Him authority, sovereign power, and worship in a kingdom over all peoples, nations, and languages (Dan. 7:13–14; Matt. 26:24).

Jesus used the name *Son of man* at His trial, and Caiaphas the high priest tore his clothes when he heard it (Matt. 26:64–65). This reaction indicated how well Caiaphas understood that the title referred to the Messiah, although he was not willing to ascribe the designation to Jesus.

Jesus told the chief priests, "The Son of Man will be seated at the right hand of the mighty God." They fully understood the implications of the statement and responded by asking, "Are you then the Son of God?" (Luke 22:69–70). By taking the name *Son of man,* Jesus as Messiah affirmed both His own personal humanity and His being the representative Man for the entire human family—and the chief priests knew it well.

Athanasius (A.D. 296–373) was the great bishop of the church in Alexandria, Egypt. Church history remembers him as a champion of New Testament christological orthodoxy. "[Jesus] became what we are" Athanasius wrote, "that He might make us what He is."[8] Said another way, Jesus took on our mortality so He could clothe us with His immortality.

The Law of Moses was explicit that Israelites were to worship God alone (Exod. 34:14), yet Jesus accepted worship and offered no protest. One such example occurred after He quieted a storm on the Sea of Galilee: "Those who were in the boat worshipped him, saying, 'Truly you are the Son of God'" (Matt. 14:33).

In His incarnation, Jesus was always fully human. However, it is a fact evidenced in the Gospels that when the Lord was on Earth, His humanity veiled His divinity. The people to whom He ministered saw Him as a mere man; it took a special revelation for people to discover His deity. Nathaniel expressed just such a revelation: "Rabbi, you are the Son of God; you are the King of Israel" (John 1:49). Jesus responded to him, "You believe because I told you I saw you under the fig tree. You shall see greater things than that. I tell you the truth, you shall see heaven open, and the angels of God ascending and descending on the Son of Man" (John 1:50–51).

The same kind of revelation came to the apostle Peter. The Lord asked him at Caesarea Philippi, "Who do you say I am?" Simon Peter answered, "You are the Christ, the Son of the living God." Jesus replied, "Blessed are you, Simon son of Jonah, for this was not revealed to you by man, but by my Father in heaven" (Matt. 16:16–18).

Jesus had a normal physical maturity with a truly human nature. He developed according to the same natural laws as all other men—from a helpless infant, through His teenage years, and into young adult manhood. Luke wrote that Jesus "grew and became strong; he was filled with wisdom: and the grace of God was upon him" (Luke 2:40). He surely received some rabbinic training as a growing child, which typically involved demanding and focused instruction. One can only imagine how avidly Jesus studied the Torah, the five books of Moses, as well as the whole of the Old Testament. He who was the living Word of God, in His humanity became so astute in the Scriptures He could turn in the scroll to the passage He wanted and read it. One such occasion is recorded (John 1:1; Luke 4:17).

Isaiah said there was "nothing in [Jesus' human] appearance that we should desire him," yet we think of Him as "radiant and ruddy, outstanding among ten thousand" (Isa. 53:2; Song of Sol. 5:10). If His physical looks did not captivate, His character certainly did. Even His enemies admitted He was impeccable in the integrity of His moral fiber (Mark 12:14).

The apostle John was explicit about any attempt to deny that God in Christ came to the earth as a human being in flesh and blood.

Dear friends, do not believe every spirit, but test the spirits to see whether they are from God, because many false prophets have gone out into the world. This is how you can recognize the Spirit of God: Every spirit that acknowledges that Jesus Christ has come in the flesh is from God, but every spirit that does not acknowledge Jesus is not from God. This is the spirit of the antichrist, which you have heard is coming and even now is already in the world.

—1 John 4:1–3

C. The Attitude That Made the Strategy Possible

"Your attitude should be the same as that of Christ Jesus," wrote the apostle Paul (Phil. 2:5). The Authorized Version renders it, "Let this mind be in you which was also in Christ Jesus." No one at any time has seen the God who is Spirit; yet, God became flesh in Jesus Christ and dwelt among men (John 1:14; 4:24). So, what was the Lord's unique mindset in His incarnation that enabled Him to serve as a human being?

We answer that *implicit trust in His Father* summarizes the overarching attitude that explains the earthly life of the Nazarene. Jesus trusted His Father completely, and that confidence is foundational to His accomplishing the plan of salvation. Paul said Jesus was "in very nature God," yet He "did not consider" in His humanity that His attributes of "equality with God" were "something to be grasped" (Phil. 2:6). Jesus "did not demand and cling to his rights as God" (Phil. 2:6, TLB). Such a choice fundamentally assumes an attitude of implicit trust. Because of precisely this confidence, Jesus lived fully as a human being, with His will freely submitted to His Father, without ever demanding the independent exercise of the prerogatives of His deity.

Jesus functioned as a lowly servant in His true humanity. From that humble status, His objective as the last Adam was to redeem "whosoever will." To that end, He "became obedient unto death, even death on a cross" (Phil. 2:7–8; 1 Tim. 2:5; 1 Cor. 15:45–47; John 3:16). Jesus felt safe in His Father's care during His incarnation, because He was safe.

Paul presented this teaching on the mind of Christ in applicational terms: "Your attitude should be the same as that of Christ Jesus" (Phil. 2:5). The great apostle was not content merely to explain how the God-man achieved the atonement. He wanted his readers to understand how it benefited them in their daily living. Every child of God who makes the choice to trust the heavenly Father completely will feel safe in His care too, because he is safe. The Lord's redemptive strategy unveils, therefore, the path for believers "to work out [their] own salvation with fear and trembling" (Phil. 2:12).

≈ A Teenager's Trust: ≈
God Won't Give Me What I Can't Handle

Missy Jenkins was one of seven students gunned down December 1, 1997, at Heath High School in Paducah, Kentucky. A bullet damaged her spinal cord, leaving Missy dependent upon braces and a walker in order to move around.

At the time of the shooting, Jenkins was 15 years old and described herself as "without direction." During her convalescence, she not only found the will to stay alive, but the determination to go forward in a positive direction with her life.

"I realized I did not die that morning. I'm all here. I'm alive," said Missy in a recent interview.

Carried by that resolve, Missy Jenkins received a bachelor's degree in social work from Murray State University on December 18, 2004. Her dreams include a master's degree, marriage, children, and a job.

Missy said, "I just don't think God is going to give me anything I can't handle."[9]

D. The Self-Emptying Strategy: Making Himself Nothing

Because of Jesus' attitude of trust in His Father, He "made himself nothing" (Phil. 2:7). The phrase can also be rendered, He "emptied Himself." The term derives from the Greek word *ekenosen*, which means "to make empty." *Ekenosen* is transliterated into English as "kenosis."[10]

The significance of the kenosis, or this self-emptying strategy, is that "when the time came, he set aside the privileges of deity and took on the status of a slave" (Phil. 2:7, THE MESSAGE). Jesus' decision to surrender voluntarily His divine prerogatives is the essence of making Himself nothing.

The bond of confidence between Jesus and His Father gave Him the strength and freedom to live out precisely this self-emptying as a man. Therefore, Jesus accepted in His incarnate manhood the sinless limitations of humanity. In doing so, He freely emptied Himself of the independent expression of His divine attributes. But He released them, not to a man, or to an angel, and certainly not to a devil. Specifically, the Lord's trusting attitude enabled Him to surrender to His Father and to the Holy Spirit the autonomous exercise of His attributes when He became a flesh-and-blood man with a sinless heart that beat to serve. Jesus knew He did not need to come "demanding and clinging to His rights as God," because His Father would be there for Him in every situation (Phil. 2:6, TLB).

Throughout His ministry, therefore, the Holy Spirit guided Him, but never took advantage of His manhood to manipulate obedience.

Admittedly, in harvesting this field of golden grain, we presume to reap the most sacred biblical truth. Understanding the Godhead will surely require sitting at the Father's feet for millennia in the ages to come (Eph. 2:7). It is important, however, that we make the effort to comprehend what the Bible does explain about the subject. The goal of this quest is to discover the marvelously successful blueprint by which Jesus lived out as a man His attitude of humble dependence on His Father.

E. The Self-Emptying Strategy and Jesus' Trinitarian Attributes

Jesus described the exercise of His coequal attributes in Trinitarian categories: "*I* will ask the *Father*, and he will give you another Counselor, who will never leave you. He is the *Holy Spirit*" (John 14:16–17, NLT, emphasis added; 1 Tim. 2:5). This interdependent relationship is exactly what He had enjoyed in the Trinity from eternity. It was natural for Him in His manhood, therefore, to yield the independent application of His attributes to His Father and to the Holy Spirit, with a commitment never to grasp for them, no matter how intense the pressure (Phil. 2:6). Such is the essence of implicit trust. The apostle Peter described His ministry in these terms: "God anointed Jesus of Nazareth with the Holy Spirit and power…he went around doing good and healing all who were under the power of the devil, because God was with him" (Acts 10:38). This meant, of course, that even though He released their self-directed application, His divine attributes never ceased to be available to Him in His humiliation. This is true because the Holy Spirit, given to Him "without measure," ministered them back through Him in His true manhood as the circumstances warranted (John 3:34; Mark 1:10).

F. The Self-Emptying Strategy and Free Will

The purpose of the Incarnation was to make it possible for the man Christ Jesus to redeem mankind (1 Tim. 2:5; Heb. 2:9–17). In accomplishing that objective, the Lord respected fully the gift of free will God gave to Adam and his seed (Gen. 2:16–17). A redemptive plan that forced man's obedience would have changed the very nature of man, because from the beginning God granted Adam and his posterity the power of choice. A strategy that altered man's free moral agency would also have been an admission that God made a mistake in creating man with the freedom to say yes or no, even to his Creator. Jesus' goal in His ministry, therefore, was not to coerce people to make the right choice, but to show them so much love they would realize their need and freely choose the gift of eternal life.

The method by which this happened was God's Son came to the earth in true humanity and became "the last Adam, a life giving spirit" (1 Cor. 15:45). His own holy life, and especially His death, mirrored the great love of God. His crucifixion is central because it showed both what was wrong with the world's way of living and the affection of God for all people. This understanding makes Paul's two statements to his Corinthian readers pivotal for comprehending the new covenant: "In Adam all die, so in Christ shall all be made alive," and "The first man Adam became a living being; the last Adam, a life-giving spirit" (1 Cor. 15:22, 45).

The writer of Hebrews chose this line of reasoning as the primary purpose for his book. He presents Jesus as "the Apostle and High Priest whom we confess," and shows what was required for Him to qualify for that lofty role (Heb. 3:1; 4:14). For example, "He had to be made like His brothers in every way," taking on true humanity (Heb. 2:17; 3:1–2). The Incarnation shows Jesus met in His manhood this qualification as the perfect High Priest and made the final sacrifice for sin. Paul's *kenosis* teaching explains how it happened (Heb. 5:1–10; 10:11–12; Phil. 2:5–7).

Jesus made atonement in his true humanity. He did it in such a loving and compelling way as to motivate people to make their own free choice to respond to His magnanimous invitation (Isa. 55:1; Rev. 22:17).

> Come to me, all you who are weary and burdened, and I will give you rest. Take my yoke upon you and learn from me, for I am gentle and humble in heart, and you will find rest for your souls. For my yoke is easy and my burden is light.
>
> —Matthew 11:28–30

G. Jesus' Love for All People

God knew from eternity just the right approach for Jesus to redeem fallen humanity and, in doing so, to destroy the works of the devil (Titus 2:14; Heb. 2:14–15). The heavenly Father did not need to create a new attitude for His Son to adopt in His incarnation; instead, the choice flowed out of the essence of the Tri-unity of God.

Each of the Trinitarian persons serves the others' interests (e.g., John 14:26). Therefore, servanthood is a cherished value in the Godhead, while the concept of independence is not in the divine vocabulary and character. God's Son stepped into time and space as the servant of all, "and was made in the likeness of men," (Phil. 2:7, KJV; Mark 9:35; John 1:14). When He did this, the very essence of God became flesh with Him, expressing itself as a loving servant (Phil. 2:5–7; Mark 10:45). Little wonder Jesus later said to Philip, "Anyone who has seen me has seen the Father" (John 14:9).

The term *agape*, defined as the love of God, expresses the core value of the Godhead (1 John 4:8, 16) *Grace* is its synonym in the Scriptures. This love of God has no selfishness in it and seeks no personal aggrandizement. Neither is it egocentric. *Agape* has nothing about it that smacks of a "holier than thou" mentality. *Agape* never seeks advantage at the expense of another; in fact, no thought even exists in the Trinity of taking advantage.

God "has showered down upon us the riches of his grace" and requires nothing in return (Eph. 1:8, TLB). His love never comes with a price tag and does not ask if you deserve it. God shares unconditionally, no questions asked. He "sends rain on the righteous and the unrighteous" (Matt. 5:45). The Father's love seeks only what is best for its beneficiary. God's great portrait of His unconditional love is the fact that Jesus "became obedient unto death, even the death of the cross" (Phil. 2:8, KJV).

This love of God sent Jesus into the world, and He voluntarily marched straight to His death at the hands of evil men. The Cross, therefore, is the core event in the life of Jesus Christ. "Christ died for us," in fact, "while we were still sinners" (Rom. 5:8). Jesus did it to serve His Father's objective—to meet humankind's deepest need for a Redeemer. *Agape*, then, is grace tailor-made for God's children to express the heart of God to their fellowmen, and it describes servanthood at its best.

Agape is the opposite of the world's system. Man is selfish and often exaggerates for personal benefit. He is ego-centered and finds it easy to justify condescension. The world system seeks the advantage and certainly will steal and take from a fellow human being. Fallen mankind does not give love freely and has reciprocal expectations. This love always has a price tag, and the giver asks every time if you deserve it. People share worldly love with many selfish conditions because they want the best for themselves, even if it is at someone else's expense.

In every generation, Adam's sons have always fought for their rights and grabbed for their privileges. After all, it is the world's way to get ahead in life. Everyone knows lions rule the jungle with their brute strength, taking what they want. People in the worldly system think the way the world thinks—the only way to fight strength is with greater strength, because might makes right; and that is the way it is.

The way the world does things disdains the *agape* love of God precisely because by its standard God's love appears to be weak and the value system of losers. Obviously, the worldly wise who lived by the world's techniques interpreted Jesus' methods as very alien. To discover the great strength of *agape*, however, one needs look no further than the cross and resurrection of Jesus. The Messiah-become-servant did not come clinging to the prerogatives of His deity, yet He had the awesome strength and perseverance to stay on a cruel cross until He died and then arose from the dead (Phil. 2:6–8, TLB; Matt. 28:6). "May the Lord direct your hearts into God's love," Paul wrote the Christians at Thessalonica, "and Christ's perseverance" (2 Thess. 3:5).

H. Living What Agape Is

Jesus chose an attitude that for Him was merely God being God. As it regards the world system, however, it was totally counter-cultural and anticipated by only a very few (Ps. 13:5; Zech. 9:9; Isa. 42:1–4). In fact, anyone who did not have an intimate understanding of the character of God would have denied the possibility. God incarnate, Jesus Christ, chose to live out the love of God in a depraved and sinful world. He treated people with the same servant heart as the persons in the Tri-unity of God treat each other (Mark 9:35; John 5:20, 30; 14:26). Total trust is at the heart of the relationships in the Trinity.

Agape love will act in the best interests of another, even if the recipient is not asking for help and does not know he needs relief. This is true because inherent in love is its own sense of obligation. Millions of fathers selflessly take a job, for example, work faithfully for long hours day after day, bring home paychecks week after week, and spend it all on the well-being of their families because their love for wife and children mandates it. Only the sense of obligation built into love explains this kind of selfless labor. This example illuminates why the heavenly Father sent His Son into the world to die as the final atonement for sin; God's love compelled it (John 3:16; Rom. 5:8; Gal. 4:4; Eph. 2:1; Heb. 9:26). It also shows why love is superior to law. Law can define right and wrong and condemn for not doing the right (Rom. 7:7). But no law has ever been written that can give life (Gal. 3:21). Love is superior because it *can* impart life. For this reason, love has an inherent sense of duty that motivates doing right, thus fulfilling the Law (Rom.13:10; 1 John 5:2–3). This principle inspired the apostle John to affirm, "We love [God] because he first loved us" (1 John 4:19).

Based on this understanding, each person in the Tri-unity of God always functions for the highest good of the other persons. While the world system thinks in terms of individual independence, *agape* love in the Godhead operates on the value system of selfless mutual submission. Such a lifestyle is the Golden Rule in full-orbed expression (Matt. 7:12). This helps to explain, for example, why the Holy Spirit always exalts the Lord Jesus and not Himself (John 15:26).

I. The Lamb, Triumph of the Defenseless

Could the humble, servant-like demeanor of Jesus succeed and actually save the world if He did not come with the qualities of a lion, demanding and taking? Could He accomplish His objectives if He lived instead by the qualities of a lamb, the polar opposite of demanding and taking? (Phil. 2:7.) Everyone knows lambs are helpless and defenseless, easy to kill. Jesus chose to adopt the weaknesses of the lamb, and in the plan of God became the lamb slain "before the creation of the world" (1 Pet. 1:18–20). Paul wrote that "he humbled himself and became obedient to death—even death on a cross" (Phil. 2:8).

From eternity, Jesus was the Lamb of God, wholly dependent upon His Father. Jesus lived out the plan of redemption with this mindset, defeating every "lion" that came up against Him. The Lord did it, even when it cost Him His life at the hands of evil men in a very convoluted world (John 1:14–18; Acts 2:23; 3:26; 14:23; 2 Cor. 5:14). The message of the Gospel admits, therefore, that lions can kill, but God's Lamb held the power of resurrection, and that makes a quantum difference (John 10:17–18). Hence, we celebrate the triumph of the Lamb (Rev. 5:5–6).

Arguably, the greatest strength of a lamb is his trust in his shepherd. It also follows that the highest goal of Christian maturity is for a believer to vest complete trust in the Nazarene (Matt. 2:23; 11:29; John 14:1; Prov. 3:5). "Your attitude should be the same as that of Christ Jesus," Paul wrote (Phil. 2:5). We too trust the Good Shepherd of our souls, who continues to hold the power of resurrection. Jesus, in fact, used this vein of thinking to teach His disciples to live the life of servants:

> You know that those who are regarded as rulers of the Gentiles lord it over them, and their high officials exercise authority over them. Not so with you. Instead, whoever wants to become great among you must be your servant, and whoever wants to be first must be slave of all. For even the Son of Man did not come to be served, but to serve, and to give his life as a ransom for many.
>
> —MARK 10:42–45

This also explains why Paul taught Christ's followers to work out their own salvation with fear and trembling so that Christ could be formed in them (Phil. 2:12–13; Gal. 4:19).

J. Jesus, the Firstfruits of Spirit-filled Men

In the hindsight of the Upper Room, it became clear to the Apostles the incarnate Jesus had lived among them as a man who was full of the Holy

Spirit (John 3:34; Acts 2:1–4; 10:38). His life is the great example, therefore, of what walking in the Spirit is all about (Gal. 5:16, 25). Having received the Spirit Himself, Jesus was the firstfruits of Spirit-empowered men (1 Cor. 15:20–23). His ministry anticipated the baptism with the Holy Spirit for all thirsty people, as well as the era of the gifts of the Spirit, which duplicate the life and ministry of Jesus Christ (John 3:37–39; Acts 1:8; Gal. 5:16, 25). At the core of Pentecostal understanding is the concept that the same Spirit who anointed Jesus' life "without limit" also anoints each of God's children (John 3:34; Luke 24:49; Acts 10:38). This understanding enlightens the Lord's teaching: "I tell you the truth, anyone who has faith in me will do what I have been doing. He will do even greater things than these, because I am going to the Father" (John 14:12–13).

As the firstfruits of Spirit-empowered men, Jesus made the commitment to live, die, and rise from the grave without even one time grasping for the independent use of His divine attributes (Phil. 2:6). This means when the incarnate Jesus performed a miracle or did any of the great works of God (e.g., healing the sick, casting out devils, raising the dead, walking on water), He acted as a man in the power of the Holy Spirit, who superintended His life. He always served in the marvelous unity of the Trinity, therefore, and was never without assistance (1 Tim. 2:5; 3:16; John 10:30).

> Have the same attitude that Christ Jesus had. Although he was in the form of God and equal with God, he did not take advantage of this equality. Instead, he emptied himself by taking on the form of a servant, by becoming like other humans, by having a human appearance. He humbled himself by becoming obedient to the point of death, death on a cross. This is why God has given him an exceptional honor—the name honored above all other names—so that at the name of Jesus everyone in heaven, on earth, and in the world below will kneel and confess that Jesus Christ is Lord to the glory of God the Father. My dear friends, you have always obeyed, not only when I was with you but even more now that I am absent. In the same way, continue to work out your salvation with fear and trembling. It is God who produces in you the desires and actions that please him.
>
> —Philippians 2:5–13, gw

What a strategy! Such a plan was uniquely a God kind of idea; no steeped-in-sin member of Adam's race would have ever even thought of it. Isaiah prophesied that the Messiah's life would have this special guidance from the Holy Spirit.

The Spirit of wisdom and of understanding, the Spirit of counsel
and of power, the Spirit of knowledge and of the fear of the LORD—
and he will delight in the fear of the Lord.

—ISAIAH 11:2–3

Precisely this fullness of the Spirit enabled Him to speak "the words of
God" (John 3:34; see also Isa. 42:1, KJV). Had Jesus as very-God-become-man
restricted the independent display of His attributes to any being lesser than
Himself, the Lord would have ceased to be truly God. In submitting Himself
in His manhood to His own Father and the Holy Spirit, He was able to serve
as a flesh-and-blood-man in full obedience to His Father. Jesus was guided by
the Holy Spirit, but without diminishing His deity. This meant that in the
marvelous unity of the two natures in one person (God and man), Jesus' deity
never coerced His humanity, and His humanity never obstructed His deity. In
this remarkable freedom, Jesus performed His miraculous works as a man in
the power of the Holy Spirit (Acts 10:38).

The goal of each of God's children must be to walk in the Spirit as Jesus did,
because He is the Firstfruits (Acts 1:8; 10:38; 1 Cor. 15:20; Gal. 5:16, KJV).
In doing so, we follow the example of the one who is "outstanding among ten
thousand" (Song of Sol. 5:10).

III. Making the Strategy Succeed

How did Jesus communicate with His Father day after day as a surrendered
servant, so that as a man He carried out His Father's will fully? How did the
kenosis, or self-emptying plan of action, work in His ministry?

A. Watching, Listening, and Talking to His Father

After Jesus healed the man at the Pool of Bethesda, He gave His critics a
powerful insight into how His Father, whom He completely trusted, was with
Him to guide His life. "I tell you the truth," He said, "the Son can do nothing
by himself; he can do only what he sees his Father doing, because whatever the
Father does, the Son also does. For the Father loves the Son and shows him all
he does" (John 5:19–20).

In His discourse on spiritual blindness after healing the man born blind,
the Lord offered a word-picture that helps to explain how this worked.

I am the good shepherd; I know my sheep and my sheep know
me—just as the Father knows me and I know the Father—and I lay
down my life for the sheep. I have other sheep that are not of this

sheep pen. I must bring them also. They too will listen to my voice, and there shall be one flock and one shepherd.

—JOHN 10:14–16

Jesus assumed His hearers understood that as sheep know the shepherd's voice or as a child recognizes his father's voice, so God's Son could discern His Father's voice (John 10:4–5). No further explanation should be needed beyond those metaphors.

Jesus lived His entire life both watching and listening to the Father whom He trusted fully, and then saying and doing exactly what He perceived from the Holy Spirit. Jesus made the claim that by Himself He could do nothing: "I judge only as I hear and my judgment is just; for I seek not to please myself but him who sent me" (John 5:30; 10:37; 12:50; 14:24, 31). Jesus asserted the singular goal of His life as a servant was to listen to His Father. "I have come down from heaven," He said, "not to do my will but to do the will of him who sent me" (John 6:38). He went on to define God's plan: "My Father's will is that everyone who looks to the Son and believes in him shall have eternal life, and I will raise him up at the last day" (John 6:40; 2 Pet. 1:3).

When Jesus healed the paralytic in Capernaum and forgave his sins, some teachers began to think the Lord had committed blasphemy. "Immediately Jesus knew in his spirit that this was what they were thinking in their hearts, and he said to them, 'Why are you thinking these things?'" (Mark 2:8). Jesus told His critics:

"When you have lifted up the Son of Man on the cross, then you will realize that I am [the one I claim to be] and that I do nothing on my own but speak just what the Father taught me. And the one who sent me is with me; he has not deserted me. For I always do those things that are pleasing to him." Many put their faith in him even as Jesus said this to them.

—JOHN 8:28–30; 14:31

Jesus' very active devotional life was also central to His strategy to talk with His Father, on whom He totally depended (John 14:31). His habits of intercession made it possible for Him to receive guidance, as well as enjoy His Father's companionship and fellowship.

Jesus was praying, for example, when he emerged from the water at His Jordan baptism (Luke 3:21–22). He often withdrew from His disciples to be alone in prayer. He liked to pray on mountains, and at times went to lonely and solitary places to communicate undisturbed with His Father. Sometimes he prayed "very early in the morning, while it was still dark" (Mark 1:35;

6:46; Matt. 14:23; Luke 5:16). Jesus prayed all night before He chose His disciples (Luke 6:12). He prayed for little children, as well as for His disciples (Matt. 19:14–15; John 17:6, 9). He interceded with the Father so that Satan would not be able to "sift [Peter] as wheat" (Luke 22:31–32).

The Twelve were so attracted to Jesus' prayer life they asked Him to teach them to pray and He gave them a model prayer (Luke 11:1). Jesus prayed with thanksgiving before feeding the five thousand (Matt. 14:19). He prayed in Gethsemane and on His cross (Matt. 26:36–46; Mark 14:32–42; Luke 23:44–46). The writer of Hebrews recorded that, "During the days of Jesus' life on earth, he offered up prayers and petitions with loud cries and tears to the one who could save him from death, and he was heard because of his reverent submission" (Heb. 5:7).

The Lord's disciples concluded early in His ministry that prayer was a vital part of His life. His prayer habits help to explain, therefore, how the Father and the Holy Spirit gave Him the support system that guided and empowered His life.

B. Depending on the Old Testament Scriptures

Jesus' capacity to watch and listen to His Father also reveals the Lord as the perfect *logos*, or Word of God (John 1:1, 14). The apostles recognized that Jesus, in His own person, was the sum total of the wisdom of godliness (Matt. 16:16; John 16:30; 1 Cor. 1:30; Col. 2:9). Jesus not only was the Word, but He also possessed the blessing of the Holy Spirit to draw out of the Scriptures just the right word for a given situation (John 1:1; 11:25–26; 1 Cor. 2:10). John the Baptist noted that, "The man whom God has sent speaks God's message" (John 3:34, GW).

The phrase "speaks God's message" uses the Greek term *rhamata*.[11] It transliterates into English as *rhema*, and is a synonym of *word*. Jesus was the *Logos* (Word) who could masterfully pull just the right word (*rhema*) from the Scriptures to speak to the specific needs of people. In doing so, He demonstrated "God [gave] him the Spirit without limit" (John 3:34, GW).

Jesus' unreserved trust in His Father enabled Him to make one of His boldest assertions: "I am the way and the truth and the life. No one comes to the Father except through me. If you really knew me, you would know my Father as well" (John 14:6–7). Philip had trouble with the statement, and asked Him, "Lord, show us the Father and that will be enough for us" (John 14:8).

The answer Jesus gave Philip opens up another insight into why Jesus could hear and see His Father so perfectly; namely, His Father really was with Him at all times.

Don't you know me, Philip, even after I have been among you such a long time? Anyone who has seen me has seen the Father. How can you say, 'Show us the Father?' Don't you believe that I am in the Father, and that the Father is in me? The words I say to you are not just my own. Rather, it is the Father living in me, who is doing his work. Believe me when I say that I am in the Father and the Father is in me.

—JOHN 14:9–11

Jesus trained His disciples to understand His heavenly Father was their Father, too, and that like Him, they should trust the Father completely. One example is how He prepared them to face persecution before judges and magistrates. When "you are arrested and brought to trial," He said, "do not worry beforehand about what to say. Just say whatever is given you at the time, for it is not you speaking, but the Holy Spirit" (Mark 13:11).

C. A Spirit-Guided Ability to Discern

Isaiah prophesied the Holy Spirit resting on Messiah would make Him "wise and understanding" and would fill Him with "the spirit of counsel and might, the spirit of knowledge and of the fear of the Lord." The Spirit also made Him "quick of understanding" (Isa. 11:2–3, KJV). The Gospels have many passages that illustrate the Lord's swiftness of thought (Mark 2:8; Luke 20:23; John 6:15)

Isaiah predicted He would not "judge after the sight of his eyes, neither reprove after the hearing of his ears" (Isa. 11:3, KJV). The reason is clear: natural senses cannot be trusted to be accurate. Isaiah saw correctly that the Spirit would guide Messiah, making Him discerning in every situation. The Holy Spirit made it possible, for example, for Him to "defend the poor and the exploited" (Isa. 11:4, TLB). Because of the Spirit resting on Him, Isaiah said, "Righteousness will be his belt and faithfulness the sash around his waist" (Isa. 11:5).

The life of the Lord demonstrated the accuracy of Isaiah's prophecy. Jesus knew the Pharisees' thoughts, for example, when they accused Him of being Beelzebub (Matt. 12:24–27; Luke 11:17). When the Pharisees, "who loved money," sneered at Jesus, He responded to them, "God knows your hearts" (Luke 16:14–15). After Jesus preached His sermon in the Capernaum synagogue, He was fully aware "that his disciples were criticizing his message" (John 6:61, GW). He also had accurate knowledge "from the beginning which of them did not believe and who would betray him" (John 6:64). His disciples had come to see clearly by the end of His life that Jesus knew "all things" and He did not "even need to have anyone ask [Him] questions" because He could answer questions before they were asked. The result was they confessed to Him, "This makes us believe that you came from God" (John 16:30).

The disciples finally came to the place they were able to appreciate from experience what Jesus taught them in the Sermon on the Mount: "Your Father knows what you need before you ask him" (Matt. 6:8). The woman with the issue of blood is an example. Without saying a word, her touching His garment motivated Him to say, "I know that power has gone out from me" (Luke 8:46).

The courts search diligently for motive in order to render justice. Jesus gave His life helping others by looking into their hearts. He is the perfect judge because the "inmost thoughts and motives" of men are open and bare before Him (Rom. 2:16, TLB; Heb. 4:12–13). He made divine judgments about people with full knowledge of their deepest motives. His amazing knowledge is the foundation, therefore, of His ability to execute judgment that always balances grace and truth (John 1:14, 17; 8:1–12). Possessing that kind of information also enabled Him to heal their illnesses and deliver them from bondage to Satan. It was abundantly evident "God was with him" (Acts 10:38; John 5:1–15; 8:44).

Such was the strategy and the mindset of the God who became a man in Jesus Christ. This approach made Him so successful in pursuit of His plan that He paid with His own blood the price for man's salvation and then triumphantly arose from the dead (Rev. 1:18; 5:9; Col. 2:9, 15).

The great lesson for all believers today is that an attitude of implicit trust in God that is anchored in the written Word, seasoned with an active prayer life, and that walks in the Spirit, is the highway to successful Christian living. Little wonder that after Paul wrote his profound Christological statement to the church at Philippi, he penned his own application.

> My dear friends, as you have always obeyed—not only in my presence, but now much more in my absence—continue to work out your salvation with fear and trembling, for it is God who works in you to will and to act according to his good purpose.
> —PHILIPPIANS 2:12–13

D. The Self-Emptying Strategy and Jesus' Divine Attributes

The following glimpse at three of Jesus' divine qualities will illustrate how the plan of action functioned.

1. Omnipresence

It is self-evident that while in flesh and blood, the Lord was not omnipresent, or everywhere at the same time. Jesus clearly accepted the limitations of time and space during His incarnation, but balance is essential. The Lord "saw" Nathaniel even though he was many miles away in his hometown of Cana, sitting under a fig tree (John 1:48). The apostle John wrote in his prologue of "God the One and Only, who is at the Father's side" and said He "has made [the Father] known" (John 1:18). Again, we must admit this to be a great mystery; for how could God in Christ, who was truly incarnate, be at more than one place at the same time? Obviously, He could not in His physical body. Passages such as this find explanation only in *kenosis* categories.

2. Immutability

"I the LORD do not change," God told Malachi, which is the essence of immutability (Mal. 3:6). The writer of Hebrews recorded that "Jesus Christ is the same, yesterday and today and forever" (Heb. 13:8). Yet, when God's Son left heaven and came into the world through the Virgin's womb, He set aside His immutability and experienced lots of change as He moved from infancy to adulthood.

> Jesus grew in wisdom and stature, and in favor with God and men.
> —LUKE 2:52

This is a wondrous mystery, that He who experienced great change as a human being remained immutable throughout His humiliation as the living Word of God.

3. His Glory

Jesus voluntarily limited the independent enjoyment of His divine glory when He stepped into time in flesh and blood. Jesus was the Son of God and merited honor in that exalted role as a member of the Godhead. The angelic hosts certainly respected His lofty estate and gave Him the worship He was rightly due (Ps. 148:2; Luke 2:9–15; Heb. 1:6).

> Praise the LORD, you his angels, you mighty ones who do his bidding, who obey his word. Praise the LORD, all his heavenly hosts, you his servants who do his will. Praise the LORD, all his works everywhere in his dominion; bless the LORD, O my soul.
> —PSALM 103:20–22

It is vital to Jesus' success that He voluntarily released His right to be welcomed with honor and freely worshiped. A bitter cross is what awaited

Him in His humanity, not a throne, and from eternity Jesus knew it well (Matt. 16:21; 20:18; 26:1–2). In His three years of ministry, a few people gave Him divine honor, but those moments were far from His daily routine (Matt. 2:11; 8:2; 9:18; 14:33; 15:25). Throughout His ministry, the priests regularly and faithfully offered the daily sacrifices in the temple—hundreds of them. However, they did not present even one sacrifice in adoration of their Messiah, who was at that time walking in their streets. When Jesus cleansed the ten lepers, only one of them returned to give Him thanks. The Lord spoke out about the ingratitude of the other nine, who did not give common courtesy to God after receiving such a gracious gift of a new life (Luke 17:17–18).

Jesus could handle insults because He knew what was in man and did not come demanding worship. He never grasped for His glory (John 2:25; Phil. 2:6). Instead, humility so characterized His attitude that He focused His life on serving His Father's plan and, through that strategy, ministered to the deepest needs of people. His goal was to function with such loving effectiveness that people would freely make a choice to give Him respect and, ultimately, worship. In this way, He earned in His manhood the honor and worship that was already His by right of His deity.

On at least one occasion as He neared His cross, Jesus made His glory an object of prayer: "Father, the time has come; glorify your Son, that your Son may glorify you.... glorify me in your presence with the glory I had with you before the world began" (John 17:1, 5). This was not a prayer of impatience; rather, it was a petition that recognized the time had almost come for the restoration of the glory the Lord so fondly remembered and for which He rightly longed.

All of God's children have so much to learn from the Servant who came from heaven. His decision to achieve man's salvation without grasping for His glory and never lording it over anybody made Him the "morning star" who rises in our hearts (2 Pet. 1:19).

❧ A King in Commoner's Garb ❧

A vivid word picture of the attitude of Jesus Christ is painted in Mark Twain's novel, *A Connecticut Yankee in King Arthur's Court*. The story tells the adventures of an ordinary 19th century man (the Connecticut Yankee), transported back to the medieval world of King Arthur.

At one point, he convinces King Arthur to dress like a peasant and take a journey through his kingdom. The results are generally laughable as the king, completely oblivious to life in the trenches, tries to carry on with all the pomp of the court while those around him simply think he is crazy. But there is a touching chapter titled "The Smallpox Hut" describing how the king and his companion happen upon a beggar's hovel. The husband lies dead, and the wife tries to warn them away: "For the fear of God, who visits with misery and death such as be harmless, tarry not here, but fly! This place is under his curse."

The king replies, "Let me come in and help you; you are sick and in trouble."

The woman asks the king to go into the loft and check on their child.

"It was a desperate place for him to be in, and might cost him his life," observes the Yankee, "but it was no use to argue with him."

The king disappears up a ladder looking for the girl.

There was a slight noise from the direction of the dim corner where the ladder was. It was the king descending. I could see that he was bearing something in one arm, and assisting himself with the other. He came forward into the light; upon his breast laid a slender girl of 15. She was but half conscious and was dying of smallpox.

Here was heroism at its last and loftiest possibility, its utmost summit. This was challenging death in the open field unarmed, with all the odds against the challenger, no reward set upon the contest, and no admiring world in silks and cloth-of-gold to gaze and applaud. Yet, the king's bearing was as serenely brave as it had always been in those cheaper contests where knight meets knight in equal fight and clothed in protecting steel.

He was great now; sublimely great. The rude statues of his ancestors in his palace should have an addition. I would see to that; and it would not be a mailed king killing a giant or a dragon, like the rest. It would be a king in commoner's garb...[12]

4. Going No Further Than the Scriptures Go

It is clear from passages like Luke 4:18–19, Acts 2:22; 10:38, and Philippians 2:5–13 that Jesus released to His Father and to the Holy Spirit the voluntary exercise of His divine attributes, and did all of His ministry as a man, the last Adam, who was filled with the Holy Spirit. His strategy for ministry was to see what His Father was doing and do that, and hear what His father was saying and say that (John 5:19–20).

It is important, however, that we do not focus our energies on seeking to explain every detail of how the kenosis principle applied to Jesus' divine attributes. Instead, it is a fundamental tenet of Biblical interpretation that the student should go no further than the scriptures do in explaining Biblical truth. Holy Scripture clearly presents the self-emptying principle, but does not answer all questions regarding it. We must be content, therefore, for the mystery of the incarnation to await full explanation in the heavenly classroom (Eph. 2:7).

Meanwhile, believers today should concentrate where the New Testament focuses. After the Lord's investiture as Messiah at Jordan River and His temptation in the wilderness, He went back to Nazareth in the power of the Holy Spirit. Jesus announced His job description in His hometown synagogue: "the Spirit of the Lord is upon me, because He has anointed me to preach..." (Acts 4:18). Peter's sermon at Pentecost has the same focus on the Holy Spirit, and so does his affirmation in Cornelius's house (Acts 2:22; 10:38). Instead of trying to comprehend all the details of the kenosis, therefore, we should give our time and energy to walking in the Spirit ourselves as we learn to hear and see what the Father is doing, and then say and do it. As the Lord emptied Himself of the voluntary exercise of His attributes, we also must focus on emptying ourselves of everything in our lives that hinders implicitly trusting the Father and walking in the Spirit, as we work out our own salvation with fear and trembling.

IV. The Incarnation as a Principle of Life

Moses, as the son of Pharaoh's daughter, lived out the life principle inherent in the Incarnation when he emptied himself of his royal wealth, power, and prestige and joined his brethren in the mud pits of Goshen. "Moses chose to be mistreated along with the people of God rather than to enjoy the pleasures of sin for a short time. He regarded disgrace for the sake of Christ as of greater value than the treasures of Egypt, because he was looking ahead to his reward" (Heb. 11:25–27; Exod. 2:10–14; Acts 7:20–23).

As the prophet far greater than Moses, the Lord Jesus Christ made an infinitely superior decision to yield Himself to His Father's will. He also made the humiliation He experienced the benchmark of discipleship in the kingdom He set out to build. In fact, He raised the bar very high (Heb. 3:3–6; Deut. 18:15).

> [Jesus] called the crowd to him along with his disciples and said: "If anyone would come after me, he must deny himself and take up his cross and follow me. For whoever wants to save his life will lose it, but whoever loses his life for me and for the gospel will save it. What good is it for a man to gain the whole world, yet forfeit his soul? Or what can a man give in exchange for his soul? If anyone is ashamed of me and my words in this adulterous and sinful generation, the Son of Man will be ashamed of him when he comes in his Father's glory with the holy angels."
>
> —MARK 8:34–38

While it is true the Lord did not come snatching for His divine magnificence, it is also accurate that His lifestyle of service earned for Him in the eyes of His followers a new splendor all its own. The apostle John said, "We beheld His glory...as of the only begotten of the Father, full of grace and truth" (John 1:14, KJV). To give two examples, this new glory was apparent when He stilled the storm on the Sea of Galilee; in fact, "the disciples just sat there, awed!" (Matt. 8:27, TLB; Mark 4:39). That same sense of wonder was also present when He raised Lazarus from the dead (John 11:40–45; Matt. 15:31).

Jesus earned the right to be "the blessed and only Potentate, the King of kings, and Lord of lords." He alone has immortality and dwells "in the light which no man can approach unto; whom no man hath seen, nor can see" (1 Tim. 6:15–16, KJV). Yet, He did not defeat the works of the devil with the pompous attitude of the world's demanding monarchs (Luke 22:25; 1 John 3:8). Instead, He served humbly, fully dependent on His Father and the Holy Spirit for guidance. Using this strategy, the King of kings manifested a new kind of royal toughness characterized by absolute trust and lived out in meek servanthood.

Every child of God, as he grows in Christ, will face his own call to empty himself of the lifestyle that has become comfortable to him, forsake his "Egypt," and walk down to his own equivalent of the mud pits of Goshen (Exod. 5:7–8, 14, 16–19; Heb. 11:24–27). This self-emptying is fundamental to what Paul meant by, "Let this mind be in you which was also in Christ Jesus" and "work out your own salvation with fear and trembling" (Phil. 2:5, 12–13, KJV).

Basic to the success of the Son of God was that He answered the call of His Father to a set-apart life. This is the spiritual principle the prophet Hosea spoke to, in the name of God, when he foretold the coming historical event: "Out of Egypt have I called my Son" (Hosea 11:1; Exod. 3:7–10; Matt. 2:15). Although in the world, Jesus set Himself apart from the world in order to achieve God's plan to redeem the world. The call to this self-emptying also recognizes "God is working in [us], giving [us] the desire to obey him and the power to do what pleases him" (Phil. 2:13, NLT).

It is appropriate now to define the specific way the incarnate Jesus became a servant.

Chapter Two

JESUS, THE SERVANT—
LIVING OUT THE PLAN

I belong to my lover, and his desire is for me.

—SONG OF SOLOMON 7:10

[Jesus] made himself nothing, taking the very nature of a servant, being made in human likeness.

—PHILIPPIANS 2:7

~ The Hard Job of Training Servants ~

Mary Louise Starkey has a difficult job. She is trying to turn ordinary people into servants. The current economic climate has fueled the need for servants. In the past decade, the number of American households worth $10 million or more has quadrupled and the newly rich want help managing their large homes and busy lifestyles.

Servants are in demand, and Mary Starkey's International Institute for Household Management in Denver, Colorado, is trying to meet the need. With household managers earning $60,000 to $120,000 a year, applications are at an all-time high. But servanthood is not easy to learn.

Those enrolled in the rigorous eight-week, $7,200 course, devote themselves to mastering the more mundane aspects of running a large household: dealing with trades and outside vendors, managing household staff, learning table manners, and taking cooking classes. Instruction is given regarding setting a formal dinner table, and ironing table linens so they are perfectly crisp and wrinkle free.

Perhaps the most difficult aspect of servanthood is the element of personal self-denial. A consulting beautician at the school recently told an attractive young female student to trim her long blond hair, lose the showy earrings, and lay off the red lip-liner. It seemed that her good looks were attracting awareness of her, and away from her employers.

Servants don't draw attention to themselves; their only goal is to meet the needs of others.[1]

I. A Servant, but in What Sense?

First and foremost, Jesus served His Father by giving His full trust, loyalty, and energy to achieve the most demanding assignment ever given to a human being—the divine plan of redemption. Speaking in the name of God, Isaiah wrote, "Take a good look at my servant. I'm backing him to the hilt. He's the one I chose, and I couldn't be more pleased with him" (Isa. 42:1, THE MESSAGE). Isaiah also said, "My servant will be successful" (Isa. 52:13, GW; see also Matt. 12:18; Phil. 2:5–7). The writer of Hebrews said that Jesus was "a merciful and faithful high priest in service to God" (Heb. 2:17–18). The apostle Peter understood this special Father-Son relationship and said, "God... glorified his servant Jesus," and "raised up his servant" (Acts 3:13, 26; see also 4:27, 30; 2 Pet. 1:17). The Lord described His servant relationship to His Father in these terms: "I have come down from heaven not to do my will but to do the will of him who sent me" (John 6:38). This commitment was so strong that Jesus also said, "My food is to do the will of him who sent me and to finish his work" (John 4:34).

In fulfilling this ministry as the servant of Jehovah, Jesus showed the nature of the heart of God the Father as being love toward all people—Jews and Gentiles (John 3:16; Luke 15:11–32; 2 Cor. 1:3–4). Hence, Jesus Christ ministered as the servant of all. "I tell you that Christ has become a servant of the Jews on behalf of God's truth," Paul said, "to confirm the promises made to the patriarchs so that the Gentiles may glorify God for his mercy, as it is written: 'I will praise you among the Gentiles; I will sing hymns to your name'" (Rom. 15:9; also Ps. 18:49; Exod. 21:5–6).

Achieving this objective as the servant of all required that Jesus:

- diagnose the human problem, even though people did not realize their predicament and vehemently opposed the very idea they had a problem (Mark 7:15–23; John 7:5; 16:8–11),
- provide the antidote (Matt. 9:12–13; John 19:30),
- serve people so convincingly that they came to accept by their own choice His diagnosis and the cure He provided, assimilating its implications into their lifestyles (John 4:42; 6:68; Rev. 1:18), and
- commission, empower, and gift His disciples to serve like Him, taking seriously the worldwide application of the gospel. The result was they committed to its ethnic implications by taking the good news of His redemption to the ends of the earth (Matt. 28:16–20; Acts 1:8).

Achieving all of this was a colossal and costly personal challenge that offers insight into Paul's phrase, "the faith of God" (Rom. 3:3, KJV). The God kind of confidence took on a task this monumental and believed so completely in the ultimate outcome that the Godhead never devised a Strategy B. The ultimate measure of Jesus' success was His staying on the cross, by His own free choice, until He died. Calvary remains to this day the centerpiece of the gospel and Jesus' most astounding achievement. Personal faith in His success on the tree and His resurrection three days later has continued through the centuries as the necessary requirement for people to accept the Lord's diagnosis and the antidote He freely offers.

The prophets understood the depth of man's quandary but were powerless to fix it. For example, Isaiah wrote, "[The Israelites] have forsaken the LORD; they have spurned the Holy One of Israel and turned their backs on him...Why do you persist in rebellion? Your whole head is injured, your whole heart afflicted. From the sole of your foot to the top of your head there is no soundness—only wounds and welts and open sores" (Isa. 1:4–6).

The Holy Spirit gave John the Baptist, as Jesus' forerunner, a message of repentance (Matt. 3:2). Hence, John joined the ranks of the prophets who correctly identified the problem but could not repair it; the chasm was far too wide. But John was endowed with the high honor to introduce the Messiah who did take "away the sin of the world" (John 1:29).

The Lord's assignment from eternity was to accomplish the plan of salvation without any fine-tuning of its design, not even one iota, no matter how intense the pressure (Luke 22:39–46; Matt. 27:39–44). In this way, He succeeded in opening the eyes of very sin-sick people. Jesus did it for men and women who did not even realize they were living with a cancer so acute it merited the ugliest of all labels: rebellion against God (John 8:34, 37, 40, 44–49, 55; Isa. 1:4, TLB). The greatest and most powerful eye-openers of all time to this deadly malignancy are the Lord's crucifixion on Calvary's knoll and His resurrection three days later.

Jesus not only served His Father's plan but also served people, blessing them with His love. The Lord did not come demanding; instead, He lived only to give Himself to others. "It is not the healthy who need a doctor, but the sick," Jesus said to the Pharisees. "I have not come to call the righteous, but sinners to repentance" (Luke 5:31–32). He was even willing to wash His disciples' dirty and smelly feet (Deut. 15:16–17; John 13:5–10). The most depraved of men felt a warm brotherhood with Jesus Christ.

When a person discovers how Jesus loved, he is motivated to shout with a heart full of passion, "I belong to my lover," even as he rejoices that "His desire is for me" (Song of Sol. 7:10).

II. Jesus, the Servant-Messiah

A. Service vs. Servility

Jesus "made himself nothing," Paul wrote, and took "the very nature of a servant" (Phil. 2:7). The term for "servant" here is *doulou*, which translates in English as "slave." Jesus "laid aside his mighty power and glory, [took] the disguise of a slave and [became] like men" (Phil. 2:7, TLB).

Slavery is arguably the greatest social evil in all history. It has always been cruel and fundamentally flawed, precisely because it violates free will, the most sacred and treasured gift God gave to all men.

> The Israelites groaned in their slavery and cried out, and their cry for help because of their slavery went up to God. God heard their groaning.
> —Exodus 2:23–24

This kind of bondage is inherently evil, therefore, because it violates free will and reduces fellow human beings to cringing servility.

The principle of service, however, is not evil. Service is actually a basic value in the Tri-unity of God; therefore, service is not what defines the wickedness of slavery. Slavery is criminal because it perverts service by making it involuntary.

B. The Golden Rule

"In everything, do to others as you would have them do to you," Jesus said (Matt. 7:12). If all men lived by this servant principle from a heart of love, society would be utopian. Little wonder Jesus' teaching is identified by the term *the Golden Rule*, which "sums up the Law and the Prophets" (Matt. 7:12).

✀ Are You Taking Care of Your Baby? ✀

Our Bible college professor impressed on us often that we are not under the law when we are in Christ. Instead, we are under a new law—the law of love. He was fond of this illustration and told it often.

All states in America, he said, have laws stating a woman must take care of her child. So, a legal representative from Social Services comes to this new mother's home. "Are you doing what the law requires and taking care of your baby?" she asks the young mother."

The woman, tenderly holding her baby, responds, "I don't need a law to make me take care of my baby."

Then our professor would ask us, "Why was this mother telling the truth?" He usually would continue without waiting for us to answer: "Because she loves her baby! She voluntarily becomes his servant. She feeds him, holds him, changes his diapers—fulfills all of the requirements of the law day and night—because she loves him."

Our teacher would always make his application: "In the same way, you and I no longer need the law when we are in Christ. Instead, we are guided by the law of love."[2]

Law can define disobedience but cannot empower obedience. This is true because no law has ever been written that can impart life (Gal. 3:21). God is love, however, and God is also life; hence, love is life-giving too (John 14:6; 1 John 4:8, 16). Love, therefore, can both define disobedience and empower obedience, because inherent in love is its own sense of obligation. So, love fulfills the law (Gal. 5:7–14, KJV; Matt. 5:17; 2 Cor. 3:6; Eph. 6:24). When we are living by the Golden Rule, we actually want to do what is right because we love Jesus Christ.

This understanding helps to explain the interrelationships of the Trinity. No sense of mastery, which makes another grovel, is present in the Godhead, nor are there even tiny flashes of the egoism that exalts oneself in pride over another. Each of the persons in the unity of the God who is One—the Father, the Son, and the Holy Spirit—acts out of *agape* love. The Golden Rule has always been golden first and foremost because it characterizes the heart of God.

The Golden Rule did not describe the Roman Empire, however. Half the people in the Mediterranean world eked out their existence under the slashing lash of stinging slavery. It was a vicious and unbearably cruel way of life.

Jesus Christ set in motion the solution to humanity's fundamental problem by serving His Father and His plan. He did it with unreserved trust, from a heart committed to the ethic of *agape* love. These qualities frame the essence of the term *the love of God*. The Lord served His fellow man with the same love He showed to His Father (John 17:23). In doing so, He taught people to love as He loved (John 13:34–35). To give the ultimate illustration of His love, Jesus collected His own strength, climbed Mount Calvary, and died to cure the slavery to sin in every man's heart. Humanity could never be the same, not after Calvary. That kind of grace changed the world.

Modeling the Golden Rule, in fact, came quite naturally for the Messiah. He had been a part of only that attitude in the Godhead from eternity. Jesus brought heaven's "normal" to the earth in the Golden Rule. When compared to the attitude of Rome, however, His ordinary life seemed unbelievably alien and utterly weak.

C. The Wisdom That Misses God's Wisdom in Christ

The wise, the scholars and the philosophers, totally missed God's visit to the earth in flesh and blood. In their foolishness they were too consumed with the wisdom of this world to see God's wisdom in Jesus Christ (1 Cor. 1:20).

The religious leaders missed His visit too. When the Servant of all rode the lowly donkey into Jerusalem, the priests demanded that Jesus stop the adulation of the crowd, especially that of the children. They failed to perceive that Israel's Messiah was actually in their streets doing wonderful things, while they were blindly demeaning Him with their silly demands. They even wanted to make the children stop being children—solely because the youngsters were honoring Jesus (Matt. 21:14–16).

D. Jesus, Servant of the Father

One of the chief requirements of a slave is that he give unquestioned obedience. Jesus was just that kind of servant to His Father. He was totally committed to God's plan (Luke 18:31–34; John 6:38; 14:31; 18:37). Jesus had made Himself a servant to the agenda from eternity, long before He gave His hands and feet to the Roman spikes (Eph. 1:4; 1 Pet. 1:20). Hence, He refused to permit anything to hinder His march to Calvary (Matt. 16:23–28). In becoming such a dedicated servant, Jesus showed His followers what it means to "serve God" (John 17:4). He also turned the world upside down (Acts 17:6, KJV). When people follow Him with the kind of trust He gave to His Father, they will turn the world upside down, too.

The Lord freely served people's needs without seeking to control them and did it whether or not they loved Him back. The result of His life-changing love was that all people chosen "in him before the creation of the world" are redeemable (Eph. 1:4–8). John wrote that "all people" means "whosoever will" (John 3:16; 4:13–14, KJV; also Joel 2:32; Isa. 55:7).

Men and women of the most humble status quickly saw God in Jesus and speedily came to feel a warm brotherhood with the lowly Nazarene. His servant heart made them sense unbelievable warmth, love, and freedom. As a result, "The common people heard him gladly" (Mark 12:37, KJV). Jesus motivated the people to perceive that God was present among them—and He was.

Paul said Jesus' strategy to redeem people was to love them so much He was willing to make Himself nothing. For this reason, He took on "the very nature of a servant, being made in human likeness" (Phil. 2:7). In His humiliation, the divine nature did not merely touch human flesh; it actually became flesh at the level of slavery, the lowest strata of society. Jesus Christ condescended not just to men of wealth and power but also to "people of low position" (Rom. 12:16).

E. The Songs of the Servant

In four passages commonly called the Servant Songs, the prophet Isaiah foretold that Messiah would come to serve. A brief summary of each hymn will illustrate the prophet's insight into Jesus' mindset.

1. The Tenderness of the Servant (Isa. 42:1–4)

Jesus was a kindhearted servant, the chosen and the delight of His Father. Isaiah foretold this very gentle servant would not raise His voice in the streets, break a bruised reed, or snuff out a smoldering wick (Matt. 12:20; 20:28); nor would He be discouraged or falter until He finished the job of establishing justice on the earth, including the remote islands of the sea.

The light in the life of Simon Peter burned dimly in Pilate's judgment hall when Peter denied three times even knowing the Lord (Matt. 26:34; Mark 14:30–31). Jesus could have easily snuffed out Peter's faith that dark night, but His goal was only to soften the very hardened wick, bringing it back to full flame—and He succeeded. Peter had been such a bruised reed at Jesus' trial that the song went out of his life. But sweet, indeed, was the "music" that came from the Apostle to the Jews in his sermon on the day of Pentecost (Luke 22:31–34; 54–62; Acts 2:14–41; Gal. 2:8).

2. The Call of the Servant (Isa. 49:1–7)

God, from eternity, gave Jesus a servant's commission. He was the sharpened sword in His Father's hand and the very special polished arrow in His quiver. Messiah's job description was to call Israel back to God. He would also be a "light for the Gentiles," successfully bringing "salvation to the ends of the earth" (Isa. 49:6). In achieving so grand an objective, Messiah's ministry displayed the Father's splendor.

3. The Obedience of the Servant (Isa. 50:4–9)

Isaiah portrayed the submission of the Servant, recording Jesus' testimony in advance: "I have not been rebellious; I have not drawn back" (Isa. 50:5). The prophet actually described the Messiah in the sharp terms of the self-emptying (*kenosis*) principle that the Incarnation revealed centuries later (John 5:19–36; Ps. 16:7–8; Acts 2:25). In fact, Isaiah put this declaration in Jesus' mouth:

> The Sovereign Lord has given me an instructed tongue, to know the word that sustains the weary. He wakens me morning by morning, wakens my ear to listen like one being taught. The Sovereign Lord has opened my ears, and I have not been rebellious; I have not drawn back.
>
> —ISAIAH 50:4–5

In the context of describing Messiah's obedience, Isaiah used His suffering to model the extent of the Lord's faithfulness: "I offered my back to those who beat me, my cheeks to those who pulled out my beard; I did not hide my face from mocking and spitting" (Isa. 50:6; see Mark 14:65). Isaiah even penned the Lord's testimony as He made His last journey to Jerusalem: "I set my face like flint, and I know I will not be put to shame" (Isa. 50:7). Some seven centuries after Isaiah's prophecy, Jesus vindicated all of Isaiah's predictions.

4. The Suffering of the Servant (Isa. 52:13–53:12)

As the Father's loyal servant, the Messiah was willing to pay the ultimate price for man's salvation. For example, Isaiah anticipated the high cost of redemption just in the disfigurement of Messiah's face and body, and wrote about it in the past tense, as if it had already happened. He was "marred beyond human likeness," Isaiah said, and was "despised and rejected by men, a man of sorrows, and familiar with suffering" (vv. 52:14; 53:3).

Isaiah's prophecy was accurate. In Isaiah 53, the prophet wrote that Messiah submitted to His Father to the point of being "pierced for our transgressions" and "crushed for our iniquities" (v. 5). He carried our punishment and healed our wounds (v. 4). The Father chose to give His Son rather than give up on humankind. Hence, God made this abused and suffering servant, who served all the way to His shameful death, the ultimate guilt offering (v. 10). By His death, Jesus achieved His goal and satisfied the requirements of His Father for the justification of all who call on God for salvation (v. 11). Indeed, the opposite demands of justice and mercy met in harmonious embrace in Christ's outstretched arms on Golgotha's tree (Rom. 3:26). At Calvary, both rested their cases in the heavenly courts and were satisfied (Isa. 53:11).

The Lord's objective, to bring the love of God to the earth, was a most challenging concept to the Hebrew mindset. The Jewish people just did not grasp that their King would come to them "gentle and riding on a donkey, on a colt the foal of a donkey" (Matt. 21:5; Zech. 9:9). This difficulty also shows how far Abraham's seed had drifted from the servant heart of God, as mirrored in the Golden Rule (Matt. 7:12).

F. The Ultimate Portrait of the Servant

Jesus demonstrated He would serve the needs of a Roman centurion as quickly as He would a son of Abraham (Matt. 8:5–13). The apostle Paul later perceived that in Jesus' great mind, a centurion with a heart to believe God *was* a son of Abraham (Gal. 3:29).

Jesus taught His followers the best way to win people to God is to serve their deepest needs selflessly, even when they do not know what their needs are. "Whoever will be great among you," Jesus said, "let him be your minister; and whoever will be chief among you, let him be your servant: even as the Son of Man did not come to be ministered to, but to minister, and to give his life as a ransom for many" (Matt. 20:26–28, KJV). In fact, a requirement for a believer to be able truthfully to say, "I belong to my lover," is to make a free and loving choice to adopt the Servant-Messiah's attitude and lifestyle (Song of Sol. 7:10; Phil. 2:5). Doing so is the best possible way to work out one's own salvation with fear and trembling (Phil. 2:12–13).

On Golgotha, implicit trust had its finest hour. The Cross, therefore, is the ultimate portrait of Jesus as the slave to His Father's plan. Could there be a greater example of a loving, servant-like attitude? No man before or since has demonstrated loyalty on that scale. This is all the more true when one comprehends Jesus could have reached for the independent display of His omnipotence and, with a word, sent His enemies into the abyss (Matt. 26:53; Luke 8:31–32; Rev. 20:1–3).

G. Engaging the Culture With Love

Jesus confronted Jewish culture to such an extent that He became a threat to the system (John 11:48). Because the priestly system could not control Jesus, they drew their weapons and conspired to kill Him. Kings invariably believe dominion and authority come by the sword, but the humiliation of Christ teaches that those "who draw the sword will die by the sword" (Matt. 20:25; 26:52). Instead of using a sword, Jesus won the throne of the universe with the qualities of a lamb (John 1:29, 36; also Rev. 5:5–6).

The Lord's plan proved that the one who serves best will also reign best. Jesus served humbly and made His way to the cross in complete trust. Marvel of marvels, while hanging on the nails, Jesus endured the fury of hell in silence (Isa. 53:7; Acts 8:32–33; 1 Pet. 2:19–25).

The bottom line was the Jewish leaders, personified in the high priest and the Sanhedrin, produced their own version of religious slavery and demanded complete loyalty. A classic example is the blind man whom the Lord healed. Though their son received sight, his parents were afraid to give honor to Jesus for fear they would be cast out of the synagogue (John 9:22).

The Jewish system did not own Jesus, however, and could not control Him. He was every bit a servant, but not their servant; He was outside their system. He submitted Himself to His Father and to hurting people in need of a physician, but not to them (Matt. 9:12; 12:34–37). They perceived if they could not bring Jesus under their domination, they would ultimately lose control over the people. The religious rulers conspired to kill Him because they feared Him (Mark 11:18).

Jesus gave His life helping people comprehend their problem and convincing them of His cure. This was without question one of the Pharisees primary issues against Him (John 11:48). Jesus was committed to serve His Father; hence, His servant heart did not adopt their values and way of living. He offered a diagnosis and cure radically foreign to their commitment to preserve the Law of Moses (John 3:14; 9:28).

Rome demanded loyalty too—political loyalty. Quite obviously, Jesus' message of spiritual freedom threatened Roman political values. With the power of the sword, Rome reduced conquered peoples like the Israelites to the most rancid levels of slavery. It was servility at its worst and totally against their will.

Political servility and religious servility, no doubt, are two of the greatest evils ever perpetrated on the human family. Arguably, the worst of these is religious servility.

H. The Love of Ordinary People for the Servant

The common people "listened to him with delight" (Mark 12:37). To them, being around Jesus was like paradise on Earth. The more they observed the great strength of His gracious servant heart, the less they liked the bondage of the Pharisees' hundreds of rules, all of which demanded performance but lacked motivating love to achieve them. As for Jesus, one needed to be around Him for only a few minutes to realize He loved people and was dedicated to serving their needs. Let it be underscored: Jesus Christ was a servant to His Father's plan, and that included absolute commitment to man's redemption.

I. Legalism and the Golden Rule

Legalism is always self-centered. It focuses on man's futile efforts to earn merit with God, and serves to *get*. Legalism is very alien to the love in the Golden Rule.

Grace, however, is the special and unmerited favor of God that concentrates on love for God and for people, and says, "I serve because I love." "You will know the truth and the truth will set you free," Jesus taught (John 8:32; Gal. 5:1). The Lord offered His followers freedom to love God and people and to live as a servant at the same time, but His own people ultimately rejected His values and nailed Him to the tree (John 1:11). Yet, Jesus died by His own choice; He could easily have stopped them (Matt. 26:53; John 18:6). The Lord hung there because of His own desire to serve humankind. He knew what He was doing would redeem God's children and bring peace between God and man (Col. 1:20).

Jesus' enemies, therefore, did not succeed in making Him grovel, even on the cross. The centurion whose soldiers crucified Him had seen many men do just that—die both cursing and begging for mercy at the same time—but not Jesus. This hardened Roman officer recognized the distinctive difference (Matt. 27:54; Luke 23:47). One of the thieves hanging on a cross beside Him saw the dissimilarity too, and made his appeal, "Jesus, remember me when you come into your kingdom" (Luke 23:42). With what little stamina He had left in His weakened body Jesus answered the thief, "Today you will be with me in paradise" (v. 43).

When Jesus' tabernacle of flesh was dangling on the nails between life and death, the Lord loved the criminal hanging beside Him so much He forgave his sins and swung the gates of heaven wide open to him. Could there be a greater example of the Golden Rule?

The believer's road of total trust in both the Father's good intentions and His strategy is always the highway that leads to peace with God. The key for all Christ's followers is to "let this mind be in you," that begins with adopting the Lord's attitude (Phil. 2:5, KJV and NIV).

III. Following the Example of the Servant

A. Yearning for Personal Guidance

Spirit-filled people have always hungered for personal guidance by the same Holy Spirit who directed the life of our Lord Jesus Christ and His holy apostles (John 5:19–20; Acts 3:4). The baptism with the Holy Spirit is the gift of the Father to help people see and hear God. Yet, human frailties cloud vision and diminish ability to listen. All of Christ's followers in the church, in fact, live with imperfect hearing and perception.

B. The Written Word—the First Priority for Guidance

The Lord inseparably linked the Scriptures with the Word of His Father and the guidance of the Holy Spirit (Matt. 4:4, 7, 10; 5:17–18; 24:35). The anchor that keeps God's children in balance is the written revelation of God. God does talk to His children (Acts 8:29). Yet, the Bible must be primary above all visions, all intuition, and all spiritual perceptions. No spiritual manifestation rises to the level of adding to the inspired Scriptures. Instead, all manifestations must bow before and be judged by the written Word of God.

❧ A Day Without the Word, a Lost Day ❧

"Because I am a Christian," said Dietrich Bonhoeffer (1906–1945), "every day in which I do not penetrate more deeply into the knowledge of God's Word in Holy Scripture is a lost day for me. I can only move forward with certainty upon the firm ground of the Word of God. And, as a Christian, I learn to know the Holy...by hearing the Word preached and by prayerful meditation."[3]

The yearning of one's soul to hear what God is saying and to see what the Holy One is doing must come first from diligent study of the sacred Canon. We elevate the primacy of the Bible for all matters of faith and practice. King David said God actually exalted His Word above His name (Ps. 138:2, KJV).

Secondarily, the Spirit talks to people through the inner voice of their spirit and enables them to see with spiritual eyes (2 Kings 6:12; Luke 2:25–27; Acts 8:29; 14:9). The primary standard for judging personal insight is the written Word of God. The Holy Spirit never contradicts the Word He inspired.

The person that is able to walk in the Spirit best is one who has diligently developed the habit of searching the Scriptures. He accepts the final authority of the Bible for all matters of faith and practice, even while he delights in the specific manifestations of the Spirit that give guidance to His life.

A child of God cherishes and devours the Bible for Christ's sake and resists wholeheartedly the temptation to devour the sacred Canon merely for intellectual knowledge. To hold the Word dear as an end in itself is the seedbed of a form of idolatry identified by the term *bibliolatry* (the worship of the book itself).

IV. The Servant-Messiah's Anointing

It is important to explore the special anointing of the Holy Spirit that functioned in Jesus' life. In doing so, this study will develop the biblical background for this anointing and show that it reached its fullest meaning in the investiture of Jesus Christ at His Jordan River baptism.

A. Understanding Terms

The first biblical use of *mashach*, which means "to anoint," is Genesis 31:13, when Jacob anointed the pillar he built at Bethel. This concept of anointing communicates the word picture of spreading a liquid, and the most common ointment was olive oil. As the meaning of the word expanded in Hebrew culture, it came to mark the anointing ceremony that set a person apart for divine service.

Moses spelled out a specific formula for the anointing oil. It included myrrh, fragrant cinnamon, cane, and cassia, mixed by a perfumer in an olive oil base. This unique blend became the sacred anointing oil for tabernacle worship (Exod. 30:22–29). Everything about the tabernacle had this oil on it, including Aaron and his sons, their clothing, and all of the furniture pieces of the tabernacle.

The Lord laid exclusive claim to this mixture and told Moses to say to the Israelites:

> This is to be my sacred anointing oil for the generations to come. Do not pour it on men's bodies and do not make any oil with the same formula. It is sacred, and you are to consider it sacred. Whoever makes perfume like it and whoever puts it on anyone other than a priest must be cut off from his people.
>
> —EXODUS 30:31–33

B. The Presence in the Tabernacle and the Temple

Without question, the special presence of God accompanied priestly ministry at the tabernacle and the temple (Lev. 9:24; 2 Chron. 7:1). When the people came to worship and offer their sacrifices, they perceived this presence and knew Jehovah was with them. The Ark of the Covenant positioned between the cherubim in the Most Holy Place of the tabernacle was God's unique dwelling place (Exod. 37:1–9).

The special anointing oil, therefore, came to symbolize a profound impartation that transferred divine power and authority for service. The people understood that a blessing of the gift of the Spirit of Jehovah should be part of this anointing (Exod. 30:30; 1 Sam. 10:9–11). The Hebrew priestly system linked the anointing closely with the nearness of the Spirit, and many who were anointed, like Saul, did experience the presence (1 Sam. 10:1, 6–7). It was never the purpose of God that the oil and the presence would be one and the same, however. A person clearly could have the anointing oil poured on him as a symbolic investiture of office without an accompanying impartation of the divine presence.

Over the centuries of Israel's spiritual decline, the anointing ceremony came to mean little more than a person receiving the authority of his office. This was true because the Spirit of God released no divine presence to honor the ceremony. Ezekiel saw a vision, for example, in which the Spirit actually departed from the temple (Ezek. 11:23).

A person could also have the blessing that imparted the divine presence of the Spirit in his life without the ceremony of the anointing oil. John the Baptist, who was filled with the Spirit from his mother's womb, illustrates the principle (Luke 1:15, KJV).

C. The Anointing as a Symbol

So what was the purpose of the anointing oil? It served as an outward symbol of an inward work of the Spirit in a new leader's life. The anointing oil itself never blessed anyone with an endowment of the presence of God. Only God could do that. It was clearly the Spirit of God, the Presence, who was the effective source of a divine anointing, so the use of the anointing oil relates only as a figure of speech. It never did guarantee the blessing of the Spirit.

D. The Christ, the Anointed One

As the anointing oil relates to Jesus, two great themes unfold. The first relates to His name, the Christ, and the second, to His anointing. Angels on the Bethlehem hillside announced that "a Savior has been born to you; he is *Christ* the Lord" (Luke 2:11, emphasis added). *Christ* is a transliteration of the Greek word *christos*, which carries the same meaning as the Hebrew *mashach*, or "anointed one."

The name *Christ* blossomed into its fullest meaning at the Lord's baptism in the Jordan River, thirty years after the angels' declaration. At the precise moment Jesus emerged from the water, the Holy Spirit descended upon Him in the form of a dove and the voice of the Father spoke from heaven, "This is my son, whom I love; with him I am well pleased" (Matt. 3:17).

That divine instant marked the investiture of the Son of God as the Messiah. At His Jordan River baptism, Jesus became the Anointed One, the Messiah, the Christ, the *mashach,* who in the heart of God had been "slain from the creation of the world" (Rev. 13:8; 1 Pet. 1:19–20). The inauguration did not result from a perfumer's oil, but from the Holy Spirit, given to Him without limit (John 3:34). At the Jordan River, Jesus was empowered to do the work of the Messiah. It did not include handing Him a seal, a ring, or a diadem; instead, the Holy Spirit in His life became the witness of His messianic office.

The prophet Isaiah specifically foretold the anointing that would be on the life of Jesus. This is another of Isaiah's first-person prophecies, as if the Messiah Himself were speaking His own testimony and job description:

> The Spirit of the Sovereign Lord is on me, because the Lord has anointed me to preach good news to the poor. He has sent me to

bind up the brokenhearted, to proclaim freedom for the captives and release from darkness for the prisoners, to proclaim the year of the LORD's favor.

—ISAIAH 61:1–2

After Jesus triumphed in the wilderness of temptation, He was free to return to His home in Nazareth. When Jesus arrived, He walked into the synagogue, accepted the scroll handed to Him, and unrolled it to Isaiah's prophecy. Then He began to read from Isaiah 61.

The Spirit of the Lord is upon me, because he hath anointed me to preach the gospel to the poor; he hath sent me to heal the brokenhearted, to preach deliverance to the captives, and recovering of sight to the blind, to set at liberty them that are bruised, To preach the acceptable year of the Lord.

—LUKE 4:18–19, KJV

Then the Holy Spirit-filled Son of man spooled up the scroll, returned it to the scribe, and sat down, saying, "The eyes of everyone in the synagogue were fastened on him, and he began by saying to them, 'Today this scripture is fulfilled in your hearing'" (Luke 4:20–21).

Jesus Christ was truly God incarnate before He left Nazareth to journey to his installation as Messiah at the Jordan. He was also the same incarnate Son of God when He returned to Nazareth. Yet, part of the mystery is that He was significantly different after that event, for He returned to Nazareth being full of the Holy Spirit. He experienced an impartation of the Spirit that exceeded measurement.

As the second person of the Trinity, Jesus always had been the Christ and Israel's Messiah. Now as the God-Man, He was regally invested as Israel's anointed, her Messiah—albeit veiled in the flesh of true humanity. In this anointing, soon to be thoroughly tested in the crucible of the wilderness, the Lamb of God launched His redemptive ministry to take away the sin of the world.

V. The Servant Makes Atonement

We now turn our attention to the Atonement—the process by which Jesus Christ brought peace between God and man, satisfying the requirements of a holy God. Achieving it was the singular goal of the Incarnation and the lynchpin of His mediatory work as the Servant of all (John 18:37; Mark 9:35; John 19:30). Everything the Lord did in His ministry ultimately focused on this objective (Luke 24:26; Acts 17:3; Heb. 9:26–28).

✺ Satisfaction, on My Behalf ✺

The film Luther traces the struggles of the young scholar to relate the message he was learning from Scripture to the rigid church of his day. Martin Luther's own religious upbringing had taught him a gospel that was an exercise in fear.

Preaching to his congregation in Wittenberg, Luther dared to proclaim the truth of the Christ of Scripture over the terrors of the institutional church.

Standing before his congregation (in the film) he says, "Terrible. Unforgiving. That's how I saw God. Punishing us in this life; committing us to Purgatory after death, sentencing sinners to burn in hell for all eternity. But I was wrong.

"Those who see God as angry do not see him rightly but look upon a curtain as if a dark storm cloud has been drawn across his face. If we truly believe that Christ is our Savior, then we have a God of love, and to see God in faith is to look upon his friendly heart.

"So when the devil throws your sins in your face and declares that you deserve death and hell, tell him this," says Luther, as his sermon rises to a crescendo, "I admit that I deserve death and hell. What of it? For I know one who suffered and made satisfaction in my behalf. His name is Jesus Christ, Son of God. Where he is, there I shall be also."

In such simple and straightforward preaching of the gospel, the Reformation was launched.[4]

A. Atonement: Provided by the God Who Feels Pain

How do the children of Adam comprehend the extent to which their sins wounded the heart of God? The prophet Jeremiah painted a gut-wrenching portrait of the Father's broken heart in his description of Israel's divorce from Jehovah, a people whom God loved deeply, having chosen them as His own (Jer. 3:1–4:4). Eight times in these twenty-nine verses the heart-rending appeal goes out, "Return!" God promised faithless Israel if she would come back: "'I am merciful,' declares the LORD, 'I will not be angry forever'" (Jer. 3:12).

Calvary itself is the masterpiece painting of how deeply our sins have injured God's heart. In fact, a person will never comprehend the pain his sins cause God until he opens his eyes and sees God's Son hanging on the cruel crossbeams to atone for his sins. Many people do not understand that the eternal God, who is Spirit, even feels pain (Gen. 6:6). How vitally important to rediscover the cross of Jesus Christ! The truth is, our sins hurt Him deeply and crucify Him afresh (Heb. 6:6).

The human family really does need help, and the fountain from which the healing comes is the wounded heart of God Himself. He gave His only begotten Son as the sacrifice for our atonement, and that gift defines the extent of His love (Rom. 3:25).

B. The Atonement as a Free Choice

It is part of "the mystery of godliness" that the sacrifice of Jesus was at the same time both a free choice and a necessity (1 Tim. 3:16). As a free choice, Jesus paid the price willingly to accomplish Calvary (John 10:17–18). He was under no necessity or obligation inherent in either His own divine essence or in His true humanity to drag His cross up Golgotha. Jesus was God before He volunteered to go to Calvary. The cross was not obligatory to remain God, and as a perfect, sinless man, Jesus did not deserve the sentence.

How, then, should one understand the Atonement? Calvary was the result of an act of free choice that sprang from the essence of the Godhead. It was a love decision of the Trinity toward sinful man. Jehovah showed that He cared so very much that the triune God planned from eternity the sacrifice to heal the breach between God and man. The atonement was a free expression of God, showing His essence to be that of love—"God so loved the world that he gave His only begotten Son" (John 3:16, KJV).

It was the good pleasure of the triune God that the Son of God would be "a Lamb without blemish or defect…chosen before the creation of the world" and "revealed in these last times for [our] sake" (1 Pet. 1:19–20; 2 Tim. 1:9–10; Rev. 13:8). As Colossians 1:19–20 explains, "God was pleased to have all fullness dwell in him and through him to reconcile all things to himself." The atonement, then, was a gift, a love gift from the heart of God. "The Son of God…loved me and gave himself for me," Paul said (Gal. 2:20). Jesus washes us "from our sins in His own blood" because He loves us (Rev. 1:5).

C. The Atonement as a Necessity

When a believer assimilates into his thinking the Atonement as the free love-gift of God, he can then begin to look at the other side of the Atonement. From the point in eternity when God's Son made the choice to achieve the Atonement, "it was necessary for the Christ to suffer and to rise from the dead the third day" (Luke 24:46, NKJV; Ps. 22; Isa. 50:6; Acts 17:3).

During His incarnation, Jesus the Servant repeatedly taught His cross was the centerpiece of the gospel. Jesus explained that a grain of wheat must fall into the ground and die or it can bring forth no fruit; but if it does die, it brings forth much fruit (John 12:24). "As Moses lifted up the snake in the desert," Jesus said of Himself, "so the Son of Man must be lifted up" (John 3:14; see also Num. 21:9; John 8:28).

To perceive that *agape* love, the love of God, acts in the best interest of others is to understand the compelling love in the heart of Jesus Christ. For example, "As the time approached for him to be taken up to heaven, Jesus resolutely set out for Jerusalem" (Luke 9:51). In this passage the Lamb "slain from the creation of the world" loved sinners to such an extent that He made non-negotiable the commitment to accomplish the atonement (Rev. 13:8).

We conclude, then, the cross of Christ was essential for man's salvation. The atonement portrays God demonstrating "his love for us in this: while we were still sinners Christ died for us (Rom. 5:8). Since we were "reconciled to God by the death of his Son," we can "also rejoice in God through our Lord Jesus Christ, through whom we have now received reconciliation" (Rom. 5:10–11).

D. The Atonement as a Covering

The term *atonement* carries the idea of a covering that hides the eyes of God from the sins of humanity (Exod. 25:17; 26:34) Man's sin affronted the righteous heart of God, but Jesus Christ surrendered His own life to provide the covering (Ps. 51:9; Micah 7:19; Isa. 38:17; Heb. 10:4–10; Eph. 2:14–18). Jesus Christ gave His blood to enable people to choose His diagnosis and His cure (Rom. 3:25; Heb. 2:17; Lev. 4:12–20; 6:2–7). The Father "made him who had no sin to be sin for us, so that in him we might become the righteousness of God" (2 Cor. 5:21).

No one inherits everlasting life because of his own personal righteousness. Salvation comes through trusting in the covering Jesus Christ provided. He alone made satisfaction before God on man's behalf, birthing eternal life (Isa. 53:11; Rom. 3:23; 5:9). Because His love covers a multitude of sins, when we love like Him, our love covers sins, too (John 20:23; James 5:20; 1 Pet. 4:8).

E. The Atonement as Reconciliation

"We rejoice in God through our Lord Jesus Christ," Paul wrote, "through whom we have now received reconciliation" (Rom. 5:11; Col. 1:21). *Reconciliation*, by its very nature, assumes a breach has occurred, so that each participant feels separation from the other and needs to be reunited. This great trait of God's character does just that, bringing together estranged parties. Let it be fully appreciated that man's sins grieve the heart of God and fill Him with pain (Gen. 6:6). Even the Holy Spirit can be grieved (Isa. 53:10; Eph. 4:30). In fact, the necessity of God's own judgments causes Him grief (1 Chron. 21:15; Ps. 78:4). God was alienated from man and man from God, yet God's pain and grief never hindered demonstration of His lavish grace, mercy, and loving kindness (Jer. 3:1, 14; 1 John 3:1). Quite to the contrary:

> If anyone is in Christ he is a new creation; the old has gone, the new has come! All this is from God, who reconciled us to himself through Christ and gave us the ministry of reconciliation: that God was reconciling the world to himself in Christ, not counting men's sins against them. And he has committed to us the message of reconciliation. We are therefore Christ's ambassadors, as though God were making his appeal through us. We implore you on Christ's behalf: be reconciled to God.
>
> —2 CORINTHIANS 5:17–20

❧ Teaching Children About the Atonement ❧

Michael takes his family out most weeks to see a game or to some other special event. When they come home, they make a fire in the fireplace and pop popcorn.

During one of these evenings, little Billy made a real pest of himself in the car driving home, so he was punished by being sent to sit in his bedroom while the family enjoyed popcorn. After the fire was blazing and the aroma of the popcorn filled the house, Billy's dad went back to his son's room and said to the precocious youngster, "You can go out now with the others. I will stay here and take your punishment!"

Billy never forgot his first lesson on the concept of atonement.[5]

Jesus Christ served His Father's interests so effectively He achieved this reconciliation between God and man, resulting in a new friendship (1 John 2:2, TLB; John 15:14; Col. 1:21–22, KJV). Paul taught that even though we were "alienated and enemies in our minds because of wicked works, yet now he has reconciled us in the body of his flesh through death, in order that He might present us holy and unblameable and unreproveable in his sight" (Col. 1:21–22, KJV). The result of His sacrifice is that all believers can "rejoice in God through our Lord Jesus Christ, through whom we have now received reconciliation" (Rom. 5:10–11). This resolution of the problem is so thoroughly comprehensive that He removes man's transgressions "as far as the east is from the west" (Ps. 103:12).

Because man is reconciled to God through Christ's death, he receives the word of reconciliation, which he is to share with the unconverted. How beautiful is that word—"that God was reconciling the world to himself in Christ"

(2 Cor. 5:19). Considering what Jesus did at Calvary, can there be a greater example of a servant heart? Surely, in the face of such love the redeemed are motivated to return it by serving as Christ's ambassadors (2 Cor. 5:20).

The concept of atonement embraces more than the forgiveness of an estranged relationship. It also includes a change in the nature of the offender, enabling him to cease living his life of alienation from God. Jesus' atoning blood creates a new man "like God in true righteousness and holiness" (Eph. 4:24). In this relationship, the believer is "shielded by God's power" (1 Pet. 1:5). Christ's blood provides that man need not sin, as well as provision that if he does sin, he has "an advocate with the Father, Jesus Christ the righteous" (1 John 2:1, KJV; Rom. 6:22).

F. The Atonement as Substitution

Jesus died in our stead as our replacement—one in the place of another; hence, His death was a substitutionary atonement (Isa. 53:6). Nowhere is this better illustrated than when Jesus Christ took the place of Barabbas, a murderer and insurrectionist, and died the death Barabbas should have died (Luke 23:13–25).

As our substitute, Jesus' sacrifice brought to an end the barrier of wrath that barred intimacy between God and the whole world (Eph. 2:14–18; Col. 1:20). The captivating portrait of Christ's sacrifice was that one "died for all.... God made him who had no sin to be sin for us; so that in him we might become the righteousness of God" (2 Cor. 5:15, 21). "While we were yet sinners Christ died for us" so that we would not suffer the wrath of God (Rom. 5:8, KJV; 1 Thess. 5:9–10). Abraham experience precisely this substitutionary atonement when he "believed the LORD, and he credited it to him as righteousness" (Gen. 15:6).

The Lord did not come to the earth primarily to set an example or to teach a philosophy. Instead, Jesus showed the full extent of His Father's love by giving His life in our place (John 3:16; 13:1). As Peter explained, "Christ died for sins once for all, the righteous for the unrighteous, to bring [us] to God" (1 Pet.3:18). Jesus' death, therefore, was not a great historical accident or a martyrdom, for no man took His life from Him (John 10:17). "The good shepherd [voluntarily laid] down his life for the sheep" (John 10:11).

"Through faith in his blood" as our "merciful and faithful High Priest," the separation between God and man ended (Rom. 3:25–26; Heb. 2:17; Eph. 2:14–18). God's own Son healed the broken heart of the heavenly Father by overlaying our sins with a coating of His own forgiving blood (1 Cor. 15:3; 2 Cor. 5:21; Rom. 5:8; John 10:11).

G. The Atonement as a Ransom

The redemptive work of Jesus Christ included paying a price, a ransom, to set free every captive to sin (1 Cor. 6:20). In Christ's atonement, the Servant Savior funded the ransom with a price so high it cost the last drop of His blood (Mark 10:45; Matt. 20:28; 1 Pet. 1:19). The result is we are "justified freely by his grace through the redemption that is in Christ Jesus" (Rom. 3:24).

Speaking of the divine provision, Paul told Timothy that Jesus "gave himself a ransom for all men" (1 Tim. 2:6). Addressing God's foreknowledge, Matthew said the Lord "gave his life as a ransom for many" (Matt. 20:28).

Setting men free who are undeserving was the purpose for which Jesus gave His own life. He disbursed the payment as His precious blood dripped on the rocks of Calvary's knoll (Heb. 9:14; 10:12). Jesus offered this costliest of all ransoms on the altar of heavenly justice. Any penitent who personally believes in Christ is enveloped by the redeeming blood of Jesus and made a co-heir of eternal life (Rom. 8:17).

❧ The Lost Boat ❧

Tom carried his new boat to the edge of the river. He carefully placed it in the water and slowly let out the string. The boat sailed smoothly. Tom sat in the warm sunshine, admiring the little boat that he had built. Suddenly a strong current caught the boat. Tom tried to pull it back to shore, but the string broke. The little boat raced downstream.

Tom ran along the sandy shore as fast as he could, but his little boat soon slipped out of sight. All afternoon he searched for it. Finally, when it was too dark to look any longer, Tom sadly went home.

A few weeks later, on the way home from school, Tom spotted a boat just like his in a store window. When he got closer, he could see—sure enough—it was his!

Tom hurried to the store manager: "Sir, that's my boat in your window! I made it!"

"Sorry, son, but someone else brought it in this morning. If you want it, you'll have to buy it for one dollar."

Tom ran home and counted all his money. Exactly one dollar! When he reached the store, he rushed to the counter. "Here's the money for my boat."

As he left the store, Tom hugged his boat and said, "Now you're twice mine. First, I made you and now I've bought you."[6]

H. The Atonement and Divine Healing

The sacrifice of Jesus Christ embraces the ministry of *Jehovah Rapha*, the God who heals. This revelation came when Israel in the wilderness had only the bitter waters of Marah to drink. Moses cried out to the Lord, and God miraculously healed their water supply. In this context, Moses interpreted the heart of God to the people, saying, "If you listen carefully to the voice of the LORD your God and do what is right in his eyes, if you pay attention to his commands and keep all his decrees, I will not bring on you any of the diseases I brought on the Egyptians, for I am the LORD [*Jehovah Rapha*] who heals you" (Exod. 15:26).

Isaiah looked through the eyes of prophecy at the Messiah's work and actually interpreted what Jesus' suffering meant some eight hundred years before the events: "Surely he took up our infirmities and carried our sorrows. Yet we considered him stricken by God, smitten by him, and afflicted" (Isa. 53:4). We know this passage refers to Messiah as a healer of the physical body because Matthew gave it that interpretation: "When evening came, many who were demon-possessed were brought to him, and he drove out the spirits with a word and healed all the sick. This was to fulfill what was spoken through the prophet Isaiah: 'He took up our infirmities and carried our diseases'" (Matt. 8:16–17; Isa. 53:4).

The apostle Peter went back to Isaiah 53:5 when he wrote about the provision of salvation in the atonement of Jesus: "He himself bore our sins in his body on the tree, so that we might die to sins and live for righteousness; by his wounds you have been healed" (1 Pet. 2:24). Jesus showed the relationship that routinely exists between spiritual healing and physical healing in the experience of the man He set free at the pool of Bethesda. Shortly after the Lord restored the man, "Jesus found him at the temple and said to him, 'See, you are well again. Stop sinning or something worse may happen to you'" (John 5:14). The man left the temple and gave testimony "that it was Jesus who had made him well" in soul and body (John 5:15).

It is appropriate to rejoice in the incredibly marvelous provision of Jesus' atonement for spiritual healing, as well as physical and emotional healing. James, for example, showed insight into the interrelationship of sin and sickness, especially the sin of unforgiveness and sickness. At times, the two can be so entwined as to be almost inseparable. James also identified a model for ministry to the sick that includes anointing with oil in the name of Jesus to bring healing to the whole man—soul, mind, and body.

Is any one of you sick? He should call the elders of the church to pray over him and anoint him with oil in the name of the Lord. And the prayer offered in faith will make the sick person well; the Lord will raise him up. If he has sinned, he will be forgiven. Therefore, confess your sins to each other and pray for each other so that you may be healed. The prayer of a righteous man is powerful and effective.

—JAMES 5:14–16

I. The Atonement as Redemption for Nature

Jesus Christ, the last Adam, covered with His blood everything that came under condemnation because of the sin of the first Adam. Ultimately, this blessing of redemption extends to nature itself. The natural order groans "as in the pain of childbirth," Paul said, waiting "eagerly for our adoption as sons" (Rom. 8:22–23). Followers of Jesus should find it easy to be good ecologists, therefore, respecting and preserving nature as the creation of God, but without worshiping the natural order (Rom. 1:21–23).

J. The Atonement as Cause of Rejoicing

The apostle Peter taught that even though we cannot physically see our ascended Lord Jesus Christ, we believe and love Him. The result of this firm confidence is that we "rejoice with joy unspeakable and full of glory, receiving the end of [our] faith, even the salvation of [our] souls" (1 Pet. 1:8–9, KJV). The great cause of celebration is that on His cross, Jesus satisfied the wrath of God and brought peace between God and man. He died to enable me to enter into a right relationship with His Father (Gal. 2:20). The fact that Calvary sealed the fate of the devil and all demonic powers was but the byproduct of the Atonement (Luke 10:17–24; 15:7; 1 John 3:8).

Before Jesus Christ, as the Servant of all, could become the Great Physician and cure the cancerous sin that so pervasively plagues all men, Jesus had to walk through the crucible of testing and temptation. Could the devil maneuver Him into a set of circumstances that would motivate Him to break His bond of unqualified trust in His Father? Was there a pressure that just might be strong enough to get Him off track and fog His focus on the Holy Spirit?

~≪ **Chapter Three**

THE COLOSSAL EFFORT
TO BREAK THE SERVANT

Who is this coming up from the desert leaning on her
lover?...Place me like a seal over your heart.

—SONG OF SOLOMON 8:5–6

Consider him who endured such opposition from sinful men, so
that you will not grow weary and lose heart.

—HEBREWS 12:3

Physician, heal yourself!

—LUKE 4:23

~≪ Knowing the Strength of Temptation ≫~
By C. S. Lewis

No man knows how bad he is till he has tried very hard to be good. A
silly idea is current that good people do not know what temptation means.

This is an obvious lie. Only those who try to resist temptation know
how strong it is. After all, you find out the strength of the German army
by fighting it, not by giving in. A man who gives in to temptation after five
minutes simply does not know what it would have been like an hour later.

That is why bad people, in one sense, know very little about badness.
They have lived a sheltered life by always giving in. We never find out the
strength of the evil impulse inside us until we try to fight it.[1]

I. The Servant: Facing Venomous Treatment

Jesus' objective was clear: He was committed to serve both His Father and
the needs of people. His service to His Father focused on His commitment,
with unqualified trust, to accomplish the plan of salvation framed in eternity
by God's love. He intended to achieve the goal without changing it in any
way. Jesus based His commitment to serve people on His understanding of

every man's sinfulness. The Lord's diagnosis of man's problem meant that humankind desperately needed a redeemer, and Jesus came committed to fulfill that role and make the atonement that would cure the problem.

The opposition Jesus faced doing it was vitriolic. It required Him to stay on the alert throughout His ministry and maintain His concentration at all times. He had to resist every pressure intended to divert His attention. For example, the Jews claimed Abraham as their physical and spiritual father, but Jesus denied the claim that they were Abraham's spiritual descendants. The Lord's reason was they were rejecting Him as their Messiah, something Abraham would have never done (John 8:40).

The Jews' reaction was lethal: "'We are not illegitimate children,' they protested. 'The only Father we have is God himself'" (John 8:41). The statement shows how blind they really were. The Son of God was standing face to face with them, speaking the truth into their lives, and they were rejecting Him with murder in their hearts (John 8:37, 48).

Jesus confronted their unbelief after He freed the woman caught in the act of adultery. He bluntly told the Pharisees they did not know Him or His Father, otherwise, they would not have treated the woman so brutally. Jesus' analysis was so foreign to the thinking of the Jewish religious leaders, they were convinced He was a Samaritan and was possessed by a devil—and said so to His face (John 8:48).

Jesus' finding was accurate, however. The Pharisees' Messiah was physically standing in front of them, but they were not the children of His Father. The Lord boldly spoke the truth: "You belong to your father, the devil, and you want to carry out your father's desire. He was a murderer from the beginning, not holding to the truth, for there is no truth in him" (John 8:44; also Luke 4:28–30). It was a forthright judgment from the Messiah who knows the hearts of all men (John 16:30; 21:17). The gospel message is that outside the redemption of Jesus Christ, every man has the devil as his father. Little wonder these spiritual leaders responded to His diagnosis with murderous anger.

People become accustomed to the world system and fit into its mold (Rom. 12:1–2, THE MESSAGE). Said another way, they accept that sickness, pain, and disease, as well as pride, arrogance, and brutality, are status quo in life, so they learn to live with it. By this standard, the values of Jesus Christ actually looked demonic. They could not see they had literally made the satanic the norm for their lives, having accepted it as "just the way it is" and concluding, "It is never going to change," "There is no solution," or "Just make peace with it." Worldly wisdom does come to accept the barnyard lifestyle, expecting nothing better.

❧ Fred and Frank ❧

One summer I worked on a farm, caring for a hundred chickens and two goslings, Fred and Frank, who grew up in a chicken's world. They ate the same food as the chickens and shared a shed with them. One day I formed a plan to set the geese free in a nearby pond. They were uncooperative as I hauled them out of the pen.

Fred and Frank landed in the pond with wings flapping and their feet treading water. For the first time they were enjoying the freedom of what it meant to be geese, not chickens. Even though Fred and Frank were free, they could not ignore the calls of a hundred chickens.

It took the geese no time at all to find their way back to the chicken pen. They squawked and honked, trying to find a way into the enclosure. Even though I took them back to the pond, the geese once again returned to the familiarity of their chicken world.

At times, many of us are like Fred and Frank. We struggle to accept and live in the freedom God offers, but something holds us back. Still, God keeps opening the gate and offering new life. He delights to see us live in abundant freedom.[2]

Jesus challenged Jewish culture with a set of penetrating questions: "How does a man benefit if he gains the whole world and loses his soul in the process? Is anything worth more than his soul?" (Mark 8:36–37, TLB). The wisdom of fallen man can teach a person how to gain the world, but it cannot present to him the gift of eternal life (John 17:2–3). Only Jesus has the wisdom to do that (1 Cor. 1:21). "I am the way and the truth and the life," He said. "No one comes to the Father except through me" (John 14:6; see also John 8:32).

The venomous treatment the Messiah received from the Pharisees and Jewish leaders in Jerusalem continued throughout His ministry (John 8). This reality motivated the writer of Hebrews to admonish his readers to "consider Him who endured such opposition from sinners," lest they grow weary mentally and lose heart (Heb. 12:3).

It is to the spiteful and malicious, even murderous, antagonism Jesus faced day-in and day-out that we now turn our attention.

II. The Servant: Tempted in the Wilderness

Jesus was full of the Holy Spirit following His baptism in the Jordan. He could not yet go back to Nazareth, however, to announce in His hometown synagogue, "The Spirit of the Lord is on me," because there can be no testimony without a test (Luke 4:18). Instead, Jesus was "led by the Spirit in the desert, where for forty days he was tempted by the devil" (Luke 4:1–2).

Jesus served with a moral commitment of total obedience to His Father's plan to redeem the world. But would the commitment of God's Son-become-truly-man hold amid the crucible of forty days' fasting in the wilderness? The devil tempted Adam in the Garden of Eden, but the Son of man underwent His own moment of truth in a far more challenging environment—the wasteland of Judea.

The wilderness temptation demonstrated just how high the stakes really were. Satan knew that steel bond between the persons in the Tri-unity of God had to be penetrated. Some way, some how, Satan had to isolate this new breed of man—the God-man, the Son of man, the last Adam—from The Trinity as His support base. If Satan could do that, he would win. His weapons had always focused on the weaknesses of the flesh, and they had always worked. Surely, there was at least one crevice somewhere in Jesus' manhood that Satan could successfully pry into a open door, and the devil intended to find it.

A. The Appeal to His Flesh—for Bread

"Immediately the Spirit drove him into the wilderness," records Mark 1:12 (KJV). There He fasted for forty days and "ate nothing during those days" (Luke 4:2). Other than the Spirit of God, who never left Him, His companions were the angels who attended Him and the wild animals (Mark 1:13).

It was at the end of those forty days, when Jesus was very hungry, that the devil came to Him. Satan made three appeals to the Lord's physical appetites. The trilogy of answers Jesus gave the tempter came out of the life experiences of Moses, the eminent lawgiver and emancipator. These no doubt constituted the three most important conclusions of the great liberator's life:

> Fear the LORD your God, serve him only.
>
> —DEUTERONOMY 6:13

> Do not test the LORD your God.
>
> —DEUTERONOMY 6:16

> Man does not live on bread alone but on every word that comes from the mouth of the LORD.
>
> —DEUTERONOMY 8:3

Satan first appealed to the desire of Jesus' flesh through His craving for food: "If you are the Son of God, tell this stone to become bread" (Luke 4:3).

Satan intended that his appeal would motivate Jesus, because of His acute hunger, to grasp for His deity and miraculously provide food for Himself extra to the Father's plan (Phil. 2:6). So, the issues in this temptation become obvious:

- Could Satan take advantage of Jesus' acute need for nourishment so that it would become a greater stimulus than His absolute trust in the Creator of the bread?
- Would the demands of His stomach become more important to Him in those moments than faithfulness to the God who formed His stomach?
- Would Jesus worship the thing God made (the bread) or would He remain loyal to the God who is the creator of bread?

Jesus' craving for food was a legitimate physical desire. Honoring Satan's instructions, however, would require Him to grasp for His deity independently of His Father's plan to satisfy His hunger and meet His basic human need (Phil. 2:6).

It also called for an attitude change that would have broken Jesus' bond of absolute trust in His Father, transforming Jesus into the servant of Satan. The result of the attitude change would be that Jesus would reject His Father's special arrangements made in eternity to give nourishment to His hungry and very weak Son. God's plan was that angels would renew His strength after it was all over (Matt. 4:11), so meeting the need Satan's way required turning what was good (the stones) into the food of the devil. It would have changed a basic human need into a carnal and sinful desire, which is the essence of the lust of the flesh (1 John 2:16, KJV).

Moses learned that same lesson well in Israel's wilderness sojourn. He knew what it was like to have a whole nation in the wilderness with no bread or water. He also knew their murmurings that sprang out of their hunger and then turned into the lust of the flesh. They grumbled for the bread they craved instead of entrusting their needs to the Lord of the bread. Moses summarized the experience like this: "[God] humbled you, causing you to hunger and then feeding you with manna, which neither you nor your fathers had known, to teach you that man does not live on bread alone but on every word that comes from the mouth of the LORD" (Deut. 8:3; Num. 11:20; Exod. 17). God does indeed sometimes use circumstances to mirror to His children the condition of their hearts, but He does not tempt them to sin (James 1:2–4, 13–15).

The Lord was with Moses in the harsh Sinai Desert (1 Cor. 10:4). It was He who gave the Israelites daily manna to eat and water out of rocks. The Old Testament record offers no hint, however, that Moses comprehended he had discovered in the wilderness the foolproof answers to the temptations of the devil. Nor does the record show that Moses perceived he was recording what would become, centuries later, his Messiah's responses to Satan's enticements, when the Lord faced His own fiery trial in the wilderness.

Jesus quoted Moses' conclusion to silence the devil: "It is written, 'Man does not live on bread alone but on every word that comes from the mouth of God'" (Matt. 4:4).

B. The Appeal to His Eyes—a Shortcut

The second temptation in Luke's chronology was Satan's effort to show Jesus a plan that would bypass the Cross (Luke 4:5–8). The devil led Jesus to a high place and in an instant flashed before Him all the kingdoms of the world. In essence, his argument was, "Jesus, you are much too special to follow a path that leads to a cross; let me show you a far easier way." Satan proceeded to promise Jesus all the "authority and splendor" of the world's kingdoms (v. 6). Satan also claimed with a subtle falsehood that "it has been given to me and I can give it to anyone I want to. So if you worship me, it will all be yours" (Luke 4:6–7). Daniel spoke to the same issue in very different terms, saying to Nebuchadnezzar: "The Most High is sovereign over the kingdoms of men and gives them to anyone he wishes" (Dan. 4:17).

The Israelites showed lots of willingness to bypass their Lord because they wanted to get through the desert with their own strategies (1 Cor. 10:4–6). It was this precise attitude, in fact, that resulted in raw idolatry during the time Moses was up on Sinai in forty days of intercession. Moses' prayers were rewarded with the Ten Commandments from the finger of God, commandments that became bedrock for the values of the whole of Western culture. Israel's idolatry produced a golden calf, a god that had no future and brought them only death. But it did appeal to their senses; they could look at their lifeless metal calf and touch it (Exod. 32:8; Deut. 9:11).

The lust of the eyes, which longs for what can be seen, led the Israelites to reason they deserved better guidance than what the invisible Spirit was giving them. "As for this fellow Moses who brought us up out of Egypt," their eyes told them, "we don't know what has happened to him" (Exod. 32:1). Their seemingly logical conclusion was that they had to figure out for themselves how to get out of the desert.

"Let me alone," God said to Moses, "so that I may destroy them and blot out their name from under heaven. And I will make you into a nation stronger and more numerous than they" (Deut. 9:14). Moses the intercessor perceived correctly that accepting this alternative plan would have meant bypassing the destiny God promised to Abraham and His seed. Moses' response was to go on his face in a second forty-day season of intercession. He did it because he "feared the anger and wrath of the LORD, for he was angry enough with [them] to destroy [them]" (Deut. 9:19). The following summarizes his petition to God over the next almost six weeks:

> I prayed to the LORD and said, "O Sovereign LORD, do not destroy your people, your own inheritance that you redeemed by your great power and brought out of Egypt with a mighty hand. Remember your servants Abraham, Isaac and Jacob. Overlook the stubbornness of this people, their wickedness and their sin. Otherwise, the country from which you brought us will say, 'Because the LORD was not able to take them into the land he had promised them, and because he hated them, he brought them out to put them to death in the desert.' But they are your people, your inheritance that you brought out by your great power and your outstretched arm."
>
> —DEUTERONOMY 9:26–29

The result, Moses said, was that "again the Lord listened to me" (Deut. 9:19).

During the wilderness sojourn, the Israelites paid a severe price time and again for the lust of the eyes, which broke faith with Jehovah God, whom they could see only with the eyes of faith. On one occasion some of them seriously considered returning to Egypt, remembering its leeks, onions, and garlic. How deceptive is human memory; they actually said Egypt's food had been theirs "at no cost" (Num. 11:5).

Moses expressed his conclusion about Israel's rebellions saying, "Fear the LORD your God, serve him only and take your oaths in his name. Do not follow other gods" (Deut. 6:13–14).

What would Jesus do in the face of the same kind of temptation? Would He take a shortcut that would bypass the cross? To the eyes, it surely looked easier. After all, God's plan included the horrible rigors of crucifixion. Jesus could clearly see the kingdoms Satan placed before Him. Was Jesus dedicated fully to God's one and only plan, framed from eternity? Would His moral commitment to serve His Father hold at a time when the devil presented everything to Him so deceptively as an easier way, promising Him, "If you worship me, it will all be yours" (Luke 4:7)? Would He opt for a less demanding plan that would bypass the cross? Could He be tempted to tinker with His Father's strategy to save the world? Would He turn the kingdoms Satan showed him into the lust of the eyes? Would He short-circuit His servanthood? Would He grasp for His destiny on the promise of a shortcut?

No, Jesus gave the devil the same answer He had guided Moses to express in the wilderness: "It is written, 'Worship the Lord your God and serve him only'" (Luke 4:8; Deut. 6:13–14). Moses did not opt to amend the strategy God offered to him because He feared the honor of God's name. Jesus did not take a shortcut either; He was too loyal to His Father even to entertain it. In doing so, He demonstrated there is no bypass on the highway of life superior to the plan of God.

C. The Appeal to His Pride—"You Deserve Better"

1. The Test for Jesus

For the third temptation, the devil sought to tempt Jesus to turn His legitimate pride into the illegitimate pride of life (Luke 4:9–12; 1 John 2:16). He stood Jesus on the highest point of the temple and said to Him, "If you are the Son of God, throw yourself down from here. For it is written: 'He will command his angels concerning you to guard you in all your ways; they will lift you up in their hands so that you will not strike your foot against a stone'" (Luke 4:9–11; Ps. 91:11–12). It was a bold effort to penetrate Jesus' bond of absolute trust in His Father. "Go ahead, Jesus, and jump," whispered the deceiver. "You are so special to your Father you will not even have to reach for the prerogatives of your deity. Your Father loves you so much He will dispatch His angels to take care of you just as the Scriptures say; you will not even 'strike your foot against a stone.'"

To do what Satan said, however, Jesus would also have been testing His Father, trying to make Him prove if He would keep His word. Even to consider doing that presumed Satan could successfully plant in Jesus' mind mistrust of His Father. If Jesus trusted His Father perfectly, He had no need to challenge Him to prove His word. The stakes were very high. If Jesus could be motivated to jump from the pinnacle of the temple, it would break the bond of trust between Him and His Father. That action would have stopped in its tracks Messiah's march to Calvary.

2. The Test for Moses

Moses knew this situation too. The pride of life as an attitude among the people came to a head in the wilderness at Rephidim (Exod. 17:1, 7). The people needed water; their bodies were dehydrating rapidly in the desert sun. With what attitude would they handle the crisis? They could have humbly trusted Yahweh as the Creator of all things, believing He would lead them to springs of cool water. After all, it was a legitimate need, and God had promised not to destroy them but to lead them into the Promised Land (Exod. 3:7–8; 12:25; Deut. 6:3; 9:28). Instead, in their pride they chose to challenge Him: if you really are God, prove it and save us in this wilderness.

By its very nature, to test God is to mistrust Him. The people chose not to believe the promises of the God who created water and knew exactly where it was in the wilderness. In fact, God already had a plan to open a new oasis in the desert, right before their eyes. It is a striking fact that the pride of life always births the unbelief that mocks and jeers.

While the Lord was on His cross, even the highest spiritual spokesmen of the nation withstood Him.

> The chief priests, the teachers of the law and the elders mocked him. "He saved others," they said, "but he can't save himself! He's the King of Israel! Let him come down now from the cross, and we will believe in him. He trusts in God. Let God rescue him now if he wants him, for he said, 'I am the Son of God.'"
> —MATTHEW 27:41–43

In their spiritual blindness, these leaders did not believe Jesus had the power to get off the cross. They could not foresee that Jesus' big heart of love *chose* to ignore their scoffing. In fact, love alone is what held Him on the tree. Doing what their ridicule demanded would have defeated His making atonement for the sins of the very high priests and elders who were testing Him with their taunting insults. Jesus did have a marvelous plan, however, and it included staying on the cross.

The essence of the Israelites' attitude in the wilderness was, "It is Moses' job to give us water, and he is not doing it, which means he can not do it. We deserve better." Since Moses had not led them to water, they reasoned, neither Moses nor Moses' God knew where any water was. Raw taunts followed. They claimed Moses has brought "us up out of Egypt to make us and our children and livestock die of thirst" (Exod. 17:3). They blamed him for not knowing where the oasis was as they challenged Moses and God to save them from the wilderness.

3. The Lesson of Pride—the Failure of God

Because they were convinced they deserved better, their pride led them to believe God had failed them. The natural conclusion was to trust only what they could see with their eyes, so they goaded Jehovah by grumbling against Moses, the leader God raised up to represent Him to them (Exod. 17:2). Their sin was raw human pride, the pride of life. The people concluded their God and His representative, Moses, could not deliver them.

The pride of life always has its roots in reasoning that says things like, "God can no longer be trusted, so I am on my own. I have to frame my own plan and get out of this wilderness the best way I can, by my own wits. And, I can do it.

I do not need to give any more time seeking guidance from the invisible God, when I can see there is no water anywhere near here. Moses' God obviously does not have the power to help me. To follow Moses' God is to trust what I cannot see, and any fool can see trusting the invisible will never get us out of this wilderness alive."

For the Israelites, that pride meant they wanted the water their bodies craved more than they wanted the Living Water their parched and dehydrated souls so desperately needed (Exod. 17; Ps. 95; John 4:10; 7:38; Rev. 7:17).

4. The Irony—Rebellion a Few Steps From the Oasis

The paradox of their situation was that through Moses, God was at that moment graciously leading them, even amid their unbelief, to an abundant water supply (Ps. 23:2; Rom. 5:8). Their Guide knew exactly where the water was, and they were on the verge of it. Jehovah knew all of the subterranean rivers under the desert and just the right rock that would flood into a new lake.

Even when they did not trust Him to get them to it, in His mercy, God was already taking them to just the right spot. They obviously were following, albeit grumbling in unbelief because their eyes could not see it. Moses could not see it either, but Moses trusted God to know where it was; so Moses walked by faith.

How poignant that at the precise time when the pride of life peaked as full-blown rebellion in the hearts of the people, they were literally standing at their oasis. Fallen man always exalts himself in pride, and the pride of life is universally blind to the Holy Spirit. It cannot see what is perfectly clear and visible to the eyes of faith.

> The LORD answered Moses, "Walk on ahead of the people. Take with you some of the elders of Israel and take in your hand the staff with which you struck the Nile, and go. I will stand there before you by the rock at Horeb. Strike the rock, and water will come out of it for the people to drink." So Moses did this in the sight of the elders of Israel. And he called the place Massah and Meribah because the Israelites quarreled and because they tested the LORD saying, "Is the LORD among us or not?"
> —EXODUS 17:5–7

When Moses struck the rock, a geyser of water gushed out, and Israel's Messiah stood by the rock watching the whole scene with delight, just as He had said: "I will stand there before you by the rock" (Exod. 17:6; Num. 20:1–13). Moses knew the Messiah was there because He was looking with the eyes of faith. It is reasonable to conclude very few of the Israelites, however, realized He was at hand. If only they had trusted their God and His chosen leader!

5. Three Days from History's Greatest Miracle

At the crucifixion of Jesus, the spiritual leaders of Israel were a mere three days away from witnessing the greatest miracle of the ages—the resurrection of the Son of man. However, they gave their time at the foot of His cross, while His atoning blood was dripping, to challenging, taunting, and insulting their own Messiah. Then, when the resurrection happened, the leaders of the Sanhedrin paid bribe money to try to hush up the breathtaking good news (Matt. 28:11–15; Zech. 7:11–14).

6. Testing God

Moses' great conclusion from the people's tragic mistake was, "Do not test the Lord your God" (Deut. 6:16). The Lord is worthy of complete and loving trust; He can be counted on to be faithful (1 Cor. 10:13; 2 Tim. 2:13; Ps. 33:4). Arrogant pride, though, always seems to lead to the risky business of provoking God. In fact, Israel taunted Jehovah repeatedly.

❧ Tempting God ❧

The St. Petersburg Times reported in 2002 the death of a Ukrainian man who was mauled by a lioness at the Kiev Zoo. He encountered the animal on purpose, believing God would protect him.

A zoo official said the man lowered himself by a rope into a concrete enclosure holding four lions. Shouting, "God will save me, if he exists," the man took off his shoes and strode toward the animals.

One lioness came to meet him. She knocked him down and quickly severed his carotid artery. Zoo officials stated that the incident—that occurred in front of a large crowd—was the first of its kind.[3]

What would Israel's Messiah do in His own wilderness temptation? Could His legitimate sense of His deity be corrupted into the pride of life, so that He would doubt the promises of His Father and jump from the temple to test His Father's love and support? Could the devil induce Him to act on His own, at least one time, doing it free from the guidance of His Father and of the Holy Spirit?

The moral commitment of the Son of man held firmly: "Jesus answered, 'It says: "Do not put the Lord your God to the test"'" (Luke 4:12; Deut. 6:16). It was the same answer Jesus had blessed Moses to express in the wilderness.

What a profound victory! Amid each of these three temptations, the Lord Jesus demonstrated His commitment to depend on the Word of God in the Old Testament for His answers, as guided by the Holy Spirit. He did it without breaking with His Father and grasping for the independent exercise of His deity, not even one time (Phil. 2:6).

With this humble mindset, Jesus triumphantly demonstrated that all sons of God must rely completely on the written Word of the Father, as enabled by the Holy Spirit, so they can overcome the very seat of Satan's power: "the lust of the flesh, the lust of the eyes and the pride of life" (1 John 2:16, KJV; Luke 10:18; Rom. 8:14).

With this achievement in the wilderness of temptation, Jesus Christ as the Son of man demonstrated He was also the victorious "last Adam, a life-giving Spirit;" there would never be a need for another (1 Cor. 15:45). He had won the clear right as the Son of man to be the leader of a new kingdom of redeemed sons of God (1 Cor. 15:22, 45).

A meal prepared by angels speeded up the restoration of Jesus' physical strength (Matt. 4:11; see also 1 Kings 19:3–9). With that new energy, Jesus walked out of the wilderness of Judea ready to launch His ministry to take away the sins of the world (John 1:29; Heb. 9:25).

Yes, there can be no testimony without a test.

"Who is this that cometh up from the wilderness?" (Song of Sol. 8:5). It is the triumphant Messiah, leaning upon the strong arm of His Father and walking in the Spirit. The Savior of the world understands the wilderness well. Because He does, He can also walk with His followers, leading them through their own desert places.

D. The Wilderness, Valid as Temptation?

The question is surely appropriate, was it even possible for the incarnate Christ to sin in His wilderness temptation? Asked another way, how could temptation be valid as temptation when the person being tempted is God Himself?

If the point of the wilderness temptation was to demonstrate the mastery of the second person of the Trinity over Lucifer, then the wilderness experience was certainly no ordeal and no contest. God had already settled that issue: "I saw Satan fall like lightning from heaven," Jesus said (Luke 10:18; Isa. 14:12). That, however, was not the point during those forty lonely days of temptation.

The central issue of Jesus' wilderness experience was to test if the devil could induce God-become-man to sin, and this was a very different matter, because that had never been tested. The devil had never squared off against a man like Jesus, because Jesus was God incarnate, the God-man, the firstborn of the new covenant, "the second man...the Lord from heaven" (1 Cor. 15: 47; John 1:14; Luke 22:20).

Would God's incarnate Son succumb to the demands of His flesh? Would His moral commitment to do the will of His Father succeed with the independent and voluntary exercise of His divine attributes yielded to His Father and to the Holy Spirit? Could the Spirit-filled Son of man be induced to change His attitude of total loyalty to His Father?

These questions frame the central issue at stake in the wilderness of temptation. Satan tried in every way he could to test the deity of Jesus and to tempt the God-man in His true humanity, but the bond between Jesus and His Father held. Satan's three juicy "apples" just were not attractive to the taste buds of the Savior. Jesus lived out His commitment to trust the Word of God as He walked in the Spirit.

The lesson is applicable to all Christ's followers. A Spirit-filled life lived with an attitude of firm moral commitment to serve obediently the written Word of the Father is the foundation of what it means to work out one's salvation (Phil. 2:12). That standard continues to this day to be more than a match for Satan's powerful appeal to the appetites of the flesh. Jesus' strategy for triumph has become every believer's blueprint. The plan worked for Him, and it will work for all who "follow in His steps," because "it is God who works in you to will and to act according to his good purpose" (1 Pet. 2:21; Phil. 2:13).

The apostle Peter described the believer's victory with great jubilation.

> Praise be to the God and Father of our Lord Jesus Christ! In his great mercy, he has given us new birth into a living hope through the resurrection of Jesus Christ from the dead, and into an inheritance that can never perish, spoil or fade—kept in heaven for you, who through faith are shielded by God's power, until the coming of the salvation that is ready to be revealed in the last time.
>
> —1 PETER 1:3–5

The triumph of the Servant of Jehovah motivated Paul to make the application, "Each of you should look not only to your own interests, but also to the interests of others," because that is what *agape* love always does (Phil. 2:4).

Jesus understood fully that He really had only one choice—obedient service to His Father and His plan. By living this commitment and teaching His followers this overcoming grace, He has won the undying affection of His followers in all generations (Eph. 6:24).

When the wilderness temptation ended, "angels came and attended Him" (Matt. 4:11). The devil walked away in dismal defeat, but he remained

determined to fight again at "an opportune time" (Luke 4:13). Satan had
many more poison arrows in his quiver for the last Adam. Jesus' plan to
convince people of His verdict and solution would be a hard and uphill
struggle. The wilderness temptation settled only the first round.

III. The Servant: Opposition During His Ministry Years

A. The Devil's Strategy

Lucifer's plan of action for the remainder of Jesus' ministry was to keep the
pressure on the God-man, whom the Holy Spirit declared to be Messiah at
His Jordan River baptism (Luke 3:21–23). The devil had a formidable array
of weapons against man's fleshly appetites that had effectively held all people
in the world's system century after century. It is for good reason that Satan
carries the name "the god of this age" (2 Cor. 4:4).

The all-out war to bring Jesus Christ into Satan's dominion had as its goal
creating a situation that would tempt Him to misspeak in some way or become
angry, upset, or offended. Satan was willing to try anything, no matter how
vicious and cruel or unfair and dishonest that might cause Him to do something independently of His Father and of the Holy Spirit.

As for Jesus, He used two weapons in the ongoing struggle, and He wielded
them masterfully: a Spirit-filled life and an unyielding commitment to serve
only the word of His Father.

What follows first is a survey of the ministry years of the Lord, and then
a look at the events of Passion Week. This study will include ten areas of
continuing temptation in each phase of His ministry. Episodes such as these
show the very high personal price Jesus paid to redeem all men. He was
successful because He lived to obey the Word of His Father. The demands of
His fleshly appetites were always secondary priorities to Him.

1. Plots to Kill Jesus

The devil actually drew the battle lines at His manger. Satan planned the
first death scheme against Israel's Messiah while He was in the cradle, but
Satan was not able to take out the infant Jesus in one preemptive strike.

"Get up," the angel said to Joseph, "take the child and his mother and
escape to Egypt. Stay there until I tell you, for Herod is going to search for the
child to kill him" (Matt. 2:13). Satan's scheme did not work. God had even
pre-arranged that the gifts of the wise men would finance Joseph, Mary, and
the Baby in Egypt.

The important principle here is that the foreknowledge of God is broader than merely understanding what individual men will choose. The Lord knew in advance the strategies of the devil, too; hence, from eternity God planned for all eventualities.

The birth of Jesus so veiled God's Son in flesh and blood that Herod had to order the murder of all of the Bethlehem babies to try to get the One and Only; his soldiers just could not tell the difference (John 1:14, 18). Even in the Garden of Gethsemane, the only way the temple guards knew for sure the one to arrest was Judas' kiss of betrayal (Matt. 26:48).

After the wilderness temptation, Jesus "returned to Galilee in the power of the Spirit" (Luke 4:14). This statement unveils much more than the fact He went back home to Nazareth. It also reflects the extent to which the Holy Spirit guided His life. When Jesus arrived home, on the next Sabbath He announced Himself to His relatives and longtime friends as their Messiah. He went into the synagogue, as was His custom and the scene unfolded like this:

> The scroll of the prophet Isaiah was handed to him. Unrolling it, he found the place where it is written: "The Spirit of the Lord is on me, because he has anointed me to preach good news to the poor. He has sent me to proclaim freedom for the prisoners and recovery of sight for the blind, to release the oppressed, to proclaim the year of the Lord's favor." Then he rolled up the scroll, gave it back to the attendant and sat down. The eyes of everyone in the synagogue were fastened on him, and he began by saying to them, "Today this scripture is fulfilled in your hearing."
>
> —Luke 4:17–21

Livid anger welcomed Jesus' claim. Regarding the furious response of His countrymen, Jesus said to them, "Surely you will quote this proverb to me, 'Physician, heal yourself! Do here in your hometown what we have heard that you did in Capernaum'" (Luke 4:23). The people of Nazareth felt such resentment toward Him, in fact, that "they got up and drove him out of the town and took him to the brow of the hill on which the community was built, in order to throw him down the cliff" (Luke 4:28–30; Mark 6:3).

When Jesus made His first ministry trip to Jerusalem, the Jews persecuted him and "tried all the harder to kill him" because, they alleged, He was "breaking the Sabbath" and "was even calling God his own Father, making himself equal with God" (John 5:16–18). In fact, Jesus purposely stayed away from Judea for a season because "the Jews there were waiting to take his life" (John 7:1). He did it as part of the plan, however, and not out of fear. Killing Jesus prematurely would have been a victory for Satan because the Lord would not have fulfilled all of the prophetic Scriptures and achieved the Atonement. This meant Jesus had to control the timing of His death (John 13:1). Jesus, however, had no personal fear of death because He understood fully that He came to this earth to die (John 18:37).

On His next visit to Jerusalem, "the Pharisees sent temple guards to arrest him" (John 7:32). They "went back to the chief priests and Pharisees" and reported, "No one ever spoke the way this man does" (John 7:45–46).

In His teaching on this visit, Jesus claimed, "Before Abraham was born, I am!" At that the Jews "picked up stones to stone him, but Jesus hid himself, slipping away from the temple grounds" (John 8:58–59). Luke 13:31–33 tells of another similar occasion:

> Some Pharisees came to Jesus and said to him, "Leave this place and go somewhere else. Herod wants to kill you." He replied to them: "Go tell that fox, 'I will drive out demons and heal people today and tomorrow, and on the third day I will reach my goal.' In any case, I must keep going today and tomorrow and the next day—for surely no prophet can die outside Jerusalem!"

The fox had been outfoxed.

Each time the Lord was in Jerusalem, in fact, death threats swirled around Him. Luke recorded their plotting, saying, "The chief priests, the teachers of the law and the leaders among the people were trying to kill him" (Luke 19:47). Jesus fundamentally threatened their hold on the people (John 11:48).

These kinds of serious death threats hounded Jesus His whole life, but He was much too wise to let them work until the Father's time (Heb. 12:3). The bond of implicit trust held between Jesus and His Father, and He continued to live the life of the lowly Servant who loved all people.

2. The Charge of Blasphemy

The indictment that Jesus, seemingly a mere man, was showing gross irreverence for God by making Himself equal with God came early in His ministry (John 5:18; 10:33). The social stigma that surrounded such a charge was so shameful that an innocent person would invariably defend himself with deep anger.

Jesus lived with a clear knowledge of who He was and who His heavenly Father was; therefore, the blasphemy charge must have been heartbreakingly onerous to Him. After all, "He came to...His own, but His own did not receive Him" (John 1:11). Adding to the pressure was the fact that the charge never seemed to go away. It kept surfacing throughout His ministry.

When four men brought a paralytic on a stretcher and lowered him through the roof to Jesus, the Lord told the poor man, "Take heart, son, your sins are forgiven" (Matt. 9:2; Luke 5:20). The Pharisees and teachers of the Law immediately started thinking to themselves, "This fellow is blaspheming" (Matt. 9:1–3; Mark 2:6–7).

At the wintertime Feast of Dedication in Jerusalem, the Jews actually picked up stones to kill the Lord "for blasphemy," because He, "a mere man, claim[ed] to be God" (John 10:33). Ultimately, Caiaphas, the high priest, used that very charge to sentence Him to death, but it took place on the Lord's timetable, when Jesus had fulfilled all righteousness (Matt. 3:15; 26:65).

Each time the accusation came, the insult cut to the core of who He was as the Son of man, but He never once struck back matching insults with insults. Jesus had no disposition to get even or to teach them a lesson (1 Pet. 2:23). He just continued to love and serve people.

What a wise man! How right we are to rejoice and delight in Him (Song of Sol. 1:4).

3. Evil Spirits Screaming Out His Identity

The piercing squeals of demons obviously had the goal to unnerve Jesus by prematurely revealing His divinity, which the devils knew was veiled in humanity (James 2:19). On one such occasion, a man in the Capernaum synagogue possessed by an evil spirit cried out, "What do you want with us, Jesus of Nazareth? Have you come to destroy us? I know who you are—the Holy One of God!" (Mark 1:24).

Jesus sternly ordered him to "Be quiet!" and "Come out of him!" Then "the evil spirit shook the man violently and came out of him with a shriek" (Mark 1:25–26). "Whenever the evil spirits saw him," in fact, "they fell down before him and cried out, 'You are the Son of God'" (Mark 3:11–12).

These evil spirits were false advertisers. Their goal was to push the timeline forward for the revelation of Christ as the Son of man, and get His plan out of sync. Jesus' response was not to become angry, but calmly to give "them strict orders not to tell who he was" (Mark 3:12). Even the perverted testimony of demon spirits could not make Him irate enough to lose His self-control, although they were deliberately trying to destroy the Father's strategy.

4. The Accusation of Demon Possession

Accuse God's Son of being full of demons? Unthinkable! It must have been a particularly odious charge to Him, knowing how much He loved His Father and how deeply He was committed to obeying Him.

Israel's Messiah was right there in their midst, doing the work of Messiah before their eyes, but the Pharisees and teachers of the Law—some of the very people He came to save—interpreted His actions as being demonic. The apostle Paul understood the principle when he told the Corinthians "the god of this age" has the power to blind the minds of those who do not believe. They "cannot see the light of the gospel of the glory of Christ, who is the image of God" (2 Cor. 4:4).

When a group of "teachers of the law…came down from Jerusalem" to Galilee to confront Him, they accused Him in the strongest terms: "He is possessed by Beelzebub!" they told the crowd. They charged Him with teaching and driving out demons "by the prince of demons" (Mark 3:22). It was a patent effort to embarrass and humiliate Him before His audience and make Him react angrily. Later, at the Feast of Tabernacles, even the crowd bluntly said to Him, "You are demon-possessed" (John 7:20).

Such a bitter and utterly false accusation would typically make a person furious, causing him to retaliate in defense. Instead, the Lord denied their charge, but without losing control of Himself or the situation.

The charge of demon possession surely challenged the Lord and troubled Him deeply, but it did not hold the power to make Him angrily do something prematurely, nor did it change His attitude of unconditional trust in His Father, depending on the guidance of the Holy Spirit. This wicked, accusatory spirit had worked against so many over the centuries. The spirit of the accused, responding in great resentment, routinely could be depended on to become like that of the accuser. It did not succeed, however, against the God-man.

5. Unbelief

The kind of mistrust that fundamentally challenges a person's credibility has also worked countless times for Satan, keeping people bound tightly in the world system. It is tough to handle one's emotions when slapped with angry mistrust, especially when you know you are telling the truth. Jesus met just that kind of evil heart among His home folk at Nazareth and "was amazed at their lack of faith." In fact, He "could not do any miracles there except lay his hands on a few sick people and heal them" (Mark 6:5–6).

After Jesus fed the five thousand with five barley loaves and two small fish, the crowd was quick to pick up the prospect of a free food supply. "So the people began to say, 'Surely this is the Prophet who is to come into the world.' Jesus, knowing they intended to come and make him king by force, withdrew again to a mountain by himself" (John 6:14–15).

The multitude saw His ability to make bread miraculously as too good to be true, and the people were eager to sign up on the spot as His subjects. The crowd found Him the next day and asked Him, "What must we do to do the works God requires?" Jesus' answer shook them: "The work of God is this:

to believe in the one he has sent" (John 6:28–29). The throng welcomed the benefits of free bread, but they were not equally eager to make Jesus Lord of their personal lives. To do that, they would have to accept that He had been sent by His Father.

With the bar set that high, many people started pulling away from Him. They believed in bread they could see and eat, but were not at all tuned to the invisible God who could end the famine in their souls. When Jesus began to teach them He had actually come to sacrifice His body so they could eat spiritual bread that would give never-ending nourishment to their souls, "Many of his disciples turned back and no longer followed him" (John 6:66). They were very much like their fathers in the wilderness who missed seeing their Messiah standing by the rock (Exod. 17:6). The multitude with Jesus wanted bread but were blind in their unbelief to the fact that the true Staff of Life was right there among them, offering them food that is everlasting (Exod. 16:1–10). Hence, they continued to give their loyalty to the world system because it gave them the food that satisfied their stomachs.

The Author of the bread—the Maker of the sunlight, the soil, the rain, and the very seed that produced the crops that actually fed them—was in their midst to love them and bless them. He wanted to give them timeless bread so they would never hunger again, but they showered him with raw skepticism and walked away. It was cold unbelief.

Jesus turned to His disciples and asked them, "Will you go also?" Simon Peter answered, "Lord, to whom shall we go? You have the words of eternal life. We believe and know that you are the Holy One of God" (John 6:68–69).

Jesus had a few followers, like Peter, who were growing in faith, but He also had many curious onlookers around Him who walked in unbelief. They hounded Him everywhere He went. The writer of Hebrews said there is indeed such a thing as an "unbelieving heart that turns away from the living God" (Heb. 3:12). ·

Jesus even met unbelief in the members of His own family. On one occasion, "they went to take charge of him, for they said, 'He is out of his mind'" (Mark 3:21). At times His own disciples showed lack of faith. When they could not help the poor man at the foot of the Mount of Transfiguration, Jesus said it was because of their "unbelief" (Matt. 17:19–20, kjv). After He came out of the tomb, the Lord actually "rebuked them for their lack of faith and their stubborn refusal to believe those who had seen him after he had risen" (Mark 16:14; see also Mark 8:17–21; Luke 24:25).

One could think having to fight unbelief on this scale day after day would wear a person down, causing him to throw in the towel and give up. The load of leading the people did ultimately get at Moses, near the end of his life. He responded in anger when the church in the wilderness needed water a second time (Acts 7:38, KJV).

> Moses and Aaron gathered the congregation together before the rock, and he said to them, Hear now, ye rebels; must we fetch you water out of this rock? And Moses lifted up his hand, and with his rod he smote the rock twice.
> —NUMBERS 20:10–11, KJV

The water gushed out, but God was displeased with Moses. The great liberator had perceived His Messiah standing by the rock when the water surged at Rephidim, but He failed to trust God in the Desert of Zin. Therefore, he did not comprehend the rock he angrily struck was his Messiah (Num. 20:1–12; Exod. 17:5–7; 1 Cor. 10:4).

Jesus lived full of grace and never made judgments based in anger, nor was revenge ever in His heart (John 1:14; Rom. 12:19). He never stopped loving His people when they were rebellious and actually forgave them, even when they nailed Him on a cross (Luke 23:34). On the contrary, when Moses angrily struck the rock, he showed how he felt at that moment about the people, which also meant he was striking at the very heart of God. "The LORD said to Moses and Aaron, 'Because you did not trust in me enough to honor me as holy in the sight of the Israelites, you will not bring this community into the land I give them'" (Num. 20:12).

The tool that worked successfully against Moses—repeated attacks from the enemy until he was worn down—has destroyed so many sons of Adam. Reformers all too often become weary and finally decide, "You can't fight city hall." Sooner or later, most visionaries see so much doubt and unbelief they conclude it is not worth the effort and make peace with the world system. But not Jesus. His moral commitment to trust His Father and the Holy Spirit held firmly in the daily grind of the battle against unbelief. Unbelieving people just could not tire him out and make Him drop His guard. Instead, Jesus continued to watch and listen to His Father, doing and saying only what He saw and heard (John 5:19–20, 30).

6. Keeping Bad Company

The rumor spread rapidly: something must be very wrong with Jesus because of the kind of people He enjoyed being around. The Pharisees thought they had good evidence to feed the rumors. Levi held a great banquet for Jesus at his house and a large crowd of tax collectors and other disreputable characters were eating with them (Matt. 9:10). So, "the Pharisees and their religion scholars" who belonged to their sect complained to his disciples, "Why do you eat and drink with tax collectors and sinners?" (Luke 5:29–30, THE MESSAGE; Matt. 9:10–13).

Jesus did not respond with an equally cutting and angry retort. Instead, He honestly answered their question: "It is not the healthy who need a doctor, but the sick. But go and learn what this means: 'I desire mercy, not sacrifice.' For I have not come to call the righteous, but sinners" (Matt. 9:12–13).

The Pharisees hurled the same charge at Him when the Lord invited Himself to dinner at Zacchaeus' home. It did not matter that "the tax collectors and sinners were all gathering around to hear him," or that Zacchaeus showed the true fruit of repentance when he committed to pay fourfold restitution to anyone he had cheated (Luke 15:8; 19:8). In their twisted minds, if you eat with tax collectors and sinners, you must have something to hide. "Bad company corrupts good character" was a commonly understood proverb in that time (1 Cor. 15:33).

In the home of Simon the Pharisee, a woman brought an alabaster jar of expensive perfume into the house. She walked up to Jesus, knelt before him, poured the perfume on his feet and began to wipe his feet with her hair. That act of adoration suggested too much guilt by association for Simon. "If this man were a prophet," Simon murmured to himself, "he would know who is touching him and what kind of woman she is—that she is a sinner" (Luke 7:39). Simon did not understand what Paul later taught, that in Christ there is a pure state of mind that regards no one from a worldly point of view (2 Cor. 5:16). Instead, in the eyes of Simon the Pharisee, Jesus was staining Himself with the reputation of the woman. Simon did not comprehend that Jesus was giving her a brand new reputation.

Most people will fight to preserve their good name. Lawsuits involving slander are not unusual in the courts. However, the rumors that spread about Jesus did not unnerve Him. He knew His works of righteousness were much greater news than the lies of the gossipers.

All believers in Christ need to know their reputation ultimately stands or falls with the judgment of God (1 Cor. 4:4). When that realization blossoms, the Word of God truly becomes their blueprint for living. With the blessing of that discovery, believers can sit with sinners without becoming one of them. Instead, they will lead them to Christ.

7. Breaking the Law

Most people will bow to the world system because it is the law of the land, and Satan knew that. The law is a potent weapon, even when it is unjust law, precisely because the law can punish lawbreakers. Part of the punishment is the shameful social stigma that goes with being a lawbreaker. Mothers and dads ingrain in their children from the cradle the principle that "if you are to get along in life you must respect the law." Because that is true, people truly fear being caught breaking the law. The overwhelming majority will go to any length to clear their good name in the courts.

Jesus Christ came to this earth to fulfill the Law, not to break it. Throughout His incarnation, therefore, Jesus kept the Law fully. But He also knew in total recall what was in the Law. He had been there to inspire Moses to write it (John 8:58; Exod. 17:5–7; see also the many "God said" passages, as Exod. 3:12). This meant He knew authoritatively when the Pharisees made up their own laws and then tried to force them on the people.

Accusing people of being lawbreakers was a powerful weapon the Pharisees used regularly and effectively. Most people so feared the charge they bowed to interpretations of Law that sound authoritative, even if they were not truly rooted in the Scriptures.

"Isaiah was right when he prophesied about you hypocrites," Jesus said to them. "These people honor me with their lips, but their hearts are far from me. They worship me in vain; their teachings are but rules taught by men" (Mark 7:6–7; Isa. 29:13). The Lord had such personal command of the Law, in fact, that He actually indicted the Pharisees, telling them, "You have let go of the commands of God and are holding on to the traditions of men" (Mark 7:8).

When Jesus appeared on the scene, He knew the details of the Law of Moses, Israel's Law, better than the Pharisees. Therefore, they could not control Him with their legal interpretations. Ordinary people realized the distinction and loved Him for the liberty His life demonstrated. Neither is it surprising the leaders of the Pharisees wanted to kill Jesus, because He fundamentally threatened their power and status in society (John 11:48).

A few Pharisees were actually kind to him, however:

- While on one of Jesus' visits to Jerusalem, some Pharisees sought to befriend the Lord, telling Him, "Leave this place and go somewhere else. Herod wants to kill you" (Luke 13:31).
- Nicodemus was a member of the ruling Jewish council who came to Jesus by night, asking Him the sincere questions that resulted in the Lord's teaching on the new birth (John 3:1–8).
- On at least one occasion, Nicodemus also spoke up trying to defend Jesus, and in the process earned for Himself a very strong rebuke from his fellow Pharisees (John 7:50–52). Nicodemus also paid the bill for the seventy-five pounds of spices used to anoint the body of Jesus for burial (John 19:39–42).

- After Jesus' death, Nicodemus accompanied Joseph of Arimathea to the site of Joseph's empty burial cave, where they laid the Lord's body in Joseph's own tomb.
- As for Joseph of Arimathea, he was a secret disciple of Jesus who kept his faith under wraps "because he feared the Jews" (John 19:38).

Neither Herod's threats nor the Pharisees' charges of breaking the Law made Jesus fearful; instead, He continued to reject their false interpretations of Moses' Law (Matt. 12:1; Mark 7:5; Luke 6:6–11). The tactic did not work on Jesus because He knew both the letter of the Law and the spirit of the Law, and they could not catch Him in anything He said or did. Instead, He could confront His accusers with His own challenge, "Can any of you prove me guilty of sin?" (John 8:46). No man could.

8. Challenges to His Authority
When an authority figure defies a person's right to do what He is doing, it can be very disconcerting and unnerving. "The chief priests and the teachers of the law, together with the elders" came to Jesus to try the tactic on Him: "By what authority are you doing these things?" they wanted to know. "Who gave you this authority?" (Luke 20:1–2).

Those two questions make for a compelling, double-barreled weapon, especially if a person believes authority flows from man-made institutions. But Jesus knew His power came from His Father. Because Jesus walked in the authority of His Father, He was actually able to unnerve Pilate at His trial. "You would have no power over me if it were not given to you from above," Jesus said to the governor. "'Therefore, the one who handed me over to you is guilty of a greater sin.' From then on, Pilate tried to set Jesus free" (John 19:11–12).

The critics doing this questioning clearly thought Jesus was amenable to them and their authority. They were blind to the fact they really were under Jesus' command. The result was their weapon fizzled against Jesus; in fact, Jesus marvelously neutralized it and kept on doing what He saw the Father doing and saying what He heard His Father saying (John 5:19).

9. Trap Him in His Speech
When the Lord told the parable of the tenants, especially the part about the tenants killing one emissary after another and then murdering the landlord's son, Jesus' enemies knew well the parable was directed at them. For that reason, the teachers of the Law and the chief priests "looked for a way to arrest him...but they were afraid of the crowd" (Matt. 21:46). They did keep "a close watch on him" however, and sent spies, hoping "to catch Jesus in

something he said so they might hand him over to the power and authority of the governor" (Luke 20:20). His enemies made numerous efforts.

- "The Sadducees, who say there is no resurrection, came to Jesus" to trip Him up with a question about Levirate marriage (Luke 20:27–33; Mark 12:18–23; Matt. 22:23–25).
- The Pharisees tested Him with the query, "Is it lawful for a man to divorce his wife for any and every reason" (Matt. 19:3; Mark 10:2–3).
- The Pharisees and the Herodians teamed up and "laid plans to trap him in his words" regarding paying taxes to Caesar (Matt. 22:15–17; Mark 12:13–15).
- "The Pharisees got together" and had one of their legal experts test "him with the question: 'Teacher, which is the greatest commandment in the Law?'" (Matt. 22:34–36).
- On another occasion, the Pharisees began to probe Jesus, testing Him by asking for a sign from heaven (Mark 8:11–13).

It must be tough for a leader to have people on his trail all the time who are spies hoping to catch him in something—anything. Jesus lived under that pressure day after day (Heb. 12:3). What was the secret that enabled Him to silence all of them so they did not dare ask him any more questions (Luke 20:40)? The answer surely goes to the moral bond of unqualified trust He enjoyed with His Father and the guidance He received from the Holy Spirit. Isaiah had prophesied the anointing of the Holy Spirit on His life would make Him "wise and understanding," filling Him with "the spirit of counsel and might, the spirit of knowledge and of the fear of the Lord." The result was the Spirit made him "of quick understanding" (Isa. 11:2–3, KJV; Luke 5:29–32, THE MESSAGE). Jesus, the God-man, could think faster on His feet than any man who has ever lived (Matt. 9:12, THE MESSAGE; Luke 20:23–24).

The third of Isaiah's four Servant Songs speaks to the principle of how the Holy Spirit prepared Him for the challenges of each day. This kind of guidance was routine in Jesus' life.

> The Sovereign Lord has given me an instructed tongue to know the word that sustains the weary. He wakens me morning by morning, wakens my ear to listen like one being taught. The Sovereign Lord has opened my ears and I have not been rebellious; I have not drawn back.
> —ISAIAH 50:4–5

The wisest and brightest of the Pharisees, Sadduccees, and the Herodians were not a match for the Holy Spirit who guided the life of the Servant who came from God. They did not catch Him off guard even one time, making Him speak something He would regret later. Jesus never had to apologize for a thing He said.

10. Rejection

Repudiation is among the bitterest responses a person can give to his fellow human being. The typical person finds it very difficult to handle it wisely. The Lord prophesied to His disciples "the Son of Man, must suffer much and be rejected" (Mark 9:12–13). One of the key reasons He could handle rejection was He really did expect it; He saw it coming (Luke 9:22; Isa. 53:3).

When Jesus visited the eastern side of the Sea of Galilee, the land of the Gadarenes, He healed a demon-possessed man who was stronger than chains. The man wore no clothing and lived amid the tombs. He was so demented he regularly cut himself with stones (Luke 8:27–39). The demons spoke out of the man, asking the Lord's permission to go into a large herd of pigs feeding nearby. Jesus granted their request, and the pigs ran headlong over a cliff, plunging to their deaths in the water below. When the people of the town came out to inquire what had happened, they experienced the wonder of the man clothed and in his right mind—but they also recognized the pigs that had drowned were their livelihood.

The Lord knew the man was worth infinitely more than the pigs, but the Gadarenes did not agree. Perhaps that is the reason Jesus sent the demons into their pigs—to hit them in their pocketbooks and cause them to ask questions about the true value of life. Their response was to plead with the Lord to leave their region, and He did (Luke 8:37). To them, neither Jesus nor the poor man was worth their pigs. It was a raw rebuff of the Messiah, who could have changed for the better the lives of every person in their village and at the same time rebuilt their economy on a stronger foundation.

Toward the end of His ministry, "As the time approached for [Jesus] to be taken up to heaven, the Lord resolutely set out for Jerusalem. He sent messengers on ahead, who went into a Samaritan village to get things ready for him; but the people there did not welcome him because he was heading for Jerusalem" (Luke 9:51–53). Racial prejudice explains why the Samaritans rejected Jesus. Their sole reason was that He was a Jew. James and John were so upset about it they wanted to call down fire from heaven in the tradition of Elijah, but the Lord refused to strike back (Luke 9:54–56; 2 Kings 1:10–12; 1 Pet. 2:21–24). Instead, He continued on His journey to the next village. Yes, the Lord knew well the stabbing rejection of racial prejudice.

B. The Lord's Overcoming Strategy

Without any effort to be exhaustive, this study has looked at ten weapons that Satan used against Jesus in the three years of the Lord's ministry leading up to Passion Week, the week of His crucifixion. Each of the ten was powerful and intended to tempt Him to strike back in some way and break the bond with His Father. Each had worked on countless people before, but the devil had never waged war against a man like Jesus. He was a new breed—the last Adam, the Son of man, the God-man, and the firstfruits of Spirit-filled men (1 Cor. 15:45; Matt. 8:20; John 3:34). We can only conclude that a person far greater than Adam had become flesh and blood and was walking the dusty roads of Israel.

What a man! So wise and tough, yet so tender and caring. Men and women cheerfully place Him as the seal over their hearts (Song of Sol. 8:6).

It is appropriate to summarize some strategies the Lord used during His ministry years to resist the many temptations He faced, enabling Him to defeat the devil:

1. An attitude of total trust that was stronger than steel welded the heart of Jesus to His Father. It was the core moral principle of His life.

2. Jesus humbled Himself in His manhood, the key expression of which was emptying Himself of the voluntary exercise of His divine attributes (Matt. 11:29; Phil. 2:6–7). The guiding star of His ministry was that He submitted to the direction of His Father and the empowering of the Holy Spirit, given to Him without limits (John 3:34; Acts 10:38).

3. Because He knew who His Father was, He also understood who He was. This knowledge meant the many weapons Satan used so successfully on millions through the centuries did not work on Jesus. A key reason was the Lord surrendered to His Father and to the Holy Spirit the glory He had enjoyed with the Godhead in eternity. During His incarnation, He greatly restricted His expectations of honor and worship. The very fact that He came from God as the selfless and humble Servant headed to Calvary, also meant His expectations were low. Yet, He loved people with no strings attached, and not because of any personal benefit He could get out of them. Instead, His love, divine love, was entirely unselfish. Even the

rawest wickedness subtly expressed against Him through the hearts of fallen men just could not offend Him enough to make Him react. "He knew what was in man" and did not expect any better (John 2:25; Matt. 9:12).

With that stroke of divine genius, Jesus neutralized one of the devil's most effective strategies. When a person believes someone has violated his rights, he feels offended and will normally strike back in some way to protect himself. However, the weapon did not work on Jesus, not even once. His lifestyle of selfless love limited His expectations of honor and worship, so He came with full anticipation of denunciation and rebuff. Even crucifixion itself did not make Him strike back; He knew that was coming, too.

The Lord handled the massive rejection He received precisely because He limited His expectations and came to Earth as a servant, demanding no honor. In fact, this strategy was central to the genius of His plan.

The apostle Paul made the Lord's attitude his own in his missionary journeys, and it worked for him, too (1 Cor. 2:16). He expressed the secret to the Corinthians:

We are fools for Christ, but you are so wise in Christ! We are weak, but you are strong! You are honored, we are dishonored! To this very hour, we go hungry and thirsty, we are in rags, we are brutally treated, we are homeless. We work hard with our own hands. When we are cursed, we bless; when we are persecuted, we endure it; when we are slandered, we answer kindly. Up to this moment we have become the scum of the earth, the refuse of the world.

—1 Corinthians 4:10–13

4. Jesus lived by the ethic of love and taught His disciples to do the same. He modeled that it is actually a blessing "when people insult you, persecute you and falsely say all kinds of evil against you because of me." The Lord went on to say, "Rejoice and be glad, because great is your reward in heaven, for in the same way they persecuted the prophets who were before you" (Matt. 5:11–12). Jesus understood well the love that is *agape* (i.e., real servanthood) actually sparkles at its best when gratitude ends.

Paul taught this love ethic has telling characteristics even in a person's hour of great duress and stress:

Love is patient, love is kind. It does not envy, it does not boast, it is not proud. It is not rude, it is not self-seeking, it is not easily angered, it keeps no record of wrongs. Love does not delight in evil but rejoices with the truth. It always protects, always trusts, always hopes, always perseveres.

—1 CORINTHIANS 13:4–7

The apostle Peter saw this powerful principle in action as He watched the Lord handle Himself amid all the tension of the assaults of evil men, attack after attack, day after day. He summarized Jesus' self-control by saying He did not strike back or threaten. "Instead, He entrusted himself to him who judges justly" (1 Pet. 2:23–25). The same principle works for any child of God.

The love ethic also matures an attitude of trust into a bond stronger than steel between a believer and his heavenly Father. Such a disciple of Christ learns God "judges justly;" therefore, he can walk through profane mistreatment without reviling and through suffering without threatening (1 Pet. 2:23). Instead, amazingly, he will feel blessed! In the process, he will watch the most dependable bombs of evil men launched against him turn into duds. Hence, Jesus' followers achieve the impossible as they fight the good fight, finish the course, and keep the faith (John 19:30; 2 Tim. 4:7).

5. The Lord never desired to please Himself. The apostle Paul tucked this great nugget into his concluding remarks to the believers in Rome. It, too, has *agape* written all over it.

We who are strong ought to bear with the failings of the weak and not to please ourselves. Each of us should please his neighbor for his good, to build him up. For even Christ did not please himself, but as it is written: "The insults of those who insult you have fallen on me." For everything that was written in the past was written to teach us, so that through endurance and the encouragement of the Scriptures we might have hope.

—ROMANS 15:1–4

The Lord never had a strategy to pursue self-gratification. No *me-ism* is in the Tri-unity of God; instead, Jesus lived to delight His Father. Servants do not even hope to get what they want. Knowing who you are to make happy in life is a fundamental key to neutralizing the temptation to strike back when insulted. A person with evil intent cannot insult you unless you believe in some way you are amenable to him. Therefore, slurs became unexploded shells at the feet of Jesus. He chose not to take them personally because His heart was set to please His Father (Luke 22:42; 2 Cor. 5:9; Gal. 1:10; Col. 1:10; 1 Thess. 2:4; Heb. 11:6). The apostle Paul learned that principle too. "I care very little if I am judged by you," Paul said, "[because] it is the Lord who judges me" (1 Cor. 4:3–4).

The Lord's followers must know the same key. When they understand this principle, their capacity to endure takes a quantum leap. The result is encouragement and hope for daily living.

6. Jesus was able to run His race successfully because He kept His eyes fixed on the joy that was ahead of Him, depending on the Holy Spirit to replenish His emotional batteries (Hebrews 12:2, The Message; John 4:34; 5:36; Acts 20:24). The overcoming principle is this: if the reward is worth it, then the sacrifice to get there is worth it. To this end, the writer of Hebrews calls on his readers:

Since we are surrounded by such a great cloud of witnesses, let us throw off everything that hinders and the sin that so easily entangles, and let us run with perseverance the race marked out for us. Let us fix our eyes on Jesus, the author and perfecter of our faith, who for the joy set before him endured the cross, scorning its shame, and sat down at the right hand of the throne of God. Consider him who endured such opposition from sinful men, so that you will not grow weary and lose heart. In your struggle against sin, you have not yet resisted to the point of shedding your blood.
—Hebrews 12:1–4

No one should conclude the work of redemption was easy for Jesus; it was not. The road was rough, and the repeated confrontations with evil men took their toll. Yet, the destiny ahead for

Jesus Christ was to sit down again at the right hand of God and, ultimately, to enjoy eternity in heaven as the Savior of the redeemed hosts. Because of the great magnitude of that future, Jesus deemed it worth the price of on-going contradiction. Ultimately, it meant enduring the cross, the shame of which He so despised (Heb. 12:2–3; Isa. 53:11).

The apostle Paul absorbed this great theme into his own life, too. He taught the congregation at Corinth they were all runners in a race, and the whole point of the strenuous effort was to win the prize (1 Cor. 9:24–27). Paul understood the strength of endurance blossoms out of its persevering attitude, without which even powerful muscles soon become useless.

The reward ahead, in fact, was what made the rigors of the cross worth it to Jesus Christ. The marvelous message of the gospel is that Jesus successfully faced it all; He endured. His methods must become ours as we work out our salvation (Phil. 2:12–13).

Let this mind [or attitude] be in you.

—PHILIPPIANS 2:5, 8–11

⊰ An Old Elm—the Survivor Tree ⊱

A sprawling, shade-bearing, 80-year-old American elm has become a special symbol in Oklahoma City. Tourists drive from all across America to look at it. People enjoy taking pictures beneath it. This elm adorns many posters. Oklahoma City has lots of more beautiful trees, but no other is equally celebrated. This old elm is special because of endurance, not appearance.

The elm survived the Oklahoma City bombing on April 19, 1995.

All visitors to the Oklahoma City Bombing Memorial hear the story of Timothy McVeigh, who parked his death-laden truck only yards from this elm. His bitterness at 9:02 that morning killed 168 people and wounded 850. The explosion destroyed the Alfred P. Murrah Federal Building, and buried the elm in rubble. Everyone thought the tree would die; no one expected it to survive. No one, in fact, gave any thought to the dusty old elm stripped of its branches.

But new buds began to pop out. Sprouts pushed through damaged bark; green leaves wiped away dirt and soot. Life resurrected from a field of death.

People started noticing.

That elm now has the name, the Survivor Tree.[4]

IV. The Servant: Temptations During His Passion

A. Satan's All-Out Stand

In addition to the many temptations that Jesus faced in His ministry, it is important to examine the unique challenges that confronted Him in the last seven days of His life. The devil really did make his last stand against the Son of man during that final week, and especially during His crucifixion. It was a gory struggle; Jesus actually resisted to the point of "shedding [His] blood" striving against sin (Heb. 12:4). Satan's goal was clear: stop Him in any way possible, no matter how ugly and bloody the fight, and prevent His making the atoning sacrifice for all people and all sin.

1. Raw Terror

While on His way for His final visit to Jerusalem, "Jesus took the Twelve aside and told them, 'We are going up to Jerusalem, and everything that is written by the prophets about the Son of Man will be fulfilled. He will be handed over to the Gentiles. They will mock him, insult him, spit on him, flog him and kill him. On the third day, he will rise again'" (Luke 18:31–33). But the Lord's statement was more than the disciples could comprehend because "its meaning was hidden from them and they did not know what he was talking about" (v. 34).

The ugly horror of these six pitiless cruelties that lay ahead was very real, however.

- **"Handed over to the Gentiles"**—It was rare indeed for a Jew to choose Roman justice. Jews hated Romans and Romans returned the hatred with a vengeance; their cruelty against Jews was proverbial. Just the thought of being turned over to the Romans and placed in the hands of angry pagans was enough to strike the rawest terror in the hearts of most. The typical person would go to any lengths to avoid that sentence—and all the more so if he were innocent. Jesus knew He would not escape it even though He was innocent; His own people would surrender Him to the Romans (Mark 15:1).
- **"Mock Him"**—Jesus was the Son of God. The very prospect of submitting to the mockery of men—Jews and Gentiles— must have been tough for Him.
- **"Insult Him"**—Jesus knew how to avoid taking the insults of men personally, but the mere thought of what was ahead was

painfully sobering to Him. Isaiah prophesied for good reason that Messiah would be a "man of sorrows and familiar with suffering" (Isa. 53:3).

- **"Spit on Him"**—Many a fight has started because an angry person spits on another. Most people find spittle highly offensive, and people routinely come to blows because of it. In Jesus' case, soldiers spit on their own Redeemer. Can anyone doubt the devil perched on His shoulder and said to Him, "You don't deserve this and you don't have to take it"?

- **"Flog Him"**—Roman flogging was one of the cruelest punishments of the ancient world. The sentence was tantamount to being beaten to death—minus a blow or two. Most people would pay any price to avoid it. Jesus knew He would not escape that, either.

- **"Kill Him"**—In the Lord's case, He was well aware His end would be a brutal and bloody death.

The suffering ahead was enough to tempt most people to strike back in any way possible to defend themselves and avoid the horrendous pain. Jesus knew "all that was going to happen to him," so He understood what was coming (John 18:4). He also knew He would receive no mercy.

Would these six ruthless agonies tempt Him to change His attitude toward His Father to avoid the Cross? We know the answer; they did not. The Servant of all just kept on serving as He continually poured out divine love, asking nothing in return.

The fact that Jesus knew what was ahead and was willing to face it does not at all mean He enjoyed it. Quite to the contrary, the writer of Hebrews said He "endured" what He "despised" (Heb. 12:2, KJV). How did He do it? Jesus' big secret was He knew the rest of the story—on the third day He would rise again (Luke 18:33). The resurrection on the other side of crucifixion is what made the ordeal worth it.

Jesus taught His disciples that He owned His own life. The Father gave Him the choice, therefore, to lay His life down (John 10:17–18). In this context, the Lord's incredible sense of timing deserves attention. For Jesus to accomplish the Atonement and fulfill all righteousness, He had to be in full control of the timeline leading up to His crucifixion. The Lord's ownership of the timing was all the more striking when one considers just how thick the hatred was against Him in the religious establishment in Jerusalem. Since Jesus was God's Paschal Lamb, it meant His crucifixion needed to occur at the time the priests in the temple offered the morning Passover sacrifice (1 Cor. 5:7).

The situation called for precision. Jesus had to be sovereign over the overall situation, including the timing, so that nothing happened prematurely. It was for this reason that Jesus "withdrew to a region near the desert, to a village called Ephraim, where he stayed with his disciples" until six days before the Passover (John 11:54–12:1). After that all-too-brief respite, built into the plan from eternity, He returned to Jerusalem—exactly on the timeline.

2. Putdowns

After Jesus raised Lazarus from the dead, Mary and Martha gave a dinner in the Lord's honor to express their love for Him. At the meal, "Mary took about a pint of pure nard, an expensive perfume; she poured it on Jesus' feet and wiped his feet with her hair. And the house was filled with the fragrance of the perfume" (John 12:3).

Her act infuriated Judas Iscariot, who started grumbling that Mary should have sold the fragrance for a year's wages and given it to the poor. To Judas, Mary wasted all of that very valuable essence because, in his mind, Jesus was not worth a year's wages. It must have been an offensive put down to the Lord, but He did not respond in kind. Instead of defending Himself, He shielded and honored Mary, saying, "Why are you bothering this woman? She has done a beautiful thing to me.... When she poured this perfume on my body, she did it to prepare me for burial. I tell you the truth, wherever this gospel is preached throughout the world, what she has done will also be told in memory of her" (Matt. 26:10, 12–13).

Hatred really will sink people to the lowest depths of moral depravity. The chief priests so despised Jesus that he actually "made plans to kill Lazarus as well" since because of Lazarus' testimony "many of the Jews were going over to Jesus and putting their faith in him" (John 12:10–11). What bitterness! They would put Lazarus through the agony of death a second time just to try to get at Jesus. In reality, every homicide is an effort to get at God. Murder is an attitude of deadly pride that at its root says, *I know better than God who does not deserve to live, and my superior knowledge gives me the right to take life.*

3. Murderous Plots

"The chief priests and teachers of the law were looking for some way to get rid of Jesus," but fear of the people slowed their progress (Luke 22:2). Mark offers the insight they were looking for a "sly way to arrest Jesus and kill him" (Mark 14:1). In their frustration, Caiaphas, the high priest, called a meeting of the Sanhedrin. "'What are we accomplishing?' they asked. 'Here is this man performing many miraculous signs. If we let him go on like this, everyone will believe in him, and then the Romans will come and take away both our place and our nation'" (John 11:47–48). One cannot help but believe they were more concerned about preserving their place of power and privilege than caring for the people or the nation.

It was during this discussion that Caiaphas spoke up: "It is better for you that one man die for the people than the whole nation perish" (John 11:50). John wrote that Caiaphas had no intention to prophesy, "Jesus would die for the Jewish nation, and not only for that nation but also for the scattered children of God to bring them together and make them one"—but that's exactly what he did prophesy (John 11:51–53).

It must be unnerving to know people you really do love are looking for ways to kill you, and Jesus did know it. He also knew He came to die. Jesus was able to handle it because He understood perfectly that to love people at all is to take the risk of being disappointed and even wounded by their choices.

Jesus knew from eternity His death would be the price for our sins, so He came expecting to die as the sacrifice for all. Therefore, the plots did not demoralize Him. They were not motivation enough to break His bond with His Father and His dependence on the Holy Spirit.

It was important to Jesus that His disciples understand why He would submit to the brutality of evil men. He did it because of His commitment to obey His Father, whom He loved. He wanted the disciples to appreciate fully that when His arrest came, it would not happen because Satan held control over Him.

> The prince of this world is coming. He has no hold on me, but the world must learn that I love the Father and that I do exactly what my Father has commanded me.
>
> —JOHN 14:30–31

Trust cannot possibly be more absolute than the obedient service Jesus offered to His Father in the face of His crucifixion.

❧ The Risk of Love ❧
By C. S. Lewis

To love at all is to be vulnerable. Love anything, and your heart will be wrung and possibly broken. If you want to be sure of keeping your heart intact, you must give your heart to no one, not even an animal. Wrap it carefully around with hobbies and little luxuries, avoid all entanglements. Lock it up safely in the casket of your selfishness. And in that casket, safe, dark, motionless, airless, it will not change, it will not be broken. It will become unbreakable, impenetrable and irredeemable. The only place outside of heaven where you can be perfectly safe from the dangers of love is hell.[5]

"If it is possible, may this cup be taken from me," Jesus prayed to His Father in the Garden of Gethsemane, "yet not as I will, but as you will" (Matt. 26:39). No sane human being would relish what was ahead, and Jesus was human. Little wonder Jesus wrestled in Gethsemane with the cup He was to drink. His sweat became as great "drops of blood falling to the ground" as he anticipated the next few hours (Luke 22:44). Nonetheless, wisdom always lies in obedience to God. It was a principle the Son of man had learned well from the many attacks of evil men who doused His life with suffering even up to the cross (Heb. 5:8).

The first Adam failed in the Garden of Eden, but Jesus came through that long hour of prayer in the Garden of Gethsemane. He was determined to finish His life in firm obedience to His Father's strategy, as developed in eternity. There really was no other way. Jesus understood from eternity that the love of God provided no substitute plan, although in His true humanity He prayed to escape the horrendous suffering, if it were possible. In Gethsemane, Jesus made the choice final: He would drink the cup His Father had given Him, although it would be indescribably bitter (Isa. 51:17–22; Matt. 26:37–39; John 18:11). Love for His Father and for humankind defined His sense of obligation. The servant of Jehovah, who came to give His life for the sheep, kept on serving (John 10:15). Only complete loyalty to His Father motivated Him to submit to the path ahead.

4. Betrayal

The emotions associated with betrayal are devastatingly traumatic for most people. The courts of many nations routinely sentence traitors to capital punishment. Some cultures, in fact, summarily execute them. Nobody likes a defector. When the turncoat is a person close to you, it becomes all the harder to accept. Many a person has taken justice into his own hands to deal with a traitor.

Judas was one of the Lord's twelve disciples and the treasurer who maintained Jesus' funds. In reality, he was also a thief who was stealing from Jesus, helping himself to what was in the money bag (John 12:6). Judas deserved dismissal from the Twelve, but Jesus tolerated the thief in His ranks because of a higher objective—the role Judas would play in His passion.

Then one of the Twelve—the one called Judas Iscariot—went to the chief priests and asked, "What are you willing to give me if I hand him over to you?" So they counted out for him thirty silver coins.

—MATTHEW 26:14–15

It is interesting that all thieves are traitors; they are betraying a trust just by being a thief. Then, as their greed grows, they will almost invariably escalate their thievery to higher levels of betrayal.

The Lord dealt tenderly with Judas, showing Him special attention and lots of love even while Judas was looking for a way to surrender Jesus to His enemies (Matt. 26:16). How in the world did the Lord knowingly welcome the man to His table who would betray His very life in a few short hours? Why did Jesus wash *his* feet? (John 13:1–17). Why did Jesus give him a special "piece of bread" after the meal (John 13:26–28)? And above all, why did He permit the traitor to kiss Him? (Luke 22:47–48).

Jesus demonstrated "the great love wherewith He loved us" and "the love that passes knowledge" by doing each of those for Judas (Eph. 2:4; 3:19, KJV). The horror of betrayal did not tempt Him to change His attitude of perfect trust in His Father or His love for Judas. Instead, the Servant of all performed an act that can only spring from *agape* love—He became even Judas' bondservant.

At the Last Supper, Jesus announced that the "hand of him who is going to betray me is with mine on the table" (Luke 22:21). Jesus also predicted, "The Son of Man will go as it has been decreed, but woe to that man who betrays him" (Luke 22:22). It was an admonition spoken from a heart of love; His tone of voice communicated no anger. The warning did not deter Judas, who had already arranged a signal with the chief priests: "The one I kiss is the man; arrest him and lead him away under guard" (Mark 14:44).

Judas kept his word. In the Garden of Gethsemane that night, he walked up to Jesus, addressed him as Rabbi and kissed Him. At that, "the men seized Jesus and arrested him" (Mark 14:45–46). It is an interesting fact of the Incarnation that the Son of God became so completely the Son of man that the guards would not have known who to arrest, but for that kiss.

5. Denial in His Inner Circle

At the same Last Supper, Simon Peter vowed that if all men forsook the Lord, He would remain faithful. But Peter was wrong. "Before the rooster crows today, you will deny three times that you know me," the Lord told him (Luke 22:34). Jesus was committed to His Father with a bond like steel, but His disciples were not so committed to Jesus, at least not yet. In the face of His trial they all fell away, and Peter did it with cursing and swearing, saying, "I don't know the man!" (Matt. 26:31, 74; Luke 22:57). After his third denial, "the Lord turned and looked straight at Peter. Then Peter remembered the word the Lord had spoken to him: 'Before the rooster crows today, you will disown me three times.' He went outside and wept bitterly" (Luke 22:61–62).

Teachers have feelings too; they want to believe their students are learning their lessons. But for Jesus, the dominoes were falling fast. When one of His disciples betrayed Him, they all "deserted him and fled" (Mark 14:50). In that scenario of deep emotional pain, how did Jesus avoid feeling like a failure? Was there not temptation to think, it was of no use and give up?

Surely such temptation was present, but Jesus overcame it. The Lord could handle denial in His inner circle because of what He was certain was ahead. Jesus knew in advance that Judas, the son of perdition, would betray Him and then commit suicide (John 17:12; Matt. 27:5). He also had foreknowledge that the eleven would make a striking comeback after His resurrection. The Lord actually gave that as a prophecy to Peter.

> Simon, Simon, Satan has asked to sift you as wheat: But I have prayed for you, Simon, that your faith may not fail: and when you have turned back, strengthen your brothers.
>
> —Luke 22:31–32

What love! In that one, intimate statement, Jesus used Peter's name three times. The Lord also taught all of His disciples about His suffering before it happened, so that when it did happen, they would believe (John 14:29).

The Lord also knew this denial in His inner circle was not the final chapter. Jesus was certain that when His disciples discovered His tomb was empty and He was alive, they would begin to assimilate all He had taught them in a new way. And, when they received the Holy Spirit, each of them would be empowered for effective Christian service. It was because of this foreknowledge that the Lord felt compassion for His disciples and not anger, knowing the tragedy they were walking through was but another lesson in the curriculum—albeit a very important and painful one.

For the Lord personally, this kind of foreknowledge meant He did not feel like a failure as their Teacher. Instead, He knew He had achieved all of His objectives in training His disciples up to that point. The fickle character of His students, including His inner circle, did not come close to motivating Him to break faith with His Father, or to lose trust in His disciples. His Father, in fact, was the one stable rock of dependability in His life in the shadow of Golgotha. Jesus *knew* He could count on His Father. Jesus also knew the time was near when He would be able to count on His disciples.

❧ Always Be Prepared ❧

Twenty years ago, my wife and I were vacationing in Estes Park, Colorado, and had breakfast in a coffee shop. It was empty, except for four men at another table. One was mocking Christianity, in particular, the resurrection of Christ. He went on and on about what a stupid teaching that was.

I could feel the Lord asking me: "Are you going to let this go unchallenged?" However, I was thinking, *But I don't even know these guys. He's bigger than me. He's got cowboy boots on and looks tough.* I was agitated and frightened about doing anything. But I knew I had to stand for Jesus.

Finally, I told Susan to pray. I took my last drink of water and went over and challenged him. With probably a squeaky voice, I said, "I've been listening to you, and you don't know what you're talking about!"

I did my best to give him a flying rundown of the proofs for the resurrection. He was speechless, and I was half dead. I must have shaken for an hour after that. But I had to take a stand.

We cannot remain anonymous in our faith forever. God has a way of flushing us out of our quiet little places, and when he does we must be ready to speak for him. [First] Peter 3:15 says, "Always be prepared to give an answer to everyone who asks you to give the reason for the hope that you have."[6]

6. The Sting of False Evidence

When an innocent person who is on trial for his life has to sit and listen to people spewing raw lies as sworn testimony, their words can leave deep stab wounds. As the Lord's trial got underway, "the chief priests and the whole Sanhedrin" were scrounging around, "looking for false evidence against Jesus so they could put him to death" (Matt. 26:59). Many false witnesses came forward, "but their statements did not agree" (Mark 14:56). Jesus' keen ability to think on His feet could have easily silenced all of His critics, but He chose not to defend Himself (Isa. 53:7; Matt. 26:63; Mark 14:61; Luke 23:9). The pain of false evidence did not make Him change course. He had adjusted His expectations from eternity so that He was not shocked when the people whose problem He had accurately diagnosed lied about Him. Instead, He "entrusted himself to Him who judges justly" (1 Pet. 2:23).

7. Blasphemy

The charge that Jesus desecrated God and all things sacred in His speech and actions (the essence of blasphemy) dogged the Lord throughout His ministry, but it climaxed in His nighttime trial. As part of the process of the trial, Jesus endured mockery and beating by the religious leaders themselves, as well as the temple guards. They even slapped their own blindfolded Judge, then demanded that He prophesy and tell them who slapped Him (Mark 14:65; Luke 22:64; Micah 5:1). They "made fun of Him as they beat Him" (Luke 22:63, gw). Some of the chief priests started spitting in His face and pounding Him repeatedly in the face with their fists while yanking out His beard (Mark 14:65; Matt. 26:67, The Message; Isa. 50:6, The Message). One can only imagine, while Jesus was in the custody of the guards, the many other insulting and humiliating things done to Him not detailed in the record (Luke 22:65, gw).

Caiaphas and the other members of the Sanhedrin made no headway that long night at finding a charge against Him, but when the Passover dawn was first streaking across the sky, their big chance came.

> At daybreak, the council of the elders of the people, both the chief priests and teachers of the law, met together, and Jesus was led before them. "If you are the Christ," they said, "tell us." Jesus answered, "If I tell you, you will not believe me, and if I asked you, you would not answer. But from now on, the Son of Man will be seated at the right hand of the mighty God." They all asked, "Are you then the Son of God?" He replied, "You are right in saying I am." Then they said, "Why do we need any more testimony? We have heard it from his own lips."
>
> —Luke 22:66–71

Jesus was in control of both the timing and the evidence in the trial. He and He alone gave the Sanhedrin the testimony the members used to convict Him. The charge was blasphemy. The accusation worked that morning only because Jesus allowed it, and His timing was perfect for His crucifixion to take place simultaneous to the Passover sacrifice in the temple that very morning (1 Cor. 5:7). "He came to…his own," but they really did love "darkness instead of light, for their deeds were evil" (John 1:11; 3:19). As for Jesus, He was in command of His own life and laid it down on His own terms (John 10:18).

It is an interesting detail of the Gospels that Matthew, Mark, Luke and John focused their primary attention on the facts of the crucifixion but said little about Jesus' emotions. To get His feelings, the student must study the psalms. For example, David wrote several songs that are clearly Messianic; Psalm 69 is one of them.

> Save me, O God, for the waters have come up to my neck. I sink in the miry depths, where there is no foothold. I have come into the

deep waters; the floods engulf me. I am worn out calling for help; my throat is parched. My eyes fail, looking for my God. Those who hate me without reason outnumber the hairs of my head; many are my enemies without cause, those who seek to destroy me...You know how I am scorned, disgraced and shamed; all my enemies are before you. Scorn has broken my heart and has left me helpless; I looked for sympathy, but there was none, for comforters, but I found none. They put gall in my food and gave me vinegar for my thirst.

—PSALM 69:1–4, 19–21

Did His spirit break in the face of a formal Sanhedrin charge of blasphemy, motivating Him to try to plea bargain with the Sanhedrin to save His life? It did not. In this panorama of unfolding ruthlessness, Jesus knew there was only one rock on which He could find safety: obedience to His Father, as directed by the Holy Spirit. And there He stood.

8. Roman Cruelty
A few more blood-curdling missiles remained to try to prevent Jesus' sacrifice.

Early in the morning, all the chief priests and the elders of the people came to the decision to put Jesus to death. They bound him, led him away and handed him over to Pilate, the governor.

—MATTHEW 27:1–2

It was the religious leaders—the chief priests and elders of the land—who hustled Jesus to Pilate's court. Self-righteousness has always been a deadly enemy of Jesus Christ and His church. These hypocrites would not swat a mosquito or eat an egg a hen laid on the Sabbath, but on the day of their annual Passover celebration, they would kill with impunity "the Sun of righteousness" who had risen "with healing in His wings" (Mal. 4:2).

Pharisees are alive and well in the church today. They attend every service, tithe faithfully, and work hard, but none of them love Jesus Christ or their neighbor, and especially not lost souls. And they all will go to hell unless they discover the heart of Jesus.

The Jewish religious leaders did the unthinkable; they placed their Messiah in the hands of Roman justice. Pilate the governor began to question Him and quickly learned He was a Galilean, so Pilate turned Him over to Herod, who was in Jerusalem that very day.

When Herod saw Jesus, he was greatly pleased, because for a long time he had hoped to see him. From what he had heard about him, he wanted to see him perform some miracle. He plied him with many questions, but Jesus gave him no answer.

—LUKE 23:8–9

The chief priests and the teachers of the Law were standing there "vehemently accusing him" (Luke 23:10). Then Herod's soldiers began to ridicule and mock him. Their final charade was to dress him in an elegant robe and send him back to Pilate. How ironic that on the day of Jesus' trial for His life, "Herod and Pilate became friends—before this they had been enemies" (Luke 23:11). Jesus the peacemaker brought them into relationship again.

Pilate called together the chief priests, the rulers and the people, and said to them, "You brought me this man as one who was inciting the people to rebellion. I have examined him in your presence and have found no basis for your charges against him. Neither has Herod, for he sent him back to us; as you can see, he has done nothing to deserve death. Therefore, I will punish him and then release him" (Luke 23:14–16).

It was the governor's custom at the Passover Feast to "release a prisoner chosen by the crowd," and Pilate's plan was to release Jesus. He knew it was because of envy they had Jesus on trial (Matt. 27:18). Pilate was also holding in a cell a notorious insurrectionist and murderer named Barabbas (Matt. 27:15–16). The chief priests anticipated the opportunity and stirred up the crowd. In response, "With one voice they cried out, 'Away with this man! Release Barabbas to us!'" (Luke 23:18). Jealousy. What a green-eyed monster! Jealousy will even commit murder!

Pilate made the trade—Barabbas for the Son of God, the last Adam. Pilate ignored Roman law, his own better judgment, and the counsel of his very troubled wife in passing the sentence. "Don't have anything to do with that innocent man," she had pleaded with her husband, "for I have suffered a great deal today in a dream because of him" (Matt. 27:19). Even Romans did not want innocent people killed, and Pilate knew Jesus was innocent. Yet, he gave the order anyway (Matt. 27:18; John 18:38; 19:4, 6).

Then the scene began to unfold that made Roman cruelty so proverbial. Pilate took Jesus and had him flogged. He was lashed and lashed and lashed; they nearly beat Him to death—short just a few blows. Then the soldiers added mockery to the beating. They "twisted together a crown of thorns and set it on his head." These warriors "put a staff in his right hand, and knelt in front of him and mocked him. 'Hail, King of the Jews!' they said." (Matt. 27:29).

Although His flesh had been repeatedly gashed open by the flogging, "they clothed him in a purple robe" so that the blood and the robe clotted together. Then they "went up to him again and again, saying, 'Hail, king of the Jews!'

And they struck him in the face" (John 19:1–3). Although the bloody flesh coagulated on His clothing, they ripped the robe off and tore loose lacerated flesh, producing even more excruciating pain. "Then they led Him out to crucify Him" (Mark 15:20). It was cruelty guaranteed to make a man curse and swear at his captors. The soldiers had never seen it fail. If a man had any capacity to hate in his heart, that kind of punishment would pull it out, wrapped in the black invectives of vile profanity.

Undoubtedly, Satan perched on Jesus' shredded, bleeding shoulder and said with the reassuring voice of calculating deception, "Jesus, you really do not have to take this!" Surely, the experience of Roman cruelty would break His bond with His Father. Yet amazingly, Jesus neither cursed nor threatened, although He was literally "disfigured" by the cruelty and "marred beyond human likeness" (Isa. 52:14; 1 Pet. 2:23). Why did He go through with it? Why did He allow it?

The only possible answer is that love is stronger than hate; in fact, love always trumps hate. Love did have to take it, because love contains its own sense of duty. Love absorbed the worst the curse of sin could muster. Little wonder Paul later "reasoned with [the Thessalonians] from the Scriptures, explaining and proving that the Christ had to suffer and rise from the dead. 'This Jesus I am proclaiming to you is the Christ,' he said" (Acts 17:2–3).

When David penned Psalm 22, for example, he probably did not comprehend he was describing the sentiments of his Messiah's crushed heart on the cross, but he certainly did:

> My God, my God, why have you forsaken me? Why are you so far from saving me, so far from the words of my groaning? O my God, I cry out by day, but you do not answer, by night, and am not silent. Yet you are enthroned as the Holy One; you are the praise of Israel. In you our fathers put their trust; they trusted and you delivered them. They cried to you and were saved; in you they trusted and were not disappointed. But I am a worm and not a man, scorned by men and despised by the people. All who see me mock me; they hurl insults, shaking their heads: He trusts in the LORD; let the LORD rescue him. Let him deliver him, since he delights in him.
>
> —PSALM 22:1–8

9. Crucifixion

> When they came to the place called the Skull, there they crucified him, along with the criminals—one on his right, the other on his left.
>
> —LUKE 23:33

When the soldiers crucified Jesus, they took his clothes, dividing them in four shares, one for each of them, with the undergarment remaining. This garment was seamless, woven in one piece from top to bottom. "Let's not tear it," they said to one another. "Let's decide by lot who will get it."

—JOHN 19:23–24

The Savior suffered the final, humiliating mortification—public crucifixion, probably in the nude, without even a mere cloth to cover His loins and give Him a modicum of privacy. The Romans were too cruel to allow even that little scrap of dignity.

Satan had already used his every weapon short of crucifixion, but Jesus had not buckled. Hanging Him on the cross was the last temptation. Satan did not want Jesus actually to die on the cross, however, for then His sacrifice would be complete as the Savior of the world. Satan wanted the furnace called crucifixion heated so hot it made the pain unbearably horrific and sickening. (See Daniel 3:19.) Surely, the multiplied intensity of the suffering would motivate Jesus to stop the sacrifice and come down from the cross.

As for Jesus, if He could not bear up under the load in His true humanity, He knew He could call on His Father to come to His aid. "More than twelve legions of angels" were available to Him to take Him down from the cross, but He did not ask, demonstrating that love for His Father was a greater force than the horrendous pain of His screaming nerves (Matt. 26:53). Satan just could not make the furnace hot enough for *pain* to overcome *love*. Because Jesus did not come down from the cross, neither did flesh triumph over spirit. Instead, the Lord set a new example of faithfulness unto death and demonstrated a new definition of human endurance (Heb. 12:2; Rev. 2:10). By staying on the cross, He also sealed Satan's doom.

Even though the rulers were acting in ignorance, their hatred was so strong they could not let the Physician of their own eternal souls die in peace (Luke 23:35; Acts 3:17). They hurled insults at Him, and "the elders mocked him" (Matt. 27:39, 41; Mark 15:29–32). As the people stood watching, "the rulers sneered at Him. They said, 'He saved others; let him save himself if he is the Christ of God, the Chosen One'" (Luke 23:35). It was skepticism and cynicism run amok. They were gleefully certain the Great Physician could not heal Himself—not in this situation (Luke 4:23).

Matthew 27:44 records that "the robbers who were crucified with him also heaped insults on him." One of the thieves stopped hurling His slurs, however, and broke through to the realm of faith. He said to the other crook, who was still cursing, "'Don't you fear God, since you are under the same sentence? We are punished justly, for we are getting what our deeds deserve. But this man has done nothing wrong.' Then he said, 'Jesus, remember me when you come into your kingdom.' Jesus answered him, 'I tell you the truth, today you will be with me in paradise'" (Luke 23:40–43).

Even on His cross, amid all of the pain, suffering, and opposition, Jesus bestowed the gift of redemption on a repentant thief. What a great physician!

King David wrote Psalm 22 about a millennium before the event, prophetically describing the Lord's feelings at Calvary.

> Strong bulls of Bashan encircle me. Roaring lions, tearing their prey, open their mouths wide against me. I am poured out like water, and all my bones are out of joint. My heart has turned to wax; it has melted away within me…My tongue sticks to the roof of my mouth…Dogs have surrounded me; A band of evil men has encircled me, They have pierced my hands and my feet. I can count all my bones; People stare and gloat over me. They divide my garments among them and cast lots for my clothing.
> —PSALM 22:12–18

10. Forsaken by His Father

The last Adam in His manhood handled every technique tried against Him. It just was not in the power of the devil to break the steel bond between Jesus and His Father, thus preventing the success of the Savior's sacrifice. Everything Lucifer undertook to stop Calvary failed. Jesus was the Servant both of His Father and of all people. He did not even one time step out of His servant role, nor did He show any inclination at all to act independently in His own divinity and come down from the cross.

One more barrage remained, though, and it did not spring from Satan's arsenal. This missile came from His Father. Without question, it was the toughest of them all. The explosion hit when the Lord was the weakest. He had lost so much blood and expended so much energy just trying to breathe. The throes of death were already settling in, and His holy body was beginning to shut down. Could His pure mind handle one last struggle—and of all places, coming from His Father?

Jesus had always given absolute loyalty to His Father. He knew He could depend on Him—anytime, all the time.

But this time?

The ears of history have never heard a gut wrenching cry pierce the soul quite like this one: "My God, my God, why have you forsaken me?" (Matt. 27:46). It marks the only time in Jesus' incarnation that He referred to His Father with language other than that of a son to a father.

God's "eyes are too pure to look on evil" or to tolerate treachery, and Jesus was hanging there with the sins of the world on his shoulders (Hab. 1:13). His Father responded to His Son with silence as He hung on the cross. Separation and abandonment from God—it was the worst test of all, by far the worst. In all the others, Christ had known His Father was right there with Him; He could see Him and hear Him. Morning after morning He had awakened, talking with His Father (Isa. 50:4). They had enjoyed such a close relationship.

In these extreme moments of His holy life, when the shroud of death was slowly moving over Him, Jesus hung there *alone*. From eternity, He had never experienced separation from His Father. God had always been there for Him in His incarnate ministry, too. It is part of the mystery of the Incarnation that for the first time, in this moment, Jesus felt abandonment.

What would He do in this hour of His soul's black midnight? If the raw pain of crucifixion could not make Him buckle, would this separation push Him over the edge so that He would grasp for His omnipotence? Would He change His attitude toward His Father and break the bond to release Himself from the cross, when His Father and the Holy Spirit were not there to help Him? After all, those twelve legions of angels were no doubt standing on tiptoe, just waiting for the Father's order (Matt. 26:53).

Understanding Christ's redemptive work requires deep appreciation of the bond between the heavenly Father and His incarnate Son. As the High Priest of our confession, Jesus fulfilled that attachment by healing on the cruel cross the breach between His Father and fallen men, "reconciling the world to himself in Christ" (2 Cor. 5:19; Heb. 3:1–3; Isa. 53:10). He did it as our substitute, with the sins of all humankind on His heart (Isa. 53:10; Rom. 10:10; Heb. 6:20). Jesus became every man's guilt offering (Lev. 5:17–19).

It should never be forgotten that it was "the Lord's will to crush him and cause him to suffer, and though the Lord [made] his life a guilt offering, he [saw] his offspring and [prolonged] his days, and the will of the Lord [prospered] in his hand" (Isa. 53:10). "God made him who had no sin to be sin for us," Paul said, "so that in him we might become the righteousness of God" (2 Cor. 5:21). Peter added that Jesus Himself "bore our sins in his body on the tree, so that we might die to sins and live for righteousness; by his wounds you have been healed" (1 Pet. 2:24).

Love is a greater force than pain, shame, or abandonment. Because love mandated it, Jesus had to stay on the cross all alone until He died. We should remember Jesus taught in the parable of the unjust judge, "Men always ought to pray and not give up" (Luke 18:1; 2 Cor. 4:1, 16; Heb. 12:3). Hanging there in history's greatest miscarriage of justice amid the greatest stress of His incarnate life, Jesus kept His clarity of mind (Luke 23:43). He demonstrated that unconditional trust in God always trumps isolation and aloneness.

B. The Triumph of Implicit Trust

The spotless Lamb made the decision that even if His Father forsook Him in His death, He chose to continue obediently to trust that His Father would be waiting for Him on the other side of the grave (1 Pet. 1:21). The faith of God motivated Him to act in faith, even at a time when He could not see His Father's hand or feel the security of His voice (Rom. 3:3, KJV; Heb. 11:1). Jesus walked on, alone, through the murky Jordan of death, unflinchingly the bondservant to the Father's plan for our salvation.

❧ When the Lights Go Out ❧

When I was a student at Harvard Divinity School, I learned preaching from Dr. Gardner Taylor, a pastor in New York City. I'll never forget those lectures. I remember his telling us a story from when he was preaching in Louisiana during the Depression. Electricity was just coming into that part of the country, and he was out in a rural, black church that had just one little light bulb hanging down from the ceiling to light up the whole sanctuary. He was preaching away, and in the middle of his sermon, all of a sudden, the electricity went out. The building went pitch black, and Dr. Taylor did not know what to say, being a young preacher. He stumbled around until one of the elderly deacons sitting in the back of the church cried out, "Preach on, preacher! We can still see Jesus in the dark!"

Sometimes we get our best picture of God in the dark. And the good news of the gospel is that whether or not we can see him in the dark, He can see us.[7]

Amid this deep isolation, both the humanity and the divinity of Jesus came through again. "Knowing that all was now completed, and so that the Scripture would be fulfilled, Jesus said, 'I am thirsty'" (John 19:28). In His divinity, He knew the victory was His. Yet, in the true humanity of the Son of man, a mere thimble full of cool water would have felt like a deluge of rain on His dehydrated body and swollen tongue. The very lonely God-man, the Prince of paradise, was hanging between Earth and heaven as Jehovah's trustworthy servant. He was faithful, even in death.

The last Adam was almost dead. His sanctified life was clicking down to its final moments. Paul later wrote to Timothy, "There is one God and one mediator between God and men, the man Christ Jesus, who gave himself as a ransom for all men—the testimony given in its proper time" (1 Tim. 2:5–6). What a loyal servant!

How can one say that God died? We answer that death for a Christian does not imply cessation of being, but change of form of being. The God-Man left this natural world in the moment of death and joined the world of the supernatural. Paul later picked up this theme, too, when he explained, "To be absent from the body is to be present with the Lord" (2 Cor. 5:8, KJV). In the death of Jesus Christ, faith triumphed over the dreadful darkness of doubt, and trust prevailed over the emotional devastation that comes with being forsaken. "It is finished," Jesus said, in speech greatly weakened by blood loss (John 19:30).

The ancient Greeks boasted of being able to say much in a word. Hellenists considered it the perfection of oratory to give an ocean of meaning in a drop of language. Jesus did it here; He condensed the whole plan of redemption into one word: *tetelestai*. "It is finished." One word said it all!

Jesus had no strength left. The clock of His holy life was ticking not in minutes, but in seconds. Yet, Jesus maintained control of His mental faculties until the very end; He never became irrational. Instead, He reached into the depths of His holy soul and found His last reservoir of energy. By this time, His face and head had probably swollen twice their normal size (Isa. 52:14), yet His very parched tongue moved one last time as He cried out in "a loud voice, 'Father, into your hands I commit my spirit.' When he had said this, he breathed his last" (Luke 23:46).

The Lord's attitude of implicit trust held to the very end; it yielded to no pressure. The apostle Paul admonished his readers to work out their salvation with fear and trembling, by making that attitude their own (Phil. 2:5, 12–13).

This triumph also explains why Jesus has always been so attractive to men. They love His tough willingness to take on the impossible, and then pay the price to achieve it. Jesus was dedicated to the bold vision of obediently serving His Father's plan to save the world. He committed Himself totally to it and risked everything for it, including His life. Millions of men since then have chosen to follow Him in total trust, giving Him their full loyalty and allegiance—even dying for Him. Women, too, find security for life in His robust strength and tender compassion.

In the moment of Jesus' death, the veil in the temple was torn from top to bottom, making it possible for all to enter the holy of holies (Matt. 27:51; Heb. 6:19–20; 9:7; 10:19–20; Exod. 30:10). Little wonder Gabriel gave Mary's baby the name *Jesus*, meaning, "He will save his people from their sins" (Matt. 1:21).

1. The Conquest of Satan

In spite of all the effort allied against Him, the Lord achieved on Golgotha's knoll the primary purpose of the Atonement—reconciliation between God and man (Rom. 5:11; 2 Cor. 5:18–19; Matt. 27:39–44; Luke 23:35–37). Jesus proved in the process that spirit really is victor over flesh.

Achieving His primary objective presupposed the success of His secondary purpose. The conquest of Satan at Calvary was a wonderful byproduct of Jesus' atoning sacrifice. It was vitally important to the plan of salvation, but a derivative of the primary purpose (1 John 3:8; Isa. 53:10; Col. 1:20–23). Satan realized Jesus had crushed his kingdom when it became obvious He could not prevent Jesus' death. No one should think Satan and his fallen angels went into celebration when Jesus said, "It is finished," and died (John 19:30). It is far more likely the forces of darkness, full of fear, went into deep mourning over their eternal defeat.

2. What Kept Jesus on the Cross?

Again, without any effort to be exhaustive, it is appropriate now to look at some additional principles by which Jesus lived that enabled Him to stay on the cross until He died, surely the most stunning success among the many accomplishments of His incarnate life.

a) "What Jesus Knew"

John 13 is a marvelous chapter to explore the knowledge Jesus had as He went into His passion. Because of what He knew, Jesus was able to walk the friendless road ahead. His foreknowledge enabled Him to squeeze out to the last drop a winepress that was chock-full of throbbing pain and tormenting agony.

- Jesus knew "the time had come for Him to leave this world and go to the Father" (John 13:1).
- "Jesus knew the Father had put all things under His power, and that he came from God, and was returning to God" (v. 3).
- Jesus "knew who was going to betray Him" (v. 11); in fact, Jesus knew this information from the beginning of His ministry (John 6:64, 71). Judas' choices did not catch Jesus off guard. John takes this understanding even further: Jesus knew "all that was going to happen to him" (John 18:4).
- Jesus knew those He had chosen (John 13:18). His disciples would all forsake Him and flee, but He knew after His resurrection they would come back and, after Pentecost, become utterly loyal powerhouses of courage and boldness. His instruc-

tion had not been a failure; in fact, He was exactly on schedule as the master Teacher.

Throughout history, Jesus' followers have found extra strength for the journey by identifying with what Jesus knew. When a person's attitude is one of unreserved trust in Christ, he knows:

- who his Father is
- that His Savior has given him a job to do and the power to do it
- the road ahead will be rough and there will be people who will disappoint and even betray him, but Jesus will be with him and will give him people to help him

Just knowing these facts imparts great strength for the voyage for any child of God (Phil. 2:12–13). Jesus also knew His pending return to His Father was the ultimate reward of a job well done (John 13:1; Luke 19:17; 20:42–43; Ps. 110:1). That hope gave Him great endurance in the face of His crucifixion; it has always filled Christ's followers with strength, too. Paul wrote to the Christians at Rome, "I consider that our present sufferings are not worth comparing with the glory that will be revealed in us" (Rom. 8:18).

Jesus also knew that premeditated crimes can be committed in ignorance (Acts 3:17; 1 Tim. 1:13–16). The chief priests plotted against Jesus in the cold blood of malice aforethought, but they acted out of their lack of knowledge. Peter assimilated this great truth after the Lord's resurrection and addressed the theme in his sermon on Solomon's porch:

> Now, brothers, I know that you acted in ignorance, as did your leaders. But this is how God fulfilled what he had foretold through all the prophets, saying that his Christ would suffer. Repent, then, and turn to God, so that your sins may be wiped out, that times of refreshing may come from the Lord, and that he may send the Christ, who has been appointed for you—even Jesus.
> —Acts 3:17–20

b) A New High Priest

The Lord knew that when he stayed on the cross and triumphed over everything the devil threw at Him, He would be established as "a merciful and faithful high priest in service to God," who is able "to help those who are being tempted" (Heb. 2:17–18). This new High Priest has taught us with His own example that one of the golden keys to successful living is the power of adopting His own attitude—total commitment to God.

Isaiah looked forward some seven centuries and predicted His victory:

The will of the LORD will prosper in his hand. After the suffering of his soul, he will see the light [of life] and be satisfied; by his knowledge my righteous servant will justify many, and he will bear their iniquities. Therefore, I will give him a portion among the great, and he will divide the spoils with the strong, because he poured out his life unto death, and was numbered with the transgressors. For he bore the sin of many, and made intercession for the transgressors.
—ISAIAH 53:10–12

The Holy Spirit anointed the apostle Paul to look back at the Lord's cross and describe the great reward that followed Jesus' striking success: "God exalted him to the highest place and gave him the name that is above every name, that at the name of Jesus every knee should bow, in heaven and on earth and under the earth, and every tongue confess that Jesus Christ is Lord, to the glory of God the Father" (Phil. 2:9–11).

"Who is this that cometh up from the wilderness, leaning upon [his] beloved?" asked the wise king (Song of Solomon 8:5). His name is Jesus, and He triumphed because of His total dependence on the Word of God. The same, strong arm of the Father on which Jesus depended is available to every one of God's children to bring them out of their wilderness places too.

❧ Prayer as Comfort ❧

Author Garry Friesen writes: "When my friend Reilly told me about his first visit to our church, I learned something about prayer. Reilly says that after the service he lingered, talking to this person and that. When he stepped outside, his four-year-old daughter, Melody, did not come out. By then the building was empty, and the door was locked, and could be opened only with a key."

Reilly called through the mail slot in the large oak door, "Melody are you in there?"

A small frightened voice answered, "Yes, Daddy."

Then Melody put her hand through the mail slot so Daddy could hold it until someone fetched a church key. Melody could not see him, but she knew her father was there, and she was comforted.[8]

c) The Importance of Focus—to the End

Jesus kept His concentration on the will of His Father throughout His incarnation. That laser beam focus was a vital factor at Calvary that kept Him on the cross. It was this that allowed Jesus to complete every assignment given to Him from eternity.

For the Lord's followers, this achievement shows that perseverance to the end is the measure of a successful walk with Christ (2 Thess. 3:5; Heb. 12:1; James 1:3–4; 2 Pet. 1:6; Rev. 2:2, 19). Few in a lifetime get to see all of their spiritual harvest. The victory in the ups and downs of life, therefore, is that we do not give away our confidence. Instead, we keep our focus and pursue faith to the last breath (Heb. 10:35).

In the same way that the Lord's attitude held toward His Father, we conclude that keeping the faith is itself our ultimate victory, too. The writer of Hebrews listed such great Biblical personalities as Abel, Enoch, Noah, Abraham, Sarah, Isaac, and Jacob, and then said about them, "These all died in faith, not having received the promises, but having seen them afar off, and were persuaded of them, and embraced them" (Heb. 11:13, KJV). Peter said the trial of our faith is much more precious than gold that perishes (1 Pet. 1:7). Paul wrote to Timothy, "I am now ready to be offered, and the time of my departure is at hand. I have fought a good fight, I have finished my course, I have kept the faith: henceforth, there is laid up for me a crown of righteousness which the Lord, the righteous Judge, will award to me on that day" (2 Tim. 4:6–8, KJV). "This is the victory that has overcome the world, even our faith," wrote the apostle John (1 John 5:4).

With this understanding of how the Lord endured and how believers persevere, the children of God can rejoice "with an inexpressible and glorious joy" that the Messiah never broke faith with His Father and committed even one presumptive act. Instead, He lived the ethic of love faithfully to the end (John 13:1, GW; 2 Thess. 3:3; Heb. 3:2, 10:36; 1 Pet. 1:8).

V. The Sovereignty of God

We have seen in this study that the colossal effort to break the Servant of Jehovah included a wide range of temptations, each of them designed to motivate Jesus in some way to lose faith in His Father and take matters in His won hands by grasping for the prerogatives of His deity. Nonetheless, the Lord's bond of unreserved trust in God held amid them all. Now it is appropriate to look at how the sovereignty of God operated in the march to Calvary and contributed to the Lord's triumph.

A. Who Killed Jesus?

It is a good question. The Romans knew they did (Mark 15:24, 39; John 19:16). The Jewish leaders also knew they did (Mark 15:13–14, 20; 1 Thess.

2:14–15). In a very personal sense you and I did, as all of our sins were on His shoulders. Isaiah described the participation of Jesus' own Father: "It was the Lord's will to crush him and cause him to suffer" and to "make his life a guilt offering" (Isa. 53:10). Jesus added that He voluntarily gave His life. "No one takes it from me," He said. "I lay it down of my own accord" (John 10:18). Each of these affirmations is the truth. It is patently wrong, therefore, to blame only the Jews for Jesus' death, as has so often been the case through the centuries since the Lord's crucifixion (Matt. 27:25).

B. Blending Sovereignty and Foreknowledge

In His magnificent sermon on the Day of Pentecost, Peter proclaimed, "Him, being delivered by the determinate counsel and foreknowledge of God, you have taken, and by wicked hands have crucified and slain" (Acts 2:23, KJV). Hence, both the sovereignty and the foreknowledge of God merged into one at Calvary. The triune God Himself planned the event and brought together the whole jigsaw puzzle of circumstances and people, with all of their personal agendas and emotions. He did it without violating the free will of a single player in the drama. In this context, *free will* means each of Christ's enemies made a personal choice to participate in Jesus' death. The Father manipulated the participation of no one, not even Judas. Each took part by His own decision, making his choices out of his own desire (Matt. 26:21–25, 46–50; Luke 22:3–6; John 6:70–71). In His foreknowledge, God anticipated all the decisions of the people involved. In doing what they freely chose to do, each participant helped fulfill the Father's plan to save the world.

God had one plan, a grand design, an intentional strategy for all ethnicities, and purposed from eternity to fulfill it. The Godhead framed no backup model in the eternal counsels. Jesus Christ remains to this day the one and only blueprint of the Father. In achieving the magnificent plan, the Father brilliantly allowed the autonomy of every actor in the drama to be truly unrestricted, and yet that broad and unhampered display of free will achieved God's very purpose in Jesus' sacrifice. Such is the mirror image of God's sovereignty.

⊰ Ocean Voyage Illustrates ⊱
Free Will and Sovereignty

In *Knowledge of the Holy*, A. W. Tozer attempted to reconcile the seemingly contradictory beliefs of God's sovereignty and man's free will.

"An ocean liner leaves New York bound for Liverpool. Its destination has been determined by proper authorities. Nothing can change it. This is at least a faint picture of sovereignty. On board the liner are scores of passengers. These are not in chains, neither are their activities determined for them by decree. They are completely free to move about as they will. They eat, sleep, play, lounge about on the deck, read, talk, altogether as they please; but all the while the great liner is carrying them steadily onward toward a predetermined port. Both freedom and sovereignty are present here, and they do not contradict.

"So it is, I believe, with man's freedom and the sovereignty of God. The mighty liner of God's sovereign design keeps its steady course over the sea of history."⁹

C. Fulfilling the Prophets

After the Sanhedrin summoned Peter and John, they went back to their brethren and reported what had happened. When they heard the report:

> They raised their voices together in prayer to God. "Sovereign Lord," they said, "you made the heaven and the earth and the sea, and everything in them. You spoke by the Holy Spirit through the mouth of your servant, our father David: 'Why do the nations rage and the peoples plot in vain? The kings of the earth take their stand and the rulers gather together against the Lord and against his Anointed One.' Indeed Herod and Pontius Pilate met together with the Gentiles and the people of Israel in this city to conspire against your holy servant Jesus, whom you anointed. They did what your power and will had decided beforehand should happen."
> —Acts 4:24–28

On his first missionary journey, Paul preached a sermon in Pisidian Antioch that brings this whole panorama together:

> Brothers, children of Abraham, and you God-fearing Gentiles, it is to us that this message of salvation has been sent. The people of Jerusalem and their rulers did not recognize Jesus, yet in condemning him, they fulfilled the words of the prophets that are read every Sabbath. Though they found no proper ground for a death sentence, they asked Pilate to have him executed. When they had carried out all that was written about him, they took him down from the tree and laid him in a tomb. But God raised him from the dead, and for many days he was seen by those who had traveled with him from Galilee to Jerusalem. They are now his witnesses to our people.
> —Acts 13:26–31

Every person who had any part in the drama of the ages—the crucifixion of Jesus—acted out of his own free will. The sovereign God brought all of these willing participants together to fulfill the predictions of the prophets and to achieve the death of Jesus Christ. The result is the gospel of God (Rom. 1:1; 1 Thess. 2:8–9).

> We tell you the good news: What God promised our fathers he has fulfilled for us, their children, by raising up Jesus. As it is written in the second Psalm: "You are my Son; today I have become your Father." The fact that God raised him from the dead, never to decay, is stated in these words: "I will give you the holy and sure blessings promised to David." So it is stated elsewhere: "You will not let your Holy One see decay." For when David had served God's purpose in his own generation, he fell asleep; he was buried with his fathers and his body decayed. But the one whom God raised from the dead did not see decay. Therefore, my brothers, I want you to know that through Jesus the forgiveness of sins is proclaimed to you.
>
> —ACTS 13:32–38

VI. The Resurrection of the Servant

On the third morning, Jesus received the reward of His faithfulness. The Father did not leave His Son in hades, but instead raised Him from the dead (Acts 2:27, 31; Eph. 4:8).

> After the Sabbath, at dawn on the first day of the week, Mary Magdalene and the other Mary went to look at the tomb. There was a violent earthquake, for an angel of the Lord came down from heaven and, going to the tomb, rolled back the stone and sat on it. His appearance was like lightning, and his clothes were white as snow. The guards were so afraid of him that they shook and became like dead men. The angel said to the women, "Do not be afraid, for I know that you are looking for Jesus, who was crucified. He is not here; he has risen, just as he said. Come and see the place where he lay. Then go quickly and tell his disciples: 'He has risen from the dead.'"
>
> —MATTHEW 28:1–7

Calvary both vindicates Jesus' explanation of man's fallen condition and demonstrates the Father's cure. The Lord not only identified the core of man's problem, He also provided the solution with His own blood, pulling God and man together in passionate embrace. Because of Christ's death and resurrection, we "put our hope in the living God, who is the Savior of all men, and especially of those who believe" (1 Tim. 4:10). Jesus demonstrated full loyalty to His Father. He also loved fallen men enough to die for them. It is only proper, in return, that we should place Him like a seal over our hearts (Song of Sol. 8:6).

Chapter Four

JESUS, WHAT A SAVIOR

He has taken me to the banquet hall, and his banner over me is love.

—SONG OF SOLOMON 2:4

He himself bore our sins in his own body on the tree, so that we might die to sins and live for righteousness.

—1 PETER 2:24

I. Sin, the Curse

A. The Fall

God created man with a holy nature, placed him in the Garden of Eden, and endowed him with a free will (Gen. 2:15–17). Our first parents could actually say yes or no, even to their Creator, and so can all their children. Eve made her choice and said no to God when she ate the forbidden fruit, and Adam joined her in the rebellion (Gen. 3:6; Rom. 5:12). They decided to make what they could see with their eyes and discern with their minds a higher priority than unconditionally trusting the invisible God, whom they could see only with the eyes of faith (Gen. 3:1–6; John 4:24; 1 Tim. 1:17).

Our first parents' fateful decisions violated the heart of God and broke the intimate fellowship between God and man. In that moment of rebellion, Adam died a spiritual death, and the lust of the eyes, the lust of the flesh, and the pride of life were birthed in his life (Gen. 3:6; 1 John 2:16). The byproduct of the rebellion was the birth of idolatry. Man would henceforward actually worship the things God made and forget about the God who made the things man chose to adore (Lev. 26:1; Ps. 106:20; Rom. 1:23). The impact of this death left Adam hopelessly addicted to sin. The corruption, like yeast, reached into his heart, the seat of his willpower as well as his mind, and his strength, and soaked through the entire inner sanctuary of his soul (Isa. 1:4–6).

All people since have found it easier to focus on the creation, including themselves and their own corrupted physical desires, rather than the Creator, who is an invisible Spirit and can be seen only with the eyes of faith (Rom. 1:18–23; 2 Tim. 3:2–4). After that sin, Adam could effortlessly see his world, but his vision of God was dreadfully blurred.

Sin keeps a blinding veil over the eyes of the soul. This condition means man "is dead in trespasses and sins" (2 Cor. 3:13–16; Matt. 15:14; Eph. 2:1, 5). With his willpower now bound in addiction to sin, a person cannot choose to revel in fellowship with God and has no inherent righteousness to commend him to God. Nor does he gaze adoringly on the Lord who made him and loves him so much He even rejoices over him with singing (Zeph. 3:17; Mark 8:18; Luke 24:16, 31). Instead, this addiction requires man to glory in himself (self-centeredness), and the created order he can see (Gen. 4:23–24; Judg. 17:4–6; Luke 12:16–20). All of Adam's children since then have inherited this same estrangement from God the creator.

1. The Birth of Independence

The rebellion and first transgression birthed a new attitude of self-sufficiency, expressed as proud selfishness. This independence engulfed Adam and displaced his trust in God. Just a short time earlier, he had been so responsive to the Holy Spirit. After the rebellion, the new addiction resulted in the lusts that produce idolatry, adultery, murder, and so many other inordinate desires and deeds of the flesh (Matt. 15:19). All of Adam's children since then have been plagued with the same evil "free will" (Gen. 4:6–8; 1 John 2:16; Gal. 5:19–21; Col. 3:5).

With the fellowship severed between God and Man, Adam began to use his new self-sufficiency to chart his own course. From this fountain flowed the blinding power of a new and colossal pride that has continued to convince people they can make it on their own without the loving care of the God who created them.

2. "Adam, Where Are You?"

The Sovereign Adam and Eve so violated in their rebellion lovingly came "walking in the garden in the cool of the day," calling to Adam, "Where are you?" When he answered, Adam's reply summed up both the death that already reigned in his soul and the future condition of all his seed: "I heard you in the garden, and I was afraid because I was naked; so I hid" (Gen. 3:8–10).

"I heard…I was afraid…I hid." Such is the universal condition of man. Adam felt for the first time the corruption of his will that made him try to hide from God; in fact, fallen man always runs from God:

- Adam and Eve actually felt fear. Their sins made them feel exposed.
- They felt guilt when they heard the voice of God calling them and actually wanted to avoid Him. Their choices had shattered the intimate fellowship they enjoyed with God.

- Adam and Eve also felt shame. Basic to this sense of humiliation was realizing they were naked. In fact, all of Adam's seed are "uncovered and laid bare before the eyes of him to whom we must give account" (Heb. 4:13).

The Bible describes the emotions of Adam and Eve, but the record of the Fall does not disclose the feelings of God. One can imagine, however, that if the sins of Noah's generation grieved God to the extent that "His heart was filled with pain," it was with a very broken and crushed heart that God called out to Adam in the Garden, "Where are you?" (Gen. 3:9; 6:6).

Moses the great lawgiver and emancipator summed up the principle centuries later, "You may be sure your sin will find you out" (Num. 32:23).

3. The Threefold Sin Curse

The curse of sin bore devastating results (Gen. 3:14–19; Ps. 9:16; Zech. 9:9, KJV; Rom. 3:26; Rev. 15:3). Spiritual death occurred immediately. Its essence is separation from the holy environment of God's Spirit. The natural death of the physical body followed this spiritual death. Adam lived for almost a millennium, but the penalty came true—"he died" (Gen. 5:5). Eternal death, also described as the second death, is the final step in the sin curse, the very essence of which is everlasting separation from God and His Holy Spirit in a burning hell (Luke 16:23; Rev. 20:14). Sin is the cancer of the spirit that kills vision, hope, and, ultimately, life itself.

God cursed the serpent above all the animals of the field, condemning him to crawl on his belly (Gen. 3:14). Eve's penalty was that she would bear children in sorrow, a distress that extended to child rearing (Gen. 3:16). The curse of sin also tainted their marriage relationship: "Your desire will be for your husband, and he will rule over you," God said to Eve (Gen. 3:16). Ever since, women have typically functioned on a feeling level ("desire"), while men think and operate on an authority level ("rule"). This gap between wife and husband is huge. Wise is the couple that understands it and works hard to build a bridge over the chasm.

Physical work actually predates the Fall, because God made Adam responsible from the beginning to dress and keep the Garden (Gen. 2:15). After the Fall, God cursed the ground for Adam's sake, for how could he function any longer in a perfect environment? (See Genesis 3:17–18.) God also told Adam he would earn his living by the sweat of his brow until he returned to the dust from which he came, and the toil of making a living was made even harder because thorns and thistles would start growing in nature (Gen. 3:18–19). God then drove Adam and Eve out of paradise and placed cherubim with flaming swords at Eden's gates to guard the tree of life (Gen. 3:24).

Of all the effects of the curse of sin, surely the most significant aspect of Adam's immediate spiritual death was his deprivation of the presence of God. A deep crater of emptiness opened up in his soul, and his new sense of self-sufficiency could not fill it. What had been a magnificent cathedral in Adam's heart was now but a desolate chasm, empty and cold, and delusional in its perceived independence. God had created Adam in His own image, but Adam's choice utterly corrupted his free will and disfigured the image of God in his soul (Gen. 1:26–27; 3:17–24; Eccl. 3:11).

How desperately man needed help.

4. A Violated but Merciful God

Adam's generous God, whom the choices of these first parents had so desecrated, responded with both firm judgment and loving grace (John 1:14). "I will put enmity between you and the woman," God said to the serpent, "and between your offspring and hers; he will crush your head and you will strike his heel" (Gen. 3:15). The pronouncement meant their Messiah would also be their Savior. This was God's first promise that He had already arranged a plan to heal the deep rift between Himself and them. This pledge marvelously reveals the great heart of God. Even in these earliest moments of the rebellion, God promised His plan to reconcile to Himself Adam and Eve and their seed (Gen. 3:15; 6:6). His objective ever since has been to save lost people, not to condemn them (John 3:17). The great storyline of the Bible, in fact, is that God lovingly continues in every generation to seek a restored relationship with fallen man, even while He judges sin (Exod. 34:5–7; Matt. 18:11, KJV).

B. Messiah's Diagnosis

"When the time had fully come," God's Son arrived in flesh and blood with the goal to face squarely man's fallen condition and redeem all that Adam lost (Gal. 4:4; 1 Cor. 15:45). One of Jesus' primary objectives was to explain the human problem in such a clear way that any fair-minded person could grasp it. Just the diagnosis itself is good news, because it is essential for establishing the cure. Knowing the facts, therefore, is a big first step. When people hear the diagnosis, the Holy Spirit convicts their hearts, making them know it rings with truth (Gen. 6:5; 15:6; Ps. 51:5; Rom. 1:17, 25, 28; Phil. 2:15; Eph. 2:5).

The Son of God summarized the lost condition of all people worldwide in His conversation with Nicodemus and presented Himself as the only solution.

> God so loved the world that he gave his one and only Son, that whoever believes in him shall not perish but have eternal life. For

God did not send his Son into the world to condemn the world, but
to save the world through him.

—John 3:16–17

The attention given to these verses usually focuses on the three great themes
that frame the *antidote* to man's addiction. They are the love of God, the
redemptive death of His Son, and the faith in Christ that redeems. These three
express the gospel cure. It is an interesting fact that the Lord expressed the
cure to Nicodemus before He stated the diagnosis: that God loves every fallen
person and offers "whosoever" the one and only road back home through the
sacrificial death of His "only begotten Son."

Jesus summarized His diagnosis of man's fallen condition with the phrase
"Whoever believes in Him should not perish." The implication is that all people—
"whoever"—all are under the same curse and are perishing (Matt. 19:16–26, lb).
Hence, all are facing the second death of eternal separation from God because
of their broken relationship with God and their active state of mutiny, which so
violates Him. The matter is deadly serious and the condition is universal. This
verdict is authoritative because it comes from God's Son, the living Word "by
whom all things were made," who became flesh in Jesus Christ (John 1:1–3, 14).

⚘ Wabush: One Way In, and One Way Out ⚘

Wabush, a town in a remote portion of Labrador, Canada, was
completely isolated for some time. But recently, a road was cut through
the wilderness to reach it. Wabush now has one road leading into it, and
thus, only one road leading out. If someone would travel the unpaved
road for six to eight hours to get into Wabush, there is only one way he or
she could leave—by turning around.

Each of us, by birth, arrives in a town called Sin. As in Wabush, there
is only one way out—a road built by God himself. But in order to take
that road, one must first turn around. That complete about-face is what
the Bible calls repentance, and without it, there's no way out of town.[1]

After Jesus launched His ministry, Pharisees from Jerusalem challenged
Him because they observed His disciples did not wash their hands before
eating. In that exchange, He identified the collective spiritual condition of
humanity, with which every man lives. Jesus said:

"Listen to me, everyone, and understand this. Nothing outside a
man can make him 'unclean' by going into him. Rather, it is what

comes out of a man that makes him 'unclean.'" After he had left the crowd and entered the house, his disciples asked him about this parable. "Are you so dull?" he asked. "Don't you see that nothing that enters a man from the outside can make him 'unclean'? For it doesn't go into his heart but into his stomach, and then out of his body"... He went on: "What comes out of a man is what makes him 'unclean.' For from within, out of men's hearts, come evil thoughts, sexual immorality, theft, murder, adultery, greed, malice, deceit, lewdness, envy, slander, arrogance and folly. All these evils come from inside and make a man 'unclean.'"

—Mark 7:15–23

The Pharisees' big concern was that an individual wash his hands before a meal. With Jesus, the primary issue was not unclean hands but dirty hearts, because all people live with a corrupted will that is in rebellion against God (Matt. 12:34; 15:2, 11, 18–20; 23:25–28; Gal. 5:19–21; Heb. 3:8, 15).

Jesus boldly confronted the Pharisees, saying to them, "You belong to your father, the devil, and you want to carry out your father's desire" (John 8:44). This was so true that even though their Messiah at that moment was standing in front of them, physically talking with them, His message was so foreign to their thinking they slandered Him as a demon-possessed Samaritan (John 8:48).

Not all people take their rebellion against God to the ultimate extreme of these Pharisees, but the diagnosis fits the condition of every man. This verdict is the whole reason why the love of God sent Jesus into the world (Mark 7:21; Matt. 15:11, 18–20). The truth is that all people in varying ways want to carry out Satan's desires (John 8:44). Jesus' conclusion, therefore, has universal application (John 3:16).

C. Depravity

In the Tri-unity of God, the members of the Trinity operate on the principle of mutual interdependence. Sinful man in his fallenness operates out of independence. The rebellion in Eden meant Adam and his descendants, as spiritual beings, would henceforward be "dead in [their] transgressions and sins" (Eph. 2:1). *Depraved* is the term that best fits this spiritual condition (Rom. 1:28–32; Phil. 2:15). Adam lost his original righteousness in the Fall, and was left with an utterly marred image of God in his soul that meant he had no capability to contribute anything to correcting his problem (Gen. 1:27; 3:1–19; Ps. 14:3; Ezek.18:20; Matt. 16:26; Rom. 3:10–12).

A new self-sufficiency that retained no holy affection toward God controlled Adam's will after the Fall. He lived with an addiction that made love for the things God made more attractive than love for the God who made everything (Exod. 34:17; Deut. 6:4–5; Matt. 22:37; Acts 17:16).

In his fallen condition, Adam could do nothing of merit to regain a right standing with God; he was completely devoid of the love God required (Gen. 6:5–6; Rom. 7:18). All people since Adam's fall have lived with the same bias that regularly blossoms into outright hostility toward God: "in Adam all die" (1 Cor. 15:22). In fact, sin has corrupted every faculty of man's being (Eph. 4:18). In his feelings, willpower, and choices, Adam went into a downward spiral. The verdict is that there is no righteousness before God in any of man's decisions or attitudes (Rom. 1:18–32). Paul reduced mankind's condition to a single sentence: "Not one person has God's approval" (Rom. 3:10, GW; Ps. 14:1–3; 53:1–3).

Understanding how evil our sins truly are in the eyes of God is vital to appreciating how our choices continue to wound the heart of God. Yet, so many people choose to minimize their sinfulness and maximize their righteousness. How much wiser to stand under the truly bitter cross where Jesus died and take in the real picture—how totally lacking we are of a right standing with God (Jer. 17:9; see Ezek. 16 for another graphic description of mankind's utterly fallen condition).

Depravity does not mean a person can have no pleasing qualities toward his fellow men. He can indeed have high moral character in the eyes of the world (Mark 10:21; Rom. 2:14). Nor does every person carry his rebellion toward God as far he could. Jesus affirmed that even the Pharisees did some good things (Matt. 23:23).

All men since Adam's fall have lived with gnawing emptiness in their souls, a nagging sense that something important is missing. Solomon explained that spiritual hole by saying, God has "put a sense of eternity in people's minds" (Eccles. 3:11, GW). People live with an incredible frustration. They have no independent drive to run to the cross of Jesus for help. Yet, an inner sense of the eternal makes them know God has set a day "when he will judge the world with justice," which means they know their own judgment day is coming (Acts 17:31).

II. Christ, the Cure

A. The Love That Surpasses Knowledge

The Messiah knew His diagnosis was correct: all people, everywhere, have corrupted hearts toward God (Matt. 15:18–20; Mark 17:15–23; John 3:16–17). Hence, Jesus gave His precious blood as the antidote (John 10:15; Rom. 1:28–32; 3:25). The apostle Paul later offered this petition: "I pray that you, being rooted and established in love, may have power, together with all the saints, to grasp how wide and long and high and deep is the love of Christ, and to know this love that surpasses knowledge—that you may be filled to the measure of all the fullness of God" (Eph. 3:17–19).

⚒ The Great Lie of Auschwitz— ⚒ "Work Makes Free"

When I was a teenager, I became fascinated, appalled, and grieved by the literature of the Holocaust...One scene that haunts me is a picture from Auschwitz. Above the entryway to the concentration camp were the words, *Arbeit macht frei*. The same thing stood above the camp at Dachau. It means, "work makes free"—work will liberate you and give you freedom.

It was a lie—a false hope. The Nazis made the people believe hard work would equal liberation, but the promised "liberation" was horrifying suffering and even death.

Arbeit macht frei. One reason that phrase haunts me is because it is the spiritual lie of this age. It is a satanic lie. It's a *religious* lie. It is a false hope—an impossible dream...People believe their good works will be great enough to outweigh their bad works, allowing them to stand before God in eternity and say, "You owe me the right to enter your heaven."

It is the hope of every false religion—*arbeit macht frei*.

It's the love of God that liberates. It's the blood of Jesus Christ that liberates. He died in my place, and I am free.[2]

B. The Method of Salvation

1. The New Birth

Jesus chose a member of the Jewish ruling council, a man named Nicodemus, to be the first person to hear the Lord's redemptive plan. Jesus expressed it with great earnestness: "Unless you are born again you can never get into the kingdom of God" (John 3:1, 3, 16, NLT). In this new birth, when people repent, God gives them a new heart. The Lord made very clear, therefore, that His objective was not to rebuild man's utterly sinful, old heart; instead, God said, "I am making everything new" (Rev. 21:5; Ezek. 18:31; 36:26; 2 Cor. 5:17; Gal. 6:15).

Jesus was equally explicit that He expects His followers to believe passionately with Him both the diagnosis He identified and the cure He offers through the new birth. His language is precise: "Those who want to follow me must say no to the things they want, pick up their crosses, and follow me. Those who want to save their lives will lose them. But those who lose their lives for me and for the Good News will save them" (Mark 8:35, GW).

Although sin is the universal curse on all men, Christ is the universal cure (Gal. 3:13; John 3:16; Rev. 22:17). The gospel is all about how the love God demonstrated at Calvary produces this new birth.

Postmodernism clearly rejects this diagnosis as truth that applies equally to all people worldwide. In fact, postmodernism denies that any universals exist and is especially quick to reject the Christian belief that every person has a corrupted heart at enmity toward God. Nonetheless, the proof is in the diagnosis; sins emerge out of the hearts of all people because all people have a spiritual heart problem that includes "evil thoughts, sexual immorality, theft, murder, adultery, greed, malice, deceit, lewdness, envy, slander, arrogance and folly" (Mark 7:21). It is so easy for even believers to be pulled into postmodernist thinking, so that the church waters down the gospel. The answer to postmodernism is not to apologize for Jesus' absolutes, but faithfully to proclaim them. When the gospel is preached, the Holy Spirit connects the Word to the sense of eternity God set in the heart of every man, and people are drawn to Jesus Christ (Eccles. 3:11).

⊰ All Roads Lead to God ⊱
By Max Lucado

All roads lead to heaven. Well, the sentence makes good talk-show fodder, but does it make sense? Can all approaches to God be correct? How can all religions lead to God when they are so different? We don't tolerate such logic in other matters. We don't pretend that all roads lead to London or all ships sail to Australia; all flights don't lead to Rome. Imagine your response to a travel agent who proclaims they do. You tell him you need a flight to Rome, Italy. So he looks on his screen, and he offers, "Well, there's a flight to Sidney, Australia, at 6:00 a.m."

"Does it go to Rome?" you ask.

"No, but it offers great food and movies."

"But I need to go to Rome," you say.

He says, "Well, let me suggest Southwest Airlines."

"Southwest Airlines flies to Rome?"

"No, but they win awards for on-time arrivals."

You're getting frustrated, so you reiterate: "I need one airline, to carry me to one place—Rome."

The agent appears offended: "Sir, all flights go to Rome."

Well, you know better. Different flights have different destinations. That's not a thickheaded conclusion, but an honest one. Every flight does not go to Rome.

And every path does not lead to God.[3]

2. *The Lavish Love of God*

Man's broken fellowship with God can be restored. It happens because Jesus has always been willing to cascade love down on the sons of Adam, never once asking if they deserve it (Eph. 1:8). In doing so, the Lord reveals that love for God is the cornerstone ethic of the life that follows this new birth. Jesus expressed the standard when He quoted the first commandment from the Law: "Love the Lord your God with all your heart, and with all your soul, and with all your mind, and with all your strength" (Mark 12:30; Deut. 6:5).

The concept of a new birth describes best the new beginning to which God calls every person. In this new relationship, each becomes a child again—a child of God. As a child loves and totally trusts his parents, so a new believer falls wholeheartedly in love with Jesus Christ, whom he now trusts completely. This includes His:

- heart, the seat of his emotions and feelings, and his will;
- soul, the spiritual dimension of his life that makes him an eternal being;
- mind, the sphere of his capability to think and reason; and
- strength, his energy and ability to move about, work, and serve.

For this to happen, the gospel also shows the heavenly Father must first pour His own love into a person's life. Hence, "we love [him] because he first loved us" (1 John 4:19). When a person makes the Spirit-motivated choice to love God in this comprehensive way, then he is ready for the second commandment: "love your neighbor as yourself" (Mark 12:31; Lev. 19:18).

The Lord Jesus loved His Father with all His heart, soul, mind, and strength, and that love motivated Him to trust and obey His Father implicitly (Matt. 22:37; 8:28–29). To read the Gospel narratives is to discover that He also loved people, according to the high standard of the Golden Rule. These twin loves—for God and people—made it possible for Jesus to redeem man's fallen condition, letting people partake of the divine nature (2 Pet. 1:4).

Based on the gift of God's love, anyone who is thirsty can come to the cross of Jesus. Even those who "have no money" are welcome to "buy and eat...without money and without cost" (Isa. 55:1). The attitude that achieves this so great salvation is unqualified faith in the heavenly Father (John 6:29; Heb. 2:3; Phil. 2:5–6).

✻ Love in Relationship Changes Us ✻

When I was dating my wife, Anna, one thing I admired about her was her love for sports. I love sports too, but there are two sports I don't like. Forgive me if you like these, but I don't.

The first is bowling. I can't understand it…the dumbest thing I've ever heard.

The other is roller-skating: four wheels, none of them turn, and they expect you to go around in circles.

This is a true story. On our first date, I knocked on Anna's door. I was so excited. I said, "Where would you like to go tonight?"

She said, "Do you like bowling?" And she picked up her own bowling ball. She had her own bag. Now, I was in love, so when she asked if I liked bowling, my answer was, "I love bowling." And we went bowling…We had a great time.

The next week I knocked on her door. I said, "Where would you like to go this week?"

She picked up her skates. She said, "Do you like skating?" I said, "I've been waiting for months for someone to ask me to go skating; I love skating." And we skated…

I look back on it now and think, what made it easy for me to change? Did I have to work up this thing to change my desire for bowling and skating? No. It was because of my relationship with that girl. Because of the love that I had in relationship with her, change was easy.

The power to change is predicated upon your relationship with God. How often I think, "God, it's hard to do what you're asking me to do, hard to change. Do I just grit my teeth?"

"No," the Lord says, "why don't you just come closer to the cross? Why don't you let me restore and renew my relationship with you? Would you come close?"[4]

---

3. Jesus Christ as God's Answer

The fall of man was a colossal tragedy, but it did not catch God off guard. His answer was Jesus Christ. When He came to this earth in the Incarnation, the Lord Jesus achieved reconciliation between God and man, all the while showing full respect for man's freedom of choice. This Redeemer, who was loved by His Father "before the creation of the world," so generously loves all people that He sacrificed Himself to restore lost humanity's fellowship with

God (John 17:24; Eph. 1:7–8; 3:17–19). Therefore, the magnanimous love of the Liberator motivates people to return His love freely, honoring their Rescuer with full loyalty and adoring worship (2 Cor. 5:14–21).

C. The Last Adam

"The first man Adam was made a living soul; the last Adam was made a quickening spirit…The first man is of the earth, earthy: the second man is the Lord from heaven" (1 Cor. 15:45–47, KJV). The Lamb of God "foreordained before the foundation of the world" became this second man (1 Pet. 1:20, KJV). The Lord "chose us in him before the creation of the world that we should be holy and blameless in his sight." And, Paul added, "He predestined us to be adopted as his sons through Jesus Christ" (Eph. 1:4–5).

Paul wrote, "Sin entered the world through one man and death through sin, and in this way death came to all men, because all sinned" (Rom. 5:12). Then the Apostle wrote:

> If, by the trespass of the one man, death reigned through that one man, how much more will those who receive God's abundant provision of grace and of the gift of righteousness reign in life through the one man, Jesus Christ. Consequently, just as the result of one trespass was condemnation for all men, so also the result of one act of righteousness was justification that brings life for all men.
>
> —ROMANS 5:17–18

The apostle Paul demonstrated in his writings a marvelous capacity to summarize the human predicament and the gospel solution provided by the last Adam. "All have sinned and fall short of the glory of God," he wrote, "and are justified freely by his grace through the redemption that came by Christ Jesus (Rom. 3:23–24). He also explained, "The wages of sin is death, but the gift of God is eternal life in Christ Jesus our Lord" (Rom. 6:23).

D. Understanding the Depth of the Problem

Jesus' ghastly crucifixion defines how bad sin is, framing the best definition of the extent of the sin curse. Jesus' death is also the best measure of God's love, revealing the servant heart of a Savior committed to curing the fallen condition of all people. Sin is an insidious cancer so evil it required the death of God's Son, the jewel of heaven, to make man well again.

Man's best works, however, are woefully inadequate to restore him to the high level of God's righteousness. No one is capable through his own efforts of breaking the addiction and approaching the expectations of divine holiness. Isaiah stated, "all our righteous acts are like filthy rags" (Isa. 64:6). "When you have done everything you were told to do," Jesus taught His disciples, you still have no choice but to say, "We are unworthy servants; we have only done our duty" (Luke 17:10).

✹ We Healed the World ✹

In 2006, Yoko Ono placed a full-page ad in the New York Times calling for December 8—the anniversary of John Lennon's death—to be made a global day of healing.

"One day we will be able to say that we healed ourselves," Ono promised, "and by healing ourselves, we healed the world."[5]

Man in his proud independence always thinks he can heal himself, and thus, the world. But Jesus' diagnosis rings true all the time: "Out of the heart come evil thoughts, murder, adultery, sexual immorality, theft, false testimony, slander" (Matt. 15:19).

Jesus Christ responded to man's condition with a passionate love that motivated Him to win lost people. "I have come into the world as a light," He said, "so that no one who believes in me should stay in darkness" (John 12:46). His death on the cross became the greatest beacon of redeeming radiance the world has ever seen (John 8:12; 9:5).

God planned from eternity to welcome His redeemed children into His banquet hall, placing His banner of love over them (Song of Sol. 2:4). The Father's design for doing this is His only Son, Jesus Christ. Little wonder men pick up His challenge and freely give Him their allegiance for life.

So, the universal problem has a universal solution in the Cross, expressed with Jesus' own blood splattered on the rocks of Calvary's knoll.

What an awesome Savior (Exod. 34:10).

What a "treasure" we have "in jars of clay" (2 Cor. 4:7).

What a story is ours to tell (Luke 2:10; 4:43; Acts 5:42; 14:21).

E. Soteriology—the Doctrine of Salvation

In this overall context, the fall of man motivates exploration of soteriology, the study of all that Jesus Christ did to make atonement and bring people back into a right relationship with God. Soteriology includes both the doctrine of salvation and provision for His followers to walk in holiness (John 3:6; Rom. 10:9–10; 2 Thess. 2:13; 1 Cor. 1:2, 30). The grace of God in the new birth enables a person to respond to the gospel, becoming a child of God and a joint heir with Jesus Christ. In sanctifying grace, he works out his salvation with fear and trembling, realizing as he does that it is God who motivates him to do what pleases the Father (1 John 3:10; Gal. 3:26; Phil. 2:13).

A baby girl in her mother's arms does not need to understand the rich nourishment in her mother's milk in order to drink to the full and start growing. In the same way, it is not necessary to comprehend the distinctive elements of the new birth in order to be born again. As an individual matures in the Word of God and learns more and more about walking in faith, however, he will surely want to understand from the Scriptures what happened in his heart when he accepted Jesus Christ as Savior and Lord. This understanding will also help him share his testimony of what God has done in his life.

It is to the strategy of redemption that we now turn our attention.

III. The Elements of the New Birth

A. Prevenient Grace

1. *Defining* Prevenient Grace

Prevenient grace is the undeserved favor of God that draws people toward Jesus Christ and prepares them for the new birth. The term derives from the Latin and suggests the grace that creates the special anticipation in the soul that precedes salvation.[6] Hence, the Holy Spirit draws a person by blessing him to anticipate the forgiveness that will follow if he responds in repentance. Prevenient grace whets a person's appetite and creates thirst in his spirit, all the while giving assurance the long night of the soul's separation from God is about over. This astronomically gracious kindness can also be described as courtship. It is love unfurled by heaven's hand, extending favors without prior conditions. Jesus sends rain on the righteous and the unrighteous (Matt. 5:45).

Prevenient grace describes the call of Jesus Christ to sinful man. It leads him to want the saving faith that opens the door to renewed personal intimacy with God in a new birth.

> When you were dead in your sins and in the uncircumcision of your sinful nature, God made you alive with Christ. He forgave us all our sins, having canceled the written code, with its regulations that was against us and that stood opposed to us; he took it away, nailing it to the cross.
>
> —COLOSSIANS 2:13–14

Paul used the illustration of death to paint this word picture of man's addiction to sin: he is actually "dead in [his] transgressions and sins" (Eph. 2:1). The condition is so desperate, Paul taught, man must experience a quickening of the

Holy Spirit, comparable to a resurrection, in order to be able to make the choice to respond to the invitation of Jesus Christ (Eph. 2:1, 5–6).

Jesus described this prevenient grace when He expressed to His disciples, "No one can come to me unless the Father has enabled him" (John 6:65). This mercy has its basis in the loving favor of God that no one deserves and is addressed to men who are dead in their sins (Col. 2:13).

2. The Role of the Spirit in Prevenient Grace

The Holy Spirit is the agent and administrator of this awakening grace. He convicts the unbeliever of his sins and urges him to accept Christ (Gen. 6:3; John 16:8; Heb. 3:7–8). The summons goes out by the Word of God through the witness of believers who become living epistles "known and read by everybody" (2 Cor. 3:2; Rom. 10:17–18; 2 Thess. 2:14). The call springs from God's providential mercies, for surely "God's kindness leads you toward repentance" (Rom. 2:4). The Lord also speaks to men through His acts of judgment: "They cried out to the Lord in their trouble and he delivered them from their distress" (Ps. 107:6).

Jesus said it is the assignment of the Holy Spirit to "convict the world of guilt in regard to sin and righteousness and judgment: in regard to sin, because men do not believe in me; in regard to righteousness, because I am going to the Father, where you can see me no longer; and in regard to judgment, because the prince of this world now stands condemned" (John 16:8–11).

This passage defines the job description of the Holy Spirit, identifying how He works to confront the guilt in the hearts of all people and convince them to turn to Jesus Christ. In doing so, the Spirit also convinces people that when they turn to Jesus Christ they will "receive mercy and find grace to help" (Heb. 4:16).

- The Holy Spirit convicts of *sin* because men do not place their trust in Jesus Christ (John 16:9). To reject the gift of God's Son who poured out His blood on the cross is without question the ultimate sin people can commit. In a very real sense, all other sins flow from this one, and the Holy Spirit works to make men and women realize it.
- The reception Jesus received at His Father's right hand at His ascension affirms the Lord's *righteousness* (John 16:7–10; Ps. 110:1; Matt. 22:44). His Father could not have received Jesus back into the heavenly glory if His personal righteousness had been impeached during His incarnation. If that had happened, Jesus' sacrifice would have been imperfect (Acts 2:34; Heb. 1:13).

- The Holy Spirit also convinces people of the *judgment* to come (John 16:11). The primary mission of the death of Jesus was to save "whosoever will" (John 3:16). The Holy Spirit uses the blood of Jesus to show God's Son has the right to judge all men. In fact, God has appointed a day for just that to take place (Acts 17:31; John 16:11). It is the work of prevenient grace to convince men not to trifle with God's mercies, lest the great Day of Judgment should fall on them unawares.
- The secondary benefit of His freely poured out blood unveils the revelation that Jesus has judged Satan. When Jesus rejected the fierce temptation to come down from His cross, man's salvation was assured and Satan's eternal punishment was sealed. The Son of man came out of the grave as the world's Redeemer, in ultimate triumph over the devil. In fact, He made a public spectacle of him (Col. 2:15). The great deceiver stands convicted in God's courtroom beyond any reasonable doubt, and the capital sentence of eternal hell awaits him.

Without this special grace that draws people to Christ, every man's condition is hopeless. This is true because he is estranged from God in his heart, "dead in trespasses and sins," and possesses no natural willpower to move toward God (Rom. 1:25; Eph. 2:1; 2 Tim. 3:2–4; 1 Pet. 3:18). His spirit is restless and lonely, but he can do nothing about it. He is powerless to escape the addiction to sin that has pulled him into its darkness.

No one should take the call of God lightly, for "man is destined to die once and after that to face the judgment" (Heb. 9:27). Indeed, "it is a dreadful thing to fall into the hands of the living God" (Heb. 10:31). The forbearance of God clearly has limits, for the Spirit of God "will not struggle with humans forever" (Gen. 6:3, GW).

3. Prevenient Grace and Saving Faith

The Spirit's courtship continues until prevenient grace results in saving faith, or until a person stubbornly determines to reject the grace offered with such kindness to him. Even if he rejects grace, God remains "patient...not wanting anyone to perish, but everyone to come to repentance" (2 Pet. 3:9).

The ministry of prevenient grace is solely the work of the Holy Spirit and precedes salvation, which comes only by grace through faith (Rom. 1:17; 4:16; 11:6; Eph. 2:5, 8; Hab. 2:4). However, grace never overpowers the free will of man, rendering him a robot or a puppet. Instead, the Spirit shows "the incomparable riches of [God's] grace expressed in his kindness to us in Christ Jesus" (Eph.

2:7). This grace manifests itself as love so overwhelming it mercifully motivates hungry souls to respond in faith to God's very magnanimous invitation.

4. Prevenient Grace and Evangelism

Jesus' heart beats for the good news to go to the ends of the earth. This understanding forms the basis of all evangelism and explains the Lord's Great Commission (Matt. 28:16–20; Luke 10:2; John 4:35). Everywhere Jesus' followers proclaim the gospel faithfully, the Holy Spirit will do His work. The Spirit is the evangelist; we are only the messengers. As Jesus was a faithful servant to His Father's plan to save the world, so His followers commit heart and soul to share the good news at home and abroad, even at the risk of their lives (Heb. 2:17; Acts 1:8; 14:19). Evangelism is all about explaining how Jesus diagnosed humanity's problem. Wherever an individual dwells anywhere in the world, he lives with alienation from God, but Jesus provided the cure for this universal condition when He shed His blood at Calvary.

> God has poured out his love into our hearts by the Holy Spirit, whom he has given us.
>
> —ROMANS 5:5

> How, then, can they call on the one they have not believed in? And how can they believe in the one of whom they have not heard? And how can they hear without someone preaching to them? And how can they preach unless they are sent? As it is written, "How beautiful are the feet of those who bring good news!"
>
> —ROMANS 10:14–15

When the Lord's faithful servants share the message, the Holy Spirit confronts people with the call of the gospel. The Spirit also empowers and motivates them to do what they could not do before—make a choice, and blesses them to anticipate the benefits that are ahead. Prevenient grace, therefore, includes all that the Holy Spirit does in preparing and cultivating the soil of the soul to expect that new freedom in Christ is at hand (Eph. 2:1, 4–5; Col. 2:13).

B. Repentance

1. Repentance as Changing Directions

Immediately following Jesus' baptism and investiture at the Jordan River, the Lord began preaching, "Repent for the kingdom of heaven is near" (Matt. 4:17). The Greek term, *metanoeo*, which means "repent," embraces the idea of turning around.[7] When a person on the highway of life realizes he has missed his street, he must go back and get on the right road; this is the essence of repentance.

Repentance also embraces a particular emotion of deep regret or contrition in which a person sincerely comprehends the depth of his sins against God. He then, in his brokenness, returns to God, offering his heart, soul, mind, and strength (Deut. 6:4–5; Luke 10:27). In this complete paradigm change, he turns away from his sins, makes the choice to open himself up to God, and seeks His mercy. He humbly pleads for forgiveness for his transgressions against God and asks for release from their condemnation.

2. Repentance and the Character of God

Moses wanted to know God during the exodus from Egypt and prayed to see Him face-to-face (Exod. 33:12–23). God did not grant that specific request, because no mere mortal can look on the pure essence of the immortal God and live. God did place Moses in the cleft of the rock on Mount Sinai, however, and caused His glory to pass in front of him.

> The LORD descended in the cloud and stood with him there, and proclaimed the name of the LORD. And the LORD passed before him and proclaimed, "The LORD, the LORD God, merciful and gracious, longsuffering, and abounding in goodness and truth, keeping mercy for thousands, forgiving iniquity and transgression and sin, and by no means clearing the guilty."
>
> —EXODUS 34:5–7, NKJV

Moses discovered what he needed to see was not the wonder of God's holy essence, but the beauty of His pristine character. Hence, the Lord revealed His essential being to Moses as Jehovah, the great I AM, the God of infinite being, who:

- is merciful,
- gracious, and
- longsuffering;
- abounds in goodness and truth;
- keeps mercy for thousands;
- forgives iniquity, transgression, and sin; and
- judges and punishes fairly.

The summary of these marvelous character traits mirrors the dazzling diamond of the gospel: God honors repentance with forgiveness. He always has. He always will. He deals with guilt at the deepest levels of depravity by forgiving evil at its worst—wickedness, rebellion, and sin.

Moses' response to this great revelation was to exclaim, "O Lord, if I have found favor in your eyes" then please guide us though the wilderness to the Promised Land. "Although this is a stiff-necked people, forgive our wickedness and our sin, and take us as your inheritance" (Exod. 34:9). The great lesson of Moses' experience in the cleft of the rock is that God did exactly what Moses requested. He passed by Moses and said, "I am making a covenant with you…the people you live among will see how awesome is the work that I, the LORD, will do for you'" (Exod. 34:10).

The experience Moses had with God was the greatest single revelation of the character of God in the Old Testament. The prophets repeatedly looked back to it (Num. 14:18; Neh. 9:17; Ps. 86:15, 103:8, 145:8–9; Joel 2:13; Jonah 4:2). Of course, the cross of Jesus Christ superseded it, but not because Moses got the message wrong. Moses heard God say who He is; Messiah, on His cross, showed the whole world who God is. Mount Sinai was limited, but Mount Calvary demonstrated without boundaries the full-orbed character of God.

3. Forgiveness as God's Most Awesome Work

The punishment Jesus took on His cross demonstrates that all men merit death. Jesus' sacrifice in our place also shows the heart of God because He can always be counted on to respond to repentance with gracious forgiveness. This is a fact fundamental to the character of God. The psalmist David said the Lord has never forsaken those who seek him (Ps. 9:10; John 6:37).

God has the answer to the plaintive cry of the heart: He can be counted on to meet repentance with forgiveness. Forgiveness, in fact, is God's most awesome work. He cleanses man's conscience and provides the solution to the great curse of guilt (Heb. 9:14). Forgiveness is so completely in the DNA of God in His dealings with fallen men that God's Son cried out amid the horrendous pain of His crucifixion, "Father, forgive them, for they do not know what they are doing" (Luke 23:34).

God's response to repentance with forgiveness is the superlative quality of Christian faith.

> As far as the east is from the west, so far has he removed our transgressions from us.
>
> —PSALM 103:12

This truth above all else explains why for two millennia the gospel has given men peace with God. God forgives. His children are never more God-like than when they follow in His steps and practice forgiveness too.

~≈ I Distinctly Remember Forgetting It ≈~

Clara Barton, the founder of the American Red Cross, was reminded one day of a vicious deed that someone had done to her years before. But she acted as if she had never heard of the incident.

"Don't you remember it?" her friend asked.

"No," came Barton's reply. "I distinctly remember forgetting it."[8]

4. The Three Elements of Repentance

a) The Role of the Mind in Repentance

The prodigal son came to his senses. He realized his bad choices had exacted a high toll on his dad and himself. He also came to appreciate fully what his sins had done to his heavenly Father. "I have sinned against heaven and against you," he said to his dad. "I am no longer worthy to be called your son" (Luke 15:18–19). The time had arrived for him to release his old way of thinking, which had produced so much pain (Luke 15:17). And the prodigal emptied it all out.

After his fall into immorality, King David showed this same profound knowledge of whom he had wronged. He committed adultery with Bathsheba while her husband, Uriah, was on the battlefield helping to fight the king's war. To try to cover up his sin, David then ordered Uriah killed (2 Sam. 11:3–26). After the prophet Nathan confronted David, the king poured out his heart to God in repentance. Psalm 51 records his prayer, including this appeal to God: "Against you and you only have I sinned and done what is evil in your sight" (Ps. 51:4). This cry was not a denial that he had grossly taken advantage of Bathsheba. Guilt had flooded David after their rendezvous, and it compounded after murdering her husband. Uriah had been a loyal subject who loved both his wife and his king.

David's prayer underscores his comprehension that his sin first and foremost violated God; he had crushed the heart of his Lord (Ps. 51:4). David's actions disappointed God, and David realized it. The fact that David violated God is what made it such a grievous sin against Uriah and Bathsheba.

b) The Role of the Emotions in Repentance

People begin to feel their sinfulness and lost condition as the Spirit of God woos and draws them toward Jesus Christ. "Godly sorrow brings repentance that leads to salvation," Paul said, "and leaves no room for regret" (2 Cor. 7:10). The word *sorrow* in this verse comes from the Greek word *lupe*, which is also sometimes translated as "grief," which is the emotional pain of great loss, as in a death.

The conviction of the Holy Spirit makes a person realize his past life has been "dead in…transgressions and sins" (Eph. 2:1; James 1:14–15). These painful feelings flood man's entire being. When a person feels convicted by the Holy Spirit, it is not unusual for him to hurt all over, feeling full of deep regret.

"Worldly sorrow brings death," Paul added (2 Cor. 7:10). When men merely regret getting caught or simply try to deal with their guilt by self-improvement ("I'll do better next time"), no fundamental change will be forthcoming. This cheapened form of repentance leaves men dead in their trespasses and sins—and still facing a fearful judgment described as the second death (Heb. 10:31; Rev. 2:11; 20:14; 21:8).

Job despised himself and repented "in dust and ashes" (Job 42:6). King David had such a genuine sense of his own sinfulness after his tryst with Bathsheba that he begged God to blot out his transgressions, appealing to Him on the basis of the multitude of God's "unfailing love" (Ps. 51:1). When the prodigal son in the parable came to himself, he issued the universal cry of a lost soul: "I am starving to death" (Luke 15:17). There was plenty of bread and extra to spare in his father's house. In his pain he probably could taste his mother's cooking. He also sensed a gnawing hunger for peace with God, because he knew he had sinned "against heaven" (Luke 15:18).

c) The Role of the Will in Repentance

"Let the wicked forsake his way and the evil man his thoughts," Isaiah wrote. "Let him turn to the Lord, and He will have mercy on him; and to our God, for He will freely pardon" (Isa. 55:7). This verse paints a word picture that is a classic definition of biblical repentance. A person is on the wrong road ("way") and badly needs someone to point out the right road. The marvelously rich grace of God touches his corrupted will and enables him to ask for the help he needs. He can then make the choice to turn around, go back, and get on the right road (John 6:44).

Repentance is more than merely changing roads, however. Isaiah also described in this passage the need to recognize the thinking patterns that drove him onto the wrong road and kept him on it. It is essential that the person then make a fundamental shift in his heart, mind, and will. He must forsake the mindset that got him on the wrong road and accept the fresh thought patterns that fit "the Holy Highway" (Isa. 35:8, TLB). The person who forsakes both the old road and the ungodly thinking that goes with the road will find overflowing mercy and abundant pardon in the arms of the heavenly Father. The Lord guarantees acceptance when the penitent turns to Him for help with this attitude. What a beautiful truth about God's character!

After the prodigal son comprehended his depraved and sad condition, he said, "I will set out and go back to my father" (Luke 15:18). With this choice, the prodigal made the paradigm shift from his pig-pen lifestyle and began his long walk home. Repentance always embraces this kind of change of direction.

The prodigal's decision, which resulted in his action, does not imply that he suddenly merited his father's forgiveness, because he did not. The prodigal's father did not restore him because he came home deserving it; his father reinstated him in the family because he never stopped loving him.

Salvation is solely a love-gift from God, an act of divine grace. A convicted felon is not pardoned and released from prison because of his own merit, because what he merited was decided when the judge sentenced him. Pardon can only come because the governor chooses to show mercy.

Only when three elements merge—the mental comprehension, the decision to commit one's will, and the emotional grief—is repentance genuine. Without the three acting simultaneously, a person might make new resolutions, but he will not repent. He can even decide to mend his ways, but will remain merely an improved sinner. When the mind, emotions, and the will blend as one, then the penitent will experience saving faith.

Repentance pounds on the door of God's mercy, and grace always answers, as in the story of the landowner who paid all of his employees the same wage, even his eleventh-hour workers (Matt. 20:1–16). When Jesus rewards, He always acts out of His divine heart that delights to lavish favors on people who do not deserve them (Eph. 2:4–10; John 1:14).

> He chose us in him before the creation of the world to be holy and blameless in his sight. In love, he predestined us to be adopted as his sons through Jesus Christ, in accordance with his pleasure and will—to the praise of his glorious grace, which he has freely given us in the One he loves. In him we have redemption through his blood, the forgiveness of sins, in accordance with the riches of God's grace that he lavished on us with all wisdom and understanding.
>
> —EPHESIANS 1:4–8

Little wonder the term *gospel* means "good news" and that God's children "sing praises to the Lord, enthroned in Zion" (Ps. 9:11).

5. Repentance and Restitution

A willingness to make amends for wrongs committed (restitution) is an important biblical theme associated with repentance. Obviously, when Zacchaeus joined Jesus on the road to his house, this tax collector quickly started picking up the thinking patterns of his new lifestyle. Compensation was an immediate fruit of Zacchaeus' changed condition. "The half of my goods I give to the poor," he said to the Lord, "and if I have taken any thing from any man by false accusation, I restore him fourfold" (Luke 19:8, kjv). These attempts to pay people back blossomed out of his changed condition. Repentance and restitution go together like sunshine and warmth. When Jesus gave Zacchaeus the gift of eternal life, Zacchaeus gave the people he had wronged the blessing of restitution.

⧽ Stealing a Few Copper Nails ⧽

After F. E. Marsh preached on restitution, a young man came to him and said, "Pastor, you have put me in a bad fix. I've stolen from my employer, and I'm ashamed to tell him about it. You see, I'm a boat builder, and the man I work for is an unbeliever. I have often talked to him about Christ, but he only laughs at me. In my work, expensive copper nails are used because they won't rust in water. I've been taking some of them home for a boat I'm building in my backyard. I'm afraid if I tell my boss what I've done and offer to pay for them, he'll think I'm a hypocrite, and I'll never be able to reach him for Christ. Yet, my conscience is bothered."

Later when the man saw the preacher again, he exclaimed, "Pastor, I've settled that matter and I'm so relieved."

"What happened when you told your boss?" asked the minister.

"Oh, he looked at me intently and said, 'George, I've always thought you were a hypocrite, but now I'm not so sure. Maybe there's something to your Christianity after all. Any religion that makes a man admit he's been stealing a few copper nails and offer to settle for them must be worth having.'"[9]

C. Saving Faith and the Love of God

Repentance brings a person to the door of saving faith, which is the particular confidence in the Lord that motivates the sinner to accept the new birth Jesus offers, transforming his life. The result will be the removal of his guilt, and the emptiness in his soul will be filled (Acts 16:31; Heb. 9:9; 10:22; 1 Pet. 3:21).

Saving faith must be clearly distinguished from the faith of demons, who believe and shudder (James 2:19). Luke recorded the story of Simon of Samaria, who showed it is possible to believe intellectually without exercising saving faith (Acts 8:13, 18–24).

Saving faith goes beyond mental assent as to who Jesus Christ is or even to a remorse for sins committed. In saving faith, a penitent concludes Christ "loved me and gave himself for me," and then actually confesses and receives Jesus as his own personal Savior and Lord (Gal. 2:20; 3:11; Rom. 10:9–10; Heb. 10:38). Saving faith is "the gift of God" because of God's "great love" for us (Eph. 2:4–8).

The vehicle that delivers this gracious provision to man is the Word of God, for "faith comes from hearing the message, and the message is heard through the word of Christ" (Rom. 10:17). The power by which people appropriate this provision comes from the Holy Spirit, who applies the blessing of Christ's sacrifice to their hearts.

Saving faith is not based on personal works of righteousness (Rom. 7:18; Titus 3:5). A person can never look at the cross and say to Jesus, "You owed it to me to suffer and die because of my moral goodness." Saving faith is solely a gift of God, a totally free love-gift (Eph. 2:5, 8).

D. Conversion

Conversion denotes the kind of paradigm change Saul of Tarsus made on the Damascus Road. One moment he was determined to exercise his authority from the chief priests to throw people in jail because of the Way (the name for the early Christian movement; Acts 9:1–2). Immediately after a blinding light knocked him into the dust, he cried out in his desperate need for help, "Who are you, Lord?" (Acts 9:5). The change was so complete in Saul that within a matter of days he began preaching that "Jesus is the Son of God" (Acts 9:20). Saul of Tarsus is a picture-perfect example of what it means to repent and then convert. Apostolic preaching declares this kind of conversion is essential for regeneration to be complete (Acts 3:19; 26:18–20).

Hand in hand with the Holy Spirit who courted him and filled him with anticipation, the sinner by his own free choice walks out of the kingdom of darkness, believing every step of the way he will be received into the kingdom of light (Ps. 9:10; 1 Peter 2:9). His faith is not in vain. The Christ who is the light of the world receives the prodigal with open arms (John 9:5; Luke 15:20). The result is that Christ's blood washes his sins away "as far as the east is from the west" (Ps. 103:12). The Lord does indeed have "compassion on his children," loving them with a "great love" (Ps. 103:13–18; Eph. 2:4).

This understanding has compelling implications for the ministry of evangelism. A fundamental characteristic of a regenerated and converted child of God is his gripping desire to share what God in Christ has done for him (Luke 10:2; John 4:34–37). Evangelistic witnessing is all about leading a person to this conversion experience. Jesus instructed Simon Peter to strengthen the brethren when Peter "turned back" (Luke 22:32; James 5:19–20).

E. Justification

1. *The Definition of* Justification

We are "justified freely by his grace, through the redemption that came by Christ Jesus" (Rom. 3:24, KJV). *Dikaioo* is the Greek word for "justified," which means to regard as legally innocent and to confer all the rights and privileges that go with sonship in Christ (1 John 3:2).[10]

Justification, then, is the legal side of saving faith. Paul wrote to the Romans, "This righteousness from God comes through faith in Jesus Christ to all who believe" (Rom. 3:22; 4:1–8). Paul said God extends this blessing even to the "wicked" (Rom. 4:5; Exod. 34:7). Justification communicates a judicial rendering that releases the guilty, permits him to walk free, and restores his status to sonship in Christ, even though he has done nothing at all to merit his new legal innocence (Gal. 2:15–16).

The heart of the Christian message is that God forgives and accepts sinners into His fellowship—all sinners, no matter how depraved—when they believe Him and His promises (Gen. 15:6). This justification is not based on their righteousness, for they have none, none at all (Isa. 64:6; Rom. 3:10). God loves sinners anyway, so much that He sent His one and only, sinless Son to die in their place and pay their debt in full (Ps. 51:14; John 19:30; Acts 13:39; Rom. 3:24).

When a person hears the message of Jesus' death as his substitute, believes His promises, and repents, the heavenly Father credits to him the righteousness of His only Son, Jesus Christ (Rom. 1:17; 4:2–6; 5:1; Gen. 15:6). Although the sinner has no righteousness of His own, in this legal proceeding he is justified in the divine court solely because of Christ's righteousness, which is freely deposited to his account (Rom. 3:22; 5:17; 2 Cor. 5:21).

a) Justification as the Foundation of the Reformation

The Protestant Reformation was built on three doctrinal pillars:

- *Sola scriptura.* The sixty-six books in the Bible are the sole source for all matters of faith and practice. We rest our eternal souls on these biblical teachings, recognizing no other books or traditions as equal to them.
- *Sola fides.* Justification before God comes solely by grace through faith alone—solely faith plus nothing else.
- *Sola sacerdos.* The priesthood of the new covenant includes all believers. Salvation is not dispensed by a select hierarchical priesthood, as in the Roman Catholic Church. Instead, salvation is a direct gift from God to a penitent's heart, without

the controlling mediation of a priest. It is the role of the clergy to accept responsibility, therefore, to teach and encourage this direct relationship between Jesus Christ and His followers.

It was conclusions like these that motivated Martin Luther to nail his Ninety-five Theses on the door of Wittenburg Church in Germany in 1517, launching his futile effort to reform the Roman Catholic Church.[11] The Protestant Reformation was the result.

If one subtracts the doctrine of justification from the Scriptures, Christianity will have lost its soul and the blood of Jesus Christ will be rendered powerless. The Bible teaches that every man on Earth is a depraved sinner and is desperately in need of a new legal standing in the courts of heaven (Rom. 3:9–19). The glory of the incarnation glows with its warmest meaning at the cross of Christ because every man has the same need for this justification, or restoration to a right standing of righteousness before God (Rom. 3:10–18, 23–24). Remove this universal need, and Christ's death has no grandeur at all; instead, it becomes meaningless and idiotic. If that common necessity is not in the hearts of all people everywhere, then Jesus died the death of a fool.

❧ Declared "Not Guilty" ❧

If you've ever tried to find a parking space at the mall a few days before Christmas, you've probably eyed some of those handicapped parking places with envy. They're right up close, and there's usually one available. Maybe you've been tempted to park in one of those spots, even though you're not handicapped and you don't have one of those tags to hang on your mirror. Don't try it. Just ask Connie.

Because of some serious health issues, her doctor has given her one of those tags. Connie can use those spaces legally, if she displays her tag—which she unfortunately forgot to do during a two-night stay in a hotel. She returned to her car only to find two tickets with a fine of $250.00 each and a demand that she appear in court, no matter how she pleaded. And Connie lives a thousand miles from the town where she got the ticket!

Well, she filled out a court affidavit and pleaded guilty to what the clerk described as a "not minor violation." The affidavit was mailed to the municipal judge along with a photocopy of Connie's handicapped tag. Just yesterday, she received the judge's response regarding her scheduled court appearance. The note simply said, "Upon review, the judge has declared you 'not guilty.'"[12]

b) Justification as a Judge's Ruling

Justification is the ruling of the great Judge of the universe in which God responds to man's repentance by erasing a penitent's record. This happens because Christ's blood covers over the wealth of truthful testimony against the offender (Rom. 3:25; 1 John 2:2; 4:10). Hence, the Judge rules the sinner is not guilty, orders his ledger cleansed of all charges, and restores him to the family with all rights and privileges (Ps. 103:2; John 1:12–13; Rom. 3:24; 5:9; 8:1).

c) Jesus as Attorney for the Defense

The woman caught in the act of adultery is a classic example of justifying grace (John 8:1–12). She was loaded with guilt when the self-appointed posse of Pharisees hauled her before Jesus and turned the courtyard of the temple into her courtroom. Her very demeanor said she was guilty and burdened with shame under the heavy load of her adultery. She knew she was culpable. She had no defense and no defender and expected to be stoned.

Then, a marvelous thing happened. Her Messiah Himself, without charging her a single drachma, graciously accepted her case and served as her defender (1 John 2:1). He did it in anticipation of the blood He would shed very soon on Calvary to cover guilt just like hers (Isa. 53:11; Acts 10:43; Rom. 5:9; Rev. 1:5). The woman's accusers were no match for the defense of her Advocate (John 14:16, 26). Right before her eyes the Pharisees' case fell apart, and as a result they dropped all charges against her. Jesus defended her on the basis of every man's utter sinfulness: "If any one of you is without sin," Jesus said to them, "let him be the first to throw a stone at her" (John 8:7; Rom. 3:9–18). Facing their own shameful guilt, one by one they dropped their stones and walked away.

The Lord not only successfully defended her; He accepted her into His family, giving her a new life based on His amazing grace: "Neither do I condemn you. Go now and leave your life of sin" (John 8:11; Rom. 3:21–24; Heb. 10:22). It was a crystal clear "not guilty" verdict that left no trace of her adulterous past.

Right there, Jesus made a lavish deposit of His own righteousness into her bankrupt account, which lacked even a single drop of the righteousness God requires (1 John 3:1; Gen. 15:6). She walked into court an adulteress with no defense and walked out a lady in God's family with no condemnation and guilt and a clean court record (Rom. 3:23–25; 8:1).

The sinless and just Savior became her justifier (Rom. 3:26). Jesus gave her a new beginning that included a fresh start with an unstained moral character— all because of His own righteousness credited to her (Rom. 3:24; 4:24).

If the Son sets you free, you will be free indeed.

—JOHN 8:36

What an awesome Savior! (See Exodus 15:11; 34:10; Romans 10:10; Galatians 2:16; Titus 3:7.)

The adulteress' story shows justification is the gracious work of a merciful God who sits as the all-knowing, universal Judge, by which He cures sinfulness (Exod. 34:5–7; Ps. 25:6; Eph. 2:4–10). This grace is outrageously, even scandalously, abundant. It is love unfurled by heaven's hand, doing favors without prior conditions for "whoever believes in him" (John 3:16; Rom. 3:21–26; Gen. 15:6).

With empty, outstretched hands, therefore, the sinner comes to God. As he does so, his faith tells him to believe God's promises. Faith keeps reassuring him Jesus really is as good as His Word; He will not throw the Law book in his face. Instead, Jesus will do for him what He did for the woman caught in the act of adultery.

Receive grace, he does! God does not pronounce the stern judgment the penitent deserves. Instead, He blesses him with the unrestrained love that erases his sins and continually transforms him into Christlikeness (Eph. 2:4–10; 1 John 3:1; 2 Cor. 3:18). Indeed! The available supply of divine favors is profuse because Jesus Christ is full of grace (John 1:14, 17). In fact, "Each of us has received one gift after another because of all that [Jesus] is" (John 1:16, GW).

2. The Holding Power of Justifying Grace

Since God lovingly responds to repentance with lavish justifying grace, what is to prevent a person from repenting today and then turning away from God tomorrow? Does love have the capability to *keep* a person in Christ?

The lavish kind of love Jesus showed to the woman caught in the act of adultery and about to be stoned to death, produces profound gratitude, and therefore has incredible holding power. It is reasonable to believe she served the Lord for the remainder of her life, telling her story to anyone who would listen.

The same was true of Mary Magdalene, out of whom the Lord cast seven devils (Mark 16:9). From that day, Mary gave Jesus complete loyalty, and followed Him all the way to His cross (Matt. 27:55–56). She also helped embalm His body and became the first recorded person to see the resurrected Lord. It was a story she did not fail to tell (Mark 16:1; John 20:18).

The power of love to hold a believer is not its use of coercion. Love holds because love imparts life and restores ones sense of moral responsibility. The love of God motivates a person to *want* to love the Lord who did so much for him. The gift of God is so great, in fact, he gives his allegiance as his free choice. So love holds primarily through the power of gratitude.

In fact, people will routinely feel overwhelmed with a sense of appreciation.

They freely choose to love the Lord because he loved them first (1 John 4:9–11, 19). Why would people walk away, considering the massive demonstration of love revealed at Calvary? It makes no sense to go back to the old way of life that was killing them (Rom. 6:23; 2 Cor. 7:10, GW; James 1:13–15). The result is that love keeps people in Christ when law never could (Ps. 139:5–7).

⚜ Showing Gratitude for Christ's Sake ⚜

Author and educator, Howard Hendricks, sat in a plane delayed for take off. After a long wait, the passengers became more and more irritated. Hendricks noticed how gracious one of the flight attendants was as she spoke with them. After the plane finally took off, he told the flight attendant how amazed he was at her poise and self-control, and said he wanted to write a letter of commendation for her to the airline.

The stewardess replied that she didn't work for the airline company, but for Jesus Christ. She said that just before going to work she and her husband prayed together that she would be a good representative of Christ.

Doing it for Christ's sake, and not for a paycheck, adds another dimension to submission. You serve not just to please your employer or husband or parent, but the Lord, because of your love and gratitude for him.[13]

Love liberates. Love emancipates. Love holds with the great power of freedom, because the gift of freedom births such incredible gratitude, people will give their lives holding onto it.

"It is for freedom that Christ has set us free," Paul wrote. "Stand firm, then, and do not let yourselves be burdened again by a yoke of slavery" (Gal. 5:1; Luke 4:18). The new freedom in Christ's love is infinitely better than the old lifestyle of slavery to sin. Hence, people respond with deep dedication and commitment to the love of God, having no desire to go back to their old life (John 6:68; Rom. 6:21–23; Exod. 14:13; Prov. 26:11; 2 Pet. 2:22).

God's love never holds people in Christ with force, however. A person can turn away (Matt. 22:5). "Demas has forsaken me," Paul said, "having loved this present world, and [has] departed unto Thessalonica" (2 Tim. 4:10, KJV).

a) Removing the Penalty of the Second Death

Unsaved people live day after day under the penalty of eternal death, with a chasm so big between themselves and God they are powerless to bridge it. But the good news is breathtaking (Gen. 3:19; Eph. 4:18; Heb. 9:27; Rev. 2:11). In justification, man faces his day in God's court with a repentant heart that trusts Jesus to defend him as He defended the woman caught in the act of adultery (John 8:4–12). Jesus has never failed to step up to the bar and make the case for the defense of one of His followers.

> Because of his great love for us, God, who is rich in mercy, made us alive with Christ even when we were dead in transgressions—it is by grace you have been saved. And God raised us up with Christ and seated us with him in the heavenly realms in Christ Jesus.
> —Ephesians 2:4–7

Paul said this justifying grace transforms because God credits faith as righteousness (Rom. 3:21–27; 4:1–25). In this transaction, we are morally bankrupt; our spiritual checkbook has nothing in it at all. But because we believe Jesus' Word, He makes a deposit of His righteousness into our accounts. What good news!

The apostle Peter wrote, "His divine power has given us everything we need for life and godliness through our knowledge of him who called us by his own glory and goodness" (2 Peter 1:3). In fact, all who cry out to the Lord in repentance "are justified freely by his grace through the redemption that came by Christ Jesus. God presented him as a sacrifice of atonement, through faith in his blood. He did it to demonstrate his justice . . . so as to be just and the one who justifies those who have faith in Jesus" (Rom. 3:24–26).

b) Gratitude for Jesus Christ, the Only Road to Freedom

Jesus Christ is the road to freedom, and the only road. Jesus said that "out of the heart come evil thoughts, murder, adultery, sexual immorality, theft, false testimony, slander" (Matt. 15:19–20). These steal freedom and actually kill. All people have only one way out: "I told you that you would die in your sins; if you do not believe that I am [the one I claim to be], you will indeed die in your sins" (John 8:24). Paul later added, "The wages of sin is death, but the gift of God is eternal life through Jesus Christ our Lord" (Rom. 6:23). Such love *from* God inspires love in return *for* God (1 John 4:19). This deeply felt gratitude for Jesus' priceless gift on the tree that gave us freedom from our sins typically expresses itself in terms of wonder. Just imagine that He loved us that much and gave Himself for us! Justifying grace, therefore, forms a tough bond of faithfulness and allegiance to the Savior who took our penalty and freed us. The gratitude is overwhelming and feels almost incredible. He actually gave us this invaluable gift of freedom in Christ (2 Cor. 8:9; Gal. 2:21).

Justified people know they have received the flawless pearl that is priceless (Matt. 13:45–46, The Message). Jesus' death cancelled the penalty of the second death and substituted in its place the gift of eternal life. They begin by choice, therefore, and out of love, to do the works that stem from the righteousness deposited into their lives (Eph. 2:10). And the work of God, first and foremost, is "to believe the one [God] has sent" (John 6:29).

The result is they dedicate themselves to a habitual lifestyle of abiding in the vine and drawing nourishment from it (John 15:5). Now they really do want to love the Lord with all their heart, soul, mind and strength and complete the process of working out their salvation (Mark 12:30; Phil. 2:13). They also love their brethren and begin to practice in faith the life of victory as they enjoy actual freedom from the bondages of the flesh (Matt. 22:37–39; 1 John 3:9; 4:7; 5:4). Freedom is such a priceless gift that people will gladly give their lives to preserve it; they clearly do not intend to go back to the old life of slavery (Rom. 6:21–23; Gal. 5:1–2; Phil. 1:21; Deut. 17:16).

> He brings me to the banquet hall, so everyone can see how much he loves me.
>
> —Song of Solomon 2:4, nlt

F. Regeneration

1. A New Creation

"If anyone is in Christ, he is a new creation," Paul said. In fact, this recreating of man is so thorough that "the old has gone and the new has come" (2 Cor. 5:17). Regeneration marks a genesis, a new beginning, in the life of each believer. Because of this act of the Holy Spirit, a justified believer experiences a new birth in Jesus Christ (Titus 3:5–6). The Spirit restores the empty chasm in the soul and turns it into a magnificent new temple of the heart (Jer. 31:31, 33; Rev. 21:5). The presence of God comes into a person's spirit again.

Before regeneration, man is dead in "transgressions and sins" (Eph. 2:1). He sees God's creation with excellent vision, but sin has greatly diminished his capacity to perceive the God who created it all (Isa. 40:19–20; Heb. 1:2). In regeneration, the Spirit creates new spiritual eyes that open for the very first time in the moment of faith to the loving gaze of Jesus. That event is like the occasion when the Lord restored Jairus' daughter to life. The child opened her eyes to gaze on the beaming face of Jesus. What a lovely face! (See Luke 8:54–55; 2 Corinthians 4:6; Ephesians 2:5; and Psalm 17:15.)

One day. That blessed day, we "will see His [actual] face" (1 John 3:2; Rev. 22:4).

2. The Analogy of a Seed

In regeneration, the Holy Spirit deposits the seed of eternal life in the soul. One of the first evidences of the change from death to life is the old, gnawing spiritual loneliness disappears. Exciting life has returned to the temple (1 Cor. 6:19; 1 John 3:14). "No one who is born of God will continue to sin," John wrote, "because God's seed [*sperma*] remains in him; he cannot go on sinning because he is born of God" (1 John 3:9). This analogy offers a word picture of conception in the womb. A father plants a seed, his sperm, which is the source of a new life. This seed unites with a mother's egg and starts to grow in the warm environment of the womb. Ultimately, that seed will give birth to a child. "The seed is the word of God," Jesus said (Luke 8:11). The apostle Peter wrote that we are "born again, not of corruptible seed, but of incorruptible, by the word of God which lives and abides forever" (1 Pet. 1:23, KJV).

A mother's love will motivate her to make whatever changes are necessary in her diet and work habits in order to give the new life in her womb optimum opportunity to develop. In that same sense, "No one who is born of God will continue to sin" because new life is now in his heart. "He cannot go on sinning" because he has been born of God (1 John 3:9). Instead, God's love motivates him to endow the new life with every blessing in the Word of God so that it can grow. And it will mature, because "the word of God is full of living power. It is sharper than the sharpest knife, cutting deep into our innermost thoughts and desires. It exposes us for what we really are" (Heb. 4:12, NLT).

A new believer will cheerfully change his attitude, values, and his lifestyle in order to give this new life in Christ favorable surroundings. Basic to these living patterns is a refusal to conform any longer to this world, because he has been transformed by the renewing of his mind (Rom. 12:2; Eph. 4:23; Col. 3:9–10).

This regeneration is available to as many as will accept Christ, for all who believe in his name are given "the right to become the children of God" (John 1:12). This is the birth from above, and it solely originates in God's love, without any merit from man (John 3:3, 7, 31). Regeneration, then, leaves no room for boasting, except in the sweet sound of the amazing grace of God that saves wretches like me (Eph. 2:9; 1 Tim. 1:15).

In regeneration, the Spirit of God is at work remaking sinners, not reforming them. The new believer is recreated in spirit and enabled both to receive Christ and to "follow in His steps" (1 Pet. 2:21). Anything less than remaking the image of God in man is actually a faulty plan, because it only reforms a sinner, and a reformed sinner is still a sinner. In regeneration, the job is total; hence, the Lord said to Nicodemus, "You must be born again" (John 3:7). This regeneration, a new genesis, is so complete, a person is actually resurrected with Christ and "renewed in knowledge in the image of [his] creator" (Col. 3:10; Eph. 2:5; Rev. 21:5).

✻ A New Boat! ✻

A friend said mournfully that he had lived his life like the professor on *Gilligan's Island*. While he found time to fashion generators out of palm fronds and vaccines out of algae, he never got around to fixing that huge hole in the boat so he could go home.

How many people actually do?[14]

God by His awesome grace does not merely repair the big hole in the bottom of the boat; He creates a new boat!

Paul made clear the only thing that "counts is a new creation," and as the seed keeps growing and maturing into the new life, a believer will continue to reject the kingdom of this world (Gal. 6:15; 2 Cor. 5:17). He will also receive grace from God to choose "the kingdom of Christ" (Acts 26:18; Eph. 5:5). This happens because love radically changes a person's values, and he begins to embrace the meaning of the kingdom of light. He feels, in fact, a compelling desire to live the life of the kingdom. He is a brand new person in his desires and his intentions because Jesus Christ has resurrected him to this new life. In regeneration, then, the Spirit of God does a work in the heart of man that he is powerless to do for himself: the Holy Spirit makes him a new creation, "born of God" (1 John 5:1). In his old life he had no real interest in God and spiritual things, but now, he really does have a heart for God.

G. Adoption

In justification the judge grants a person all of the legal rights and privileges of sonship. In adoption, he is welcomed into the family and granted the spirit of sonship (Rom. 8:15). The heavenly Father immediately, in fact, takes the new believer into His family. In this divine declaration of sonship, the Father kills the fattened calf, gives him a new robe, and welcomes his lost son to the banquet table, communicating the spirit of sonship that says, "Welcome Home" (Luke 15:23–24, 32). "I tell you," Jesus said, "there is rejoicing in the presence of the angels of God over one sinner who repents" (Luke 15:10). Jesus emphatically told His disciples to "rejoice because [their] names [were] written in heaven" (Luke 10:20).

The Holy Spirit does not adopt people into the heavenly family, and then stand back and watch their destruction by a spirit of "slavery again to fear." Instead, He showers them with "the Spirit of sonship," which motivates them to "cry 'Abba,' Father" (Rom. 8:15). God places the newborn believer in His family as a true son with full standing that includes equal rights to the inheritance (Eph. 1:14). Paul prayed that the Ephesians might know "the riches of [their] glorious inheritance in the saints" (Eph. 1:18). As adopted sons, believers have the right and title to the eternal birthright that "can never perish, spoil or fade—kept in heaven" just for them (1 Pet. 1:4). The witness of the Holy Spirit gives confidence that since we are God's "children," we are also "heirs—heirs of God and co-heirs with Christ" (Rom. 8:16–17).

To add to the wonder of divine grace, Jesus treats each new believer as though he has never been outside the family of God. "God sent his son, born of a woman, born under the law," Paul taught, "to redeem those under the law, that we might receive the full rights of sons" (Gal. 4:4–6).

In the heavenly household, the only begotten Son of God becomes man's elder Brother. As the "firstborn from the dead," He has the supremacy among the brethren (Rev. 1:5; Col. 1:18). The Father has given Him full authority to operate the house, for He is "the head over all things to the Church, which is his body" (Eph. 1:22–23, 4:15). It is Jesus Christ, then, who gives to each member of the heavenly family his spiritual gifting. Both Paul and John taught that God keeps a book of life and records in it the names of His adopted children (Phil. 4:3; Rev. 3:5, 20:15, 21:27). As sons of God, "what we will be has not yet been made known. But we know that when he appears, we shall be like him, for we shall see him as he is. Everyone who has this hope in him purifies himself, just as he is pure" (1 John 3:2–3).

This sonship includes "a better country," which is the eternal kingdom of the Lord Jesus Christ (Heb. 11:16; 12:28; Luke 12:32). It also entitles God's children to inherit an "eternal glory," as well as "a crown of righteousness," and a "crown of life" (2 Cor. 4:17; 2 Tim. 4:8; James 1:12).

"How great is the love the Father has lavished on us," declares the apostle John, "that we should be called children of God." We "should be called" because, indeed, that is what we are (1 John 3:1). In fact, He chose us "in him before the creation of the world" and "predestined [us] . . . to be adopted as his sons through Jesus Christ to himself, in accordance with his pleasure and will" (Eph. 1:4–5). Little wonder Paul exclaimed, "It is by grace you have been saved, through faith—and this not from yourselves, it is the gift of God—not by works, so that no one can boast" (Eph. 2:8–9; Rom. 1:17; Gen. 15:6).

IV. The Triumph of Love

A. The Power of Love to Save the Soul

Jesus never did produce a list of do's and don'ts for his followers to keep (Gal. 2:19, THE MESSAGE). Instead, He built His kingdom of a single commandment that summarized morality and ethics for His followers: "Love the LORD your

God with all your heart and with all your soul and with all your strength" (Deut. 6:4). The directive had always been in the Law of Moses, but its importance went unrecognized for generations. The Messiah, however, understood it fully. He is the living Word who knew the Law perfectly. Jesus was fully aware the main thing in the Law had laid there dormant in the nation's history for over a millennium. He took it off the dusty shelf of history and made it the centerpiece of the new covenant. Hence, Jesus replied to the expert in the Law: "Love the Lord your God with all your heart and with all your soul and with all your mind. This is the first and greatest commandment. And the second is like it: Love your neighbor as yourself. All the Law and the Prophets hang on these two commandments" (Matt. 22:37–40; Deut. 6:4; Lev. 19:18).

Love fulfills the Law in the same way that a mother rushes to aid her crying baby without any need of a law to tell her to do it. This metaphor of a mother and her baby explains why love needs no law to fulfill its obligations, because love contains its own motivation (Matt. 22:40; Rom. 13:10; 1 John 4:11).

The love of God, revealed in the Son of man on the cross, finds people who are dead in transgressions and sins, resurrects them in spirit, and motivates them to return love to God (Eph. 2:1–5; Titus 3:4–8). They can do nothing to save their own souls, but love draws them anyway (Rom. 2:4; 5:6; 8:3; Titus 3:5). When they respond to this grace with repentance, God generously pours His love into their hearts, forgives their sins, and saves them from their old life of condemnation and shame (Rom. 8:1; 10:11; 1 John 3:1).

The Lord commanded His followers to live by the standard of this kind of love in all of their associations, since it really does redeem relationships. In the ethics and morality of Christian faith, there is but one rule—the commandment to love. Paul made the bold assertion, "The only thing that counts is faith expressing itself through love" (Gal. 5:6).

Jesus taught that love for one another is the specific, identifying quality of a Christian, and for two millennia the principle has remained true (John 13:34–35). Love redeems and is the only force on the earth that can.

⁓ "I Ask You to Forgive Me" ⁓
By Bill Bright

I know two law partners who used to hate each other.

When one became a Christian, he asked me, "Now that I'm a Christian, what should I do?"

I said, "Why not ask him to forgive you and tell him you love him?"

"I could never do that!" he said, "because I don't love him."

That lawyer had put his finger squarely on one of the great challenges of the Christian life: On the one hand, everybody wants to be loved, but on the other hand, many people never experience it. That's why we need to learn to love as Christ loves—unconditionally. We can't manufacture that kind of love. It only comes from God; and it's a love that draws people to Christ.

I prayed with that attorney. The next morning, he told his partner, "I've become a Christian, and I want to ask you to forgive me for all I've done to hurt you, and to tell you that I love you."

The partner was so surprised and convicted that he, too, asked for forgiveness and said, "I would like to become a Christian. Would you tell me how?"[15]

B. The Failure of Rules to Save the Soul

1. The Judaizers, Defending the Law of Moses

The Judaizers of the New Testament were Pharisees who zealously held to the Law of Moses as the basis for morality and ethics (Acts 13:39; Gal. 2:12–14; Ezek. 36:22). They insisted that Gentiles who came to Christ must also submit to circumcision and keep the Law in order to be saved (Acts 15:5; Gal. 5:5–6). The Jerusalem Council centered on this tension.

The first big challenge the apostles faced, therefore, was to define the relationship between the Law of Moses and the budding gospel of salvation through Jesus Christ, based on His death and resurrection (Acts 15:1–31). Greatly influenced by the apostle Peter, the council decided not to require Gentiles to be circumcised and submit to the Law of Moses (Acts 15:24–29). The apostles realized fully that keeping rules could save no one, because no law can be written that has the power to impart life (Gal. 3:21; 6:8; John 6:63; Rom. 8:2, 6, 11; 2 Cor. 3:6; Col. 2:20–23).

Judaizers never could quite understand that love actually births life; hence, love contains its own motivation to worship God, grow in His character and agenda, and respect one's neighbor. Therefore, love will save a lost soul and fulfill the Law, while rules never can (Rom. 13:10). This is true because law can only condemn, while the Spirit of God births the new life that gives a person a heart to love and serve the Lord (Rom. 1:17; 3:20–21; 4:15; 8:1–4).

The Judaizers also missed the message of the credited grace of God that is explicit in the cross of Jesus (Gen. 15:6; Rom. 4:3–25; Heb. 10:38). Lists of requirements, in fact, fail the test every time—the Pharisees had 612 such rules. "What must we do to do the works God requires?" the people asked

Jesus. "The work of God," Jesus answered them, is one thing only: "to believe in the one he has sent" (John 6:28–29).

These Judaizers' goal, instead of walking in faith, was to pull Jewish converts to Christ back under the Law of Moses and push Gentile converts to the Law of Moses. They wanted a message that said "the Law of Moses plus Jesus Christ."

The Judaizers hounded the trail of the apostle Paul throughout his ministry (Acts 13:45; 14:19; 17:5). Paul boldly addressed the issue in the book of Galatians:

> I am astonished that you are so quickly deserting the one who called you by the grace of Christ and are turning to a different gospel— which is really no gospel at all. Evidently, some people are throwing you into confusion and are trying to pervert the gospel of Christ. But even if we or an angel from heaven should preach a gospel other than the one we preached to you, let him be eternally condemned!
>
> —GALATIANS 1:6–8

2. The Law: Motivating with Guilt

Law can define right and wrong, and it can condemn for disobeying its statutes, but law motivates with fear and never liberates a soul (Acts 13:39; Rom. 7:7; 8:15; James 2:10). Because this is true, people keep breaking the Law of God, even when they do not want to disobey (Rom. 7:15). In fact, Paul said the statutes actually set people up to violate them, because by the inherent nature of saying what *not* to do, law tempts people with the opportunity. This is so true, Paul reasoned, "apart from law, sin is dead" (Rom. 7:8; Gal. 1:6–8; Heb. 10:18–26).

C. Salvation Through Credited Righteousness

Salvation comes, not by keeping a list of rules, but trusting in the atoning merit of Christ's blood (Rom. 1:17; Heb. 9:14; 1 Pet. 1:18–23). As we believe Him in heartfelt repentance, He lavishly pours His life-giving love into our hearts, and graciously credits His righteousness to our accounts (Gen. 15:6; Rom. 4:5; Eph. 1:8; Gal. 3:21; 1 John 3:1–3). We respond in gratitude to this unfathomable grace by making the choice to dedicate the remainder of our lives to growing in His likeness (2 Cor. 3:12–18; 9:15; Eph. 2:10; Phil. 2:12–13).

As Paul evaluated the great lesson of God's Son on the cross, He also perceived that Gentiles, who have this love planted in their hearts, will keep the Ten Commandments even if they have never heard of them (Rom. 2:14–15). This is true because love contains a sense of obligation that always motivates what is best toward God and one's neighbor.

Love for Jesus Christ will encourage people to:

- worship the one, true God,
- reject idols in their many forms,
- reverence the Lord's name, and
- honor the Sabbath as a holy day (Exod. 20:1–11).

Love for a neighbor will inspire people to:

- honor their parents (as their first and closest neighbors),
- respect the life of a neighbor (including a helpless neighbor in the womb),
- refuse any desire to seduce a neighbor's wife,
- reject any impulse to steal from a neighbor,
- give truthful testimony about a neighbor, and
- eliminate any motivation to covet a neighbor's possessions (Exod. 20:12–17).

The Judaizers fought "tooth and claw" to defend the Ten Commandments, but they did not love God with their whole hearts and never grasped justifying grace based on credited righteousness (Matt. 22:37; Rom. 4:22–25). Instead, they conspired to kill God's Son on a merciless cross, violating the first four commandments they had promised to fight to the death to defend. Rather than love their neighbor as themselves, they persecuted their Messiah and those who loved Him, violating the letter and the spirit of the last six of the Commandments (Matt. 22:38–39).

Viewed from this perspective, the Great Commandment did not invalidate the moral law (John 15:12). Instead, love made it possible for a child of God to embrace it and respond to it. "Love," Paul wrote, "is the fulfillment of the law" (Rom. 13:10; 1 John 4:19). This is true precisely because it births new life (Gal. 3:21).

God's love is willful, disciplined, and tough, and embraces a strong sense of responsibility. Through Christ, this love is available to all. The Lord even chose to love the unlovely and liberates everyone who embraces His love (Rom. 5:8; Gal. 5:1).

V. Showing a Person How to Accept Christ

❧ Too High to Reach Down ❧

A man once testified in one of D. L. Moody's meetings that he had lived "on the Mount of Transfiguration" for five years.

"How many souls did you lead to Christ last year?" Moody bluntly asked him.

"Well," the man hesitated, "I don't know."

"Have you saved any?" Moody persisted.

"I don't know that I have," the man admitted.

"Well," said Moody, "we don't want that kind of mountaintop experience. When a man gets up so high that he cannot reach down and save poor sinners, there is something wrong."[16]

Many good models of the plan of salvation are available that demonstrate how to bring people to Christ. Two will be stated here.

A. The A-B-C Model

Admit your condition. "You must be born again," Jesus said. In fact, accepting this injunction is the only way the Lord's diagnosis of our fallen condition can prove to be corrective. Every person living has the same dilemma, "because all have sinned and come short of the glory of God" (Rom. 3:23). "If we say that we have not sinned," John instructs us, "we make him a liar, and his word is not in us" (1 John 1:10). The writer of Hebrews declared, "It is appointed unto men once to die, but after that the judgment" (Heb. 9:27).

Believe that Jesus died, was buried, and rose from the dead—for *you*. "God so loved the world that he gave his only begotten Son, that whoever believes in him should not perish, but have everlasting life" (John 3:16; Rom. 1:17). God cared so deeply, in fact, He gave His only begotten Son, Jesus, to bear your sin and die in your place. "God made him who had no sin to be sin for us, so that in him we might become the righteousness of God" (2 Cor. 5:21). "Christ died for our sins according to the Scriptures...he was buried...he was raised on the third day according to the Scriptures" (1 Cor. 15:3–4).

Confess Jesus Christ as Savior and Lord. "If you confess with your mouth, 'Jesus is Lord,' and believe in your heart that God raised him from the dead, you will be saved" (Rom. 10:9–10).

✄ No Longer Augustine ✄

Before Augustine of Hippo (A.D. 354–430), turned from Manichaeism
to the Lord (387), he had a mistress named Claudia. After he found
Christ, Claudia saw him one day on the street.

"Augustine! Augustine!" she cried after her old lover.

Augustine paid no heed.

"Augustine! Augustine!" she cried out again. "It's Claudia!"

"But it is no longer Augustine," he replied, as he continued on his way.[17]

B. The Romans Road to Salvation

- **Romans 3:23—"All have sinned and fall short of the glory
  of God."** We all have sin in our hearts. We all were born sinful
  and under the power of sin's control, so admit that you are a
  sinner.
- **Romans 6:23a—"The wages of sin is death…"** Sin results in
  death. We all face physical death, which is a result of sin, but
  a worse penalty is spiritual death. It alienates us from God for
  eternity. The Bible teaches that there is a place called the lake
  of fire where lost people will be in torment forever. We must
  understand that we deserve death for our sin.
- **Romans 6:23b—"…but the gift of God is eternal life
  through Jesus Christ our Lord."** Salvation is a free gift from
  God to you! You cannot earn it, but you can and must reach
  out and accept it. He will forgive you and save you if you will
  ask him.
- **Romans 5:8—"God demonstrates His own love for us in
  this: While we were still sinners, Christ died for us!"** When
  Jesus died on the cross, He paid the penalty for your sins. The
  only condition is that you believe Him and His promises to
  you. He did all this because He loved you. His love is what
  saves you. God loves *you*!
- **Romans 10:9–10, 13—Confess Jesus Christ as your Lord
  and Savior.** "If you confess with your mouth, 'Jesus is Lord,'
  and believe in your heart that God raised him from the dead,
  you will be saved. For it is with your heart that you believe
  and are justified, and it is with your mouth that you confess

and are saved.... Everyone who calls on the name of the Lord will be saved."

❦ Confessing Faith in Christ ❦

Lord Jesus, I know I am a sinner. I believe You died in my place when You were crucified on the cross. I believe You poured out Your blood for me. You were also buried and arose from the dead for me. So I open my heart to You and receive You as my Savior and Lord. Thank You for forgiving my sins and giving me the gift of salvation and everlasting life because of the abundance of your mercy and grace. In Jesus' name. Amen.

VI. Summary

The distinctive elements of the plan of salvation emerge out of a process that begins in prevenient grace and ends in the marvelous moment of salvation, and include repentance, conversion, saving faith, justification, regeneration, and adoption. They are each concomitants of the same work of grace known as the new birth. The moment of the new birth is so distinctive, it is normative for a person to know the time and place when his sins were forgiven. In the presence of such divine mercies, one can only rejoice that our God is an awesome God (Ps. 47:2; Dan. 9:4).

❦ Trusting That We Don't Owe Anything ❦

I was having breakfast with my dad and my younger son at the Real Food Café in Grand Rapids. As we were finishing our meal, I noticed that the waitress brought our check, then took it away, and then brought it back again. She placed it on the table, smiled, and said: "Somebody in the restaurant paid for your meal. You're all set." And then she walked away.

I had the strangest feeling sitting there. The feeling was helplessness. There was nothing I could do. It had been taken care of. To insist on paying would have been pointless. All I could do was trust what she said was actually true and then live in that—which meant getting up and leaving the restaurant. My acceptance...gave me a choice: to live like it was true or to create my own reality in which the bill was not paid.

That is our invitation—to trust that we don't owe anything. To trust that something is already true about us, something has already been done, something has been there all along.

To trust that grace pays the bill.[18]

George Matheson wrote a hymn to describe this grace:

O love that wilt not let me go,
I rest my weary soul in Thee.
I give thee back the life I owe,
That in Thine ocean depths its flow,
May richer, fuller be.

The amazing grace of God so overwhelms with the matchless love of God, some people find it hard to accept the new freedom. But for those who do, this love motivates and even compels the children of God to do what pleases their Lord. Paul taught Titus:

The grace of God that brings salvation has appeared to all men. It teaches us to say "No" to ungodliness and worldly passions, and to live self-controlled, upright and godly lives in this present age, while we wait for the blessed hope—the glorious appearing of our great God and Savior, Jesus Christ, who gave himself for us to redeem us from all wickedness and to purify for himself a people that are his very own, eager to do what is good.

—Titus 2:11–14

The ultimate test that a person has come to Jesus Christ is his new lifestyle of complete trust in God that yields loving and voluntary obedience. Paul said to the believers at Ephesus: "It is by grace you have been saved, through faith—and this not from yourselves, it is the gift of God—not by works, so that no one can boast. For we are God's workmanship, created in Christ Jesus to do good works, which God prepared in advance for us to do" (Eph. 2:8–10).

The result is that the Lord's redeemed children place their trust absolutely in the Christ and volunteer to become servants of His plan to save the world (Matt. 28:16–20; Phil. 2:12–13). They view themselves as channels of grace. Someone loved them enough to take the risk and share with them the good news. The gospel they heard diagnosed their condition correctly, opened their eyes, and gave them a new beginning. The result is they now look for ways to do favors for other people, even those who abuse and spitefully mistreat them (Matt. 5:10–12).

- "You will be my witnesses," Jesus said, "to the ends of the earth" (Acts 1:8).

- "Be on your guard," Paul wrote. "Stand firm in the faith; be men of courage; be strong. Do everything in love" (1 Cor. 16:13–14).
- "If your enemy hungers, feed him. If he thirsts, give him drink: for in doing so you shall heap coals of fire on his head. Be not overcome by evil, but overcome evil with good" (Rom. 12:20–21, KJV; Prov. 25:21–22).
- Act wisely toward outsiders, making "the most of every opportunity," with conversation that is always "full of grace" (Col. 4:5–6).

Our Lord Jesus Christ took on the challenge of providing redemption for the whole world. He tackled an idea so big it can only be described as a "God vision." As a man Jesus overcame all the odds and achieved it. Little wonder that "God exalted him to the highest place and gave him the name that is above every name, that at the name of Jesus every knee should bow, in heaven and on earth and under the earth, and every tongue confess that Jesus Christ is Lord, to the glory of God the Father" (Phil. 2:9–11).

What an example! What an achiever! What a plan of salvation!

What an awesome Lord (Exod. 34:10).

We have noted that the study of soteriology has two aspects: the new birth and sanctifying grace. We will now focus on the second dimension, also referring to it as set-apart living.

Chapter Five

JESUS, WHAT A SANCTIFIER

My lover is mine and I am his.
—SONG OF SOLOMON 2:16

I am the LORD who makes you holy.
—LEVITICUS 20:8

In your hearts set apart Christ as Lord.
—1 PETER 3:15

Work out your salvation with fear and trembling.
—PHILIPPIANS 2:12

THE LORD JESUS lived with a moral commitment to trust His Father implicitly and serve Him in all things, as superintended by the Holy Spirit (Phil. 2:5–8; Acts 10:38; Isa. 42:1). With that strategy, God "set Him apart as His very own and sent him into the world" to achieve man's redemption (John 10:36; Col. 1:13–14). Jesus "appeared once for all...to do away with sin by the sacrifice of himself" (Heb. 9:26). Hence, Jesus came to achieve the plan of salvation. It includes both the new birth and a second work of grace, identified by the term, *sanctification*.

I. Defining Terms

A. The New Birth
In the new birth, a person recognizes his sins and repents. He makes this choice as his response to the compelling love of Jesus Christ. The Lord "bore our sins in his own body on the tree," so that "we might die to sins and live for righteousness" (1 Pet. 2:24; Isa. 49:5–6).

Motivated by the wooing of the Holy Spirit, an individual makes a fundamental lifestyle change. He turns his life around, leaves his sins behind, and opens his heart to God. The experience is so life-changing that the analogy of a second birth is appropriate (John 3:3–7; 2 Cor. 5:17; Gal. 6:15).

B. Sanctification

The master key that unlocks the Scriptures on the subject of sanctification is the idea of separation, or of the consecration that sets a person apart unto divine service.

The Hebrew verb *qadash* carries the root meaning of this separation that breaks forth in shining consecration. (In Exodus 19:10, the word *consecrate* is used to translate the Hebrew *quadash*.) The Greek equivalent of *qadash* is *hagios*, which is translated in John 10:36 as "set apart." *Hagios*, therefore, carries the meaning of "separation" or a state of being set-apart in personal consecration unto God that results in outshining devotion to Jesus Christ.

The image of separation, therefore, is the common thread woven throughout the Bible on this theme. Hence, the test that a person is sanctified must not be is he living in sinless perfection, but rather, is he actually set apart unto Jesus Christ—heart soul, mind, and strength. And, to be set apart unto Jesus Christ is to live in the best interests of one's neighbors (Luke 10:27).

The intent of this chapter is to show what the set-apart lifestyle embraces. The following chapter will be dedicated to illustrating it from Scripture.

⤛ The Vocabulary of Set-Apart Living ⤜

Every area of study—computers, science, math, medicine, astronomy, etc—has its own vocabulary, its special way of using terms. This is also true with the study of the Scriptures. As the reader walks through this chapter and the next, sensitivity to how terms are used will be important. A disciple of the Lord might even consider making a list of the new concepts as they emerge and writing out the definitions as used in this study.

The following will include enough of the new vocabulary to make the point.

the corrupted will, the old self, old man, sin nature, inbred sin, evil heart; and the futility of self effort

slave to sin, slave to righteousness

the desires of the flesh as the root of sin

symptoms vs. condition

the path of death as the road to life; crucified with Christ; resurrected with Christ

separation from and unto, separation as self emptying, separation as death

crisis and process

love that compels and decrees

the profound mystery of marriage

identification principle

coexistence thinking
bodily sacrifice
sinless perfection, angelic perfection, glorification

---

1. The Need for This Separation

In the new birth, a person becomes a son in the family of God. In sanctification, he "works out [his] salvation with fear and trembling" (Phil. 2:12). In the new birth, a person converts and, in deeply felt repentance, turns his life over to Jesus Christ. In sanctification, he sets apart Jesus as Lord of the many "thrones" of his life (1 Pet. 3:15). These include, but are not limited to, his:

- money,
- sex life,
- devotional life,
- family life,
- church life,
- work life,
- recreational life,
- possessions,
- generational curses and bondages, and
- sinful habits.

In each of the many areas of influence that make up his life, it remains for him to work out his salvation. The salt of the gospel must blend through his whole being so that the values of Jesus permeate each dimension of his life (Matt. 5:13). He comes to the cross in the new birth, bringing all of this old baggage with him, including his habits and strongholds, and lays it all at the feet of Jesus.

Then, to settle successfully the lordship question in all areas of an individual's life, a believer must confront his inner willpower. Jesus described it in these terms: "I tell you the truth, everyone who sins is a slave to sin" (John 8:34). The only conclusion to be drawn from the Lord's statement is that all people ("everyone") commit sins because they are born with a corrupted will, and, "a slave [to sin] has no permanent place in the family" of God (John 8:35). The Lord clearly taught the core of man's problem is this corrupted freedom of will (Mark 7:21). Sin always begins in the heart and expresses itself in choices that produce actions.

The Lord's atonement dealt decisively both with the sins people commit and the sin nature that binds them in addiction to sin. The result is freedom and liberation. "If the Son sets you free [from the nature of sin and the sins it produces], you will be free indeed" (John 8:36).

Paul picked up the Lord's diagnosis and wrote that in the soul of every person is this root of rebellion against God, that Paul identified with the term *the sinful nature* (Rom. 7:5; John 8:23–36). People commit sins because this nature is in them, and all people inherit it from Adam's first sin in Eden (Rom. 7:5). This understanding proved to be very important in the writings of the apostle Paul. He used the term *sinful nature* eleven times in Romans, for example, and six times in Galatians. Paul also identified this corrupt, natural tendency in the heart of every man with the term *palaios anthropos* (literally, "old man"). The Authorized Version uses the term *old man* (Col. 3:9, KJV; Eph. 4:22, KJV). The translators of the NIV rendered it the "old self" (Rom. 6:6).

Paul did not teach that most people die in Adam, while some escape the penalty because of their moral goodness (Rom. 3:12). Instead, Paul wrote, "In Adam all die" (1 Cor. 15:22). The judicial sentence of death is universal because everyone has a corrupt heart that is addicted to rebelling against God (Rom. 5:17; John 8:34). The apostle also penned a gripping description of the struggle:

> When I want to do good, evil is right there with me. For in my inner being I delight in God's law; but I see another law at work in the members of my body, waging war against the law of my mind and making me a prisoner of the law of sin at work within my members. What a wretched man I am! Who will rescue me from this body of death? Thanks be to God—through Jesus Christ our Lord!
> —ROMANS 7:21–25

This old self that remains active after conversion has its powerbase in the cravings and appetites of the flesh (Rom. 7:18, KJV; 1 Cor. 1:29; Gal. 5:17; 5:24; 6:8; Eph. 2:3). When we "have the desire to do what is good, but…cannot carry it out," we demonstrate that we are dominated by an evil will (Rom. 7:16–19). The tension between the new self and the old self continues, therefore, until sanctifying grace breaks the controlling domination of this addiction to sin.

A boiler in a basement that births the steam to heat a building is an apt description of the way the old self, or the sin nature, produces sins (Eph. 4:22; Rom. 6:6, KJV; Col. 3:9). As long as the boiler is producing steam, turning off the radiator is merely a short-term solution. The only way to stop the heat is to turn off the boiler.

Jesus taught, and Paul followed Him, that the nature of the problem is much deeper than merely what we do, or the sins we commit. The root of the predicament is an inherited addiction. The Lord said each person by nature is a "slave to sin" (John 8:34; Rom. 7:14, 18). This sin nature defines what we *are*, and the addiction is the same for every human being worldwide (Matt. 15:15–20; John 3:16; 8:34; Rom. 3:19).

a) The Witness of Noah

The very old story of Noah recognizes this corrupt heart condition, sometimes referred to as *inbred sin*. Just before the flood, "The LORD saw how great man's wickedness on the earth had become and that every inclination of the thoughts of his heart was only evil all the time. The LORD was grieved that he had made man on the earth, and his heart was filled with pain" (Gen. 6:5–6). The problem was so widespread as to be universal because "all the people on earth had corrupted their ways" (Gen. 6:12). The punishment awaiting every person was capital: "I am going to put an end to all people," God said to Noah, "for the earth is filled with violence because of them" (Gen. 6:13, see also Rom. 6:23; Heb. 9:27).

b) Trying to Achieve Holiness with Self-Effort

Many choose to believe this age-old, inherited problem can be resolved by doing enough works of righteous to break the authority of the old self, but if a person tries to achieve holiness before God by his own efforts, he will probably emerge as a Pharisee, hopelessly wrapped in the chains of legalism. He will also be frustrated, because how does one know when he has done enough good deeds to qualify as righteous before God? Hence, bound by his lists of do's and don'ts, he never enjoys personal victory over his sinful nature (Rom. 7:5–6, THE MESSAGE).

⨳ Uncle Ben's Cough: ⨳
Curing the Symptoms or the Condition

It seemed like it was just a head cold. Then Uncle Ben's chest started to hurt, and a serious cough developed. Soon even minor activity made it hard for him to breathe. We suggested that he see a physician, but he was a typical man who did not like going to doctors. Eventually he was so miserable, he let his wife call for an appointment.

"You've got pneumonia, Ben!" the doctor told him.

The chest X-ray showed it—this dark film of stuff, glued to his lung, was causing all his trouble. Thankfully, the doctor knew what to do to cure the condition.

Uncle Ben's problem was not the coughing or the chest discomfort or the breathing difficulty. Those were merely the symptoms, and all the treatments for those symptoms couldn't solve his problem. The culprit was the deadly pneumococcus bacteria growing in his lung, and it had to be destroyed for Uncle Ben's life to be saved.

---

c) Believing No Cure Is Possible

Many conclude the condition described as *the old man* or the *nature of sin* has no cure. This reasoning says there is no way to stop the "pneumonia;" victory over the addiction to sin is not possible. These believers battle temptation and live in the bondage of doublemindedness throughout their lives (Rom. 7:15–25). They also typically reason they cannot help what they feel and do, making it much easier for them to justify their sins. They will instead excuse themselves, saying something like, "It is just my old dark side coming through." This kind of thinking reasons that grace merely patches a person up. The result is a life doomed to devastating defeat, discouragement, and doubt.

However, Jesus taught victory *is* possible.

> I tell you the truth, everyone who sins is a slave to sin. Now a slave has no permanent place in the family, but a son belongs to it forever. So if the Son sets you free, you will be free indeed.
> —John 8:34–36

2. The Solution: the Path of Death

The cross of Jesus shows the solution is personal identification with the death of Jesus. Parents who have lost a child in a tragic accident will give testimony to how they identify so closely with the accident they relive it in vivid detail time and time again. In this same sense, we connect intimately with the crucifixion of Jesus. "I have been crucified with Christ," Paul said, "and I no longer live" (Gal. 2:20). The word *crucified* in this verse is the translation of the Greek word *sustauroo*, which also means "impaled." The concept here is vivid and strong: to identify with Christ's crucifixion is like being impaled with him.

What follows is resurrection to a new life—"Christ lives in me." The path of death, then, is a word picture that communicates a believer's intensely personal connection with the Lord's crucifixion. It actually has the power to shut the boiler down and cure the "pneumonia," breaking the old self's control. The many thrones or power centers in a person's life will never be brought under the lordship of Jesus Christ without this dying. Good intentions will not achieve it, nor will new resolutions. The control of the old self is too strong; only the path of death will conquer it. A child of God must surrender his evil way in a spiritual death and burial. Only then can he experience resurrection to the Lord's way. The issue boils down to who will be Lord over one's:

- money,
- sex life,
- devotional life,
- family life,
- church life,
- work life,
- recreational life,
- possessions,
- generational curses and bondages, and
- sinful habits.

And the list goes on.

As the child of God relives the death of Jesus on the cross—the death he should have died—he discovers the whole point of Christ's death was to save sinners and set them apart unto divine service (Gal. 2:20; 5:24; 6:14). This understanding opens the door for God, by the Holy Spirit, to pour into his heart the same love that nailed Jesus to the cross. Jesus overcame sin at Calvary, and so can God's children.

The evil of humankind's sinful condition is horrendous and massive. In fact, "The heart is deceitful above all things and beyond cure" (Jer. 17:9; Matt. 18:24–35). Because of this inherited nature, the heavenly Father expressed His great love by sending His own Son to die our death and set us free (John 3:16; 8:36; 1 Cor. 15:3; 1 Pet. 3:18). It is truly awesome that the sinless Savior, the Lord Jesus Christ, loved me so much He paid my debt in full with His own blood (Matt. 18:27; Col. 1:20; Heb. 4:15–16; 9:12).

When people fall in love with the Lord who sacrificed His life, the Holy Spirit meets them on their own path of death. On that road, God's love changes them at the deepest level of their will, providing the cure. People really do become like what they love (2 Cor. 3:18; 4:18). The antidote of God's love, demonstrated at Golgotha, goes to the root of man's problem. Jesus carried both my sins and my sin nature up the hill that ended at the crest of Golgotha (1 Pet. 2:24). It was horrifying beyond description what happened to the Lord on Golgotha, but He took it all so all who believe in Him could go free. Jesus' success, therefore, means my triumph too. When I identify in faith with His death to the point that I picture myself impaled and dying on the cross with Him, a quantum change occurs inside me.

This kind of grace is just amazing! The response of gratitude for this divine kindness is so compelling it actually produces an undying love for Jesus Christ and inspires people to make Him Lord of all areas of their lives (Eph. 6:24). The result is the domination of the old self is broken and believers are resurrected with Jesus because of the power of the "Spirit of life in Christ" (Rom. 6:5; 8:2).

The gospel cure for the nature inherited from Adam, therefore, is not at all based on performance, or a list of requirements. The solution is death itself, through identification with the crucifixion of Jesus Christ. This new bond ultimately settles the lordship question in all of the complex areas of one's life and makes it possible to work out one's salvation (John 20:28; Gal. 2:20; Phil. 2:12–13). It is part of the genius of the gospel to admit openly that good deeds alone can never crush the old man's dominance (Gal. 2:16; Eph. 2:8). Association with the horrible death of Jesus, who conquered all of the cravings of the flesh in His death, provides the spiritual solution to the sinful corruption of the physical appetites (John 6:63; Rom. 6:19; 7:5–6; 8:3–9; 1 Cor. 1:29, KJV).

> What actually took place is this: I tried keeping rules and working my head off to please God, and it didn't work. So I quit being a "law man" so that I could be God's man. Christ's life showed me how, and enabled me to do it. I identified myself completely with him. Indeed, I have been crucified with Christ. My ego is no longer central. It is no longer important that I appear righteous before you or have your good opinion, and I am no longer driven to impress God. Christ lives in me. The life you see me living is not "mine," but it is lived by faith in the Son of God, who loved me and gave himself for me.
> —Galatians 2:19–20, The Message

Jesus' sacrifice would have been woefully incomplete if His death on Calvary had left untouched the inner inherited nature that He Himself acknowledged produces sins (John 8:34–36). Jesus did provide a road of victory, and it is the path of death. The journey down that road, made in faith, always results in a powerful, life-changing encounter with the risen Christ of Calvary.

3. Separation From and Unto

This understanding of the set-apart lifestyle always has two sides, embracing what a believer walks away *from* on the path of death and what he *goes toward*. Because of the wooing power of God's grace, a person makes the decision he wants freedom from the nature and the deeds of the old man of sin (Gal. 5:1). The apostle John commanded his readers:

> Stop loving this evil world and all that it offers you, for when you love these things you show that you do not really love God; for all these worldly things, these evil desires—the craze for sex, the

ambition to buy everything that appeals to you, and the pride that comes from wealth and importance—these are not from God. They are from this evil world itself.

—1 JOHN 2:15–16, TLB

A child of God receives the actual strength to turn away because of the overwhelming love of God, expressed at Calvary, that motivates him to do what he could never have done before (Eph. 1:6–8; 1 John 3:1). Hence, he makes the choice to break from the old life and walk the path of death to the cross, in full faith the Holy Spirit is making every step of the journey with him. This confidence assures him that Jesus will be there, full of love, waiting with a heart overflowing with acceptance just for him (Ps. 9:10).

This separation assumes a crisis and an ongoing process. It is termed a crisis because getting on the old, rugged cross through spiritual identification with Jesus and visualizing this kind of awful death by impalement with Him, yields significant emotional pain. Coming back to life in this kind of glorious resurrection also embraces an ongoing lifestyle of growth in the outshining love of Jesus, as a believer matures in his capacity to live in freedom from his old way of life.

⪧ The Testimony of Hudson Taylor, ⪦ Missionary to China

In a letter to his mother, Hudson Taylor (1832–1905) described his point of spiritual crucifixion.

"My own position becomes continually more and more responsible, and my need greater of special grace to fill it, but I have continually to mourn that I follow at such a distance and learn so slowly to imitate my precious Master. I cannot tell you how I am buffeted sometimes by temptations. I never knew how bad a heart I had. Yet I do know that I love God and love His work, and desire to serve Him only in all things… Do pray for me. Pray that the Lord will keep me from sin, will sanctify me wholly, will use me more largely in His service."

Mr. Taylor's testimony is that he discovered Galatians 2:20 and it changed his life. "I am crucified with Christ: nevertheless I live; yet not I, but Christ liveth in me…"

John 15 also became a reality to him: "Abide in me, and I in you. As the branch cannot bear fruit of itself, except it abide in the vine; no more can you, except you abide in me. I am the vine, you are the branches: He that abides in me, and I in him, the same brings forth much fruit: for without me you can do nothing" (John 15:4–5, KJV).

When the great missionary to China discovered the principle of crucifixion through identification with Christ, a resurrection to a new life of abiding in Christ immediately began to blossom, as he wrote to his sister:

"The last month or more has been perhaps the happiest of my life and I long to tell you a little of what the Lord has done for my soul. I do not know how far I may be able to make myself intelligible about it, for there is nothing new or strange or wonderful—and yet, all is new! In a word, 'Whereas once I was blind, now I see.' The sweetest part...is the rest which full identification with Christ brings. I am no longer anxious about anything, as I realize this; for He, I know, is able to carry out His will, and His will is mine. It makes no matter where He places me or how. This is rather for Him to consider than for me; for in the easiest positions He must give me His grace, and in the most difficult His grace is sufficient."[1]

4. Separation as Two Great Streams

In sanctification, two tributaries flow together into one, majestic river. The first is what God does: "I am the LORD that doth sanctify you" (Exod. 31:13, KJV). The second is what the believer does: "In your hearts set apart Christ as Lord" (1 Pet. 3:15). Paul expressed it, "Train yourself to be godly...godliness has value for all things, holding promise for both the present life and the life to come" (1 Tim. 4:7–8).

A heartfelt experience that identifies, in faith, with Christ's death and resurrection will be met by the Holy Spirit and will be life changing. The results will be commitment to the attitude and values of Christ. The believer will be "conformed to the likeness of [God's] Son," who humbled himself and served His way to the cross (Rom. 8:29; Phil. 2:5, 8). Paul was confident "that he who began a good work in you will carry it on to completion until the day of Jesus Christ" (Phil. 1:6).

5. Separation as Sacrifice

Many people who come to Christ in repentance stop short of actively pursuing Jesus' way of thinking in their own lives (John 14:31; Phil. 2:5). Instead, they are content to live on milk as "mere infants in Christ," never working out their salvation with fear and trembling (1 Cor. 3:1–2; Phil. 2:13). Neither do they ever commit heart and soul to the Lord's worldwide agenda (Matt. 28:16–20).

Countless individuals believe, for example, that their time, treasure, possessions, entertainment, diet, and sexuality belong to them, and that the gospel merely spices enjoyment of them at one's personal discretion. This narcissism, or self-love, is very different from the message of the Cross. The Lord's call to holiness places Jesus at the center of a believer's possessions, treasure, time, entertainment, diet, and sexuality (Matt. 5:48; 19:21; Eph. 1:4–8). In this new relationship, the whole person belongs to the Lord and serves at His pleasure. Only when a child of God has forsaken all to be the Lord's disciple can he discover the rich freedom of a lifestyle set apart unto God (Matt. 19:29).

Leaving behind the values of the world for the standards of Jesus Christ calls for a dedication that is deeply meaningful and assumes a commitment to a diet of solid food in the Word of God (1 Cor. 3:2; Heb. 5:12–14). Little wonder Jesus called on His disciples to count the cost: "If anyone would come after me, he must deny himself, and take up his cross, and follow me. For whoever wants to save his life will lose it, but whoever loses his life for me will find it. What good will it be for a man if he gains the whole world, yet forfeits his soul? Or what can a man give in exchange for his soul?" (Matt. 16:24–27; Luke 14:28–33).

II. Set-Apart Living Through the Scriptures

"Without the shedding of blood" there can be no forgiveness and no new lifestyle that is set apart unto the Lord (Heb. 9:22). For this reason, a scarlet cord weaves its way through the redemptive annals of Holy Scripture. This crimson path leads straight to Jesus Christ, as Israel's Messiah and the final sacrifice for sin.

> By one sacrifice he has made perfect forever those who are being made holy. The Holy Spirit also testifies to us about this.
> —HEBREWS 10:14–15

A. The Old Testament

This study presents four Bible stories that portray a second spiritual blessing, subsequent to experiencing the credited righteousness that comes by grace through faith (Gen. 15:6). In doing so, the story of Israel's founder will receive special attention.

1. Abraham

a) Credited Righteousness: the Golden Key

"Do not be afraid, Abram," God said to him in a vision, "I am your shield and your very great reward" (Gen. 15:1). The vision he saw was that he would have a son and from that son would come a multiplied host of sons and daughters, like the sand on the seashore and the stars in the sky. They would share His faith, loving God as Abraham did (Gen. 15: 2–5; 18:18; Gal. 3:8–9).

"Abraham believed the Lord" amid that great encounter, "and he credited it to him as righteousness" (Gen. 15:6; Ps. 32:2). This righteousness came to Abraham because He trusted what God said and looked forward in faith to the coming Messiah who would pay the price in His own blood to restore all people to a relationship of intimacy with God (Acts 10:43). "Abraham—your 'father'—with jubilant faith," Jesus said, "looked down the corridors of history and saw my day coming. He saw it and cheered" (John 8:56, The Message).

The key to making the vision come true is expressed in Genesis 15:6, and it embraces a bookkeeping word picture. God responded to Abraham's faith in anticipation of the cross by depositing the righteousness of the Messiah into his account (Acts 10:43; Rom. 3:21–22; 4:6). In fact, every individual, Jew and Gentile, who becomes part of the fulfillment of Abraham's grand vision must come to God the same way (Rom. 10:3–13). When a person makes the choice to trust God, the Lord graciously responds by making this same unearned deposit. This truth is the golden key to the Bible (Rom. 4:3–5, 9–11, 22–24; James 2:23; Heb. 11:7).

Two millennia after Abraham's great experience with God, the apostle Paul carefully analyzed the meaning of the cross of Jesus. Paul comprehended that the plan of salvation anchors in God's grace and comes through faith in Jesus Christ (Eph. 2:8). When Paul also studied the life of Abraham through the bifocals of the cross and the resurrection of Jesus, he discovered this same truth had been in Abraham's story from the beginning. Out of this understanding, the Holy Spirit blossomed in Paul's mind that the new birth has always been about grace, the righteousness of Jesus Christ credited to every believer's account. The Lord makes the deposit with full knowledge the person has no personal merit with God.

When writing Galatians and Romans, Paul made Genesis 15:6 foundational in both books (Rom. 4:1–5; Gal. 3:6–9). In doing so, he demonstrated from the life of the father of the faithful that salvation has always been a loving gift of God that is freely deposited to a believer's account and received by grace through faith (Matt. 11:28–30; Rom. 4:16; Eph. 2:8).

Paul also preached that God's promise to give Abraham the nations for his inheritance certainly embraced every Israelite who trusted God like Abraham did (Gen. 15:4–5; Rom. 4:12). But it also included the uncircumcised (the Gentiles), and was actually the announcement of "the gospel in advance" (Gal. 3:8–9; Gen. 12:3–5; 15:4–5; 18:18; 22:18). God would raise up on the basis of Abraham's faith, sons and daughters who would see it as their mission to love God implicitly and take the message of His Son, Jesus, to all ethnicities, even to the islands of the seas. Hence, they would fill the earth with even more children of God. One day they would become a host so large no man could count them (Gen. 18:18; Gal. 3:8–9; Rev. 7:9).

b) Discovering the Set-Apart Walk With God

Some fourteen years after God credited His generous gift of righteousness to Abraham, when the patriarch was ninety-nine years old, a historic year unfolded in his life. In a twelve-month period, Abraham received both the covenant of circumcision and the promise of the birth of Isaac. In this short time, Abraham also saw the death of the city-states of Sodom and Gomorrah, and his ninety-year-old wife became pregnant and birthed through Isaac the new nation of Israel. Forty-two generations later, her son's seed brought the Messiah into the world. His sacrifice insured that the whole earth would be blessed through Abraham's faith (Matt. 1:17; Gen. 15:4–5; 18:18; Gal. 3:8–9).

"I am God almighty," the Lord said in that great revelation. "Walk before me, and be blameless" (Gen. 17:1). The very nature of God's command indicated that Abraham was not walking faultlessly with the Lord. To encourage Abraham to move toward the perfection God was seeking, the Lord showered him with generous promises. God would make Abraham "very fruitful" (Gen. 17:6). From him would spring nations and kings, and Canaan would be the homeland of his descendants as "an everlasting covenant" (Gen. 17:7). This unfolding story is a marvelous illustration of how the love of God motivates and even compels, but without violating one's freedom of choice (2 Cor. 5:14).

The covenant between God and Abraham had to be a two-way street. God's part was the gift of the land and fruitfulness in Abraham's home. Abraham's part was to walk before the Lord in complete trust, living the set-apart lifestyle of the covenant. "Abraham entered into what God was doing for him," Paul said, "and *that* was the turning point. He trusted God to set him right instead of trying to be right on his own" (Rom. 4:3, THE MESSAGE).

The symbol of this faith was circumcision; Abraham agreed to the surgery for himself and all the males in his household. Circumcision would also be required of any male descendant of Abraham for perpetual generations, as well as of any foreigner who chose Israelite citizenship (Gen. 17:8–14). It was to be strictly enforced so that anyone in Israel who refused the rite had to be cut off from the people (Gen. 17:14). The surgery itself physically separated Abraham and his descendants from the pagan peoples living around them.

Abraham submitted to the revelation and proceeded with the circumcision (Gen. 17:23). That choice meant Abraham set himself apart in the inward condition of his heart unto the massive vision God had given him (Gen. 15:1–6).

c) Israel's Big Mistake

The great example of the Lord's crucifixion helped Paul realize that with the passing of their generations, his forefathers came to place their hopes in the "sign of circumcision" in utter disregard for the "seal of the righteousness that [Abraham] had by faith while he was still uncircumcised" (Rom. 4:11; Gal. 5:6). In addition, the sons of Abraham interpreted their father's vision in national terms—solely as God's promise to Israel. They failed to comprehend that through their Messiah, God meant for Abraham's vision to bless all nations (Gen. 22:18). The errors were serious.

Paul fully understood a surgical cutting of the foreskin did not make Abraham holy; instead, the separation of his heart to believe the great vision is what God sought (Gen. 15:4–5; 18:18). Only then could he break forth shiningly. Circumcision was merely the sign; total separation unto God in his heart by faith was the seal (Rom. 4:11). The prophet Jeremiah in a later generation captured succinctly the spiritual significance of circumcision. "Circumcise yourselves to the Lord," Jeremiah wrote, "and take away the foreskins of your heart, you men of Judah and inhabitants of Jerusalem" (Jer. 4:4, KJV; Deut. 30:6).

What God intended when He told Abraham, "Walk before me and be blameless," as symbolized in circumcision, is a captivating story (Gen. 17:1).

d) The Unworkable Strategy

At the time Abraham received this covenant, his family was largely dysfunctional. It had been about fourteen years since he had taken Hagar to himself, at Sarah's urgings, in a surrogate motherhood relationship that was culturally acceptable for producing an heir. Ishmael, the child born from that union, was already a young teenager in his father's tent. The problem was not that Abraham had staggered through unbelief over these years at the celebrated vision God gave him (Gen. 15:1–5; Rom. 4:20). Abraham had always been convinced God would perform what He promised; he clearly believed God (Gen. 15:6; Heb. 11:8–12). The problem was he had concluded that the solution Sarah contrived, and in which he had been a willing participant, was the correct one: Ishmael would be his heir (Gen. 16:1–4). After all, Ishmael had come from his loins (Gen. 15:4). What both Abraham and Sarah failed to see was that in the heart of God, to qualify as a child from "his loins" the infant had to come also from the womb of his wife, Sarah. Monogamous marriage has been God's intent from the beginning, and the Lord did not permit Canaanite culture to offer a substitute for His plan for marriage (Gen. 2:24; 12:5–6; 17:16).

At this stage in his journey of faith, Abraham had no way to realize just how far off course his strategy was. Dependence on Ishmael as his heir would have never birthed the world's Messiah; instead, it would have made sure the Messiah would not be born. Man's goodness never does come close to the just requirements of a holy God. Our works of righteousness are always off course.

Abraham had been walking in faith, albeit imperfectly, for many years since the vision in which he saw the great host of his descendants like the stars, and believed the vision (Gen. 15:4–5; 18:18. The result was God had honored his faith and credited righteousness to his account (Gen. 15:6; 16:3; 17:1).

Jehovah was now calling him, at ninety-nine years of age, to a new walk. In this experience, the Lord wanted him to come fully into line with the vision God gave him, which would bring him to perfection in their covenant relationship (Gen. 15:3–4; 17:1; 18:8; Gal. 3:8–9; Rom. 4:3). The point is that Abraham had believed God years earlier, but he continued to lack total separation unto the ultimate destiny God had planned for him. To be set apart totally unto God, he had to become willing to give up Ishmael and cast his lot with his barren wife, and believe God for a miracle. Only then could the grand vision come true ultimately through the sacrifice of his Messiah, birthing a family of faith from all nations like the stars in the sky and the sand on the seashore (Gen. 15:4–5).

e) The Promise of Isaac

Amid this new revelation of circumcision, God promised the patriarch He would bless his ninety-year-old wife, Sarah, and give him "a son by her" (Gen. 17:16–17). Ishmael had been Sarah and Abraham's plan. Isaac, the gift from the Lord, was God's agenda. Abraham's very emotional response was to fall facedown and laugh, saying in his heart, "Will a son be born to a man a hundred years old? Will Sarah bear a child at the age of ninety?" (Gen. 17:17). It was clear that Isaac could come into the family only as a gift from Abraham's faithful God (Heb. 11:11). Little wonder Abraham fell facedown and laughed at the pronouncement.

Abraham's next realization was instinctively to understand the price tag: it would cost him Ishmael as his heir. So he pleadingly prayed, "If only Ishmael might live under your blessing" (Gen. 17:18). Abraham's full alignment with God's agenda came at the significant price of self-emptying his own plans and agenda, which included his firstborn son. It was Abraham's path of death.

> Then God said: "No, Sarah your wife shall bear you a son, and you shall call his name Isaac; I will establish my covenant with him for an everlasting covenant, and with his descendants after him. And as for Ishmael, I have heard you. Behold, I have blessed him, and will make him fruitful, and will multiply him exceedingly."
> —GENESIS 17:19–20, NKJV

God gave Abraham the promise of the birth of Isaac a second time that year when three men who were heavenly visitors came to him at Mamre to tell him about the pending destruction of Sodom and Gomorrah. This time Sarah "was listening at the entrance of the tent" (Gen. 18:11). When she heard the promise of the birth of Isaac from her dead womb, she laughed in her astonishment and then lied about her laughter. God's response was to confront her and then boldly say, "Is anything too hard for the Lord?" (Gen. 18:14).

Sarah did give birth to the child of promise, and Abraham appropriately named him Isaac, meaning "laughter" (Gen. 17:19; 21:1–3). A major flaw remained in the family, however. Abraham believed he could keep the two families united with Isaac and Ishmael under the same tent. This conclusion made the road bumpy for the next few years, but the course ahead was now clearly set that ultimately would lead to Messiah. Abraham knew God's agenda to fulfill the vision was Isaac and not Ishmael (Gen. 15:2–5). He had that much right. It was Abraham's coexistence strategy that was the fly in the ointment, and it made the journey ahead tense and emotionally unstable in his household (Eccles. 10:1, KJV).

f) Negotiating With God

The great struggle between the perfect walk in God's agenda by faith and the walk in man's own agenda presupposes futile negotiating with God and double-minded struggle (James 1:8, 4:8). For Abraham, the timeline continued until Isaac's weaning party, at least another three years. This part of the story illustrates that crucifixion of self normally is an agonizingly slow death. No one wants to release his solutions quickly, even when he knows the plan of faith is infinitely better. People serve the agenda of the world because they want to; it is their choice. Clearly, Abraham wanted to hold onto both boys, which meant he had conflicting loves in his life.

In this overall scenario, Sarah had mixed emotions that tore at her, too. One was fervent love for the covenant God had made with Abraham, which she embraced wholeheartedly. In fact, Sarah is one of the two women listed in the great Hall of Faith in Hebrews 11, because "she judged him faithful who had promised" (Heb. 11:11–12). (The other is Rahab.) Another passionate love that ran deeply in Sarah was jealousy for her husband's love and loyalty. In that swirl of family conflict, she was the first to recognize her husband's coexistence strategy could not continue. However, the two opposing loves remained a blind spot in her husband's mind.

g) Hagar's Influence

Even though Ishmael was growing up under Abraham's tent, his mother largely shaped his values, and she never adopted the covenant promises into her heart. Abraham's God was not the god Hagar worshiped. Her influence meant that Abraham would never be able to train Ishmael to fear God and embrace the covenant wholeheartedly. As for Sarah, she respected Abraham's God and enthusiastically embraced the covenant promises.

After Isaac, as the child of promise, had matured enough to have his weaning party, the predicament that had been brewing in the family for a long time finally came to a head. When Sarah saw Ishmael mocking her young son at his party, her patience ran out. The moment of truth had arrived (Gen. 21:8–9).

h) Separation as the Solution

Sarah's conclusion is one of the greatest lessons of the walk of faith for all children of God: "Get rid of that slave woman and her son, for that slave woman's son will never share in the inheritance with my son Isaac" (Gen. 21:10). Every child of God who wants to walk with the Lord must face the same moment of truth on his own path of death, because in some form there is at least one sinful entanglement in every person's life (Heb. 12:1). The solution that comes by faith and the human solution that comes by the works of the flesh cannot live together in the same house. Faith and works never coexist for long in the same heart. They will be in constant conflict until one overcomes the other (Rom. 12:1–2; Heb. 12:1).

Sarah misread the heart of God when she gave her bondwoman to Abraham to birth a surrogate child and heir (Gen. 16:2). She got it exactly right regarding what it would take to correct the problem. To her credit, she faced up to it before her husband did.

In this crisis experience, Abraham had to make a choice that was gut-wrenchingly painful, like a spiritual crucifixion. Would he try to hold onto Hagar, who had never accepted the covenant, and their son, Ishmael, whom the bondwoman so greatly influenced? Or, would he cast his lot with his loyal wife, who fully shared with him the promises of the covenant and who was already helping him train Isaac in its values? Would he work through his feelings for Ishmael and climb higher in trusting the God who called him out of Ur, the God who miraculously gave Isaac to him?

i) The Path of Death: Releasing Ishmael

Amid that sharp family crisis, Abraham squarely faced the price tag. (Forsaking one's love for the world always comes at a price and includes a decisive moment [see Gen. 21:10; 1 John 2:15].) "The matter distressed Abraham greatly" because it did concern "his son" (Gen. 21:11). Giving up Ishmael meant dying to the prospect of having in the family circle his firstborn son, who had been the apple of his eye for perhaps as many as eighteen years. Only the grace of God could motivate him willingly to release Ishmael from the family. Many centuries later the apostle Paul expressed it by saying, "Put to death, therefore, whatever belongs to your earthly nature" (Col. 3:5).

Sanctification is never solely a human work, however. First and foremost, it is a gift of God. "I am the Lord that doth sanctify you," God told Moses in a later generation (Exod. 31:13, kjv). The Lord did Abraham a big favor that night. He graciously appeared to him again amid this acute family crisis when his emotions were so torn and conflicted. The revelation was a loving reaffirmation of the disclosure that had come to him earlier in the covenant of circumcision (Gen. 17). This time, "God said to him, 'Do not be so distressed about the boy and your maidservant. Listen to whatever Sarah tells you, because it is through Isaac that your offspring will be reckoned. I will make the son of the maidservant into a nation also, because he is your offspring'" (Gen. 21:12–13).

Abraham needed to hear exactly that word of encouragement. It motivated him to make his decision to launch out on the wings of faith and believe God. Amid that crisis of dysfunctional family circumstances, his heart changed (Heb. 11:11). Right there Abraham latched onto the complete agenda of God for himself and his family. He chose to surrender Ishmael, and stake his claim on the promises of Jehovah God, with only Isaac in the tent. The love God poured extravagantly into his heart in that revelation was greater than the grief of what would be his loss in a few short hours (1 John 3:1).

Abraham made up his mind sometime before dawn to do what many parents have had to do through the centuries in dysfunctional family situations: surrender a child to find his own future in God. Abraham probably would never have found the strength to do it, but for God's gracious promise to make Ishmael into a great nation too. Abraham had to release Ishmael to his destiny and trust his firstborn to God. This meant that henceforward he was to embrace Isaac alone in his heart. God's love does indeed motivate people to make right choices.

Abraham experienced a death that night when he gave up Ishmael, but he broke forth shiningly with the dawn of the new day. It took him some years to get there, but with God working in him, motivating what he was willing to do, Abraham finally worked out God's will for his life (Phil. 2:12–13). At that point, he was set apart as a servant to a new and mature walk with God that pointed straight to the cross of Jesus via Bethlehem's manger. The result would be a host of followers who would share his faith and number like the stars in the sky and the sand on the seashore (Gen. 15:4–5; 18:18). From that crisis event forward, he was committed solely to God's character and agenda, but it took this new transfusion of the love of God to get him there.

This situation however, like a death, was surely not the last death he would die, because Abraham loved his firstborn son. The path of death continued in the weeks ahead, which turned into months and then into years. Abraham surely died many more deaths dealing with his loss of Ishmael.

Two millennia later, the apostle Paul said of His own walk with Abraham's Messiah, "I die every day" (1 Cor. 15:31). Paul understood fully this meant he would experience the most intense persecution, even facing wild beasts in the arena. His commitment motivated him daily to reaffirm his total fidelity to Jesus Christ (1 Cor. 9:24–27).

j) Separation as Self-Emptying

Abraham's story illustrates that walking with God presupposes willingness to give up and surrender one's personal wants, desires, and loves in order to be Christ's disciple. The life story of Abraham illustrates the separating grace of God that followed his experience of credited righteousness by faith (Gen. 15:6). The list that follows demonstrates some of the ways in which Abraham was required to empty himself for the sake of God's call. They show sanctification as both crisis and process, and the ongoing necessity of the path of death as the highway to success with God (Gen. 21:9–14; Gal. 4:21–31).

- God instructed Abraham to surrender his homeland in Ur of the Chaldees, including its lifestyle, and search for "the city with foundations, whose architect and builder is God" (Gen. 11:27–32; Matt. 19:27–30; Heb. 11:10).
- God required him to leave behind the fellowship of his brother, Nahor, in his march to Canaan (Gen. 11:27–12:1–5; Luke 14:26–33).
- It became necessary to surrender his nephew Lot, permitting him to make his own choices, even if that meant Lot would pitch his tent toward Sodom (Gen. 13:1–14:24; 18:1–19:38). Doing so was the final step in separating himself from his "kindred" (Gen. 12:1).
- Abraham surrendered his own body to God, submitting to the painful cutting of his flesh in circumcision (Gen. 17:23; Rom. 6:12–19; Heb. 12:1).
- He gave up Ishmael, his firstborn son, whom he loved and probably never saw again (Gen. 21:8–20). Ishmael did return for his father's funeral (Gen. 25:9).
- God asked Abraham to surrender Isaac on Mt. Moriah. In showing his willingness to do so, Abraham discovered the

great hope of the resurrection of the dead (Gen. 22:1–19; Heb. 11:19).

- He also had to surrender his beloved wife, Sarah, who had been very instrumental in living out the covenant as his life-long partner. Abraham buried her in the cave of Machpelah, the site of the city of Hebron (Gen. 23).

Abraham's life, therefore, illustrates the separating grace of God that followed his experience of credited righteousness by faith (Gen. 15:6). These self-emptyings show the ongoing necessity of the path of death as the highway to success with God (Gen. 21:9–14; Gal. 4:21–31). Abraham's journey is also a penetrating example to demonstrate how the love of God compels right choices (2 Cor. 5:14; Ps. 139:5).

Centuries later in His incarnation, Jesus Christ even surrendered the voluntary and independent exercise of His divine attributes, according to the kenosis principle.

When Abraham and Sarah died, they had only Isaac as evidence of the grand vision (Gen. 15:4–5). Forty-two generations later, in the time of the Lord, the writer of Hebrews summarized the marvelous advance of God's promise to Abraham: "from one man's dead and shriveled loins there are now people numbering into the millions" (Heb. 11:12 Msg). At the center of the vision is the power of the cross to redeem and restore all people, worldwide.

k) God's Grace Extended to Hagar

As for Hagar, the Egyptian maidservant, God was fair to her. For example, the angel of the Lord, as an Old Testament manifestation of Messiah, graciously appeared personally to her twice. Sarah never received even one personal and direct revelation of her Messiah. She was content to get her revelation of Jehovah through God's manifestations to her husband.

The first revelation to Hagar was in the wilderness of Shur, when she was running away from Sarah. Hagar recognized her visitor as *El-Roi*, meaning, "the God who sees me" (Gen. 16:13), but she only partially accepted His counsel to her, namely, "Go back to your mistress and submit to her" (Gen. 16:9). She went back, but her heart did not change.

If she had only embraced the covenant in her heart and believed the revelation of *El-Roi*! God really does watch over His word to perform it (Jer. 1:12, NAS). Submission to the Word of the Lord would have enabled her to become a faithful servant in Sarah's household. It would also have meant a life of luxury and comfort for her and her son in Abraham's family. The Messiah lovingly gave His attention to Hagar, but she was not willing to treasure the rich promise of the God who watched over her, nor was she willing to serve Sarah (Gen. 16:9).

When Abraham sent Hagar and Ishmael away that morning after the weaning party, it became Hagar's path of death, too. When their supply of water ran out, Hagar placed the crying teenager under some bushes about a bowshot away, saying, "'I cannot watch the boy die.' As she sat there nearby, she began to sob'" (Gen. 21:16). In this dire situation, the Messiah appeared to her again—on this occasion as the God who hears:

> God heard [*Elohim shama*] the boy crying, and the angel of God called to Hagar from heaven and said to her, "What is the matter, Hagar? Do not be afraid; God has heard the boy crying as he lies there. Lift the boy up and take him by the hand, for I will make him into a great nation." Then God opened her eyes and she saw a well of water. So she went and filled the skin with water and gave the boy a drink. God was with the boy as he grew up.
> —GENESIS 21:17–20

Ishmael's name means "God will hear" (Gen. 16:11). In this poignant scene that dripped with pathos, the revelation of God was that God hears the child whose name means "God hears."

The Messiah was with Hagar and could have made her situation fully redemptive. His promises to her were warm and reassuring, but she never gave unconditional trust to the God who heard her (*Elohim Shama*) and was watching over her (*El-Roi*). Nor was she willing to teach her son the true meaning of his own name, "God will hear." Instead, she continued to demonstrate lack of faith. A few years later, for example, she took a bride for Ishmael from Egypt (Gen. 21:21). Hagar has become a type for all ages, therefore, of the person who is determined to live a Messiah-rejecting life, no matter how often and how graciously God reveals Himself—even if He is standing in flesh and blood in front of them (John 18:14, 24; Acts 4:6–13; Matt. 13:13–15).

In a later generation, another foreigner, Ruth the Moabite, made what was by far the wiser choice. Ruth was an alien from the commonwealth of Israel, but she had a heart like Sarah, the mother of Israel. Ruth never received a personal revelation from Naomi's God, yet she chose the God of her mother-in-law and reaped abundant blessings as the result (Ruth 1:16–18; 4:13–22; Eph. 2:12–22).

Abraham had to eject Hagar from his tent for his family's survival. Even today, many people have secret sins, bondages, and strongholds in their lives that will ultimately destroy their families and their eternal souls, if not expelled in a radical spiritual deliverance on the path of death (Rom. 12:1–2; Heb. 12:1; Gal. 4:28–31; Matt. 8:16; Mark 3:13–15).

⊰ Living With Alligators ⊱

Kevin Garvey has a thriving business in Broward County, Florida. He is the only trapper licensed by the county to remove nuisance alligators. In 2000, he received 616 alligator complaints and removed 97 reptiles. As of the end of July 2001, he had already received over 1,500 complaints and caught 130 alligators.

The top spot in his county? Weston, a meticulously groomed, planned city. Seems the homeowners there, who spent up to $700,000 for their homes, did not expect nor appreciate giant reptiles in their idyllic new community.

"That's probably gator heaven out there," says Jim Huffstodt, a spokesman for the Florida Fish and Wildlife Conservation Commission, noting that Weston and other planned communities are often built right on top of the marshlands that were previously inhabited by the offensive reptiles. Just sighting an alligator in an area like Weston—filled with families with small children—is grounds for removal and destruction.

Such a story begs the question: How could anyone who moves into prime alligator habitat be surprised to see alligators there?

In the same way, why do so many Christians settle for lifestyles that invite trouble, then act surprised when they fall into sinful conduct?[2]

1) Why Abraham?

The question is appropriate: Why did God select Abraham when He could have called others who feared God in Abraham's day? Abraham was not the only man who honored God in his generation. One such worshiper, Melchizedek, was a righteous man who became the type of the high priesthood of Jesus Christ (Gen. 14:18; Ps. 110:4; Heb. 7:1, 15–17). Yet, God did not single out Melchizedek to birth the nation. Why did God hand pick Abraham, call him out of Ur of the Chaldees, and send him to Canaan?

God selected Abraham because He knew Abraham would commit to serve the Lord's whole agenda, and emerge as a teacher and example to succeeding generations. "I have chosen him," God said, "so that he may command his children and his household after him to keep the way of the LORD by doing righteousness and justice, so that the LORD may bring upon Abraham what He has spoken about him" (Gen. 18:19, NAS).

Abraham and Sarah surely comprehended how close they came to missing God's perfect plan. Growing out of their heartfelt gratitude for the persistent grace of God that brought them to commit to God's agenda, Abraham and Sarah determined to teach the child to believe God's covenant promises to Abraham.

The key to their success with Isaac and with succeeding generations, however, was not solely their outstanding example as great teachers who demonstrated complete faith in God. In succeeding generations, God disclosed Himself repeatedly in personal revelation to Abraham's descendents as well, to reconfirm the covenant, just as He had done to Abraham (Gen. 28:10–22; 31:3; Exod. 3; Josh. 1; 1 Sam. 17:26; 1 Kings 3:4–15).

These ongoing manifestations, coupled with Abraham and Sarah's great examples as effective teachers, assured success. Each generation of Abraham's descendants, in an unbroken chain of forty-two generations, effectively handed the covenant down to their children until Messiah came (Matt. 1:17).

m) The Father of the Faithful

It is appropriate to celebrate Abraham as a great man of faith. He should also receive honor as one of the greatest teachers of all time (Gal. 3:6–9). The dream had to be perfected in Abraham's own heart, however, before it could become reality in a set-apart walk with God.

This understanding helps to explain why Abraham earned the title *the father of the faithful* (Rom. 4:11–18). At a time of major crisis in his home, Abraham by faith paid the price to lock in perfectly on the agenda of God. He forsook his own plans and began walking blamelessly before God and His strategy, then reaffirmed that original decision many times in the years ahead (Gen. 17:1). It was this faith commitment that caused him to become the great example for all who would follow, to both Jews and Gentiles, of the righteousness of God that comes by faith (Rom. 4:13; Gal. 3:9, 14; 2 Cor. 5:21).

My lover is mine, and I am his.

—SONG OF SOLOMON 2:16

2. Moses

At a time when there was no way a budding nation of Hebrew slaves could escape the mud pits of Goshen, God raised up Moses, Israel's deliverer. He believed the promises of God were exceedingly more powerful than the armies of Egypt's pharaoh (Exod. 5:1). God honored Moses' faith, became His friend, and talked with him face to face (Exod. 33:11). The Lord did what the arm of flesh could not do. The victory was so complete God Himself said, "You yourselves have seen what I did to Egypt, and how I carried you on eagles' wings and brought you to myself" (Exod. 19:4).

On Mount Sinai Jehovah gave Moses the law that expressed the mission for the Hebrew nation: "You shall be my treasured possession, although the whole earth is mine: you will be for me a kingdom of priests, and a holy nation" (Exod. 19:5–6; Deut. 14:2). Also, "You are to be holy to me: because I the Lord am holy, and I have set you apart from the nations to be my own" (Lev. 20:26).

The Law of Moses included the sacrificial law, the moral law, and the civil law. The sacrificial law, to give one example, set forth the detailed specifications prescribed for celebrating the Passover (Num. 28:16–25). Looking back over the centuries of the sacrificial system through the lens of the Cross unveils this meticulous attention to detail. The sacrifices had to be offered exactly right because they were types that the death of Jesus Christ would fulfill (Heb. 8:5; Exod. 25:9, 40; Num. 8:4).

Based on the specifications God revealed to him, Moses constructed an elaborate system of worship anchored on the sacrificial law (Exod. 25:9; 26:30). He built it around priests and blood sacrifices of animals to demonstrate God's character to the nation and the relationship of the people to Him. The Israelites so bonded to the worship that for fifteen hundred years their lives revolved around priests who offered animal sacrifices, first in the tabernacle and later in the temple. The sacrificial law ended with the perfect sacrifice of Jesus Christ (Heb. 10:12–14).

The civil law embraced the many detailed statutes that governed Hebrew life (Exod. 21). The civil law was uniquely the constitution that guided the government of the Israelite people as a nation and is obviously not binding on believers today.

The national symbol of the moral law was the two tablets Moses brought down from the mountain, which contained the Ten Commandments, written with "the finger of God" (Exod. 20:1–17; 34:27–28; Deut. 9:10). God has never abrogated the moral law; it remains in force to this day. However, the Sermon on the Mount and the ethic based on the *agape* love of God do supersede it.

In this overall context, the concept of sanctification as *separation* had broad meaning as the culture and values of the Israelite people developed into nationhood. This was true even from the early days of the exodus from Egypt. The Lord instructed Moses to consecrate the people in anticipation of receiving the Law at Sinai (Exod. 19:10).

- That act of separation at Horeb (Sinai) was so thorough it even included the Israelites' washing their clothes (Exod. 19:19).
- The Levitical code taught Hebrew couples to set apart their firstborn children unto the Lord (Exod. 13:2; Num. 8:17).

- Faithful Hebrew parents circumcised their baby boys on the eighth day after birth, a ceremony that set them apart for life as Israelites (Lev. 12:3).
- The tabernacle and all its furnishings, and later the temple, were also set apart (Exod. 40:10–11; Num. 7:1; 2 Chron. 7:16).
- Moses' Law even required fathers in Israel to sanctify their houses (Lev. 27:14, 16).

Since this separation of the people was so all encompassing among the Hebrews, it surely follows today that a believer's personal separation from sin unto the Lord is the divine expectation. Should not this spiritual separation include home, fields, bank accounts, jobs, clothes, as well as our relationships, vehicles of transportation, entertainment, diet, and sexuality? Can a person have experienced this set-apart condition unto the Lord without that separation affecting all that he is, including all that is his?

With the passing centuries, however, the people came to trust more in the sacrifices they offered and the symbol circumcision cut into their bodies than they did their personal relationship of heart-and-soul love for God (Deut. 11:1; Jer. 4:4; John 7:22–24). It was a huge error, for Jehovah did not find His pleasure in the sacrificial system, but in them (Deut. 10:15–22; Heb. 10:6). *They* were His "treasured possession" (Exod. 19:5; 1 Sam. 15:22; Ps. 40:6; Hosea 6:6).

Be holy because I the Lord your God am holy.

—Leviticus 19:2

Sanctify yourselves, therefore, and be holy; for I am the Lord your God. And you shall keep my statutes, and do them: I am the Lord which sanctifies you.

—Leviticus 20:7–8, kjv

What value, then, was the sacrificial system? It pointed them to their Messiah, for the shed blood of every sacrifice was a schoolmaster directing Israel to His coming perfect sacrifice (Gal. 3:24; 5:6; Heb. 10:10, 14). Jesus Christ affirmed what Moses said in the Law. The first commandment was not to slay animals but to "love the Lord your God with all your heart, and with all your soul, and with all your mind" (Matt. 22:37; Deut. 6:5;11:1). In fact, circumcision pointed specifically to heartfelt love for God: "The Lord your God will circumcise your heart," Moses said, "and the hearts of your descendants, so that you may love him with all your heart, and with all your soul, and live" (Deut. 30:6; Isa. 1:10–17; Jer. 7:21–23; Micah 6:6–8; Amos 5:21–24; Rom. 4:10–16).

Viewed from this perspective, this separation in their hearts gave meaning to the outward symbols of their very inward holiness. Moses set apart the tribe of Levi, out of which came Aaron's holy priesthood. Aaron and all of his subordinate priests ministered in the holy tabernacle containing both the holy place and the most holy place (Exod. 26:33–34). Aaron and his successor high priests went annually into the most holy place to make atonement at the mercy seat before the Shekinah glory of God (Exod. 25:17–22; Lev. 16:34). The high priest walked to the mercy seat carrying a bowl of blood and wearing a golden headband that read, "Holiness to the Lord" (Exod. 28:36, KJV).

This holy nation set apart the seventh day as a holy day (Exod. 20:8). The people designated every seventh year as a holy year in which the very soil of their farms was to lie fallow, growing no crops (Lev. 25:4). The year following every seventh year of seven years (the fiftieth year) was to be a golden jubilee. In that year, Israelite owners of Hebrew slaves were to free them, and land mortgaged or sold returned to its ancestral owners (Lev. 25:8–13).

This call for a moral and social separation from the nations around them permeated the total Israelite lifestyle. It characterized all of their feast days, wedded them inseparably to their sacred Scriptures, overshadowed their military ventures, and shaped their daily routine in their homes and villages. Separation became their DNA as a people.

But there was a fatal flaw.

Twin injunctions summarized the spirit and attitude of the Law: "Love the lord your God with all your heart and with all your soul and with all your strength" and "love your neighbor as yourself" (Deut. 6:5; Lev. 19:18). Jesus Himself said, "All the Law and the Prophets hang on these two commandments" (Matt. 22:40). Hence, Moses recognized the law of love, but the priestly system never linked it inseparably to the blessing of credited righteousness by faith, expressed in Gen. 15:6. By Moses' day, the people were already anchored to the covenant of circumcision in Gen. 17. The sacrificial system with its many detailed requirements blended so easily with the list in the Ten Commandments that a works-based system of worship emerged (Gal. 3:17).

It would take the death of Israel's Messiah on the cross to reveal fully the love of God that brings salvation by grace through faith for the whole world (Gen. 15:4–6; Eph. 2:8–9).

3. King David

King David compounded his blatant sin of adultery with Bathsheba by a cold-blooded attempt to cover it up through the murder of her husband. "You are the man," Nathan the prophet told the backslidden king, forcing him to admit both adultery and murder. Then Nathan announced to David, "The sword will never depart from your house because you despised [the Lord]" (2 Sam. 12:7, 10).

David's petition in Psalm 51 reveals the need he felt for cleansing. He begged God for a two-fold blessing, asking for his transgressions to be blotted out and to be washed from the iniquity that motivated him to sin. David realized he needed to be purged as with hyssop (vv. 1, 7, 9). The king cried for inner cleansing from the wicked power of sin inside him: "Create in me a pure heart, O God, and renew a steadfast spirit within me" (v. 10). His prayer demonstrated he realized he had broken both God's laws and His heart. David felt deeply the estrangement in their relationship (v. 3). He sincerely wanted the joy of his salvation restored, and prayed for deliverance from the condition of inner sin in his heart that motivated his grievous sins (vv. 5, 12). In this crisis, David revealed the greatest fear in his life: that God might withdraw His Holy Spirit from him. He humbly pled with God: "Do not cast me from your presence or take your Holy Spirit from me" (v. 11). Instead, he asked God to grant him "a willing spirit," capable of sustaining him (v. 12).

The wayward king's plea touched the heart of God, for Nathan reported to David, "The LORD has taken away your sin. You are not going to die" (2 Sam. 12:13). As a result, God gave the truly repentant king not only forgiveness for his sins but also a heart that was again steadfast before the Lord.

Psalm 51 also shows that King David saw correctly the sacrificial system in divine focus. David admitted that God did not want animal sacrifices as atonement for his exceedingly sinful "old self." Rather, "the sacrifices of God are a broken spirit," David said (v. 17). The king knew God sought from him "a broken and a contrite heart" with "righteous sacrifices" (v. 19). David offered the whole burnt offering as a sacrifice to God, indicating how strongly he wanted that old power inside him turned to ashes, but it was David's shattered and repentant spirit that made the sacrifice acceptable before God (Ps. 51:19).

4. Isaiah

In the year that King Uzziah died, Isaiah the prophet went to the temple one day to pray. While there in worship, he saw a vision of the Lord sitting upon a lofty throne with His glory filling the temple. The seraphim of the angelic host stood above God's exalted seat, singing the heavenly anthem, "Holy, holy, holy is the Lord of hosts: the whole earth is full of his glory" (Isa. 6:3). It was a vision of the Sovereign in His royal kingship, a manifestation of Messiah that Isaiah could never forget. Such was the impact of the divine presence that the posts of the door moved, and "the temple was filled with smoke" (Isa. 6:4).

Standing in the divine presence amid the smoke of God's holiness caused Isaiah to see himself in his own imperfection. He cried, "'Woe to me!...I am ruined! For I am a man of unclean lips, and I live among a people of unclean lips, and my eyes have seen the King, the LORD Almighty'" (Isa. 6:5).

Obviously, Isaiah loved God before that experience, for he was already a prophet and had gone to the temple to seek God. In the presence of the universal King whom He saw sitting on His exalted throne while the angels sang, Isaiah realized that God's primary agenda was all about the Messiah who was to come. The vision made it very clear he needed to align his life to the same agenda that motivated the heart of God.

One of the seraphim then flew to Isaiah. The angel had "a live coal in his hand which he had taken with the tongs from off the altar: and he laid it upon [his] mouth, and said, 'Lo, this has touched your lips; and your iniquity is taken away, and your sin purged'" (Isa. 6:6–7, KJV). It is always true that the more we mature in God's holiness, the more lowly we feel. The closer we are to the light, the brighter our flaws and shortcomings glow.

"Whom shall I send and who will go for us?" Isaiah heard God ask. Little wonder the prophet answered with the deepest conviction, "Here am I; send me!" (Isa. 6:8).

Isaiah made a new commitment to the Lord of hosts amid that encounter, dedicating the remainder of his life to portraying the holiness of God about which the seraphim sang. The prophet never forgot the revelation of His Messiah, whom he saw sitting in such glory on that high throne (John 12:41).

Isaiah's experience in the temple is another expression of the blessing of separation unto God. The result was the prophet broke forth shiningly as the servant who expounded in his writings the clearest prophecies regarding the coming Messiah, the King, and Lord of hosts, whom he met in the temple. No prophet saw clearer than did Isaiah the first appearing of the Messiah as the suffering Servant, as well as His second advent as triumphant and universal King (Isa. 42–66). The book of Isaiah is akin to a fifth Gospel because of the accuracy and precision of his prophecies. Philip used just this "Gospel," for example, to preach Christ to the Ethiopian eunuch in the Gaza desert (Isa. 53:7–8; Acts 8:26–38).

B. The New Testament

1. Jesus Christ

Jesus lived in a relationship of obedient service to His Father, as superintended by the Holy Spirit. His life was always wholly set apart for fulfilling this specific mission.

a) The Pharisees, the "Separated Ones"

In contrast, the Pharisees (their name meant "the separated ones") lived set apart unto their external rules and regulations. Jesus judged harshly their peripheral holiness that cleaned the outside of the cup but left untouched the inner cup—the thoughts, motives, and intents of the heart (Matt. 23:25–26). Little wonder the Lord said to some Pharisees, "Go and learn what this means, 'I desire mercy, and not sacrifice'" (Matt. 9:13). The issues of life spring out of the heart, and the living and active Word of God is very capable of discerning inner thoughts and viewpoints (Heb. 4:12; Matt. 15:19; Mark 7:21).

b) Self-Emptying Sacrifice

The life of separation that Jesus lived calls His followers to a demanding discipleship (John 17:19). It requires a fundamental self-emptying of the values and ways of the "old self." A person then takes up his own cross, as a servant, to follow Jesus in a new lifestyle of self-denial. Many people in every generation, even among those who claim Jesus as Lord, have resisted strongly this high standard. The quest for a heart like Jesus is often misunderstood, yet the enabling love of God poured into the soul by the Holy Spirit is as extravagant as the benchmark is high (Rom. 5:5; 1 John 3:1).

⊰ Servant, a Dirty Word ⊱

On a cross-country flight, a lovely attendant graciously served me. Her pleasantness so impressed me that when she gave me a meal, I said to her, "Of all the great servants in the world, you are surely one of the best."

She pierced me with her eyes and said in a curt voice, "How dare you say that to me! I am no servant!" Then she stomped away.

Every time she served me after that, she exhibited the same abrupt attitude. Finally, overtaken by curiosity to know what caused her to respond that way, I asked her.

She replied, "A servant is the worst thing anyone could ever call me."

I responded by saying, "I'm a Christian. The one I love most in the world is Jesus Christ, and Scripture says He was the greatest servant who ever lived. Therefore, when I say 'servant,' I mean someone great. That's the highest of compliments!"

Her reaction showed me how misunderstood the term "servant" is in our society.[3]

c) Mary's Lavish Gift

The Christ, who has always been so profuse with sharing His love, found it lavished on Him when Mary broke the vase containing about a pint of pure perfume worth a year's wage. She poured it all on Jesus' feet, and then wiped His feet with her hair. The fragrance filled the whole house (John 12:1–8).

As generous as Mary's act was—so magnanimous that her story continues to this day to be told worldwide—her affection was minor compared to the abundant love God demonstrated on Calvary (Rom. 5:8; Eph. 2:4). Propelled by the magnitude of God's love, believers choose to live as the servants of Jesus Christ (Exod. 21:5). The bountiful love of God motivates them willingly to forsake houses, land, mother, father, wife, children, and even their own life. They freely make lifetime commitments to grow in the character of the Lord and to participate in His worldwide agenda. Without that dedication, Jesus said, you "cannot be my disciple" (Luke 14:26). The Lord did indeed set the bar that high and called on His followers to count the cost (Luke 14:28; Matt. 16:24; 19:21). The compelling force of the abundant love of God is what makes achieving it possible (John 8:34–36; Rom. 8:38–39; 2 Cor. 13:14; Titus 3:4–5).

Jesus requires of people only what He willingly did Himself. His copious love "wherewith He loved us" motivated Him to condescend voluntarily to men of no reputation and pay the price of crucifixion to redeem them (Eph. 2:4–10; Phil. 2:7). This explains His response to His critics, who indicted Him for claiming to be God. "What about the one whom the Father set apart as his very own and sent into the world?" Jesus asked them. "Why then do you accuse me of blasphemy because I said, 'I am God's Son?'" (John 10:36).

d) Adopting Jesus' Attitude

The essence of sanctifying grace is for a believer to embrace the mind of Christ as his own (Gal. 4:19). With Jesus Christ, implicit trust in His Father framed His mindset and lifestyle (Phil. 2:5–6). Sanctifying grace produces in God's children dedication to the same trust, in a life set apart unto God's character and agenda.

2. Paul

A radical change in Paul's very nature took place after his Damascus road experience, so sweeping, in fact, that he became a new man. Until that time, he had understood his mission in life as creating havoc against anyone who was a follower of the Way (Acts 9:2, 21). After the revelation he received on the Damascus Road, He committed himself as a "servant of Christ Jesus," and for the remainder of his life understood himself as "set-apart unto the gospel of God" (Rom. 1:1). The job description Jesus gave Paul was to open the eyes of people everywhere, turning "them from darkness to light and from the power of Satan to God" (Acts 26:18). He was to motivate them to "receive forgiveness of sins and a place among those who are sanctified by faith in

[Christ]." The change in Paul was immediate: "At once he began to preach in the synagogues that Jesus is the Son of God" (Acts 9:20).

Paul's first letter to the church in Corinth addressed "those sanctified in Christ Jesus and called to be holy, together with all those everywhere who call on the name of our Lord Jesus Christ—their Lord and ours" (1 Cor. 1:2). The apostle taught the Corinthians that Jesus Christ is the One "who of God is made unto us wisdom, and righteousness and sanctification and redemption" (1 Cor. 1:30, KJV). "May God himself, the God of peace, sanctify you through and through," was Paul's prayer for his readers at Thessalonica (1 Thess. 5:23).

Paul's farewell discourse to the Ephesian brethren, given before he left them to go to the Feast of Pentecost at Jerusalem, shows that the apostle did in fact live up to his job description. "Now I commit you to God," Paul said, "and to the Word of his grace, which can build you up, and give you an inheritance among all those who are sanctified" (Acts 20:32). This use of the phrase, *are sanctified,* is translated from the Greek word *hagiasmenois,* which indicates a present condition resulting from a past action of having been set-apart.

Paul taught the Christians at Thessalonica that set-apart living was the will of God for them. This experience would enable each of them to "learn how to control his body in a way that is holy and honorable... for God did not call [them] to be impure, but to live a Godly life (1 Thess. 4:4, 7). He also prayed for them that this work of grace would be comprehensive: "May God himself, the God of peace, sanctify you through and through. May your whole spirit, soul and body be kept blameless at the coming of our Lord Jesus Christ. The one who calls you is faithful and he will do it" (1 Thess. 5:23–24).

Paul wrote to the Colossians that they were "reconciled in the body of [Jesus'] flesh through death," that Christ might "present you holy, and unblameable, and unreprovable in his sight." This would be achieved in them, he said, if they continued "in the faith, grounded and settled," and did not move "away from the hope of the gospel" (Col. 1:22–23, KJV).

When a believer yearns by faith for this kind of moral commitment, the Lord will surely be there for him, as he was with Abraham at his separation from Ishmael. He will experience a breakthrough as a new man in Christ Jesus.

3. The General Epistles

The writer to the Hebrews said that the purpose for which Jesus so shamefully "suffered outside the city gate" was "to make the people holy through his own blood" (Heb. 13:12). Hebrews 10:14 records that "by one sacrifice he has perfected [set-apart] forever those that are being made holy" [those in the process of being set-apart]. This passage teaches the initial event of set apart living ("he has perfected"), and assumes a lifetime process of growth in the holiness of the Lord ("those...being made holy"), as a believer increasingly bears the fruit that models the character of God.

The apostle Peter taught this same life of separation when he called on his readers "as obedient children," not to fashion themselves "according to the former lusts in your ignorance." Rather, "as he which has called you is holy [set apart], so be holy [separated] in all manner of conversation; because it is written, Be holy, for I am holy" (1 Pet. 1:14–16). He also taught them in their hearts to "set apart Christ as Lord" (1 Pet. 3:15). This is an explicit call for his readers to make a determined decision to walk away from the old habits of worldly living. It results in a separation that increasingly duplicates the Lord's own lifestyle, which was totally dedicated to His Father's agenda.

In his second epistle, Peter identified at least one of the motives that should inspire men to forsake the old life and commit to the Lord.

> The Lord is...patient with you, not wanting anyone to perish, but everyone to come to repentance. But the day of the Lord will come like a thief. The heavens will disappear with a roar; the elements will be destroyed by fire, and the earth and everything in it will be laid bare. Since everything will be destroyed in this way, what kind of people ought you to be? You ought to live holy and godly lives as you look forward to the day of God and speed its coming.
> —2 PETER 3:9–11

Peter focused here on a negative motivation for holy living (fear of coming judgment). Terrifying dread of the great judgment day should be a primary motivation to live a mature Christian lifestyle. No man in his right mind wants to spend eternity totally removed from God's presence in a burning hell (Luke 16:23). The Lord Himself taught Peter and the other apostles to "be always on the watch, and pray that you may be able to escape all that is about to happen, and that you may be able to stand before the Son of Man" (Luke 21:36).

The apostle John beautifully expressed the positive motivation: "Dear friends," said John, "since God so loved us, we also ought to love one another" (1 John 4:11). Such love will demonstrate of a truth that "God lives in us," with the result that "his love is made complete in us" (1 John 4:12). The positive motivation for this perfect love in the lifestyle of a believer is explicitly this: "We love him, because he first loved us" (1 John 4:19).

III. The Call to Maturity

A. Loving as Jesus Loved, With Circumcised Hearts

It should not be surprising that Jesus issued the command in the Sermon on the Mount, "Be perfect, therefore, as your heavenly Father is perfect" (Matt. 5:48). In very similar language, God called Abraham to maturity, too, and he found it (Gen. 17:1; 21:10–14).

Jesus was merely calling on His followers to duplicate the implicit trust and commitment to His Father and His agenda with which Jesus Himself lived. Flowing out of the *agape* love of God, holiness is God's nature. Not only is God perfect in both His essence and His attributes, "He is the Rock" whose "works are perfect." He is "a faithful God who does no wrong; upright and just is He" (Deut. 32:3–4). It follows, therefore, that a believer would also want to love people as Jesus loved them and serve their best interests as He served. Such a lifestyle is vital to working out one's salvation successfully (Phil. 2:12).

God calls men to Himself, to the perfection of His own essence. No middle ground is possible here, for God can only call people to what He is in His own Being. To do less is for the Lord to compromise His own holiness and impeach His own character.

How is this standard possible? Moses focused the answer when he said, "The Lord your God will circumcise your hearts, and the hearts of your descendants, so that you may love him with all of your heart and soul, and live" (Deut. 30:6). The whole objective of this circumcision of the heart (or of this "discipline," as the writer of Hebrews expresses it), is to conquer the old self so "that we may share in his holiness" (Heb. 12:10). In fact, Peter affirmed these "very great and precious promises" have come that "you may participate in the divine nature" (2 Pet. 1:4).

B. The Fruit of the Spirit

The Holy Spirit produces only holy fruit in the believer's life: "love, joy, peace, longsuffering, gentleness, goodness, faith, meekness, and self-control" (Gal. 5:22–23, KJV). No ethnic group makes laws against these. For this fruit to grow and mature, however, a qualitative change must occur in a person's inmost being, his "old self." Paul taught the believers at Rome that their "old self," or their old nature, "was crucified," bringing "a decisive end to that sin-miserable life." Hence, they were "no longer at sin's every beck and call" (Rom. 6:6, THE MESSAGE).

We can only conclude that God wants His people to mature as new men to the level of thorough soundness in Christ; in fact, He commands just that kind of servant commitment. The requirements placed on Abraham may have seemed impossible to him, but with the motivation of the lavish love of God, they were not. God's help made it possible for Abraham to fix fully on the plan of redemption that would come through Isaac, and not Ishmael.

C. Working Out One's Salvation

In sanctification, therefore, a believer "works out [his] salvation with fear and trembling," and walking the path of death is vital to its success (Phil. 2:12). A child of God must surrender his way in a spiritual death and burial (the old self); only then can he experience resurrection with a new willingness to walk in the Lord's way. When the old man loses control, Jesus becomes the Lord of his life, and this new Lordship permeates the many "thrones" or seats of power in his life. These include, among others:

- his money,
- sex life,
- devotional life,
- family life,
- church life,
- work life,
- recreational life,
- his possessions,
- generational bondages,
- and his sinful habits.

In each of these areas of influence, when the old self is dethroned, the salt of sanctifying grace seasons the lives of God's children. Therefore, the sons of God experience through Christ the end result of faith, "the salvation of [their] souls" (1 Pet. 1:9).

Little wonder we say of Jesus, "My lover is mine and I am his" (Song of Sol. 2:16).

The Scriptures give many word pictures that help comprehend set-apart living. It is to several of them that we now turn our thoughts.

ILLUSTRATIONS OF
SET-APART LIVING

When Christ calls a man, He bids him come and die.
—DIETRICH BONHOEFFER

Put to death, therefore, whatever belongs to your earthly nature.
—COLOSSIANS 3:5

You have stolen my heart...with one glance of your eyes.
—SONG OF SOLOMON 4:9

I. The Compelling Love of Christ

A. The Love of God—the Bedrock of the New Covenant

When people cry out to God in prayer, the Lord pours "his love into [their] hearts by the Holy Spirit, whom he has given [them]" (Rom. 5:5; 1 John 4:8, 16). Because "love does no wrong to anyone," it follows that "love satisfies all of God's requirements" (Rom. 13:10, NLT). This is true because love contains its own capacity to motivate, making it a magnet infinitely more powerful as an encourager than fear. The love of God, therefore, is the bedrock of the new covenant (Mark 12:30–31; Luke 22:20; Ps. 32:3; Jer. 31:31). God's love actually penetrates the arena of the inner drives of the heart and liberates the soul (John 8:36; 2 Cor. 3:18; Gal. 5:1).

~𝒞 The Power to Change
Blossoms in Relationship 𝒞~

The more you love something, the more you become like it.

For example, I have a friend that loves tennis. He wears tennis stuff. He reads tennis magazines. He does tennis talk. He has a racket, and his hair looks like a tennis ball. I have another friend that loves surfing. He dresses with surf stuff, and he reads surf magazines. He does surf talk. He's even starting to smell like seaweed. Everything about him is going that way.

But isn't it true whatever you love, you start moving toward? Some of you love food. Case closed on that one.

That's why the Bible says the greatest commandment of all is to love the Lord your God with all your heart, with all your soul, with all your mind, and with all your strength. That is the greatest commandment. Why? Because the power to change is given in relationship, and what you love you become like.[1]

B. The Conflict between the Sinful Nature and the Spirit

Paul's enemies reacted negatively to his understanding of the love of God (Gal. 5:14). They accused Paul of being against having any laws (antinomianism) because he taught the Law of Moses had no ability to create a new man with a redeemed willpower capable of growing in the righteousness of God (Gal. 5:13–25).

> The old sinful nature loves to do evil, which is just opposite from what the Holy Spirit wants. And the Spirit gives us desires that are opposite from what the sinful nature desires. These two forces are constantly fighting each other, and your choices are never free from this conflict.... But when you are directed by the Holy Spirit, you are no longer subject to the law.... When the Holy Spirit controls our lives, he will produce this kind of fruit in us: love, joy, peace, patience, kindness, goodness, faithfulness, gentleness, and self-control. Here there is no conflict with the law. Those who belong to Christ Jesus have nailed the passions and desires of their sinful nature to his cross and crucified them there.
> —GALATIANS 5:17–18, 22–24, NLT

Paul spoke to this same theme when he wrote to the believers in Rome, "You can not go wrong when you love others." This is true because "when you add up everything in the law code, the sum total is love" (Rom. 13:10, THE MESSAGE; Gal. 5:18).

The thief on the cross, for example, certainly did not gain Paradise based on his good works. Instead, Jesus loved him and did him the big favor of crediting His own righteousness to him. The Lord did it solely because the dying man pled for help and believed Jesus could and would remember him when He came into His kingdom (Luke 23:39–43).

Paul's critics, however, were convinced the apostle was undercutting the whole foundation for ethics and morality by not requiring his converts to keep the Law. How would a person know what God expects, they reasoned, if he did not have the catalog of prescriptions and proscriptions in the Law to guide him? Without those lists, the result would be raw anarchy and lawlessness (Acts 15:5; Rom. 7:6, THE MESSAGE; Gal. 3–5). The model Paul's critics used was to diligently study the Law, make a list of its do's and don'ts, and then strive to keep everything in the catalog. But James wrote, "whoever keeps the whole law and yet stumbles at just one point is guilty of breaking all of it" (James 2:10–11; Col. 2:21–22). It was an impossible standard; their own spiritual leaders could not do it (Acts 7:53; 15:10).

Man in the pride of his human nature believes he works for what he gets in life. He reasons, if that is true on his job where he makes a living, it must also be true in the realm of the Spirit. Paul comprehended that the regulations in the Law actually point to that conclusion. This happens because the precepts of the Law do "indeed have an appearance of wisdom, with their self-imposed worship, their false humility, and their harsh treatment of the body. But they lack any value in restraining sensual indulgence" (Col. 2:23).

II. Breaking the Domination of the Old Man of Sin

When Paul studied the cross, however, He discovered a new model. Jesus loved His Father and lived with an attitude of implicit trust in Him (Phil. 2:5). By that standard, He triumphed over the flesh on His cross and broke the supremacy of sin. Jesus' triumphant cry while nailed to the tree, "It is finished," rings with a victorious note of success and finality (John 19:30). Sin never conquered Jesus (John 8:46; 1 Pet. 2:22).

But what about Jesus' followers, who have an inherited sin nature and struggle with an addiction to sin? How does the gospel birth in them a new will that can say "No!" to sin and actually walk away? It is a fair question.

⊰ Killing the Spider ⊱

"After I was saved I found some things in my heart not right," the young lady said in her testimony. The analogy she used was captivating.

"There seemed to be cobwebs in the corners. I used to sweep them out by watchfulness and prayer; but they would come again. For some time I kept on sweeping out the cobwebs, only to find them soon reappear.

"But one day the Lord came and killed the spider; and there have been no cobwebs in my heart since."[2]

People walk to the cross with all of their "cobwebs"—their baggage and bondages, their weights, and besetting sins. This condition includes the many corrupted dominions of their lives. They also come to Christ with a "spider" inside them, the old self, who continually weaves his controlling web around their hearts.

In the new birth, a person experiences forgiveness of his sins in a lavish display of the love of God. Sanctifying grace breaks the dominion of the old self by giving man a redeemed will, thus making it possible to bring the many jurisdictions of a person's life under the lordship of Jesus Christ. This is what "work[ing] out your salvation with fear and trembling," is all about, "for it is God who works in you to will and to act according to his good purpose" (Phil. 2:12–13).

This study will present six biblical illustrations, each of which portrays the same biblical truth. Four of the six come from the book of Romans.

- A fruit-bearing tree
- The profound mystery of marriage
- Baptism with Christ
- Crucifixion and resurrection
- Slavery
- The law of remarriage after the death of a spouse

A. A Fruit-Bearing Tree

Jesus used a word picture drawn from nature that explains the universal problem of inbred sin. Since thorn bushes do not produce figs and briers do not bear grapes, all people bear fruit according to the "tree" that is growing in them (Luke 6:43–45). The question becomes, how can the old, diseased tree in the heart be uprooted and a new and healthy one planted?

The solution required the Messiah's love, expressed by making Himself the perfect sacrifice (Heb. 5:7–10; 7:28; 10:12–14). Jesus took my:

- fear, by showing He was not afraid of the cross (John 10:18).
- guilt, by making Himself my guilt offering (Isa. 53:10; Heb. 10:19–22).
- shame, by hanging on three crude spikes, probably without even a cloth to cover His loins and give Him a scrap of dignity (Heb. 12:2)

Because we are crucified with Christ and resurrected with Him, we can appropriate the provision He made for uprooting the old tree of inbred sin, replacing the corrupted will with the new fruit tree that can choose to enter into Christ's righteousness (Matt. 12:33; Gal. 2:20–21). "For those who mourn" in Zion, He gives "beauty for ashes, the oil of joy for mourning, and the garment of praise for the spirit of heaviness. They are called trees of righteousness, the planting of the Lord, that he might be glorified" (Isa. 61:3, KJV). This marvelous gift calls for a profound response of gratitude—and we become like what we love.

The apostle Paul never admonished his readers to get right by following a list of do's and don'ts. Instead, he preached the cross of Christ, which gave them a fresh start (1 Cor. 1:23–30, KJV). The Lord delights for all of His children to rest in the liberty He purchased with His own blood (Rom. 5:9; Gal. 5:1; Rev. 5:9). The love of the Father makes the transformation happen through the Word of God (John 17:17). In fact, love never fails to encourage people to make the free choice to grow the new "tree" joyfully (1 Cor. 13:8).

B. The Profound Mystery of Marriage

Paul used the covenant of marriage to portray the relationship between Christ and His church and spoke of it as a "profound mystery" (Eph. 5:32). An insightful truth of the Christian message is that the marriage vows themselves illustrate how identification with the love of Jesus Christ, as expressed in the gift of His precious blood, is a call to walk the path of death.

⚜ The Marriage Vows ⚜

(*Wilson Wayne McWilliams*), will you take (*Sue Ellen Wilson*) to be your lawfully wedded wife, to live together after God's ordinance in the holy estate of matrimony? Will you love her, comfort her, honor, and keep her in sickness and in health; and forsaking all others, keep thee only unto her, so long as you both shall live? ("I will.")

I, (*Wilson*) take you (*Sue*) to be my wedded wife, to have and to hold, from this day forward; for better for worse, for richer for poorer, in sickness and in health, to love and to cherish, till death do us part, according to God's holy ordinance; and this I pledge in full faith.

The applications that follow of the profound mystery show how the love of God, expressed in the sacrifice of Jesus, breaks the hegemony of the old self. The result is a wonderful new life in Christ.

In the special moment when the eyes of two young lovers connect heart to heart in courtship, the recognition blossoms with a heartfelt sense of knowing that they have finally found their "one and only"—each for the other. But they also must face the price tag of love: *death* must occur to all old suitors and explicit trust must blossom in each other. Freely releasing these prior affections often comes easily, but this death can also require time and include frustration (a previous lover may even struggle fiercely to hang on). But when love is genuine, those old flames of courtship always rapidly burn out and trust blossoms.

The analogy fits the blessing of sanctifying grace. A believer's spirit bonds with the heart of Jesus at Calvary, where his Lord died and three days later arose from the grave *for him*. When that realization blossoms, the old self with its affections quickly fades into the background. Now a person wants the new freedom that comes with loving one person, Jesus Christ. The spark of love actually develops into a new flame, deep and passionate. This love, therefore, terminates the rule and control of yesterday's inferior relationships (the old self and its bondages), and a new life of trust emerges.

The marriage in which both do not empty themselves and die to all former interests and affections, letting those old flames expire and then burying them, will surely not survive.

- Jesus said, "A man will leave his father and mother and be united to his wife, and the two will become one flesh. So they are no longer two, but one" (Mark 10:7–9; Gen. 2:24). A couple that builds a successful marriage must not only "die" to all former suitors; they must also separate from their parents and their siblings—the people who love them the most. They make the choice to walk away from the childhood relationships of home, never to return to that same connection, in order to build their own family. They are called on to "die" to what has been so right—the blessing and security of their home, with all the benefits and provisions of parental love.

  Jesus issued a call to a set-apart life that actually embraces many separations. In fact, He was very explicit: "Anyone who comes to me but refuses to let go of father, mother, spouse, children, brothers, sisters—yes, even one's own self!—can't be my disciple. Anyone who won't shoulder his own cross and follow behind me can't be my disciple" (Luke 14:26–27, THE MESSAGE; see also Gen. 21:10–14).

- At a specific moment in the ceremony, each young adult says before God and each other, "I do!" Then they live for the remainder of their lives the results of that covenant. Included in the vow is a commitment to "keep thee only unto her so long as you both shall live." This vow also assumes a willingness to die in the years ahead to all would-be attractions and to find total fulfillment for life in the arms of each other. In a good marriage, a couple will resist all temptations to infidelity, present and future. In this way a husband's love for his wife makes her holy and keeps her clean (Eph. 5:26–27). That same love also preserves his integrity.

So many examples exist of true fidelity in forty, fifty, and even sixty-year marriages that none should doubt such marriages are possible. Why doubt that sanctifying grace also produces its intended fruit?

In sanctification, the Lord demands ownership of all that we are and have, in a lifetime of implicit trust and commitment, with no rivals. In this relationship, a believer at a specific time and place pledges his fidelity to Jesus Christ, having only one Savior. He chooses for the remainder of his life to love His Lord and trust Him completely.

Jesus is forever the faithful lover who steals his heart (Song of Sol. 4:9). It is in this context that the Bible is a romance, an ageless love story, in which the bridegroom purchases His bride with His own blood. One day He will present her unto Himself, a glorious church that has no spots or blemishes (Eph. 5:27).

- Marriage requires surrender, a death to one's treasures, time, and personal rights, and a resurrection that embraces as a servant the needs of one's spouse. Anything less is a flawed union. In the set-apart life, a child of God surrenders to Jesus Christ his time, talents, and his need for pleasure, as well as his pocketbook, his dreams, and his personal rights.

- Marriage is "for better or for worse, for richer or for poorer, in sickness and in health, 'til death do us part." In the same way, a set-apart believer embraces going where Jesus wants him to go, living where Jesus wants him to live, and doing and saying what Jesus wants. It even includes suffering unto death for Christ's sake. The call to holiness is truly a call to die. As a husband who loves his wife willingly embraces suffering, even death, for her sake, so a sanctified believer will joyfully embrace hardship and even lay down his life for his Lord.

- The covenant partners in a successful marriage work at conquering a self-centered lifestyle. As their mutual bond matures, they find themselves actually enjoying helping to meet the needs and life goals of each other. In sanctification, a believer sincerely delights to grow in the mind of Christ. He wants Christlikeness in all spheres of his life, including joyfully co-laboring with the Lord in His worldwide vision (Acts 1:8). In fact, he loves doing it!

- In an ever-maturing marriage, it is normative for a couple over time to become so alike, they actually seem to favor physically. In the sanctified lifestyle, the more a child of God gazes on the Lord he loves, the more he begins to look like the Lord's character (2 Cor. 3:18).

- A marriage must be based on commitment, not on emotions. The love that achieves this blooms out of repeated choices. A married couple learns quickly that moods deceive; couples do not always feel "in love." They go forward with the conviction that love is a choice. They choose to trust and remain committed, even when they are not living hand to hand and heart to heart. Commitment sustains marriages; dependence on feelings destroys them.

In sanctification, a person learns as an act of faith to "put on love" and not "lose heart," no matter how rough the road (Matt. 25:19–23; Col. 3:14; 2 Cor. 4:16; Rev. 2:10). Holiness of heart and life is never perpetuated based on feeling the presence of God, but by a believer's faith that chooses to believe and adore the Bridegroom. A follower of Jesus makes a decision and repeatedly reaffirms his response to the Lord's lavish love expressed at Calvary. He walks by faith and not by sight, even when doubts, thorns, and uncertainties litter his path (2 Cor. 5:7; Heb. 6:8).

C. Come Die with Me—Four Illustrations in Romans

"Unless a kernel of wheat falls to the ground and dies," Jesus taught, "it remains only a single seed. But if it dies, it produces many seeds. The man who loves his life will lose it, while the man who hates his life in this world will keep it for eternal life" (John 12:24–26).

The death of Jesus Christ had intensely personal implications in the thinking of the apostle Paul. For example, the crucifixion of Jesus meant Jesus actually took Paul's sins and his sin nature to the cross. Paul's affinity with Jesus' death was just that close. It also meant Paul personally identified with Jesus' triumph. When the apostle wrote, "I have been crucified with Christ," it was a passionately individual association (Gal. 2:20). When Jesus conquered sin and Satan on the cross, this sense of personal linkage meant Paul conquered sin and Satan, too. Then, when Jesus came out of the grave on the third day, Paul accepted at face value that he was resurrected with Christ to a victorious new life over the power of sin: "*I* have been crucified with Christ," Paul said, "and *I* no longer live, but Christ lives in me. The life *I* live in the body, *I* live by faith in the Son of God, who loved *me* and gave himself for *me*" (Gal. 2:20, emphasis added).

A student of the Scriptures must comprehend the close affinity Paul felt with the crucifixion and resurrection of Jesus, or he will probably stumble trying to understand Paul's word pictures. In addition, only as a child of God today accepts the Lord's invitation and walks his own path of death, making the same personal identification with the cross and resurrection of Jesus, will he experience personal triumph.

Chapters 1–3 of the book of Romans establish the universal need for justification in the hearts of all men. Romans 4 and 5 illustrate the universal solution of justification and its fruits, using the Old Testament examples of Abraham and King David. Romans 6 and 7 provide Paul's logical follow-through on these teachings by illustrating the experience of the set-apart life. "What shall we say, then?" Paul asked. "Shall we go on sinning so that grace may increase? By no means! We died to sin. How can we live any longer in it?" (Rom. 6:1–2). In Paul's reasoning, since Jesus died to sin, Paul died to sin too, because both his sins and his sin nature, his corrupted willpower, were there on Jesus' heart when the Lord made the sacrifice.

Paul gave four graphic examples to show that the love of God revealed in Jesus' bloody sacrifice broke the dominance of sin that is inherited from Adam.

1. baptism into Christ's death
2. crucifixion and resurrection
3. slavery
4. the law of remarriage after a spouse's death

In this study, the second of these will receive the most attention. These analogies demonstrate how two streams merge into a marvelous river of triumph in a believer's life—what God does in sanctification and what man does (Exod. 31:13 KJV; Lev. 20:7–8; 1 Pet. 3:15). What Jesus did is die on the cross in our place. What man does is get on the cross with Him through identification with His death. The love of God blends these two waterways into one. When a person gazes at Jesus on the cross, he realizes that only the magnanimous love of God motivated Jesus Christ to die the death he should have died. The only reasonable response is to say, as King Solomon did to his beloved, "You have stolen my heart... with one glance of your eyes, with one jewel of your necklace" (Song of Sol. 4:9; see also 2 Cor. 3:8; Rom. 5:5–8).

1. Baptism into Christ's Death (Rom. 6:1–4)

Baptism is Paul's first word picture in Romans to portray the grace that breaks the control of the old self and births set-apart living. "Don't you know," Paul asked, "that all of us who were baptized into Christ Jesus were baptized into his death?" (Rom. 6:3; Col. 2:12). What a deeply sobering truth: the death of Jesus is the "water" into which God's love immerses His children. How can anyone experience baptism in Christ's blood without being changed for life?

When the Lord said while on His cross, "It is finished," it summarized in a brief sentence the victory over sin that was so absolute for Him (John 19:30). Paul proceeded to apply what Christ's triumph means for the believer: "We were...buried with him through baptism into death in order that, just as Christ was raised from the dead through the glory of the Father, we too may live a new life" (Rom. 6:4). With the great apostle, identification with Christ's death and resurrection was indeed just that personal.

For this reason, Paul described in this word picture a qualitative inner change having two dimensions. First, baptism into Christ's death meant Paul's old self went with Jesus to the cross, where the river of Jesus' blood washed Paul's sin nature down the crimson stream, breaking the domination of Paul's old self over his life. The second word picture that flows out of baptism is resurrection— coming up out of the water with Christ, washed and clean and set apart with a new willpower that can choose to live in freedom in Christ (Rom. 6:5).

The change takes place by grace through faith, as the Holy Spirit pours Christ's love into the hearts of the sons of God (Rom. 5:5; 8:15). This love applies the atoning power of the blood of Jesus and motivates a response of lifelong fidelity (Rom. 5:21; 1 Cor. 1:30).

❧ Dr. Godbey Has It ❧

"A preacher came to me," said Uncle Bud Robinson, "and asked me if I had ever seen anyone who was sanctified, stating that he did not believe anyone had it."

I said, "Yes, Dr. Godbey has it."

"How do you know he has it?"

"By the way he acts," I answered.

"How does he act?"

"Well," I said, "they cussed him on the street, and he did not talk back; and they broke stale eggs all over him, and he did not even wipe them off; and when he went to preach, he did not even mention the way he had been treated; but he just preached and shouted as if nothing had happened."

"I would say a man like that is crazy."
"No, he's not crazy; he's sanctified."[3]

2. Crucifixion and Resurrection (Rom. 6:6–14)

This portrait is another vivid illustration of how the triumph of the cross results in a life of separation from the power of sin.

> Could it be any clearer? Our old way of life was nailed to the cross with Christ, a decisive end to that sin-miserable life—no longer at sin's every beck and call! What we believe is this: If we get included in Christ's sin-conquering death, we also get included in his life-saving resurrection. We know that when Jesus was raised from the dead it was a signal of the end of death-as-the-end. Never again will death have the last word. When Jesus died, he took sin down with him, but alive he brings God down to us. From now on, think of it this way: Sin speaks a dead language that means nothing to you; God speaks your mother tongue, and you hang on every word. You are dead to sin and alive to God. That's what Jesus did.
>
> —Romans 6:6–11, The Message

a) The Identification Principle

Of course, a twenty-first-century believer who yearns to mirror the attitude and agenda of the Lord cannot physically get on the cross with Jesus. The word picture is a powerful portrayal, however, of how identification with Christ by grace through faith achieves a personal crucifixion and yields a set-apart lifestyle.

The Lord did not go to Calvary to conquer His own old self, because He had no sin (2 Cor. 5:21). Instead, He died to make it possible to deposit His love in His followers (2 Cor. 1:22). He actually took my sin nature to the cross and paid my death penalty (Col. 2:13–14). This kind of love really is life changing, because Jesus as the second Adam carried on His heart at Calvary the sin nature of every son of the first Adam (1 Cor. 15:45).

A believer experiences the Lord's victorious death because Jesus was his substitute. He perceives in Christ's death, as he identifies with the horrors of Golgotha, both the magnitude of the love of God and the heinous nature of his old self (Isa. 52:14; Rom. 6:6; 8:39; Col. 3:9). As a result, he experiences the unfathomable grace of God, expressed in Jesus' death for whosoever will (Eph. 1:6–7).

In the same way that a person unites or identifies with Jesus in the suffering that resulted in His death, He also unites or identifies with Him in the triumph of His resurrection.

b) Ending the Domination of the Old Self

When this identification takes place, it is always loaded with emotion. A father who loses his teenager in a tragic hunting accident, for example, will relive the circumstances often and in detail, and deeply wish he could have died in his son's place. In the same way, people who fall in love with Jesus will easily identify with His Cross, feeling deep and painful guilt because they realize their sins caused His death. Then, when they comprehend Jesus died their death for them and embrace His gift of a redeemed will, profound and life-changing gratitude blossoms into a new choice to love and serve Jesus for the remainder of their lives. It is this identification and this love that breaks the hegemony of the old self (Rom. 6:5).

Because of this affinity, the truth dawns by the Holy Spirit that the old nature inherited from Adam "was crucified with him" and that he is "no longer...a slave to sin" (Rom. 6:6). At the moment of comprehending Christ's lavish love, believing what He did on Golgotha was for *me*, faith meets grace and the shining breakthrough occurs (Eph. 1:8; 1 John 3:1). As the Holy Spirit makes this truth dawn in people's hearts, everything changes, and the victory becomes very personal. Jesus actually, as a factual historical event, took my sin to the cross and literally paid my death penalty. This realization is so redemptive, my desires change; I actually want, earnestly desire, to live out the attitude of Christ, including His values and international agenda (Phil. 2:5). I have found my beloved for life.

The Lord's church today must face the fact that the provision of Christ's death on the cross is not deficient in its power to conquer sin. The deficiency is that much of what is termed *successful Christian living* involves no path of death and especially no death-by-crucifixion. Instead, spiritual leaders turn to sociological and psychological palliatives to help people live with their pain without dealing with the "spider" that is the root cause. The apostle Paul was very clear about "killing off everything connected with that way of life: sexual promiscuity, impurity, lust, doing whatever you feel like whenever you feel like it, and grabbing whatever attracts your fancy. That's a life shaped by things and feelings instead of by God" (Col. 3:5, THE MESSAGE).

Bonhoeffer affirmed: "When Jesus calls a man, he bids him come and die."[4] Yet, many people believe they can coexist successfully with the old self of indwelling sin. Applying the analogy of marriage, they want the new love along with the old flame, avoiding the pain of sacrifice and death. Abraham surely yearned for both Ishmael and Isaac to grow up in the same tent and did not find it easy to surrender his firstborn (Gen. 17:18).

It is a jarring fact that a marriage partner who refuses to pay the price and actually die to all old suitors has written a far more painful death warrant over the marriage. It is always easier to die to every former suitor, and every present suitor, and every future suitor, than it is to walk through divorce, the graveyard of marriages (Mal. 2:16). Coexistence thinking creates the competition that kills and buries marriages. It also cheapens grace and yields no liberation from the old self. James described the state as doublemindedness and said such a person is "unstable in all he does" (James 1:8).

❧ I Love Jesus, But… ❧

I love Jesus, but want to hold on to my own friends even when they do not lead me closer to Jesus. I love Jesus, but want to hold on to my own independence even when it brings me no real freedom. I love Jesus, but do not want to lose the respect of my professional colleagues even though their respect does not make me grow spiritually. I love Jesus, but do not want to give up my writing, travel, and speaking plans, even when they are often more to my glory than God's.[5]

---

c) Separation as Death

A lifestyle that is set apart unto Jesus' attitude, character, and agenda at home and abroad presumes this dying and will not happen without it. Since Jesus gave His life on the cross for the sins of the whole world, it only follows that for the children of God to live in victory, they too must die to the world, with its affections and lusts (Gal. 5:24; 1 John 2:15–17). However, the typical person will not effortlessly forsake his carnal loves, throwing off "everything that hinders" and the sin that "so easily entangles" (Heb. 12:1). Paul affirmed the solution requires a separation so painful that only the term *death* describes it:

> Now if we died with Christ, we believe we will also live with him.
> —ROMANS 6:8

d) Crucifixion and Resurrection—Three Vital Actions (Rom. 6:11–14)

Paul presents three essential steps on the path of death necessary to set apart Christ as Lord (1 Pet. 3:15). Each pace contributes to victory over the old self of sin.

1) Count Yourself to Be Dead

"Reckon ye also yourselves to be dead to sin" is the initial step and Paul's first directive (Rom. 6:11 KJV; see also Col. 3:5). Paul's command calls to mind an analogy of a mathematical calculation. Adding up the "numbers" that signify what Jesus achieved on Calvary yields a total:

- Jesus died
- in my place and
- *paid my debt*;
- therefore, I accept by faith that I am dead to sin with Christ.

This analogy shows what counting ourselves dead to sin is all about, and it is the believer's choice by faith to count it to be so. For example, God said to a very downcast Cain after rejecting his offering that his face could again be "bright with joy." But "if you refuse to obey, watch out. Sin is waiting to attack you, longing to destroy you. But you can conquer it!" (Gen. 4:7, TLB). God did not say to Cain, "I will conquer it for you;" instead, He said, "You can conquer it."

This conquest happens when a person stands under the cross and steadfastly "counts" it to be so. We do it, trusting in the transforming power of the river of love that flows red in the blood of Christ. Jesus' atoning sacrifice is what so powerfully reveals the compelling love of God, empowering a believer's forceful "No!" to the old self (Titus 2:12).

The numbers do add up. When the believer does what he can do and in faith sincerely proclaims himself dead to sin, the Holy Spirit will be there to do what only He can do. In that crisis moment, faith embraces grace, and a death to the old lifestyle of the world occurs. With this setting apart, the door swings wide open to a new life of enthusiastic growth in the character of God and participation in the worldwide agenda of Jesus Christ (John 8:34; Rom. 6:22).

2) Count Yourself Alive to God

Paul teaches in these verses a double faith calculation. The first is counting yourself dead to sin. The second then follows of understanding yourself as "alive to God in Christ Jesus" (Rom. 6:11).

- Jesus died
- in my place
- *and arose from the dead.*
- Hence, by faith I died to sin with Christ and am resurrected with Him to a new, set-apart lifestyle.

The "numbers" add up here too. The computation shows that since He bore *my sins* in His body on the tree, *I* actually participated in the richness of His resurrection. The calculation yields the total, therefore, that He has set *me* apart from the world and raised *me* up to grow in the character and worldwide agenda of Jesus Christ. I am set apart to a new life in Christ.

Paul is not teaching the Lord's followers to practice mere positive thinking here. Instead, the apostle knew in the moment when a person in faith sincerely reckons the death of the old self, the Holy Spirit will be there, as he was with Abraham. The Spirit pours out lavishly the transforming love of Christ, love that is so compelling it demands a response of overwhelming gratitude that births total commitment (1 John 3:1; 4:9). In this sense, we are hemmed in, and our hearts are stolen forever (Ps. 139:4; Song of Sol. 4:9; Eph. 6:24). When a young lady finds her true love she will walk away from all old suitors and not look back, committing for life to one special young man. In that same sense, the hegemony of the old self is also broken in this new relationship of love, and a new, lifelong bonding to Jesus Christ takes control (Gen. 21:12; Jer. 29:13; Phil. 2:12–13).

3) Offer Yourself to God

"If you live according to the flesh, you will die," Paul said. "But if by the Spirit you put to death the deeds of the body, you will live" (Rom. 8:13). Again, the "numbers" add up, forming a powerful partnership. What the Spirit does is pour extravagantly the compelling love of God into our hearts (2 Cor. 5:14; 1 John 4:19). We respond by willingly sacrificing on the altar the old self and all old loves that hinder bonding to Christ. Hence, the Holy Spirit, because of the effectiveness of Christ's blood, crucifies our sinful nature (Rom. 6:8; 8:9; Eph. 4:22; Col. 3:9).

What is the result? Believers can now offer themselves to God in profuse gratitude for the Lord's lavish love at Calvary. This love enables them, even in the face of temptation, to "refuse to offer the parts of [their] body to sin, as instruments of wickedness." Instead, they "offer [themselves] to God, as those who have been brought from death to life." They also "offer the parts of [their bodies] to him as instruments of righteousness. For sin shall not be your master, because you are not under law, but under grace" (Rom. 6:13–14; James 1:13–14).

3. Slavery

Paul used the analogy of forced labor as his third illustration of the sancti-fied life (Rom. 6:16–23). A slave is not his own master; instead, he is "owned" by another. The person who lives the lifestyle of the old self does so because sin enslaves his wants and choices.

> You used to offer the parts of your body in slavery to impurity and to ever-increasing wickedness, so now offer them in slavery to righteousness leading to holiness. When you were slaves to sin, you were free from the control of righteousness. What benefit did you

reap at that time from the things you are now ashamed of? Those things result in death! But now that you have been set free from sin and have become slaves to God, the benefit you reap leads to holiness, and the result is eternal life.

—ROMANS 6:19–22

What hope is in the gospel! Jesus voluntarily chose the humble lifestyle of a servant, first to His Father, and then to His fellow men. His ultimate act of service was to shed His blood on Calvary to emancipate all who are in spiritual bondage (Phil. 2:7–8; Gal. 5:1). Because we become like what we love, when we fall in love with Jesus, the gratitude for His sacrifice is overwhelming. The love expressed in the fountain of His blood at Calvary actually pulls us away from our old self into the waiting arms of the Lord.

The transformed child of God can now decide to become the servant of a new master. He cheerfully and freely chooses Jesus Christ, who has stolen his heart, a bonding that is the essence of "holiness" (Rom. 6:22; Exod. 21:5–6; Song of Sol. 4:9). He trades owners and accepts the Lord's claim on his entire being, including all of the power centers of his life.

When Jesus taught on the subject, He expressed it like this: "I tell you the truth, everyone who sins is a slave to sin...so if the Son sets you free, you will be free indeed" (John 8:34, 36). Being then "set free from sin," Paul said, you become "slaves to righteousness" (Rom. 6:18). The implication is clear. In this exchange, the child of God is no longer in bondage to sin. The result is that he voluntarily gives his wholehearted loyalty to the ways of God (Exod. 21:6; Phil. 2:5–8).

~⁓ Love Motivates Service ⁓~

Sam was a control freak, and Mary's marriage to him was unhappy from the honeymoon. Sam provided well for Mary financially, but she lived in emotional poverty. He was such a demanding husband. Sam wanted his breakfast served at 7:30 and not 7:35. His dinner had to be on the table at 5:30. Sam was such a taskmaster that he actually showed Mary just how he wanted his shirts ironed and folded. Mary was slowly dying inside.

The day came Sam felt pain in his throat that he did not seem to be able to shake, and he started losing weight. Mary begged him to get a check up. When Sam finally did go to the doctor, the diagnosis was inoperable throat cancer. Sam had delayed too long to get help. His passing came three very short months later.

When he died, Mary almost felt relief that the taskmaster in her life was gone. Then she felt guilty for the thought.

In time, Mary healed emotionally and reached the place she could love again. She met a fine Christian man, and he treated her like a queen. She did not believe she would ever be loved the way Billy adored her.

One day Mary was working up in the attic. She picked up an old letter out of a trunk that Sam had written her in the early months of their marriage. In it, Sam demanded bluntly that she serve his dinner at 5:30 sharp. Just looking at the letter brought a flood of those old and painful memories.

As she pondered it all, however, something very special dawned on her. Mary realized she was still cooking breakfast, and that she and Billy ate about 7:30 every morning. She ironed Billy's shirts too, and folded them. They also enjoyed dinner together, about 5:30 every day. But those old, negative feelings she had toward Sam—she had none of them toward Billy. Then it hit her. Sam had been a taskmaster that put her in bondage. Mary had tried to meet his harsh expectations, but she never quite measured up.

The new marriage was so much better. Billy loved her for who she was and wanted her to be happy. He had freed her and given her the right to be herself. The result was she actually enjoyed doing things for Billy. His love motivated her to want to serve, loving him in return.[6]

The emancipation proclamation Jesus issued on His cross settled the issue. The new freedom is real and factual, and the relationship with Jesus Christ is exhilarating (Gal. 5:1). The yardstick for measuring this new relationship is not one of sinless perfection, but of separation unto the servant mindset of the Lord and His worldwide agenda. "Now that you've found you don't have to listen to sin tell you what to do, and have discovered the delight of listening to God telling you, what a surprise! A whole, healed, put-together life right now, with more and more of life on the way!" (Rom. 6:22, THE MESSAGE). The NIV expresses it this way: "Now that you have been set free from sin and have become slaves to God, the benefit you reap leads to holiness, and the result is eternal life."

The old life paid wages in the currency of death (Rom. 6:21). With that life, the bondage only went deeper and deeper. However, the new Master offers blessings of inestimable value: "The gift of God is eternal life in Jesus Christ our Lord" (Rom. 6:23).

The love of God turns people by their free choice into lifelong, loyal subjects of the lowly Nazarene (Eph. 4:1). In fact, God always inspires the gratitude that blesses people to love Jesus in return (1 Cor. 13:8; Col. 2:7). At the same time, the amazing love of God never forces a positive response against anyone's will. In fact, freedom is ultimately free only when people have the choice to be ungrateful, even for their Redeemer's sacrifice.

4. Remarriage

Paul's fourth illustration is the law of remarriage after the death of a spouse (Rom. 7:1–6). The Law of Moses said a woman was bound to her husband as long as he lived. His death, however, released her from that law.

> If while her husband lives she is married to another man, she shall be called an adulteress: but if her husband is dead, she is free from that law; so that she is not an adulteress, though she is married to another man.
> —ROMANS 7:3, KJV

Embraced in this analogy is the fact that by its very nature, death separates. In this same sense of separation, the love of God expressed in Jesus' death breaks the hegemony of sin over the life of a believer and sets him apart from its controlling power and condemnation. A child of God is freed to give himself in fidelity in a new marriage—a new relationship with Christ. The association with the old self or the nature of Adam was a terrible bond that was killing him. "We were controlled by the sinful nature," Paul said, because "the sinful passions aroused by the law were at work in our bodies, so that we bore fruit for death" (Rom. 7:5).

The new marriage with the last Adam, who is "a life-giving spirit," is unspeakably better (1 Cor. 15:45). The gracious love of God, poured freely into the lives of God's children by the Holy Spirit, motivates the choice to love Jesus Christ forever (Rom. 5:5; Eph. 6:24; Titus 3:6). The road is now wide open for God's children to live as servants who "bear fruit to God," so "by dying to what once bound us, we have been released from the law" (Rom. 7:4–6; Gal. 5:22–23).

The outcome is that God's children are "no longer shackled to that domineering mate of sin." Instead, they are "out from under all those oppressive regulations and fine print…free to live a new life in the freedom of God" (Rom. 7:6, THE MESSAGE).

D. Summary

Each of these six illustrations communicates the same message in its own way. The lavishly abundant love of Jesus Christ expressed in His poured-out blood is so attractive, we are drawn to it (Isa. 53:12; Luke 22:20; Rom. 5:5; Titus 3:6). The more we look at Him on His cross, the more we love Him. The more we love him, the more we want to be like Him. The loving mercy of God's grace is so overwhelming in its separating power, it motivates a free choice to walk away from the old life and to the attitude, values, and worldwide agenda of Jesus Christ.

In a shining breakthrough, therefore, believers are "set apart for the gospel of God" (Rom. 1:1). It all happens because of "the love of God that is in Christ Jesus, our Lord" (Rom. 8:39). The grandeur of this love is that nothing can separate a child of God from it—nothing (Rom. 8:35–39).

This study pulls into focus, therefore, how the love of God demonstrated so abundantly at the cross, makes it possible for a person to work out his "salvation with fear and trembling." As it happens, all the glory goes to Jesus Christ, for "it is God who works in you to will and to act according to his good purpose" (Phil. 2:12–13). The starting place is to yearn for the mind of Christ (Phil. 2:5, KJV).

1. Love—Compelling and Decreeing Without Coercing

Using the analogy of courtship, when a person walks the path of death to the cross, in that special moment his eyes meet the eyes of Jesus (Luke 22:61). Immediately he links with His Lord. He realizes right then that Jesus poured out all of His love on that cross just for him (Song of Sol. 4:9; 1 John 3:1). At that compelling instant, yesterday's old loves lose their hold on his heart and the supremacy of the old self is broken (Col. 2:13–14). Out of a deep gratitude for the Lord's literal death for his sin, he realizes the rich meaning of David's song: "You hem me in—behind and before" (Ps. 139:5). It allows him to feel God's hand of blessing laid upon him.

This love, then, is what compels people to choose Jesus' attitude and lifestyle and to continue in servant living. Amazingly, love has the power to compel without ever overruling a person's free will; therefore, it can accomplish what the Law never could (2 Cor. 5:14).

This astonishing God kind of love can also be decreed. Jesus certainly did it. "A new command I give you," Jesus said. "Love one another. As I have loved you, so you must love one another" (John 13:34; 14:15; 15:9, 12; Luke 6:27). Moses repeatedly commanded it, too (Deut. 6:5, 20; 10:12, 19; 11:1, 13, 22).

In the entire scope of sanctifying grace, including the ordeal of a spiritual death by identification with Jesus' cross, the Lord never uses force to gain fidelity. Instead, the compelling love of God inspires a believer to such an extent that he responds with deep personal gratitude for all Jesus has done.

We love because he first loved us.

—1 John 4:19

2. Love as the Cure for Doublemindedness

Death to the old self typically does not come easily and painlessly. Quite to the contrary, the will to live is so strong that people fight death to the last breath. In spiritual terms, the sinful fruit of a relationship with an old flame can sometimes be so tantalizing, some will lie and scheme and formulate elaborate cover-ups. Others will fight to the bitter end, rather than give up "the sin that so easily entangles" (Heb. 12:1–4).

Abraham, the father of the faithful, lived in doublemindedness for several years after Isaac's birth. When the moment of truth came, he struggled with it and did not find it easy to die to his plan (Gen. 21:12). The loving grace of God became his encouragement, though, enabling him to make the choice that set him and his descendents apart unto the faith that birthed a nation and the world's Messiah.

3. Love as Power to Stay on the Cross

For all the blessings this new freedom with Christ promises, a person typically will offer compromises, make new commitments to do better, pledge a reformation of habits—anything to get off his cross of spiritual crucifixion (Exod. 8:25–28; 10:7, 24; Matt. 27:40–42). But to come down from the cross leaves a person as merely a reformed, and maybe a more cautious, sinner. No death has occurred, and no resurrection to a shining new life can take place. Only love for God keeps a person on his cross until death occurs, so that resurrection can follow. Grace actually has the power to do it.

4. Love as Grace for Change

a) In Abraham

When God came to Abraham long ago in that encouraging visit, He poured into the father of the faithful the grace to honor Sarah's demand that he surrender both the child and the child's mother (Gen. 21:11–12). The separation had to happen; coexistence with sin never works.

In that instant of trust, Abraham received the encouragement that strengthened him to do what he knew he had to do. While the choice was like a death, the resurrection that followed brought him into union with His Lord, the supreme love of his life. This new relationship of adoring love also enabled him to live for the remainder of his life in fidelity to the character of God and the plan of God. Abraham discovered the romance of the ages and the Bridegroom from heaven, and with a heart of deep love, entered by faith into union with His Messiah (John 8:56). Abraham spent the remainder of his life's sojourn looking forward to the city with foundations, whose architect and builder is God" (Heb. 11:10).

The outcome of this grace for change is a blessed resurrection unto a new life of service in the sheepfold of Jesus Christ (John 10:11–14). This set-apart lifestyle is indeed a shining breakthrough of compelling love (2 Cor. 5:14). At the foot of the cross where Christ's sinless blood dripped *for me*, the lavish love of God frees a person from the grip of sin (Gal. 5:1; 1 John 3:1).

b) In the Centurion

The hardened centurion who crucified Jesus realized quickly he had crucified an innocent man. The officer had never seen a man face death like Jesus; in fact, the Lord did not hurl a single epithet at His killers (Luke 6:28; 1 Pet. 2:23–24; Isa. 53:7). As he continued to watch Jesus closely he concluded something very different was taking place on Golgotha's hill. The Lord obviously suffered unimaginable pain and shame on His cross, but He also kept His focus throughout the ordeal. He was fully in charge of why He was on the cross and of the circumstances surrounding what was such a great travesty of justice. Amazingly, although innocent, Jesus never acted like a victim.

The fact that Jesus did not curse the religious leaders who mocked and jeered at Him, nor the soldiers who crucified Him and then rolled dice for His seamless robe, must have spoken volumes to this hardened officer as "grace for change" began to work in his heart (Matt. 27:41–44; John 19:24; Ps. 22:18; 1 Pet. 2:23). The compassion Jesus showed His mother, who felt like one of the soldiers had run a sword through her heart, and the tenderness Jesus felt for the thief on the cross beside Him poured more grace on the centurion (John 19:27; Luke 2:35; 23:40–43). The three hours of darkness no doubt shook him also, and multiplied the wooing power of God as the courtship of prevenient grace worked in his rock-tough heart (Luke 23:44–45).

This pagan could never forget the statements Jesus made from the cross, especially what to him was surely an unnerving cry: "Father forgive them, for they do not know what they are doing" (Luke 23:34). Romans understood the brutal power of revenge, but they stumbled badly before the superior muscle of the love that forgives.

It is certainly true that a person can be far freer as a prisoner in jail than the officers who guard him. In this sense, Jesus was free on the cross, and the centurion who witnessed His freedom was forced to admit that he, himself, was the prisoner. These many visual demonstrations of grace motivated this Roman officer to open His heart and say, "Surely he was the Son of God" (Matt. 27:54).

If experiencing the cross of Jesus could melt in a few short hours the heart of this hardened executioner, it can also save "whosoever will" worldwide (John 3:16). And it has. Millions since have looked at the same evidence and have come to this centurion's conclusion. In our world today, the cross of Jesus suffers, not from lack of redeeming power but because so many back away from telling the full story.

When a person ponders the many aspects of Calvary, the amazing, God-kind of love Jesus demonstrated steals our hearts and welds a steel bond of mutual affection (Song of Sol. 4:9; Ps. 145:20; 1 Pet. 1:8; Rev. 1:5–6). He walks away from Golgotha having made the choice to love Jesus for the remainder of his life (Eph. 6:24). His decision also includes determination to live out the will of the Father to reach out to people, as Jesus did. Paul expressed it by saying, "I am obligated both to Greeks and non-Greeks, both to the wise and foolish. That is why I am so eager to preach the gospel" (Rom. 1:14–15). Christ died for all sin; we must die to all suitors, past, present, and future—any and all who compete with our loyalty to the Nazarene (Matt. 2:23).

When believers comprehend the unimaginably high price God's love paid on the cross to atone for sin, it also births a profound love for sinners. On the other hand, a cheapened and diminished understanding of the story of the cross of Jesus will always produce a lackadaisical and lenient view of lost people and can actually result in a denial that they are lost.

5. Love—Claiming the Triumph of Jesus

The Holy Spirit makes it possible for a person to identify with the death and resurrection of Jesus to this life-changing extent. In fact, it is normative for a believer to have a strong sense he was actually there at Calvary, too.

Jesus took *my sins* and died in my place. The Holy Spirit enables me, therefore, to stand at the foot of His cross, watch the entire bloody scene of what should have been happening to me, and perceive the unfathomable love of God. This understanding is the essence of a substitutionary atonement, the concept of Christ's death as a substitute for me, covering over my sins (Isa. 53; Rom. 3:25; 5:19; Gal. 1:4; Heb. 2:17).

Children of God recognize as they stand in faith at the cross, it was because of Jesus' righteousness that the Father placed His stamp of approval on His Son when He raised Him from the dead. Therefore, the heavenly Father delights for His sons to claim the love of God that triumphed in Jesus' death as *their* holiness (Gen. 15:6; Rom. 4:3–8). The result is, they actually "participate in the divine nature and escape the corruption in the world caused by evil desires" (2 Pet. 1:4).

6. The Love That Paid in Full

What good news! Jesus paid our entire debt with His blood, and God's Word is the receipt of payment. The Lord's cry on His cross, "It is finished," rings with the finality of a debt paid in full (John 19:30). As a medical examiner routinely identifies on a death certificate the moment a person expires, so in a crisis moment the old self is dethroned and Jesus Christ is exalted. At that instant, the shining breakthrough begins with a new resurrection life in Christ. In this relationship, the mastery of sin is broken because the Holy Spirit pours out the love of God to change them on the inside (Rom. 5:5; John 5:42). This love does what law can never do: it imparts life (Gal. 3:21).

7. *The Love That Motivates Self-Emptying*

We have noted in this study that our sinless Lord, in His incarnation, surrendered the most precious aspects of His deity—His moral prerogatives—to His Father and to the Holy Spirit. With total trust in His Father, Jesus served in the confidence that the Spirit would minister them back through Him, as needed in His ministry (Acts 2:22). Such is the essence of Peter's pronouncement in Cornelius' house regarding Jesus' method of operation: "God anointed Jesus of Nazareth with the Holy Spirit and power," and "he went around doing good, and healing all who were under the power of the devil, because God was with him" (Acts 10:38).

In sanctifying grace, a believer surrenders his heart, soul, mind, and strength to God. Paul testified to it, saying, "I have been crucified with Christ, and I no longer live, but Christ lives in me. The life I live in the body, I live by faith in the Son of God, who loved me and gave himself for me" (Gal. 2:20). This witness was possible because Paul loved Jesus Christ (Mark 12:30). In total commitment to the Lord, Paul surrendered or emptied himself of his:

- heart—the seat of his emotions and feelings, and his will
- soul—the fundamentally spiritual dimension of his eternal moral being
- mind—his ability to think and reason
- strength—his capacity to come and go with energy and power

When a person surrenders these aspects of his human nature, the marvelous reality is that the Holy Spirit will be faithful to give them back to him, set apart to divine service.

The word picture of marriage is appropriate here. At the wedding altar, a man and a woman empty themselves of all past relationships and commit for life to each other. The fact of so many fifty-year marriages, lived in true fidelity, says keeping the covenant is possible. Mutual implicit trust births the loving commitment that glues and holds marriages together for a lifetime.

As is true with marriage, there will surely be ups and downs as time moves forward in the walk of faith, but a believer's relationship with God, bonded by this mutual affection, remains solid for a lifetime.

8. Love Changes the Power Centers

At the moment that Jesus is firmly seated on the throne of his heart, the radical alteration begins and continues to mature in what a child of God loves and wants out of life. Jesus becomes his Lord. This new attitude changes how he relates to the many seats of power in his life, including his:

- money,
- sex life,
- devotional life,
- family life,
- church life,
- work life,
- recreational life,
- possessions, and
- ungodly habits.

Now they are submitted to the mission and power of the cross. In all of these areas of influence, the salt of sanctifying grace seasons the lives of God's children. Henceforward, they enjoy a compelling new yearning to duplicate in their own lifestyle Jesus' attitude and values, as well as His vision for the nations. The Lord actually becomes more than a resident in a believer's heart; He is the new president and chairman of the board. The result is a person begins to feel his new freedom in Christ. This confidence grows rapidly, assuring him that he is making progress at working out his salvation (Phil. 2:12–13).

❧ He's a Boy Again! ☙

In *The Voyage of the Dawn Treader*, C. S. Lewis tells how a young boy named Eustace became a dragon—a very unhappy dragon at that. Eustace steals a gold armband and puts it on, only to find that his greed turns him into a dragon. And the armband is excruciatingly tight on his dragon foot.

One night, in the midst of his pain and frustration, Eustace encounters a huge lion who tells the boy to follow it to a high mountain well. Eustace longs to bathe his aching foot in the cool water, but the lion tells him he must undress first. It seems silly to Eustace because dragons don't wear clothes, but then he remembers that dragons, like snakes, cast their skins.

So Eustace scratches his skin, and the scales begin falling off—and soon his whole skin peels away. But when he puts his foot in the water, he sees that it is just as rough and scaly as before. He continues scratching at the second dragon skin and realizes there is yet another underneath.

Finally the lion says, "You will have to let me undress you."

Eustace is afraid of the lion's claws but desperate to get in the water. The first tear is painfully deep as the lion begins to peel away the skin. Surely death will follow, Eustace believes. With the gnarled mess of dragon skin now cut away, the lion holds Eustace and throws him into the water.

Initially, the water stings, but soon it is perfectly delicious. Eustace swims without pain, for he's a boy again.[7]

III. The Bodily Sacrifice of the Sanctified

A. Counting the Cost

The disciple of Christ should never make the mistake of believing that developing a servant heart like the mind of Christ is easy grace. Jesus' choice to live set apart unto His Father cost Him His life, and "no servant is greater than his master" (John 15:20). The fact that He paid the supreme price bodily and then vanquished all His foes in His resurrection explains why strong men, and so many of the best intellects of the centuries, have picked up the Lord's challenge and made His approach to life their own (Luke 14:28; John 3:16; Matt. 20:28; 1 Tim. 2:6; Heb. 9:15). Therefore, Jesus earned the right to say, "If you want to be my follower, you must love me more than your own father and mother, wife and children, brothers and sisters—yes, more than your own life. Otherwise, you cannot be my disciple" (Luke 14:26, NLT).

This means we accept as a given that the work of God in our lives is often painful. Bonhoeffer expressed it:

As we embark upon discipleship...we give over our lives to death.[8]

Strengthened by the love of God, we carry our cross cheerfully, knowing the Lord's ultimate goal is to transform us into temples of the Holy Spirit (Matt. 16:24; Rom. 5:3; 8:18; 1 Cor. 3:16–17).

The love of God seals this set-apart relationship between the Savior and His people, as well as between men and their fellow men. In this process, "We're never left feeling shortchanged. Quite the contrary—we can't round up enough containers to hold everything God generously pours into our lives through the Holy Spirit" (Rom. 5:5, THE MESSAGE; Eph. 4:25–32).

B. Give Your Body to God

Many followers of Jesus believe that coming to Christ is only a spiritual transaction of the heart, but Paul's teaching was specific that commitment to Jesus Christ includes a choice to sacrifice one's body to God. The story of Abraham carrying out the rite of adult circumcision mirrors the principle forcefully (Gen. 17:9–14). To use the analogy of marriage, if the covenant vows in marriage do not extend to giving one's body to each other for life— and only to each other—then marriage is a farce. Hence, Paul wrote:

> Never let sin rule your physical body so that you obey its desires. Never offer any part of your body to sin's power. No part of your body should ever be used to do any ungodly thing. Instead, offer yourselves to God as people who have come back from death and are now alive. Offer all the parts of your body to God. Use them to do everything that God approves of. Certainly, sin shouldn't have power over you because you're not controlled by laws, but by God's favor.
> —ROMANS 6:12–14, GW

Paul called on his readers to make this sacrifice, offering one by one all the parts of their bodies to God. Doing it requires the choice to empty oneself of all old loves. When a person makes this sacrifice, a marvelous, qualitative change actually takes place in his heart (John 8:34–36; Rom. 6:19; 1 John 1:7; 2:15; Heb. 10:19–22; 13:12). He discovers he can trust in the grace of the Lord to manifest a new authority in Christ that will not offer any part of his body to sin's power (Rom. 6:13–14; James 1:13–14). Paul applied this teaching in this way: "I urge you, brothers, in view of God's mercy, to offer your bodies as living sacrifices, holy and pleasing to God—this is your spiritual act of worship" (Rom. 12:1).

The Lord inhabited a body and died bodily (John 1:14; 1 Pet. 2:24). He came out of the grave bodily, ascended into heaven bodily, and one day will return bodily to rule and reign on the earth (1 Cor. 15:3–4; Col. 2:9; John 14:3). The apostle Paul expressed the ultimate purpose of the human body in straightforward language, saying, "Do you not know that your body is a temple of the Holy Spirit, who is in you, whom you have received from God?" (1 Cor. 6:19).

~ Building a Palace ~

"Imagine yourself as a living house," wrote C. S. Lewis in Mere Christianity. "God comes in to rebuild that house. At first, perhaps, you can understand what he is doing. He is getting the drains right and stopping the leaks in the roof and so on. You knew those jobs needed doing so you are not surprised. But presently he starts knocking the house about in a way that hurts abominably and does not seem to make sense. What on earth is he up to? The explanation is that he is building quite a different house from the one you thought of, throwing out a new wing here, putting on an extra floor there, running up towers, making courtyards.

"You thought you were going to be made into a decent little cottage, but he is building up a palace. He intends to come and live in it himself."[9]

A believer who loves his Lord and desires to grow in the mind of Christ will choose to make a complete sacrifice of his *body* to God. Many people have been left in spiritual bondage because they failed to understand this great provision of the gospel—in a decisive act, give your body to God (Rom. 12:1–2). The word translated *offer* in this verse is an aorist verb, meaning the gift is actually made. As two lovers give themselves only to each other in marriage, and keep on reaffirming the gift in a lifetime relationship, so a believer offers himself to God bodily as "a living sacrifice, holy and pleasing to God" (Rom. 12:1). Paul described this sacrifice as a "spiritual act of worship." The gift of one's body to God is to be as definite as the act of circumcision is decisive (Rom. 2:29).

When a believer respects his body as his gift of worship to God, he will surely give attention to the needs of the body, such as proper dieting that avoids gluttony, as well as adequate rest, clothing, exercise, and shelter. It also embraces a continuing lifestyle that brings the appetites and passions of the body under the authority of the Spirit of God (Rom. 16:18; 1 Cor. 9:24–27; Titus 3:3). Substance and chemical abuse in its varied addictions are clearly sins against the body, the temple of the Holy Spirit. The same is true of the whole range of sexual sins, including both heterosexual and homosexual sins, with the accompanying evils of pornography (Lev. 18:22; 20:13; Rom. 1:26–27; 1 Cor. 6:9–11; 1 Tim. 1:10; Heb. 13:4; Rev. 21:8; 22:15). Paul warned believers, "Don't become so well-adjusted to your culture that you fit into it without even thinking. Instead, fix your attention on God" (Rom. 12:2, THE MESSAGE).

Paul also recognized the close connection between the body and the mind, motivating him to write that believers must, "Change the way [they] think" (Rom. 12:2, GW; Isa. 55:7). The ultimate target, of course, is training our minds to think like the mind of Christ (Phil. 2:4–5). This goal is indeed possible because Paul claimed, "We have the mind of Christ" (1 Cor. 2:16). As a marriage partner works at learning to think like one's spouse, so a follower of Jesus Christ will want to learn to think like his Lord. Paul expressed an effective method for doing this when he encouraged his Corinthians readers to bring "into captivity every thought to the obedience of Christ" (2 Cor. 10:5, KJV; Phil. 4:8).

A couple that has fallen in love will continually reaffirm the gift of their bodies each to the other in a living, ongoing sacrifice. In fact, when love reigns, it does not even feel like a sacrifice. Falling in love with Jesus makes it possible decisively to give oneself for life in fidelity to the Savior, a choice that will be affirmed and reaffirmed many times as the year's progress.

For Abraham, the life-giving love of God in his heart was greater than the pain and grief ahead as he anticipated losing his firstborn from his tent (Gen. 21:11; Gal. 3:21; John 6:63. Without that lavish love, no one will "throw off everything that hinders" and the sin that so easily "entangles" him (Heb. 12:1). Only with this love can he commit to the Lord's way of thinking (Rom. 12:2; Phil. 2:5, KJV). Set-apart living, therefore, is a choice in which God's love motivates a believer to forsake his old way of thinking, which includes giving his body to God.

This kind of transformation will reprogram into Christlikeness each of the many spheres of influence anchored in the cravings of the flesh in a person's life. The result is that a believer will break out shiningly, renewed in his heart, soul, mind (including his subconscious mind), and strength, having discovered the pearl of great price (Matt. 13:46; Deut. 6:5; Lev. 19:18; Gal. 5:22–23).

Sadly, so many people live their whole lives searching in all the wrong places, when all along the real treasure has been at the foot of the old rugged cross.

⚬ We've Found Life's Real Treasure ⚬

The Treasure of the Sierra Madre is the story of three down-on-their-luck prospectors and their search for gold in Mexico. At one point in their search, prospectors Fred, Bob, and Howard are joined by a fourth man. No sooner had the new prospector arrived than the four are involved in a gunfight with several bandits...the fourth prospector is killed. The other three approach the body, which is propped up against a large rock. They decide to find out who the man was. Howard bends down and removes the dead man's wallet and some papers. "His name is James Cody; Dallas, Texas. There's a letter from Dallas too. Must be his home," Howard says, and shows the others a photo of a woman. One of them remarks "Not bad." Howard starts reading, and then Bob takes over.

Dear Jim:

Your letter just arrived. It was such a relief to get word after so many months of silence. I realize of course that there aren't any mailboxes that you can drop a letter in out there in the wild. But that doesn't keep me from worrying about you. Little Jimmy is fine, but he misses his daddy almost as much as I do. He keeps asking, "When's Daddy coming home?" You say if you do not make a real find this time, you will never go again. I cannot begin to tell you how my heart rejoices at those words, if you really mean them. Now I feel free to tell you, I've never thought that any material treasure, no matter how great, is worth the pain of these long separations.

The country is especially lovely this year. It's been a perfect spring: warm rains and hardly any frost. The fruit trees are all in bloom. The upper orchard looks aflame, and the lower, like after a snowstorm. Everybody looks forward to big crops. I do hope that you are back for the harvest. Of course, I'm hoping that you will at last strike it rich. It is high time for luck to start smiling upon you. But just in case she doesn't, remember, we've already found life's real treasure.

Forever yours,

Callie

Fred says, "Well, I guess we better dig a hole for him."[10]

C. Respect for the Bodies of Others

Jesus was crystal-clear in His teaching, "Love your neighbor as yourself" (Matt. 22:39; Gal. 5:14). A person who loves God and loves people will respect the bodies of others. Life is precious, whether it is mine or the life of any other human being. A brother's body, a sister's body, a spouse's body, and a neighbor's body is a "temple of God," too (1 Cor. 3:16–17; 6:19).

For this reason, Paul's affirmation takes on new meaning: "This is the will of God, even your sanctification, that you should abstain from fornication: that every one of you should know how to possess his vessel in sanctification and honor" (1 Thess. 4:3–4, KJV; 1 Cor. 6:15–18, KJV).

Lack of esteem for one's own temple always expresses itself in destructive ways, first in relationship to God and then regarding one's fellow man. Using the analogy of marriage, Paul explained that a man who does not love his wife does not love himself (Eph. 5:28–29). How many have fallen by the wayside because they hooked themselves on pornography or Internet sex (to name only two), each of which is mental adultery that utterly violates God's plan for marital intimacy. This kind of moral trap breaches a husband's covenant both with his wife and with Jesus Christ, because it rejects God's plan for marriage (Matt. 19:5). It also cheapens his regard for himself, even as it reduces his wife to an object to be used, instead of an equal partner to be loved and cherished (Eph. 5:28–30).

The same is true regarding the scourge of divorce on society, which is rooted in disrespect for God's plan for the body, as expressed in marriage (Mark 10:7–9). The prophet Malachi heard the Lord say passionately, "I hate divorce" (Mal. 2:16).

Jesus explained that Moses permitted writs of divorce because of hardness of heart (Matt. 19:8; Deut. 24:1–3). It remains true to this day that any marriage problem is redeemable until one of the partners hardens his heart and walks away. God's plan is monogamous marriage, the principle of one man for one woman until death parts them. It delights a husband and wife, set-apart by the love of Jesus Christ, to practice it with true fidelity (Gen. 2:20–24; Matt. 5:28; 19:5; Rom. 7:2).

"Do you not know that the wicked will not inherit the kingdom of God?" Paul asked. "Do not be deceived. Neither the sexually immoral, nor idolaters, nor adulterers, nor male prostitutes, nor homosexual offenders, nor thieves, nor the greedy, nor drunkards, nor slanderers, nor swindlers, will inherit the kingdom of God" (1 Cor. 6:9–10). The fundamental flaw in each of these sinful lifestyles is disrespect for the human body as the temple of the Holy Spirit. It expresses itself as people taking advantage of people to gain brief satisfaction of their own lustful appetites.

The heart of God, however, is full of redeeming grace: "That is what some of you were," Paul exulted. "But you were washed, you were sanctified, you were justified in the name of the Lord Jesus Christ and by the Spirit of our God" (1 Cor. 6:11).

D. Respect for the Unborn

The doctrine of the body as the temple of the Holy Spirit reaches even to a fetus and demonstrates that life is precious from conception. John the Baptist was filled with the Holy Spirit from his mother's womb (Luke 1:15, KJV). As an unborn baby, John was already an abiding place of the Spirit of God, even before Elizabeth was filled with the Holy Spirit (Luke 1:41).

When Mary arrived at Elizabeth's house, Elizabeth was no more than six months into her pregnancy (Luke 1:36). John the Baptist, although only a fetus, leapt in his mother's womb for joy when Mary greeted John's mother (Luke 1:41, 44). This was obviously recognition by the unborn child, through the Holy Spirit, that Mary was carrying in her womb the Son of God. Elizabeth spoke out loudly in response, addressing Mary as "the mother of my Lord" (Luke 1:42–43). In this great revelation, Elizabeth perceived Jesus, still in the womb, to be her "Lord," although the Christ-child probably was no more than a first-trimester fetus.

God chose Jeremiah from his mother's womb and set him apart as a prophet to the nations (Jer. 1:5). Isaiah said God called him from the womb (Isa. 49:1). David wrote a psalm to express that God created his inmost being and knit him together in his mother's womb (Ps. 139:13). The sweet psalmist added, "Your eyes saw my unformed body. All the days ordained for me were written in your book before one of them came to be" (Ps. 139:16).

Disrespect for the life of an unborn child also violates the Lord's teaching regarding a neighbor, whom we are to love as we love ourselves (Matt. 22:39).

A child in the womb is the most helpless and defenseless of all neighbors. It is clearly unneighborly to kill a neighbor, and despicably unneighborly to kill a defenseless neighbor in the womb.

God's children must conclude that love for Christ will manifest itself in respect for the life of the unborn.

IV. Ultimate Perfection

A. Glorification

When the Lord came out of the grave as the firstfruits of the Resurrection, He arose immortal and incorruptible, never to face death again (1 Cor. 15:20). The resurrection marked the glorification of Jesus, establishing an absolute perfection that removed from Him all the limitations and restraints of fallen humanity.

In His glorified state, for example, our Lord was no longer subject to the laws of the natural order. He could suddenly appear in a room with the doors locked (John 20:26). In addition, the pull of gravity no longer held Him; He ascended bodily into the heavenly glory to take His seat as mediator at God's right hand (Luke 20:42–43; Acts 1:9; 7:56; 1 Tim. 2:5). Jesus Christ, the firstfruits of the Resurrection, promised that His children one day would experience a glorified state like their Lord (1 Cor. 15:23; Luke 24:13–35; John 17:24; 20:19–31; 21).

No child of God experiences glorification in this life. Sanctification will be consummated, therefore, in the triumph of faith that follows death, when "to be absent from the body" is "to be present with the Lord" (2 Cor. 5:8).

B. Sinless Perfection

Set-apart living is not a state of sinless perfection. It is a Christian walk in a fallen world, with lordship in the hearts of Christ's followers changed by the love of God from the nature of Adam to the demeanor of Jesus (Rom. 6:18). The incomparable love of God is the magnet that draws a person into this new relationship, and the response of gratitude "weds" him for life to the last Adam (Eph. 2:8; Rom. 7:3, 6; 1 Cor. 15:45).

Sanctified living is "holiness of heart" living, and the test is this set-apart commitment to the values and agenda of Jesus Christ. Biblical holiness does not take the children of God out of this sinful world (John 17:15). Instead, it sets them apart unto the thinking and values of Jesus Christ while in the world (Eph. 4:23). Set-apart people enter willingly and cheerfully into a servant relationship with their Lord, characterized by the heart and agenda of Jesus. This love of God applies the Lord's atoning blood and births the new life that is separated unto God (Rom. 3:25; Gal. 3:21). It is in this sense that the love of God, and not legalism, hems them in "behind and before" (Ps. 139:5).

C. Temptation

Sanctification does not remove all temptation in a fallen world, but the child of God can enjoy victory over it. Paul wrote, "No temptation has seized you except what is common to man. And God is faithful; he will not let you be tempted beyond what you can bear. But when you are tempted, he will also provide a way out so that you can stand up under it" (1 Cor. 10:13).

An old proverb says that a person may not be able to prevent a bird from landing on his head, but he does not have to permit him to build a nest; so it is with temptation. The onslaught of sinful opportunity flaunts itself daily. With Jesus on the throne of his heart pouring motivating love into his soul and with the dominion of inbred sin having lost its dominance, what a child of God wants out of life is fundamentally changed (1 John 3:9; 5:18). The world no longer appeals to him in the same old way. And if he does miss the mark, he feels very empty, experiencing no pleasure. A fundamental part of the allure of sin is *enjoying it,* at least for "a short time" (Heb. 11:25). Basic to breaking the authority of sin is this loss of merriment. Sin now makes him sick in his soul, a pain so strong he can feel it in his stomach.

To say that the control of sin is broken, therefore, is not to say that sin has no ongoing allurements. It is to say a believer can now say no to the entice-ments of sin, refusing to permit sin to reign in his body (Titus 2:11–12; James 1:13–14). A set-apart believer's new willpower includes freedom and authority in Christ not to yield his "members as instruments of unrighteousness unto sin" (Rom. 6:12–13). This new capability succeeds because sin is no longer "[his] master...[he is] not under law, but under grace" (Rom. 6:13–14). And, if he does sin, he has a defender before the Father, none less than "Jesus Christ, the Righteous One" (1 John 2:1).

D. Angelic Perfection

Neither does a set-apart lifestyle make one angelic. Far from beatific, the person who has experienced this separation unto the Lord continues to live in a sinful world and struggles with its rulers, principalities, and powers (Eph. 6:12). His response of faith is to put on the whole armor of God so that he will be able to stand (Eph. 6:13–18).

E. Human Nature

Sanctification does not make one cease to be human. A person who has been set apart lives in a body and continues to have all of the desires that are essential to human nature. However, the set-apart relationship equips a person to enjoy these appetites to their fullest potential, under the lordship of Jesus. "I keep under my body," Paul said, "and bring it into subjection: lest by any means when I have preached to others, I myself should be a castaway" (1 Cor. 9:27, KJV; Gal. 5:16, 25). Again, marriage is the apt word picture. A couple at the altar commits decisively, bringing themselves totally into subjection to each other. They do so to meet the needs of each other as their lifelong practice.

F. Perfect Knowledge

Set-apart living does not at all presume perfect knowledge. Time, learning, and development will be required for all appetites and habits to come under subjection to Christ Jesus. Our Lord is longsuffering, but He is never permissive—and understands perfectly the dividing line between the two values.

V. Conclusion

"Everyone who sins is a slave to sin," Jesus said, and concluded, "If the Son sets you free, you will be free indeed" (John 8:34, 36). Paul was explicit too: "Sin shall no longer be your master because you are not under law but under grace" (Rom. 6:9, 14). Therefore, the believer breaks forth shiningly at the empty tomb with a new will or power to choose. He is now "created to be like God in true righteousness and holiness" (Eph. 4:24; Phil. 2:13).

Paul said when a person has "put on the new self," it actually initiates the process of restoring the image of God in the soul: "the new self...is being renewed in knowledge in the image of its Creator" (Col. 3:10). Such a set-apart believer remains in the world, but he will not be dominated by the world (John 17:15).

With the corrupted will (the spider) dethroned, the seed of life first planted in the new birth can now fully blossom into the attitude, character, and ways of the Lord Jesus Christ, which is the essence of set-apart living. In this context, "working out one's salvation with fear and trembling" takes on rich and highly motivating new meaning (Col. 3:5–17).

This study began noting the plan of salvation includes both the new birth and sanctification. What started in saving grace comes to full-orbed completion in set-apart living (Phil. 2:12–13). In this new relationship, Jesus sits on the throne of his life. The result is the love of God breaks the corrupted will and redemptively penetrates all of the control centers of his life.

Jesus was clear that the old self lost the supremacy at His cross. We can therefore exult in the rich meaning of Paul's exclamation: "I have been crucified with Christ and I no longer live, but Christ lives in me. The life I live in the body, I live by faith in the Son of God, who loved me and gave himself for me" (Gal. 2:20–21).

Love always succeeds (1 Cor. 13:8).

Jesus is looking for the dedication of heart that puts on the love that "ties everything together perfectly" (Col. 3:14, GW). He welcomes it, in fact, and delights to respond to it by richly pouring the transforming love of God into people's hearts (Exod. 31:13, KJV; 1 John 3:1, GW).

Sanctified people love Jesus and they love people, and they sincerely want to learn to think the way Jesus did. They see people as they are, in their need, but also become excited thinking about who they will become when their own personal "marriage" to Christ takes place. Because they love God with their whole hearts and they love their neighbors, they revel in the opportunity to bring people to the "light of the world," who can give them a new beginning (John 8:12; James 1:17). Jesus is that light.

A Lighted World Costs More

As a child, I heard a memorable story at a holiness revival meeting in New York. It seems a certain missionary, home on leave, was shopping for a globe of the world to take back to her mission station. The clerk showed her a reasonably priced globe and another one with a light bulb inside. "This is nicer," the clerk said, pointing to the illuminated globe, "but of course, a lighted world costs more."[11]

When the chief priests arrested Jesus, all His disciples forsook Him and fled. They certainly were not set apart yet to the Lord's gracious servant demeanor and agenda, if it meant suffering. The master Teacher was on schedule with training them, but they needed more time to assimilate all they had heard and witnessed. That process came to its conclusion after the Resurrection.

Jesus gathered His little flock again the day of His resurrection and began teaching them the exhilarating new meaning His triumph brought to life. After they absorbed the Lord's instructions between Passover and Pentecost and then walked to the Upper Room via Mount Olivet, they never forsook Him and fled again—not after Pentecost. They were "wed" for better or for worse, in "undying love," to His mind-set and servant character. The disciples understood they were His ambassadors for life, entrusted with His strategy to win the world (2 Cor. 5:20; Matt. 28:18–20). Jesus had hemmed them in and stolen their hearts (Ps. 139:4–5; Song of Sol. 4:9).

Chapter Seven

FORTY DAYS WITH
THE MASTER-TEACHER

I am a rose of Sharon, a lily of the valleys.
—SONG OF SOLOMON 2:1

Beginning with Moses and all the prophets, he explained to them what was said in all the Scriptures concerning himself.
—LUKE 24:27

~≈ My Teacher Is So Near to Me ≈~

On the advice of Dr. Alexander Graham Bell, the parents of Helen Keller sent for a teacher from the Perkins Institution for the Blind in Boston, Massachusetts. They chose Anne Sullivan, a 19-year-old orphan, for the task of instructing 6-year-old Helen.

It was the beginning of a close and lifelong friendship between them. By means of a manual alphabet, Anne "spelled" into Helen's hand such words as *doll* or *puppy*. Two years later Helen was reading and writing Braille fluently. At 10, Helen learned different sounds by placing her fingers on her teacher's larynx and "hearing" the vibrations.

Helen went to Radcliffe College, where Anne spelled the lectures into Helen's hand. After graduating with honors, Helen decided to devote her life to helping the blind and deaf. As part of that endeavor, she wrote many books and articles and traveled around the world making speeches. Since Helen's speeches were not intelligible to some, Anne often translated them for her.

Their nearly 50 years of companionship ended when Anne died in 1936. Helen eulogized her lifelong friend with these endearing words:

"My teacher is so near to me I scarcely think of myself apart from her. I feel that her being is inseparable from my own, and that the footsteps of my life are in hers. All the best of me belongs to her—there is not a talent or an inspiration or a joy in me that has not been awakened by her loving touch."[1]

J ESUS CHRIST LIVED with a clear-cut agenda in His incarnation; everything He did focused on Calvary. He totally committed Himself in His humiliation to the work of redemption.

In the time interval between His resurrection and ascension, the glorified Lord's objective with His disciples was to look back and begin to help them comprehend the meaning of His spectacular triumph at Calvary. It is to these six short weeks of the Lord's ministry that we now turn our attention.

I. The Themes of the Forty Days

The term *Pentecost* means "fifty," so the time span between Passover and the Feast of Pentecost is fifty days. Jesus went to heaven on the fortieth day, and the disciples tarried in the Upper Room for ten days before Pentecost. Therefore, Jesus had about forty days of actual teaching time with His eleven disciples before His ascension (Acts 1:3). During these few days, the Lord's overarching strategy was to continue to serve His Father's plan with the same implicit trust that characterized His ministry before His crucifixion. Jesus' mission was to prepare His followers for Pentecost, spotlighting as He did the worldwide application of the stunning success His unyielding trust in His Father achieved at Golgotha. His goal included four elements:

- Giving the disciples incontrovertible proof of His resurrection.
- Teaching them to interpret the Old Testament Scriptures through the lens of His cross and resurrection.
- Preparing them for the advent of the Holy Spirit, who would birth Jesus' church and empower the Lord's worldwide strategy.
- Thoroughly instilling in them how they were to serve His agenda at home and abroad by winning people and planting them in churches.

It is important to note what was not in the Lord's curriculum. Jesus did not establish a plan of apostolic succession by appointing a successor for Judas, who betrayed Him and then committed suicide (Acts 1:15–26). He did not teach anything about church government. He did not explain how to accumulate personal wealth or to sharpen the individual self-esteem of His disciples, nor did His tutoring speak to the need to build strong marriages and families. None of these fitted His objectives; instead, the Lord sharply focused on what had to happen to launch His church. The Lord knew if:

- the disciples' faith in Him and His resurrection was absolute,

- their trust in the authority of the Scriptures was wholehearted,
- their commitment to His great command and the Great Commission was unqualified.
- they yearned to be filled with the same power for ministry that characterized His own life, so they could serve their heavenly Father and the needs of people as He did, then
- they were ready to graduate to the Upper Room to receive the Holy Spirit so the Spirit could birth the Lord's church through them.

What a curriculum!

Jesus chose to interweave His instruction on these four themes during the forty days of postresurrection ministry. This study will first offer an overview of these themes, and then give attention to each in more detail.

A. The Resurrection Appearances

1. *The Sightings on Resurrection Day.*

The New Testament writers gave specific attention to how the Lord showed Himself alive after His resurrection, leading up to His ascension.

1) The Roman soldiers guarding His tomb became the first witnesses to the breathtaking miracle. An earthquake shook the ground and an angel came down from heaven to roll away the stone. "The guards were so afraid" of the angel "they shook and became like dead men" (Matt. 28:4). The record gives no indication the soldiers actually saw the resurrected Lord, but they probably did because they clearly knew His body was missing. Some of these soldiers went into the city and shared with the chief priests "everything that had happened" (Matt. 28:11). It is striking that Gentiles—Roman soldiers—were the first to give the testimony to the chief priests that Jesus' body was no longer in the tomb. The observations of the soldiers became another gracious attempt on the Lord's part to reach out to the Jewish religious establishment—but to no avail. The chief priests' response was to bribe the soldiers "with a large sum of money" to say the disciples had stolen the body (Matt. 28:11–15). The message of these soldiers also foreshadowed that thousands of Romans would become His witnesses in the decades ahead.

2) Mary Magdalene, Joanna, Mary the mother of James, Salome, and some others who are unnamed went to the tomb with spices to assist in embalming Jesus' body (Luke 24:1, 9–10; Mark 16:1; John 19:39). Matthew wrote that they arrived almost immediately after the resurrection (Matt. 28:2–5). Mary Magdalene was the first follower of Jesus to see the resurrected Christ (Matt. 28:8–10; Mark 16:9–11; John 20:11–18; see also Matt. 28:8–10 to note that the full group of women "clasped his feet and worshiped him.")

A woman, Eve, joined her husband in bringing sin into the world (Gen. 3:6). A woman, Mary, brought Messiah into the world (Luke 2:7). And a woman, Mary Magdalene, became the first evangelist to share the resurrection story with the Lord's disciples (Mark 16:9; John 20:18). The gospel of Jesus Christ certainly elevated the status of women, making place for them in fulfilling the Lord's Great Commission (Acts 2:17–18; Gal. 3:28).

3) John outran Peter to the tomb and examined it (John 20:4). Peter also saw Jesus on resurrection day before the Lord met with the disciples that night, but the circumstances and topic of discussion at their meeting are not disclosed (Luke 24:34; 1 Cor. 15:5).

4) Jesus joined two travelers who were walking the seven-mile journey from Jerusalem to Emmaus. One of them was named Cleopas; the other is unnamed (Luke 24:13–32).

5) Jesus returned from Emmaus on the evening of the resurrection and appeared to ten of the disciples who were meeting in the Upper Room behind locked doors. Thomas was absent and a successor had not yet been named for Judas, who had committed suicide (Mark 16:14; Luke 24:36–43; Matt. 27:5).

2. Postresurrection Appearances

1) A week later, Jesus appeared to the eleven disciples when Thomas was present (John 20:26–31).

2) One evening Simon Peter, Thomas, Nathaniel, the sons of Zebedee (James and John), and two unnamed disciples went fishing on the Sea of Galilee. They worked their nets all night, but caught nothing. The next morning at sunrise Jesus met them, standing on the strand. He told them to cast their nets on the right side, and they caught so many fish they

could not pull all of them into their boat. Jesus also cooked breakfast and invited them to "come and dine." Then He reinstated Peter, after his ugly denials at the Lord's trial (John 21:1–23; Luke 22:54–62). "This was...the third time Jesus appeared to his disciples after he was raised from the dead" (John 21:14).

3) Some days later, the disciples gathered on a mountain in Galilee. They saw their resurrected Lord come walking up the mountain to meet them. On that mountaintop, where they could see for miles and envision the far reaches of their world, Jesus gave them the Great Commission (Matt. 28:16–20; Mark 16:15–18).

4) In addition to these appearances recorded in the Gospels, the apostle Paul gave his own detail in his first letter to the Corinthians.

He was seen of Cephas [Peter], then of the twelve. After that, he was seen of above five hundred brethren at once; of whom the greater part remain unto this present, but some are fallen asleep. After that, he was seen of James; then of all the apostles. And last of all he was seen of me also, as of one born out of due time.

—1 Corinthians 15:5–8, kjv

It is widely assumed that Jesus' appearance to the five hundred was on Mount Olivet at His ascension, but that is doubtful. The record states, "After that, he was seen of James; then of all the apostles" (1 Cor. 15:7). These appearances to James and to the eleven would not have been possible if the appearance to the five hundred were at His ascension. What is very clear, Luke wrote, is that "[Jesus] showed himself to these men and gave many convincing proofs that he was alive" (Acts 1:3).

The Lord did not enjoy the heartfelt devotion of all of His disciples before His crucifixion, but that changed radically after His resurrection. As their understanding of the meaning of the gospel matured, Jesus blossomed in their lives as the "lily of the valley" and the "rose of Sharon" (Song of Sol. 2:1). They would never again turn their backs on Him and run away (Mark 14:50).

B. Interpreting the Old Testament Scriptures

1. The Bifocals of the Cross and the Empty Tomb

Jesus also used those precious few days between His resurrection and His ascension to help His followers grasp the second dimension of the curriculum.

They had to learn to let the lens of the Lord's cross and empty tomb frame their vision for everything in the Old Testament. The glorified Christ to this day is the mediator of the new and better covenant, demonstrating powerfully His continuing role as Servant of all (Jer. 31:33; Matt. 26:28; 1 Tim. 2:5; Heb. 7:22; 9:15).

2. The Road to Emmaus

Jesus actually began to teach this kind of understanding on the very day He came back to life, as He made the trip from Jerusalem to Emmaus with two of his followers. Luke writes in his Gospel that "they were talking with each other about everything that had happened. As they…discussed these things…Jesus himself came up and walked along with them; but they were kept from recognizing him" (Luke 24:14–16). "What are you discussing together as you walk along?" He asked them (v. 17).

The question shocked the very downcast men, and in their incredulity, they actually stood still in the road. Cleopas spoke first and asked him:

> "Are you only a visitor to Jerusalem and do not know the things that have happened there in these days?" "What things?" he asked. "About Jesus of Nazareth," they replied. "He was a prophet, powerful in word and deed before God and all the people. The chief priests and our rulers handed him over to be sentenced to death, and they crucified him; but we had hoped that he was the one who was going to redeem Israel. And what is more, it is the third day since all this took place. In addition, some of our women amazed us. They went to the tomb early this morning but didn't find his body. They came and told us that they had seen a vision of angels, who said he was alive. Then some of our companions went to the tomb and found it just as the women had said, but him they did not see.
>
> —Luke 24:19–24

Jesus immediately gave Cleopas and his companion the explanation why they were having trouble accepting the reports. They had foolishly let their hearts become infected with a spiritual malady known as "slowness of heart to believe all the prophets have spoken" (Luke 24:25). Then He proceeded to give them His first postresurrection lesson on how the Cross is the great interpreter of the Old Testament Scriptures. He began by saying, "Did not the Christ have to suffer these things and then enter his glory? And beginning with Moses and all the Prophets, he explained to them what was said in all the Scriptures concerning himself" (Luke 24:26–27).

After reaching Emmaus, the two men urged Him to join them for dinner.

Jesus accepted the invitation, and as He prayed over the food and blessed it, "their eyes were opened, and they recognized him, and he disappeared from their sight" (Luke 24:31). (The statement, "He disappeared from their sight," is one of the first expressions after the Lord's resurrection that shows how time and space no longer limited the glorified Christ.) Cleopas and his unnamed friend asked each other, "Were not our hearts burning within us while he talked with us on the road and opened the Scriptures to us?" (Luke 24:32).

The record does not tell what Scriptures Jesus explained, but the story is clear He had a keen interest in teaching His followers to interpret the Old Testament through the lens of His Cross.

Luke's account of the walk to Emmaus also shows how invigorated Jesus was in His glorified body. Only three days earlier, He had been cruelly beaten, "disfigured...and marred beyond human likeness" (Isa. 52:14). But Jesus did not have the appearance of a man who had been brutalized some seventy-two hours earlier. Instead, He was so full of energy He kept the pace with these two men on at least a three-hour walk of about seven miles.

Luke does not tell the method Jesus used to return to Jerusalem that same night after He disappeared from the meal at Emmaus. However, "on the evening of that first day of the week"—resurrection day—"when the disciples were together with the doors locked for fear of the Jews," Jesus appeared in their midst (John 20:19). Neither the distance from Emmaus nor the bolted doors placed limitations on the Lord in His resurrected glory. In fact, Jesus is the key to any lock that exists.

"This is what I told you while I was still with you," Jesus said to them. "Everything must be fulfilled that is written about me in the Law of Moses, the Prophets and the Psalms. Then he opened their minds so they could understand the Scriptures" (Luke 24:44–45).

The apostle Peter learned the lesson so well he placed the whole era of the Old Testament prophets in crucifixion focus with two summary statements. The first was in his sermon in Cornelius' house. It included an insightful expression about the Messianic expectations of the prophets: "All the prophets testify about [Jesus] that everyone who believes in him receives forgiveness of sins through his name" (Acts 10:43). The Lord surely taught Peter this conclusion during the teaching of the forty days. Every person in the Old Testament who looked forward in faith and believed in the coming Messiah experienced salvation at the cross, just as all believers today look back on the Christ of the cross and experience the forgiveness of God. So the cross of Jesus links the message of the prophets with the message of the Lord Himself and His holy apostles—that Jesus Christ is the one door to eternal life (Acts 4:12).

Peter's second summary statement showed the spirit of the Messiah that was in the prophets filled them with intense desire to comprehend the time and circumstances of the Lord's appearing.

> Concerning this salvation, the prophets, who spoke of the grace that was to come…searched intently and with the greatest care, trying to find out the time and circumstances to which the Spirit of Christ in them was pointing when he predicted the sufferings of Christ and the glories that would follow.
> —1 PETER 1:10–11

While the quest of the prophets was diligent, Peter understood that correct interpretation of the old covenant was possible only in the hindsight of Calvary and the empty tomb.

3. The Thomas Principle

A key prerequisite to the Lord's forty-day curriculum was the necessity to settle the matter of faith versus doubt. Jesus trusted His Father implicitly, and His love led His followers to the same conclusion. But when Jesus appeared to the disciples on resurrection night, Thomas was absent. The disciples later told Thomas the Lord had appeared to them behind locked doors, but Thomas responded, "Unless I see in his hands the print of the nails, and put my finger into the print of the nails, and thrust my hand into his side, I will not believe" (John 20:25, KJV; Mark 16:14). Thomas got his chance a week later when the Lord appeared again to the disciples.

> Though the doors were locked, Jesus came and stood among them and said, "Peace be with you!" Then he said to Thomas, "Put your finger here; see my hands. Reach out your hand and put it into my side. Stop doubting and believe." Thomas said to him, "My Lord and my God!" Then Jesus told him, "Because you have seen me, you have believed; blessed are those who have not seen and yet have believed."
> —JOHN 20:26–29

In Jesus' eyes, both faith and unbelief are choices made in response to the enormity of the evidence for His resurrection. So much proof existed, in fact, that Jesus commanded Thomas, "Stop doubting and believe" (John 20:27). So, the Thomas principle says faith in the physical and bodily resurrection of Jesus Christ is not a question of credible evidence; of that, there is abundance. If a person does not believe and accept the resurrection of Jesus as a historical event, he refuses to do so because in his own heart he makes the choice to deny the evidence. Unwillingness in the face of the evidence is the tipping point in the Thomas Principle. The bodily resurrection of Jesus is beyond dispute to a person of reasonable mind (John 7:17; Heb. 3:12). Hence, the Lord's command to Thomas was for him to make the right choice: "Stop doubting and believe!" The implication of the command is that Thomas could change his mind and choose to believe the evidence, and he did.

"My Lord and my God," was Thomas' answer to Jesus (John 20:28). Thomas believed because the evidence was standing there in front of him. He could see Jesus and touch Him.

All of God's children since the Lord's ascension have found it necessary to believe the evidence based on the historical records in the Bible, witnessed to by the Holy Spirit. Hence, Jesus spoke a special blessing on all of His followers since the resurrection. He said to Thomas, "Because you have seen me, you have believed; blessed are those who have not seen and yet have believed" (John 20:29).

The Thomas principle is at work to this day. Not to honor the wealth of the evidence, however, in the language of the psalmist, is to play "the fool" (Ps. 14:1).

C. Preparation for Pentecost and the Lord's International Vision

When Jesus appeared among them on resurrection night, He said to them:

> "Peace be with you!" Then he showed them his hands and side. The disciples were overjoyed when they saw the Lord. Again, Jesus said, "Peace be with you! As the Father has sent me, I am sending you." And with that he breathed on them and said, "Receive the Holy Spirit. If you forgive anyone his sins, they are forgiven; if you do not forgive them, they are not forgiven."
>
> —JOHN 20:19–23

Twice in this statement the Lord said, "Peace be with you." The first affirmation carried the proof of His nail scars in his hands and His side. The second embraced the promised gift of the Holy Spirit that empowers believers and births churches. When a believer knows Jesus has been raised from the dead and that he has received the gift of the Holy Spirit, he will be at peace about the meaning and direction of his life.

Preparing His disciples for Pentecost was just this critical to the teaching of the forty days. Receiving the Holy Spirit meant the apostles would actually be empowered to proclaim forgiveness of sins through Jesus Christ. It also meant they would have the assignment to develop the church Jesus had prophetically foretold at Caesarea Philippi (Matt. 16:18). The prophets had announced the diagnosis of man's sinfulness, which called for repentance, but they enjoyed only minimal understanding of the remedy. The apostles after Pentecost knew the cure and proclaimed it boldly, offering in Jesus' name actual forgiveness of sins (John 20:23).

The crucifixion and resurrection demonstrate the specific work of the Holy Spirit is to draw men to Christ, with Jesus alone holding the authority to forgive sins (Matt. 9:6; John 20:23). The Lord's followers cooperate in that forgiveness by affirming what the Holy Spirit will do in their lives if they believe and repent. It is often true, however, that an individual who has repented of his sins needs to hear a servant of the Lord whom he trusts affirm to him that God has, in fact, forgiven his sins. It really is an awesome authority.

⊰ Brother, Your Sins Are Forgiven! ⊱

"Years ago in Guatemala," wrote Luis Palau in *Discipleship Journal*, "a man came to me who had dishonored our Lord's name. He was truly broken and had repented. Yet he was still without joy. It was obvious he needed to be assured that he was forgiven; otherwise Satan would have gained an advantage over him.

"I did something then which until that day I had never done. I put my arm around him and said, 'Brother, you've repented; your sins are forgiven. Let me pray with you.'

"And this broken, humble Guatemalan said, 'Oh, thank you, thank you. Now I'm free!'

"With tears running down our faces, we hugged each other. He was so excited, because a fellow brother in Christ had reassured him.

"But this man should have been reassured earlier by his local church. When someone is obviously broken and repentant, the church must stand up and say, 'In the name of the Lord Jesus, rejoice! He has forgiven you, and we forgive you too.' The assurance from such corporate forgiveness brings healing and joy to the entire congregation."[2]

Jesus actually began to teach His disciples to expect the gift of the Holy Spirit before His crucifixion (John 24:16–18, 26). On the very evening of His resurrection, He picked up the theme again as the first item on His agenda and took it to a new level. The matter was urgent because the Feast of Pentecost was only a few weeks away. Jesus showed them the inseparable link between the baptism with the Holy Spirit and the birth of the church He had prophesied at Caesarea Philippi. In fact, without the baptism with the Spirit, there would be no church, and the disciples would be powerless before the challenges that would come against the Lord's agenda to reach all people.

When Jesus "breathed on them" that night, He demonstrated that receiving the Holy Spirit would be like experiencing a refreshing gust of cool air (John 20:22). The Greek term *emphusao* indicates that He actually puffed, or blew, on them (Gal. 5:25, KJV).

The Lord knew the baptism with the Holy Spirit was an absolute necessity if they were to fulfill His international mission. The implications were huge. For example, without the Spirit that empowered His own life residing in the disciples, they would not be able to interpret the Scriptures correctly. In fact, while Jesus was among them, He had to open their minds in order to explain the Scriptures to them (Luke 24:45). In addition, without the baptism with the Spirit, they would be powerless before the challenges of His worldwide agenda.

Regarding His international vision, Jesus said to the disciples on resurrection night, "As the Father has sent me, I am sending you" (John 20:21). The revelation of His plans to save the world would certainly get more of His attention as the six weeks of teaching progressed.

⊰ Love Sets the International Agenda ⊱

Beyond the Gates of Splendor is a documentary film that tells the true story of five American missionaries: Jim Elliot, Pete Fleming, Ed McCully, Nate Saint, and Roger Youderian, who in January 1956 were speared to death in the jungles of Ecuador by the Auca Indians, an isolated tribe known as the Waodani.

At first, the missionaries found acceptance among the Auca, but eventually they experienced their fierce hostility.

In a testament to the love of Christ that sets people apart to the Lord's worldwide agenda, family members of the slain missionaries returned to live among the tribe. They evangelized the very people who had killed their loved ones.

In one riveting scene, Kathy and Steve Saint, the children of Nate Saint, speak of their own baptisms administered by the Aucas who now believe.

Kimo, a participant in the killings and the baptisms, refers to Steve's baptism. "By his father's grave we did it when Steve was a little older. It was right up the river there. He brought his mother too."

"I was in the same water where my dad's body had been thrown," Kathy says, "and at either side of me were the two men that in their youth had killed dad. And all I knew was that I really loved these two guys."[3]

II. "Beginning With Moses and All the Prophets" (Luke 24:27)

With this overview in place, we begin to explore how the Lord opened up the things in the Scriptures concerning Himself, beginning on the Emmaus Road (Luke 24:13–27). Because the Holy Spirit did not make the specific Emmaus conversation part of the biblical story, what the Lord shared with them must be discovered another way. By looking at what the apostles taught as they laid the foundation for the Lord's church, it becomes clear how the Cross and the resurrection of Jesus brought new meaning to the Old Testament Scriptures (Eph. 2:20).

A. The Law

The Cross and resurrection refocused the Law of Moses. The Ten Commandments given to Moses from the finger of God provided opportunity for the Israelites to live their lives attuned to the Spirit of God. In fact, the ultimate design of the Law was to assist the people in discovering their Messiah, "that [they] might be justified by faith" (Gal. 3:24; see also Gen. 15:6; Exod. 33:12–23). The Hebrew people were responsible to look past the Law to see and love the Lord of the regulations and live in the hope of their coming Redeemer. Regarding Him, Moses prophesied, "The Lord your God will raise up for you a Prophet like me from among your own brothers. You must listen to him" (Deut. 18:15). To worship this Messiah, they would have to receive Moses' specific teaching and make the spirit of the commandments their center of attention: "Love the Lord your God with all your heart and soul and strength," and "your neighbor as yourself" (Deut. 6:5; Lev. 19:18).

Over time, the focus of national attention in their history fixed on the Law itself and its outward forms, to the neglect of the love of God that gave them their laws (Joel 2:13; Ps. 51:17; Isa. 1:11; Jer. 6:20). This helps to explain why the nation rejected her Messiah when He finally came, even though He demonstrated a perfect balance between the letter of the Law and the spirit of the Law (2 Cor. 3:6).

Even with this limitation, the Law provided a dependable standard by which to execute judgment. The code achieved this by making clear to the people their personal and their national guilt. In addition, the sacrificial system became a veritable university in which Israel could learn of her coming Savior and receive justification by faith (Gal. 3:24, KJV).

B. The Jewish Feasts

The Passover Feast, the Feast of Firstfruits, and the Feast of Weeks provide excellent opportunities to show how the cross and resurrection of Jesus refocused the Scriptures.

The Passover Feast began on the fourteenth day of the first month of the Jewish calendar and continued for seven days. It was normally an April celebration (according to our modern calendar). Passover reminded the people of their miraculous exodus from Egyptian slavery, which took place after each family had sacrificed their first Passover lamb (Exod. 12:1–13; Lev. 23:4–8; Deut. 16:1). Jesus was Himself offered through the eternal Spirit as the Passover Lamb (1 Cor. 5:7; Heb. 9:14). Christ's crucifixion occurred on the first morning of the Passover Feast at the precise time of the Passover sacrifice in the temple.

The Feast of Firstfruits came on the sixteenth day of the first month, or on the third day after the start of the Passover Feast. God designed the annual festival for the people to acknowledge that their sustenance came from the land itself and had its origin in God. Jehovah generously blessed their fields with grain and produce (Lev. 23:9–14). The Feast of Firstfruits taught that God was their nourishment, providing them with honey, grapes, olive oil, and wheat. Therefore, they were to bring to God an offering of the harvest from their fields (Lev. 2:12).

The Feast of Firstfruits, coming three days after Passover, enjoyed its ultimate fulfillment in the resurrection of Jesus Christ, who arose on the third day as the "firstfruits of those who have fallen asleep" (1 Cor. 15:20, 23).

God was the life of the people, imparting to them His own life in their grain and produce. In the same sense, Jesus Christ is our Bread of Life (John 6:35, 48). He is our manna come down from heaven, our Living Water, and our meat (John 4:10; 4:34; 6:48; 6:55–58). Because Jesus arose from the dead as the firstfruits of the Resurrection, He is our assurance that we will be raised in His likeness (Rom. 6:4; 8:11).

The Feast of Weeks came on the fiftieth day after Passover (Lev. 23:15–16; Deut. 16:9–12). The occasion was termed the Feast of Pentecost in the New Testament because the Greek word *pentakosta* means "fiftieth." At this feast, the men of the nation gathered annually before the Lord at the end of their May wheat harvest to present their gifts to Him. They offered God praise in gratitude for the sustaining life that came from their crops.

By the time Jesus was born, the Feast of Pentecost had developed into one of the most important events on the Jewish calendar. Jews, by the tens of thousands, made their annual pilgrimages to Jerusalem to celebrate the great festival, swelling the population of Jerusalem and straining its tourist facilities.

The heavenly Father poured out the Holy Spirit in New Testament fullness exactly fifty days after Jesus Christ became the Passover Lamb. As the grain and produce of their fields gave the people life and energy to serve God, so the Holy Spirit gives believers strength and vigor to obey the Lord's Great Commission in the spirit of the great command (Matt. 28:18; Luke 24:45–49; Acts 1:8). He is the Spirit of Life who indwells or tabernacles with those who receive Him. This empowering is necessary, for the harvest truly is great. Indeed, the fields "are ripe for harvest," but "the workers are few" (Luke 10:2; John 4:35).

C. The Prophets' Predictions About the Messiah

The seers in the Old Testament gave a host of predictions about Israel's Messiah, and the New Testament writers of the Gospels were careful to record their fulfillment. At the time of the Lord's resurrection, however, the disciples had only minimally begun to link these prophecies with Jesus. The Savior opened up each of them as He taught them. Some of the many passages that Jesus' life and ministry explained included the following:

- Messiah was the offspring of the woman—Mary was Jesus' mother, through Eve, the first mother (Gen. 3:15; Matt. 1:16; Luke 3:23; Gal. 4:4)
- As the descendant of Abraham, Jesus, the Messiah, was the One through whom everyone on Earth is blessed (Gen. 12:3; 18:18; Acts 3:25, 26; Gal. 3:16)
- Messiah was a descendant of Judah (Gen. 49:10; Matt. 1:2; Luke 3:33)
- He was also a descendant of David (Ps. 132:11; Jer. 23:5; 33:15; Luke 1:32)
- A virgin brought Him into the world (Isa. 7:14; Matt. 1:18; Luke 1:26–27)
- Bethlehem was His birthplace (Micah 5:2; Matt. 2:1; Luke 2:4)
- His ministry began in Galilee (Isa. 9:1; Matt. 4:15)
- He entered the temple with authority (Mal. 3:1; Matt. 21:12; Luke 19:45)
- He was the Son of God (Ps. 2:7; Matt. 3:17; Luke 3:22; John 20:28–29)
- He came as our Savior and Redeemer (Ps. 130:8; Matt. 1:21)
- He was the great sanctifier (Exod. 31:13; Heb. 2:11)
- He was the baptizer with the Holy Spirit, a gift available to everyone (Joel 2:28; John 14:16, 26)

- Messiah healed all of the sicknesses and diseases of the people, including the blind, the deaf, and the lame, as well as casting out devils (Ps. 103:3; Isa. 35:5; Matt. 4:23; 10:8; 11:3–5; John 11:47)
- He came to the earth first as a suffering Servant and will come a second time as a reigning King (Isa. 53; 1 Thess. 4:16; Zech. 14:4; Rev. 19:16)
- The authorities brutally mistreated Him (Ps. 22; 35:11; Matt. 26:59–60; 27:34–50; Luke 23:11, 35–39; John 19:31–36)
- The hatred poured on Him was without cause (Ps. 41:9; 69:4; John 15:23)
- He expected a friend to betray Him (Ps. 41:9; John 13:18)
- He entered Jerusalem riding a donkey (Zech. 9:9; John 12:15)
- Messiah was sold for thirty pieces of silver (Zech. 11:12; Matt. 26:15; 27:3)
- He was forsaken by His disciples (Zech. 13:7; Matt. 26:31, 56)
- He was a stone the builders rejected; yet He became the Cornerstone (Ps. 118:22; Isa. 28:16; Matt. 21:42; 1 Pet. 2:6)
- Israel's Savior was silent in front of His accusers (Isa. 53:7; Matt. 26:62–63)
- He died with criminals (Isa. 53:12; Matt. 27:38)
- He was buried with the rich (Isa. 53:9; Matt. 27:59–60)
- He arose from the dead (Ps. 16:10; 49:15; Isa. 52:13; Matt. 28:5–9)
- He instituted a new and everlasting covenant that communicates the life giving love of God (Jer. 31:31; Luke 22:20; John 6:63; Gal. 3:21; Heb. 8:6)
- Messiah continues to serve as an eternal priest in the order of Melchizedek (Ps. 110:4; Heb. 5:6)
- He was an intercessor (Isa. 59:16, KJV; Heb. 7:25; 9:15)
- He baptizes any thirsty believer with the Holy Spirit and sends His message even to the remote islands of the seas (Num. 11:29; Joel 2:28–32; Matt. 3:11; Acts 2:16–21; Isa. 42:4)

D. The Holy Spirit in the Prophets

Jesus wanted His disciples to comprehend the work of the Holy Spirit in their ancient seers through the lens of His crucifixion and resurrection. Throughout the long legacy of the prophets, the Spirit was the presence who energized their ministries and made miraculous things happen (Josh. 6:20; 1 Kings 18:36–38).

Moses surely enjoyed the presence of the Spirit of God while leading the nation. The Lord even told Moses He would give the same Spirit that was on him to the seventy elders whom Moses appointed to assist in judging Israel (Num. 11:16–17). When the Spirit of the Lord actually came on the seventy, they began to prophesy (Num. 11:25). Moses also expressed an earnest desire that all of God's people would be prophets, and that the Lord would put His Spirit on them (Num. 11:29).

Both David and Isaiah understood Him to be the Spirit of holiness who develops the character of God in men (Ps. 51:11; 143:10; Isa. 30:1). Isaiah also perceived that the Holy Spirit has feelings and said sin grieves the Spirit (Isa. 63:10).

The psalmist perceived the impossibility of running away from the presence of the Spirit (Ps. 139:7). Nehemiah understood that during the long wilderness journey, the "good Spirit" had been sent by God to the nation to instruct the people (Neh. 9:20).

Isaiah said the Messiah would possess "the Spirit of wisdom and understanding, the Spirit of counsel and might, the Spirit of knowledge and of the fear of the Lord" (Isa. 11:2). One result of the Spirit in the Messiah's life would be His "quick understanding" (Isa. 11:3, KJV).

Ezekiel the prophet lived as a captive in Babylon. While there, "The Spirit took me up," Ezekiel wrote, transporting him in the vision to Jerusalem (Ezek. 8:3). Ezekiel even witnessed in a vision the Spirit depart from the temple (Ezek. 3:12; 8:3; 11:23).

Nebuchadnezzar and the queen mother of Babylon recognized that the "spirit of the holy gods" was in Daniel (Dan. 4:8; 5:11). The anointing of the Spirit to govern was the only valid explanation for his long tenure of civil service in Babylon and Persia, in which he maintained an untainted character. Except by the Spirit of God, how else can one explain Daniel's accurate prophecies regarding the international circumstances at the time of the Messiah's birth (Dan. 2:34–45)?

Haggai said God's covenant with Israel included the promise of the abiding presence of the Spirit. "My Spirit remains among you. Do not fear," wrote the prophet (Hag. 2:5).

Zechariah knew that Israel's success depended on the Spirit. He expressed that reliance as a word from God for Zerubbabel: "'Not by might, nor by power, but by my Spirit,' says the Lord Almighty" (Zech. 4:6).

When John the Baptist and then Jesus came talking about the baptism with the Holy Spirit and with fire, plenty of evidence was already in the Jewish heritage to accept the new aspects of the revelation (Matt. 3:11).

E. The Manifestation Gifts of the Spirit in the Old Covenant

The gifts of the Spirit enumerated in 1 Corinthians 12:8–11 find expression in the Old Testament prophets. In each of these pre-age of the Spirit manifestations, God, by the Holy Spirit, demonstrated Himself in mighty power. But for all of the marvelous ways that the Spirit worked through the prophets, using them to meet particular needs on special occasions, they were only types and forerunners of the dispensation of the Spirit (Heb. 10:1; 11:40).

- Joseph told Pharaoh in a *message of wisdom,* how Egypt should prepare for the famine that was coming (Gen. 41:14–57).
- Elisha spoke a *message of knowledge* in his counsel to the confederated kings before the Moabite War (2 Kings 3:10–17). Elisha manifested the gift again when he accurately announced the troop movements of the Syrian army (2 Kings 6:8–12). Through the Holy Spirit, Nathan knew the details of David's sin (2 Sam. 12:1–14).
- Abraham powerfully demonstrated the *gift of faith* when he offered up Isaac (Gen. 22:9–12). Elijah showed it again in the contest with Baal on Mount Carmel (1 Kings 18:1–39).
- Moses manifested *gifts of healing* when he placed the serpent on a pole in the wilderness. All of the Israelites who looked on the serpent were cured (Num. 21:8; John 3:14). The same was true in their experience with the bitter waters at Marah. On that occasion, Jehovah revealed Himself as Jehovah-Rapha, "the Lord that heals you" (Exod. 15:26).
- The Holy Spirit demonstrated the gift of *working miracles* through Moses at the Red Sea (Exod. 14). Moses also wrought many other miracles, such as the ground opening up to swallow Korah and his followers in the most significant rebellion of the wilderness sojourn (Num. 16:31–33).
- Each of the prophets exercised the *gift of prophecy.* This was so self-evident it warrants little discussion. A greedy, pagan prophet like Baalam could only speak what the Lord gave him, although Balak promised him many bribes to curse Israel (Num. 23 and 24).
- An Old Testament type of the *gift of tongues* and of the *interpretation of tongues* was expressed at drunken Belshazzar's feast, when a finger wrote on the wall, "Mene, Mene, Tekel, Upharsin" (Dan. 5:25, KJV). Clearly the handwriting came from God, and it was a language unknown to Belshazzar and

all of his wise men. Only Daniel could interpret the message that weighed Belshazzar in the balances of divine justice and found him wanting (Dan. 5:11, 27).

F. The Outpouring of the Spirit in Prophecy

The plan was for the gift of the eternal Spirit to come at Jesus' request, as a gift from the Father, after the ascension of Jesus (John 14:16). The Spirit Miriam experienced at the Red Sea and the elders saw in action at the "Pentecost in the wilderness" was the same Spirit present in the Upper Room (Exod. 15:19–21; Num. 11:24–30; Acts 2:1–4).

Israel met God in the sacrificial system as the Shekinah glory manifested in their many offerings. The Spirit resided in the most holy place, dwelling between the cherubim. The priests knew it and the people were aware of it, but experiencing this presence was a blessing enjoyed by only a minority of the people, not the masses. In this context, Moses' prophetic insight surely took on a rich new meaning when he said to Joshua, "Are you jealous for my sake? I wish that all of the Lord's people were prophets, and the Lord would put his spirit on them!" (Num. 11:29).

Isaiah foresaw the day when a downpour of the Spirit would come on the people from on high, and it would be very refreshing to them, like water on a parched tongue (Isa. 32:15). The blessing on their offspring would be as floods on thirsty land (Isa. 44:3).

The first covenant had a corporate and representative nature. The Spirit came on the prophets, priests, and kings, but on very few individual Israelites. Jeremiah understood that would change, because the Lord planned to frame a new relationship with Israel. A striking individualism would mark this innovative new covenant. "I will put my law in their minds and write it in their hearts," God said to Jeremiah. "I will be their God and they will be my people" (Jer. 31:33; see also Ezek. 36:27; 39:29; Heb. 8:10; 10:16).

The prophet Joel was the seer who most clearly foresaw this individualism would express itself as an outpouring of the Spirit "on all people" (Joel 2:28). Israel was surely to be included, but so were all other peoples worldwide. The Father's promise would be a universal gift. The backdrop of the cross and the empty tomb was necessary, however, to discover this new meaning.

Joel vividly foretold a famine that would devastate Judah. The locusts would eat everything, he predicted, and a long drought would follow. Conditions would become so difficult that offerings on the temple altar would be suspended (Joel 1:13). Joel used this ominous prophecy to call the people to God. Joel also saw the day when the rains would return and their fields would be productive again. This backdrop became his analogy to proclaim the outpouring of the Holy Spirit as the former and latter rain (Joel 2:23–27, KJV).

According to the apostle Peter, the Acts 2 outpouring of the Holy Spirit on the Day of Pentecost was a direct fulfillment of Joel's prophecy, a conclusion he surely learned from the Lord during Jesus' forty days of teaching. Joel said the blessing would come to their sons and daughters, their old men and young men. Even the servants and the handmaids would receive this outpouring (Joel 2:28–29; Acts 2:18). Peter preached this same doctrine of both the individualism and universality of the Spirit when he said in his Pentecost sermon, "The promise is for you and your children and for all who are far off—for all whom the Lord our God will call" (Acts 2:39).

G. The Role of John the Baptist

The bifocals of the cross and the empty tomb also opened up the significance of the life of John the Baptist. Gabriel had announced the news of John's birth when he visited Zechariah, a Levite of the priestly division of Abijah, as he was offering incense in the temple (Luke 1:5–20). The angel proclaimed that God had chosen Zechariah and Elizabeth, a childless elderly couple, to be the parents of the forerunner of the Messiah. They "were both righteous before God...walking blamelessly in all the commandments and ordinances of the Lord" (Luke 1:6, KJV).

Gabriel said John would "go on before the Lord in the spirit and power of Elijah...to make ready a people prepared for the Lord" (Luke 1:17; Matt. 3:3). John did prepare the way for Messiah's arrival (John 1:29). He foretold Christ's coming, announced His appearance when Jesus arrived at the Jordan River, and baptized the Lord "to fulfill all righteousness" (Matt. 3:15; Mark 1:7). Jesus Himself said none of the prophets were as great as John the Baptist (Matt. 11:11; Luke 7:28).

John's baptism in the Jordan was a baptism that called on the people to "produce fruit in keeping with repentance" (Luke 3:8). He also told the people bluntly not to even begin to say they were relying on Abraham as their spiritual father (Matt. 3:9). John insisted instead on personal repentance and personal faith, if they were to make straight paths for the Messiah about to be revealed (Matt. 3:3; Luke 3:4).

John the Baptist, as a Spirit-filled man, also predicted the age of the Spirit, which the redemptive accomplishments of Messiah would launch. Moses had wished for it and Joel had foreseen it (Num. 11:29; Joel 2:28). John the Baptist followed in the footsteps of these great prophets. He announced to the crowd assembled at the Jordan to hear him that the gift of the Spirit was for all of them and not merely a select few. Addressing himself to the throng from

"Jerusalem, all of Judea, and the whole region of the Jordan," John explained, "I baptize you with water for repentance. But after me will come one who is more powerful than I, whose sandals I am not fit to carry. He will baptize you with the Holy Spirit and with fire" (Matt. 3:5, 11; Mark 1:8; Luke 3:16).

Before Jesus' crucifixion, John the Baptist's teaching had been a marvel wrapped in mystery in the eyes of so many (Luke 3:1–18; John 1:19–27). But after the resurrection, John's message made plenty of sense. Indeed, life always makes sense at the foot of the cross.

III. The Ministry of the Spirit

During the Lord's forty days of teaching, it is reasonable to assume Jesus rehearsed with His disciples what He shared with them before His crucifixion about the Father's gift of the Holy Spirit. The clear message of the New Testament is that every believer should make his way from Mount Calvary to his own Upper Room to receive the infilling of the Spirit.

A. The Humility of the Spirit

God is love and love "keeps no record of wrongs" (1 Cor. 13:5; 1 John 4:8). Rather, love is always content to act in humility with the best interests of others in mind. This attribute finds its perfect expression in the Godhead. Each coequal member of the Trinity exists for the others and lovingly submits to the others (John 15:26; Acts 10:38). This understanding of the basic nature of the Godhead explains why there can never be division or selfishness in the Trinity.

The church as the body of Christ desperately needs to learn this lesson of humility, which the Trinity so absolutely mirrors. Surely doing so would resolve many problems in the household of faith. How much better to yield oneself fully to God as a vessel filled with the Holy Spirit, earnestly desiring to be directed by the Spirit!

B. The Spirit as Living Water

It was on the final day of the Feast of Tabernacles in Jerusalem that Jesus stood and cried, "If anyone is thirsty, let him come to me and drink. Whoever believes in me, as the Scripture has said, streams of living water will flow out of him" (John 7:37–38). The apostle John explained this passionate statement: "He spoke this of the Spirit which they that believe on him should receive: for the Holy Spirit was not yet given; because Jesus was not yet glorified" (John 7:39, KJV).

The burning desire of Jesus' heart was for everyone at the feast to receive the gift He promised. In fact, Jesus gave the prophecy at the temple in Jerusalem that this experience would be available to "any thirsty man" (John 7:37, KJV). The Lord planned to pour out these blessings regardless of age, gender, social status, race, or national origin. As the apostle Paul expressed, "There is neither Jew nor Greek, slave nor free, there is neither male nor female: for you are all one in Christ Jesus" (Gal. 3:28). It is required, however, if a person would receive the Holy Spirit, that he be "thirsty" enough to "come to [Christ] and drink" (John 7:37). "If you knew the gift of God and who it is that asks you for a drink," Jesus said to the woman at Jacob's well, "you would have asked him and he would have given you living water" (John 4:10).

C. The Spirit as a Comforter

Jesus ate His final Passover Feast with His disciples and used the occasion to prepare them more thoroughly for His departure and for the coming of the Holy Spirit. "Let not your heart be troubled," Jesus said. "Ye believe in God, believe also in me. In my Father's house are many mansions: if it were not so, I would have told you. I go to prepare a place for you. And if I go and prepare a place for you, I will come again, and receive you unto myself; that where I am, there ye may be also" (John 14:1–2, KJV).

This great affirmation obviously seemed bittersweet to the disciples. It was bitter because Jesus clearly intended to leave them. It was also sweet because the Master was thinking of their interests (going to prepare a place for them and promising to come back to get them). For the disciples, who had learned to love His presence, it is easy to understand their thoughts as they began to feel acute separation anxiety.

Jesus perceived their concern, reaffirmed to them that He and His Father are One, and reminded them that if they would ask in His name, He would do it (John 14:13). Then He gave this marvelous promise:

> If you love me, you will obey what I command. And I will ask the Father, and he will give you another Counselor to be with you forever—the Spirit of truth. The world cannot accept him, because it neither sees him nor knows him. But you know him, for he lives with you and will be in you. I will not leave you as orphans; I will come to you.
>
> —JOHN 14:15–18

Paraclete is the English word for the Greek term *parakletos* that means "counselor or comforter" (John 14:16). The same word is also translated "advocate," or one who pleads the case of another (1 John 2:1, KJV). The Holy Spirit is the divine Advocate who indwells the believer and pleads his case. As was true with the woman caught in the act of adultery, the child of God has a heavenly attorney, the Holy Spirit. He is the Spirit of truth who never forsakes His own to a life of orphans (John 14:18). The Lord's plan is for the Holy Spirit, the Spirit of truth, to tabernacle continually with man. As the Spirit does so, He does not speak of Himself. Rather, He shows the believer things to come, giving all the glory to Jesus (John 1:13–16; 16:13–14). This Attorney sent from God certainly showed His mettle in His defense of the woman caught in the act of adultery (John 8:3–11).

The Paraclete

In the book *Healing the Masculine Soul*, Gordon Dalbey says when Jesus refers to the Holy Spirit as the Helper, he uses a Greek word, *paraclete*, an ancient warrior's term. "Greek soldiers went into battle in pairs," says Dalbey, "so when the enemy attacked, they could draw together back-to-back, covering each other's blind side. A soldier's battle partner was the Paraclete.

"Our Lord does not send us to fight the good fight alone. The Holy Spirit is our battle partner who covers our blind side and fights for our well-being."[4]

The word translated "another counselor" in John 14:16 indicates that the Holy Spirit, who would take Jesus' place, would be just like Himself. The disciples must have often wondered what these precrucifixion teachings meant, but the death and resurrection of Jesus, coupled with the Lord's teaching in the forty days, quickly cleared the fog out of their hearts and prepared them for His ascension and for Pentecost.

D. The Spirit as a Teacher

Jesus showed His disciples during His Last Supper that the coming Holy Spirit would be their Teacher. His curriculum would be the person and ministry of the Lord Jesus. The Spirit will teach "you all things," Jesus said, "and will remind you of everything I have said to you" (John 14:26).

As a teacher, the Holy Spirit is the true interpreter of the Scriptures. He illuminated the Bible as the written Word to enable the disciples to learn who Jesus Christ is. It took Pentecost, however, with portraits of Calvary and the empty tomb hanging on the wall of their memories, to help them get the full picture.

IV. The Lord's Worldwide Agenda

A. Servants of His Blueprint

Sensing Jesus' burning passion as He shared His international vision must have been a great experience for the disciples during the last forty days of the Lord's ministry among them. They not only needed to *hear* Jesus teach the vision, they also had to comprehend it, and then assimilate into their lives that the Lord had selected *them* as His witnesses. Jesus had actually set them apart as the servants of His blueprint for the salvation of the world (Matt. 16:18; 28:16–20).

The strategy of the Godhead from eternity was that the Holy Spirit would administer the work of the Lord's agenda for the nations. Nothing less than a baptism or infilling of the Holy Spirit was necessary to enable the disciples to commit successfully to Jesus' servant character and worldwide plan to win people and fold them into churches.

After Pentecost, with the resurrection fresh in their minds, they began to comprehend just how much spiritual and moral influence the Lord had given them, and spiritual and moral authority will always ultimately trump political and financial authority. The Spirit became to the disciples "the power of God and the wisdom of God" (1 Cor. 1:24).

B. The Great Commission

Two prophecies highlight the Lord's vision for the nations. The first came at Caesarea Philippi, before His crucifixion, when He announced, "I will build my church" (Matt. 16:18). The second occurred at an unnamed mountain site in Galilee, about a week after His resurrection. Jesus had arranged to meet them there before His crucifixion (Matt. 28:16). The eleven remembered the conversation and went to the appointed mountain. It was there that Jesus expressed the profound prophecy known as His Great Commission, which frames the mission of all believers in every generation of the Lord's church:

> When they saw him, they worshiped him; but some doubted. Then Jesus came to them and said, "All authority in heaven and on earth has been given to me. Therefore, go and make disciples of all nations, baptizing them in the name of the Father and of the Son and of the Holy Spirit, and teaching them to obey everything I have commanded you. And, surely I am with you always, to the very end of the age."
>
> —MATTHEW 28:17–20

(See Psalm 96 and 1 Chronicles 16:23–33 for poetic expressions of the Great Commission).

A commission is actually a "co-mission." In resurrection power, the Lord who holds all authority in His hands gives His followers opportunity to serve with Him in reaching the whole world. This makes it an exciting and fulfilling "co-mission." The Lord enters into a joint effort with Spirit-filled believers, doing His work *together*, no matter the hardships. This is true anywhere ministry takes place, even on the far-flung islands of the sea. "I will be with you always," He promised, "to the very end of the age" (Matt. 28:20).

God's promises to Abraham would be fulfilled; his spiritual descendants would be like the sand on the seashore and the stars in the sky, and all nations would be blessed by his "seed, which is Christ" (Gal. 3:16, kjv; Gen. 15:4–5; 22:17–18, kjv).

V. The Ascension of Jesus

The disciples had only a short six weeks after the resurrection to sit at the feet of the master Teacher. During this time He "showed Himself alive to them after his suffering by many infallible proofs and [taught them] . . . things pertaining to the kingdom of God" (Acts 1:3, kjv). He also gave them instructions through the Holy Spirit (Acts 1:2).

A. The Event

At the end of the forty days, "God exalted him to the highest place and gave him the name that is above every name, that at the name of Jesus every knee should bow, in heaven and on earth and under the earth, and every tongue confess that Jesus Christ is Lord, to the glory of God the Father" (Phil. 2:9–11).

In His incarnation, Jesus had only been on loan to mankind. His eternal throne in the unity of the Trinity sat beside His Father's and was waiting for Him. The earth was but His footstool (Ps. 110:1; Acts 2:34).

When the final day arrived for the Lord to be on the earth with them, He assembled His followers on Mount Olivet. Jesus summarized once more the teaching content of the forty days, addressing the great concerns He felt for them.

> When they met together, they asked him, "Lord, are you at this time going to restore the kingdom to Israel?" He said to them: "It is not for you to know the times or dates the Father has set by his own authority. But you will receive power when the Holy Spirit comes on

you; and you will be my witnesses in Jerusalem, and in all Judea and
Samaria, and to the ends of the earth."

—Acts 1:6–8

They were to accept Jesus' ministry as the Baptizer, return to the Upper
Room in Jerusalem, and stay there until they received the power of the Holy
Spirit. It was the master Teacher's last lesson on earth with His disciples.

The Lord knew they were ready to graduate; they had learned their lessons
well. He could count on them to do what He had taught them.

When He gave these final instructions, the people saw another of the
mighty acts of God—a grand release of divine energy.

He was taken up before their very eyes, and a cloud hid him from
their sight.

—Acts 1:9

Surely, it was a moment that lived with them for the remainder of their
lives and a memory they handed down with delight to their grandchildren and
great-grandchildren.

King David penned a psalm for the Ascension a thousand years before the
event. In the poetic imagery of a Hebrew royal inauguration, he painted a
portrait of the ascent of David's greater Son to His Father's right hand:

Lift up your heads, O you gates; be lifted up, you ancient doors,
that the King of glory may come in. Who is this King of glory? The
LORD strong and mighty, the LORD mighty in battle. Lift up your
heads, O you gates; lift them up, you ancient doors, that the King
of glory may come in. Who is he, this King of glory? The LORD
Almighty—He is the King of glory.

—Psalm 24:7–10

King David also wrote the poetry that describes the moment the heavenly
Father welcomed Jesus back to the heavenly throne room. The passage has
such significance to the gospel that the New Testament writers referred to it
five times: "The LORD says to my Lord: 'Sit at my right hand until I make
your enemies a footstool for your feet'" (Ps. 110:1; Matt. 22:44; Mark 12:36–
37; Luke 20:42–44; Acts 2:34–35; Heb. 1:13).

The great reward for a job well done in Jesus' ministry was that "God exalted
him to the highest place and gave him the name that is above every name"
(Phil. 2:9). The impact of the exaltation of Jesus is that "at the name of Jesus

everyone in heaven, on earth, and in the world below will kneel and confess that Jesus Christ is Lord to the glory of God the Father" (Phil. 2:10–11, GW).

B. The Messengers After the Event

Jesus' followers watched their resurrected Lord go into heaven. The nature of the experience was such that their gaze riveted on the clouds that took Him out of their sight.

> They were looking intently up into the sky as he was going, when suddenly two men dressed in white stood beside them. "Men of Galilee," they said, "why do you stand here looking into the sky? This same Jesus, who has been taken from you into heaven, will come back in the same way you have seen him go into heaven."
> —ACTS 1:10–11

The intent of this angelic message was clear: You have a job to do, so stop gazing into the sky. Do what Jesus said. Pentecost is at hand and you have a world to win. Get on with it!

First things must always come first. The way for them to get busy for God was to obey the commands of Jesus, as their Baptizer. They were to walk down the Mount of Olives, cross the Kidron Valley, and go into Jerusalem to the Upper Room.

And they did it: "They returned to Jerusalem from the hill called the Mount of Olives, a Sabbath day's walk from the city. When they arrived, they went upstairs to the room" (Acts 1:12–13). Their assignment was to wait until the Father sent them the gift of the Holy Spirit. About 120 people were in the group that went to the Upper Room to tarry and pray.

Jesus Christ is affectionately remembered as "the servant of all" because He successfully served the agenda of His Father and met the same root need common in the soul of every person worldwide (Isa. 42:1; 49:5–6; Mark 9:35; John 3:16; Rom. 15:8; Heb. 3:2). Achieving His objective of restoring peace between God and man required that Jesus:

- diagnose the core human problem, even when people did not realize they had the problem and vehemently opposed the very idea (Mark 7:15–23; John 16:8–11);
- pour out His own blood as the antidote (John 19:30; 1 John 1:7);
- love and serve people so convincingly, even amid their vicious opposition to His help, that they came to accept His love by

their own choice, including His diagnosis, His cure, and the worldwide application of His vision (Rev. 1:18);

- commission, empower, and gift His disciples to serve like Him by taking the good news of His diagnosis and His cure to the ends of the earth (Acts 1:8).

It is to this fourth dimension that we now turn our attention.

Chapter Eight

THE GIFT OF THE HOLY SPIRIT
BIRTHS THE CHURCH

My heart began to pound for him.

—Song of Solomon 5:4

All of them were filled with the Holy Spirit and began to speak in other tongues, as the Spirit enabled them.

—Acts 2:4

≈ Azusa Street Revival Births ≈ Pentecostal Movement

The power of God now has this city agitated as never before. Pentecost has surely come and with it the Bible evidences are following, many being converted and sanctified and filled with the Holy Ghost, speaking in tongues as they did on the day of Pentecost. The scenes that are daily enacted in the building on Azusa Street [in Los Angeles, California, in 1906] and at missions and churches in other parts of the city are beyond description, and the real revival has only started, as God has been working with His children...getting them through to Pentecost, and laying the foundation for a mighty wave of salvation among the unconverted.

The meetings are held in an old Methodist church that had been converted in part into a tenement house, leaving a larger unplastered, barn-like room on the ground floor...

Now the meetings continue all day and into the night and the fire is kindling all over the city and surrounding towns. Proud, well dressed preachers come to "investigate." Soon their high looks are replaced with wonder, then conviction comes, and very often you will find them in a short time wallowing on the dirty floor, asking God to forgive them and make them as little children.

It would be impossible to state how many have been converted, sanctified, and filled with the Holy Ghost. They have been and are daily going out to all points of the compass to spread this wonderful gospel.[1]

I. Understanding Doctrine and Mission

Jesus' teaching during the forty days proved marvelously successful in preparing the disciples for Pentecost. A primary reason for their readiness was the Lord had spent adequate time teaching them to balance doctrine and mission.

A. The False Dichotomy: Separating Knowing From Doing

Many falsely believe it is possible to separate the teachings of the faith from its evangelistic mission (John 14:15; 15:14; James 1:22–25). Hence, they give their lives to learning the beliefs of the gospel, thinking their knowledge releases them from responsibility to help fulfill the Lord's mission in the world. Such thinking sets up a false dichotomy and demonstrates they do not yet know the doctrine of Jesus Christ (1 John 2:3). As a mother cannot separate her love for her children from sacrificially serving them, so doctrine cannot be separated from the evangelistic mission of the Lord's church. Jesus made very clear He does not allow separating doctrine and mission in His kingdom; in fact, to know the doctrine is to listen to and obey it, living it out in one's experience (Matt. 28:20; Luke 11:28; John 14:22–24). Anything less fits the analogy of a man so unwise he built his home for his wife and children on a foundation of sand. Jesus said:

> Everyone who hears these words of mine and puts them into practice is like a wise man who built his house on the rock. The rain came down, the streams rose, and the winds blew and beat against that house; yet it did not fall, because it had its foundation on the rock. But everyone who hears these words of mine and does not put them into practice is like a foolish man who built his house on sand. The rain came down, the streams rose, and the winds blew and beat against that house, and it fell with a great crash.
> —Matthew 7:24–27

Information alone has no power to transform a life (2 Cor. 3:5–6, The Message). The apostle James spoke to this theme when he wrote, "Anyone, then, who knows the good he ought to do and doesn't do it, sins" (James 4:17; Luke 12:47; John 9:41). When a person tries to separate doctrine and mission, at a minimum he demonstrates his anemic understanding of the "gospel of God" (Rom. 1:1). It can also mean he is living in willful disobedience.

Before the Lord's ascension, for example, the triumphant Savior met with His disciples for a meal. In that conversation, "he gave them this command: 'Do not leave Jerusalem, but wait for the gift my Father promised, which you have heard me speak about'" (Acts 1:4). Jesus did not invite them to wait, nor did He advise them to wait; He ordered them. Waiting in Jerusalem for the promise of the Spirit was not optional for the disciples. It was a necessity. Surely if the Lord's disciples could not separate doctrine from mission, believers must not try to do it today.

Yet, many people read the Bible but never permit the Bible to read them. It is certainly possible to quote the Scriptures without knowing the Lord of the Scriptures.

⚜ Evangelical Rationalism ⚜
By A. W. Tozer

There is today an evangelical rationalism which says that the truth is in the Word and if you want to know truth, go learn the Word. If you get the Word, you have the truth. That is the evangelical rationalism...in fundamentalist circles: If you learn the text, you've got the truth.

This evangelical rationalist wears our uniform...and says what the Pharisees...said: "Well, truth is truth and if you believe the truth you've got it." Such see no beyond and no mystic depth, no mysterious or divine. They see only, "I believe in God the Father Almighty, Maker of heaven and earth; and in Jesus Christ His only Son, our Lord."

They have the text and the code and the creed, and to them that is the truth. So they pass it on to others. The result is we are dying spiritually.

To know the Truth, we must "know" the Son.[2]

B. The Ministry of the Spirit in the Resurrection

The cornerstone teaching of Christian faith is the death and resurrection of Jesus Christ. Paul wrote to the believers in Galatia that "God the Father...raised [Jesus] from the dead" (Gal. 1:1). Jesus said His life was His own; He laid it down and took it up again (John 10:18). Paul said to the Christians in Rome, "the Spirit...raised Jesus from the dead" (Rom. 8:11). Obviously, the Trinity was wholly involved in bringing Jesus Christ back from the grave.

Since the Holy Spirit is the Spirit of life, Paul reasoned the presence of the Spirit in the life of a believer is the believer's pledge that he, too, will one day rise from the dead. We have the "deposit" of the Spirit in our hearts, Paul said, "guaranteeing what is to come" (2 Cor. 1:22; 5:5). This down payment assures that a child of God will have an inheritance on the great day of redemption (Eph. 1:14). The point of the pledge is obvious: "If the Spirit of him who raised up Jesus from the dead is living in you, he who raised Christ from the dead will also give life to your mortal bodies through his Spirit, who lives in you" (Rom. 8:11). This is the heart of the Christian story and the good news of the gospel that always blends knowing and doing, or theology and mission.

C. Developing Powerful Witnesses

The message of such a wonderful story deserves to be understood, told, and obeyed. The Godhead is committed, in fact, that people around the world hear the good news of the death and resurrection of Jesus. With Jesus Christ, therefore, knowing and telling the story go together like hand and glove.

Jesus charged His disciples to tarry in Jerusalem for a specific reason: "You will receive power when the Holy Spirit comes on you; and you will be my witnesses in Jerusalem, and in all Judea and Samaria, and to the ends of the earth" (Acts 1:8). The term rendered "power" is *dunamis*, meaning "strength, ability, or energy." When God the Holy Spirit descended on them, the third person of the Trinity who anointed the Christ also made the disciples His dwelling place. The Spirit in them provided strength, ability, and wisdom to serve people and advance the Lord's agenda (John 14:12). In that energy, the disciples were Christ's first storytellers "to the ends of the earth" (Acts 1:8) Like their Lord they did not try to separate knowing and doing.

The Greek term for *witnesses* in Acts 1:8 is *martures*, meaning a person who believes his testimony so strongly he will even give his life to tell the story. The English word *martyr* comes from the term. Paul wrote toward the end of his ministry, "When the blood of your martyr Stephen was shed, I also was standing by" (Acts 22:20, KJV). Then, at the end of his sojourn, while in the Mamertine Prison in Rome, Paul penned what became his epitaph:

> My life is coming to an end, and it is now time for me to be poured out as a sacrifice to God. I have fought the good fight. I have completed the race. I have kept the faith. The prize that shows I have God's approval is now waiting for me. The Lord, who is a fair judge, will give me that prize on that day. He will give it not only to me but also to everyone who is eagerly waiting for him to come again.
> —2 TIMOTHY 4:6–8, GW

The great apostle never separated doctrine and mission. He always blended them, even to the point of dying a martyr's death in Rome.

A set-apart believer today who tarries in his own "Upper Room" for the baptism with the Holy Spirit must count the cost. Becoming a servant of the Lord's agenda includes this witnessing or storytelling, even if it embraces laying down one's life. We conclude, therefore, that a person who understands the message of Christian faith will blend knowing and doing, becoming one of the Lord's advocates in the contemporary church.

⊰ "I Am God's Wheat!" ⊱
By Ignatius, Bishop of Antioch, A.D. 110

I am writing to all the churches to let it be known that I will gladly die for God if only you do not stand in my way. I plead with you: show me no untimely kindness. Let me be food for the wild beasts, for they are my way to God. I am God's wheat and shall be ground by their teeth so that I may become Christ's pure bread. Pray to Christ for me that the animals will be the means of making me a sacrificial victim for God. No earthly pleasures, no kingdoms of this world can benefit me in any way. I prefer death in Christ Jesus to power over the farthest limits of the earth. He who died in place of us is the one object of my quest. He who rose for our sakes is my one desire.

The time for my birth is close at hand...Come fire, cross, battling with wild beasts, wrenching of bones, mangling of limbs, crushing of my whole body, cruel tortures of the devil—only let me get to Jesus Christ![3]

The two verbs in Acts 1:8 deserve brief attention: "you *shall receive* power and "you *shall be* witnesses" (emphasis added). Both are future tense verbs, stating what will be the inevitable reality after Pentecost. The mission of Spirit-filled people is clear—when the Holy Spirit comes on them, their routine practice will be to spread the story of the Lord's resurrection (Acts 1:8). These twin affirmations coming from the last teaching of the Lord before His ascension have remained in force to this day.

For the disciples to live that lifestyle successfully, however, they had to begin in the Upper Room, where Jesus was the baptizer with the Holy Spirit (Matt. 3:11; Acts 1:4). The road to effective servant ministry always wends its way up Golgotha, then to the empty tomb, and via Mount Olivet to the Upper Room. People who make this journey receive so many wonderful blessings from God they become joyful storytellers. They move out to share the good news with all the nations of the earth on their ultimate journey to the New Jerusalem.

D. The Birth of the Church

The Lord's ascension occurred on the fortieth day after His resurrection, and the Feast of Pentecost took place fifty days after Passover (Acts 1:3; 2:1, GW). Therefore, the Upper Room prayer meeting continued for about ten days.

The Day of Pentecost marked the birth of the church. The Father, the Son, and the Holy Spirit in the Tri-unity of God were participants in the grand occasion. The Lord had promised before His crucifixion, "I [Jesus] will ask the Father, and he will give you another Counselor to be with you forever— the Spirit of truth" (John 14:16–17). From this perspective, the powerful significance of Acts 2:1 comes into clear focus: "When the day of Pentecost came, they were all together in one place." The disciples were in unity with the Trinity. In fact, they were right in the center of the will of God. They had received the Lord's teachings, but needed the baptism with the Holy Spirit to be able to do what Jesus said.

II. The Role of the Holy Spirit

A. The Investiture of Jesus as Messiah

The Lord Jesus Christ received from His Father at the Jordan River an impartation of the Holy Spirit that was unlimited (John 3:34). The occasion was His investiture as Messiah, enabling Him to launch His ministry to save the world.

B. Vesting the Disciples, as Storytellers

Through prayer and supplication during the ten days after Jesus' ascension, this faithful little group sought God for a successor to Judas, who by transgression had fallen (Acts 1:13–26). Then, as thirsty vessels, they continued their earnest intercession in the Upper Room for the promise of the Father (Luke 24:49; Acts 1:4–5).

John the Baptist, the greatest of the prophets, announced Jesus as the Messiah and proclaimed Him as the baptizer with "the Holy Spirit and with fire" (Luke 3:16). The impartation John foretold happened on the Day of Pentecost. Jesus kept His promise to His disciples to send the Holy Spirit (John 16:7).

> Suddenly a sound like the blowing of a violent wind came from heaven and filled the whole house where they were sitting. They saw what seemed to be tongues of fire that separated and came to rest on each of them. All of them were filled with the Holy Spirit and began to speak in other tongues as the Spirit enabled them.
>
> —Acts 2:2–4

This occasion marked the investiture of the Lord's disciples as His storytellers of what they had seen and heard. It was a message destined to go to the ends of the earth.

C. The Baptism With the Holy Spirit as a Spiritual Experience

The Holy Spirit first comes to a person in prevenient grace, wooing Him to Christ in the saving faith that produces the new birth. Sanctifying grace continues this work of the Spirit, applying the blood of Jesus to break the dominion of the old self. A child of God is set apart unto the Lord to mature as a new person in the attitude, character, and mission of Jesus for evangelizing the world. This can only happen as the power centers in a person's life come under the Lordship of Jesus Christ. A visit to the Upper Room, therefore, always assumes a vital stopover at Calvary that deals with the old self.

When the grace of God has done its work in these spiritual experiences, the believer then becomes a candidate for the third blessing—the baptism with the Holy Spirit. In this encounter, the Holy Spirit comes to empower justified and set-apart believers to live out their new attitude of complete trust in the heavenly Father. Jesus' mother expressed it best when she said, "Do whatever he tells you" (John 2:5; see also 1 Cor. 6:19).

Our Lord never reversed His great command for all believers to go to their own Upper Room. Rather, the baptism with the Holy Spirit is an experience available for all thirsty people of every generation who come to Christ to drink (John 7:37–38). This is not to say these experiences with God must occur at three distinctly different times of spiritual intercession. They can occur simultaneously when a person comes to Christ in repentance. It is also possible to be born again, and simultaneously experience sanctification and the baptism with the Holy Spirit. We believe the norm, however, is for the three experiences to occur on three different occasions. While the Pentecostal blessing is received at a particular moment, it is appropriate to expect definite renewals over the course of a lifetime (Acts 4:31). "Be filled with the Spirit" in Ephesians 5:18, for example, is in the present tense, having the sense of "be being filled." It implies ongoing expectation of renewal.

D. Jesus as the Intercessor

The disciples that Pentecost morning received from the Father at Jesus' request their own impartation of the Holy Spirit. When a believer comprehends it happened because of Jesus' request of His Father, he can begin to appreciate the incredible power of Jesus as the intercessor at God's right hand: "I will ask the Father and he will give you another Counselor to be with you forever" (John 14:16; 16:26; Rom. 8:34). The occasion marked their investiture as servants of the Lord's plan for the nations. So, the Great Commission frames Jesus' worldwide strategy, and the great command expresses His love, which motivated the agenda (John 13:34; 14:16).

Jesus dragged His cross up Golgotha to save all people everywhere, restoring them to a right relationship with His Father. He also died to establish a church in which His followers can find family and fellowship as they mature in Christlikeness (John 3:16; Acts 20:28; Eph. 5:25). His doing so paved the way for this great act of intercession when He went back to heaven. At His Father's side, He made the petition as He promised, for all who believe in Him to receive the Holy Spirit.

E. Revealing the Father's Gift

The heavenly Father intended that the Holy Spirit would be His special blessing to all who place their trust in His Son. The believers who had been with the Lord at His ascension were the first to experience this impartation. The baptism with the Holy Spirit remains to this day the Father's gift to any thirsty person who comes to Christ to drink (John 7:37–38; Acts 2:39). Like Jesus, the Holy Spirit does not have an independent agenda (John 14:26). The primary element in the job description of the Spirit is to teach people about Jesus and wed them to His vision.

The 120 followers of Christ in the Upper Room perceived the Spirit they experienced that morning was identical to the presence that emanated from Jesus in His ministry. They knew that anointing well; it had characterized the Messiah's life the entire time He had lived with them.

In fact, the Spirit in the Upper Room was so familiar they caught themselves thinking Jesus Himself was in the room, although they had seen Him go into the heavens ten days earlier. They could not touch Him that morning, but it really did begin to dawn on them that Jesus was there.

The 120 were right; Jesus was in the room. They recognized Him by the presence, and He made all the difference. The Holy Spirit always makes Jesus known (John 14:26). To receive the Spirit is to receive Jesus, and when one experiences Jesus, he also receives the Father (John 14:9). The Spirit is life, divine energy, and anointing to enable God's children to be storytellers, showing the great power of the Lord's cross and resurrection.

⚜ If the Holy Spirit Were Withdrawn... ⚜

In many Christian circles the Holy Spirit is either neglected, forgotten, or misunderstood. The One given to unite the body of Christ is the center of controversy. This is a nettle which ought to be firmly grasped. So often Christian work is so rigidly programmed that it seems we need no longer depend on Him—yet Jesus said, "Without Me you can do nothing."

The late Dr. A. W. Tozer, author and pastor, said, "If the Holy Spirit were withdrawn from the church today, ninety-five percent of what we do would go on and no one would know the difference. If the Holy Spirit had been withdrawn from the New Testament church, ninety-five percent of what they did would have stopped, and everybody would have known the difference."[4]

Three unusual phenomena accompanied the sudden appearance of the Father's gift. It all began with a sound like a strong, rushing wind (Acts 2:2). Then, fire-like, cloven tongues miraculously sat on each of them (Acts 2:3). The result was "all of them were filled with the Holy Spirit and began to speak in other tongues as the Spirit enabled them" (Acts 2:4). The wind and the cloven tongues happened in the atmosphere of the Upper Room. The third phenomenon of "speaking in other tongues" or languages flowed from their Spirit-filled hearts and was the symbol that the Spirit had actually indwelt them.

The first two of these three phenomena did not occur again in the apostolic church; therefore, the sound like wind and the fiery, cloven tongues that sat on them, are understood best as tokens or signs of the new dispensation. Spirit-filled believers routinely spoke in other tongues in the apostolic era, however (1 Cor. 14:18). Speaking in tongues must continue to be recognized as the first indicator of the Spirit's indwelling.

The divine power present that morning gave the apostle Peter lion-like boldness, and in that new anointing, He stood to preach to the crowd that gathered. Peter had soaked up like a sponge Jesus' teaching in the forty days between His resurrection and ascension, and was ready for the day of Pentecost.

The Spirit that morning did not merely drop Joel's and David's prophecies into Peter's mouth as he spoke. Instead, it is much more plausible that Jesus had already interpreted these specific prophecies for the disciples. Little wonder Peter could say:

> This is what was spoken by the prophet Joel: "In the last days, God says, I will pour out my Spirit on all people. Your sons and daughters will prophesy, your young men will see visions, your old men will dream dreams. Even on my servants, both men and women, I will pour out my Spirit in those days, and they will prophesy."
> —ACTS 2:16–18

The overwhelming response to Peter's message must have been exhilarating, as three thousand people that morning accepted Jesus as their Messiah. Just fifty days earlier, Peter had denied the Lord with cursing and swearing. Everything changed, however, as these set-apart followers allowed the Lord's cross and empty tomb to help them get to know their Savior. It is always true that to know Jesus is to discover ourselves.

F. Jesus, the Chief Cornerstone of the Church

The 120 would never forget that occasion—what they heard in the room, what they saw resting on each other's heads, and the very presence of Jesus they felt. In the Incarnation, Mary gave birth to the Messiah (Luke 2:11). In the Upper Room, the Holy Spirit gave birth to the Lord's church, with Jesus Christ as its head (Acts 2:1–4; Eph. 1:22; 5:23).

The church was built on the foundation laid by the Lord's apostles and prophets, with Jesus "as the chief cornerstone" (Matt. 16:18; John 14:16; Eph. 2:20). After Pentecost, the disciples no longer worked under the guidance of the incarnate Christ. Rather, they served under the tutorship and the power of the Holy Spirit (John 14:26; Acts 1:8; 16:13–15). Christ's followers were anointed by the same Spirit who empowered the ministry of Jesus (Luke 4:1, 18; Acts 10:38). The whole mission of the Holy Spirit is to exalt the Lord and make Him known (John 14:26).

G. Launching the Era of Spirit-filled People

How does one comprehend the awesome river of divine love into which Jesus baptized His followers that very celebrated morning in Jerusalem? The Holy Spirit created the heavens and the earth (Gen. 1:2), inspired the Scriptures (2 Pet. 1:21), parted the waters of the Red Sea, and took Israel across on dry land (Exod. 14:10; 15:18). He is the same Spirit that miraculously enabled the Virgin Mary to conceive Jesus in her womb (Matt. 1:18). The Spirit also guided and empowered the life of Jesus Christ in His humiliation and ministry (John 3:34; Acts 10:38), and ultimately raised Jesus from the dead (Rom. 8:11).

That Spirit was there on the scene in the Upper Room in Jerusalem precisely at nine o'clock on this historic Pentecost morning (Acts 2:15). The Spirit that entered the Upper Room is the same Spirit that anointed Jesus as the Messiah, making Him the firstfruits of Spirit-filled men (Matt. 4:16; John 3:34; Rom. 8:23). It was a massive and awesome concentration of Shekinah glory and authority. The era of Spirit-filled men in the Lord's church began that day. It has continued for two millennia since that first-century Pentecost, and shows no signs of abating. In this context, one can appreciate the universal implications of God's promise to Abraham – his spiritual descendants would be innumerable, like the stars and the sand on the seashore (Gen. 15:4–6).

H. The Abiding Presence

After the Spirit-filled flock finally left the Upper Room, to their great delight, the Spirit did not leave them (John 14:17–18). They each felt like Jesus was walking with them, going wherever they went—and He was! Moses' prophecy was coming true right before their eyes: "Are you jealous for my sake? I wish that all the Lord's people were prophets and that the Lord would put his Spirit on them!" (Num. 11:29).

Jeremiah's proclamation of the new covenant had also begun to bloom— the Law now was "in their minds and written on their hearts" (Jer. 31:31–33; 32:40). Joel's prophecy was unfolding, too: "The promise is unto you and to your children and to all that are afar off, even as many as the Lord our God shall call" (Joel 2:28–32; Acts 2:39, KJV).

I. A Gender-Blind Gospel

Jesus the great Baptizer poured out the Holy Spirit and imparted the gifts and callings of the Spirit on women, as well as men (John 14:16; Acts 2:16–18). One of the striking implications of Joel's prophecy was that the Father's gift of the Holy Spirit was destined to break gender barriers, elevating the status of women. Joel's prophecy was clear, for example, that in the new covenant women would receive the gift of prophecy (Joel 2:28; Acts 21:8–9). Since the biblical record is specific on this subject, does it not also follow that God can use women to manifest the other gifts of the Spirit, as well? With Jesus Christ, "There is neither…male nor female, for you are all one" (Gal. 3:28).

J. Making a Temple Switch

The Jewish people worshiped at their tabernacle for about five hundred years and at their temple for an additional millennium. But something completely new happened in Jerusalem that Pentecost morning. A great "temple switch" unfolded. The day ended of a temple made with the hands of skilled craftsmen to which all must come to worship: "'This is the covenant I will make with them after that time,' says the Lord. 'I will put my laws in their hearts, and I will write them on their minds'" (Heb. 10:16; Jer. 31:33).

Early in His ministry, Jesus entered the temple King Herod built with a whip in His hand to cleanse it of the merchants who were buying and selling. He claimed it as His Father's house and then indicted the whole temple system because it had become a den of thieves and was no longer a house of prayer (John 2:16; Matt. 21:13). After He cleansed the temple, the disciples remembered David had prophesied Messiah's exact sentiments: "Zeal for your house consumes me" (Ps. 69:9; John 2:17).

The Father did not pour out the Holy Spirit in the most holy place of Herod's temple; instead, God relocated the new and vibrant temple of the Holy Spirit to the inner sanctum of the individual believer (1 Cor. 3:16). The Spirit was right there in their hearts, the temple made without hands. And the striking zeal the Lord had once felt for the Jerusalem temple, He transferred to the new "temple of the heart" (John 2:17). What had been the dark chasm of the soul resulting from Adam's fall in the Garden of Eden was again full of life, energy, and purpose. As for Herod's temple, the Roman general Titus in A.D. 70 ordered his soldiers to tear it down, stone by stone, and burn it, fulfilling Jesus' prophecy (Matt. 24:1–2).

The heavenly Father's plan from eternity was in full swing. Every believer can be filled with the Spirit and have direct access to the Lord Jesus Christ. He is the great High Priest who enters into personal relationship with each of God's children (Heb. 4:14–15).

Built on this strong individualism, the gospel of the kingdom had all the ingredients necessary to go to the ends of the earth. An ordinary person on the backside of the Roman Empire, far removed from Jerusalem and the Upper Room, who had never met Jesus, and who had never heard one of the Lord's twelve apostles preach could receive this same baptism with the Holy Spirit. When He did, he would become aware of the identical love and experience the same sensation of divine anointing and presence that was in the Upper Room. This new believer also would become aware that Jesus was with him, and he would be correct. The gospel births just that kind of personal relationship between Jesus and each of His followers, whom He knows by name (John 10:3).

The Lord's teaching had come true: "On that day you will realize that I am in my Father, and you are in me, and I am in you" (John 14:20–21). Empowered by this dynamic strategy of the "indwelling of the Spirit," the gospel of Jesus Christ really could go to the ends of the earth (Matt. 28:16–20). And it has.

K. The Nature of the Indwelling

How does the Holy Spirit tabernacle with a believer? The Holy Spirit is the third Person of the triune God, who indwells a human person. When the Spirit tabernacles with an individual, the Spirit does not undergo an incarnation or take a human nature like Jesus did. Rather, He unites with a believer in a spiritual union.

In this indwelling, the individualities unique to both the human personality and the divine Spirit are respected and maintained. They become two wills that function in a mutually reciprocal relationship. When a believer submits himself totally to Jesus' way of thinking in a firm moral commitment to obey the Father in all things, the Holy Spirit responds (reciprocates) by energizing and empowering him to grow in the Lord's character and mission. In other words, as a person yields to the Holy Spirit all that he is, the Spirit opens up to him the manifold possibilities inherent in the agenda of Jesus Christ. This includes positioning him in ministry in the church and gifting him to serve the body of Christ.

This relationship is obviously different from the concept of the incarnation of Jesus Christ. The Holy Spirit conceived Jesus in the womb of the Virgin Mary. Jesus was the God-man, two natures in one person. In the baptism with the Holy Spirit, man's spirit is the tabernacle the Holy Spirit indwells. In this relationship, man retains his free will and the Spirit preserves His divine prerogatives. The key to the indwelling relationship is a mutually cooperative, divine-human reciprocity of one divine person indwelling one human person. The marvel of Pentecost is that each Spirit-filled believer is empowered to live a victorious life in the presence of Jesus Christ as he awaits the Lord's second appearing (John 14:2–3).

A word of caution is appropriate. The Spirit is also extra and apart from each believer whom He indwells. This is true because the eternal Spirit is also greater than the composite of all the people He indwells.

- The Lord taught His disciples that the Spirit "lives with you and will be in you" (John 14:17).
- Jesus also recognized the temple Herod built as His "Father's house" (John 2:16).
- He taught where "two or three gather together in my name, there am I with them" (Matt. 18:20).
- Jesus told His disciples that His own body was a temple that would be destroyed and raised up the third day (John 2:19).
- Paul explained that the whole body of believers, the saints of all ages, form "a holy temple" for "a dwelling in which God lives by his Spirit" (Eph. 2:20–22).

The Holy Spirit is fully capable of baptizing and empowering every man on Earth; yet if that happened, it would not exhaust His great being. This is true because He is also the third person of the triune Godhead who inhabits eternity, even while He tabernacles in time with man (Acts 5:3–4; 1 Cor. 3:16; 2 Cor. 3:17; Ps. 104:30).

This understanding of His powerful, universal capability is a source of great comfort. No man monopolizes the Spirit of God, and no institution, church, denomination, or governmental system places Him under lock and key.

Where can I go from your Spirit? Where can I flee from your presence? If I go up to the heavens, you are there; if I make my bed in the depths, you are there. If I rise on the wings of the dawn, if I settle on the far side of the sea, even there your hand will guide me, your right hand will hold me fast. If I say, "Surely the darkness will hide me and the light become night around me," even the darkness will not be dark to you; the night will shine like the day, for darkness is as light to you.

—Psalm 139:7–12

In His worldwide ministry, the Holy Spirit has never applied for a passport at any Department of State. Instead, as eternal Spirit, He goes where He wills to comfort and tend His sheep (Heb. 9:14; John 14:16). While He does His work as the Executive Officer of the Godhead, He never speaks of Himself or acts with an independent attitude. Rather, in the mutuality of submission that characterizes the Tri-unity of God, His total mission is to exalt the Baptizer, Jesus Christ, as Savior and Lord (John 14:25; 16:13).

The divine Wind blows where He wills, permitting no one to quarantine Him. Little wonder the might of the Roman Empire proved powerless to halt the forward advance of the Lord's church. Civil governments cannot stop a church that at its most essential essence is invisible and spiritual, residing in the hearts of men.

L. The Purpose of This Indwelling

The central core of the Pentecostal message is that Jesus Christ ascended to the Father and no longer tabernacles with man in the flesh. Meanwhile, God the Holy Spirit, given by the Father at Jesus' request, continues this blessed Divine-human companionship. As He does, He reveals Jesus to each person He indwells (John 14:26; Phil. 2:5). In fact, the Spirit motivates people to take seriously the three indivisible persons in the Tri-unity of the God who is one. The third person of the Trinity, the Holy Spirit, continues to serve in the contemporary church as the administrator of the Godhead who carries out the mind of Christ in the church. This understanding in no way diminishes the redemptive accomplishments of Jesus, for, as John the Baptist taught, the Lord is Himself the baptizer with the Holy Spirit (Matt. 3:11; Mark 1:8; Luke 3:16). The whole ministry of the Spirit as the Executive Officer of the Godhead—the complete function of the gifts He administers and the fruit He grows—is to exalt Jesus Christ, God's only Son, and make Him known (John 16:13–15; Gal. 5:22). In doing so, the Holy Spirit matures the mind of Christ in the lives of contemporary believers just as He did in the apostolic church. Pentecostalism, therefore, is all about enjoying a personal and intimate relationship with the living God.

The heavenly Father gave the Holy Spirit to take Jesus' physical place on Earth (John 16:7). He enables every believer to mature in the attitude of implicit trust that Jesus vested in His Father, so that God's children learn to think like Jesus (Phil. 2:5). The Lord was the committed servant of His Father's plan. Spirit-filled believers, too, become heart-and-soul servants of Jesus' agenda (John 14:16, 25–26). This, in fact, is the essence of what it means to live victoriously in Christ Jesus (1 Cor. 15:57; 1 John 5:4; Rev. 15:2). In doing so, the Spirit draws men to Christ and prepares them for His second coming.

Because God made man in His own image, the divine Spirit fulfills the yearning for God in man's heart (Gen. 1:26–27; Ps. 42:1; Eccles. 3:11). Both men and women feel at peace when indwelt by the Holy Spirit (John 20:21). The Spirit also gives people rest as they learn to obey the Lord, the great object of all worship and adoration (Heb. 4:9).

The more a child of God dies to himself, the more he becomes alive to Christ. As his knowledge grows of who Jesus is, so will his commitment mature to see all people born again (John 3:3; 7; 1 Pet. 1:23). Paul expressed it by saying, "I am obligated both to Greeks and non-Greeks, both to the wise and the foolish. That is why I am so eager to preach the gospel also to you who are at Rome. I am not ashamed of the gospel, because it is the power of God for the salvation of everyone who believes: first for the Jew, then for the Gentile" (Rom. 1:14–17).

⚜ Free to Love Jesus in Front of People ⚜

God's Holy Spirit orchestrates our lives to touch others—strangers, friends, work-related people, service-industry workers and more—if we would just open up and be ourselves.

How?

Be free to be in love with Jesus in front of people. Be an ambassador through whom He can introduce himself. There is a world out there, hungry and searching for Jesus and his love. Don't keep Him to yourself.[5]

M. Tongues as the Initial Evidence

Speaking in tongues is the first indication a believer has received the Holy Spirit baptism. Study of the five accounts of receiving the Spirit in Acts of the Apostles will make the point.

The first is the outpouring on the Day of Pentecost, recorded in Acts 2: "They were all filled with the Holy Spirit, and began to speak with other tongues as the Spirit gave them utterance" (v. 4).

In the revival at Samaria, Luke made no specific statement regarding any phenomena accompanying the Holy Spirit baptism. However, Luke did record that Simon "saw" something: "When Simon saw that through the laying on of the apostles' hands the Holy Spirit was given, he offered them money" (Acts 8:18). What Simon observed made him know the people had received the Holy Spirit. It is reasonable to conclude he watched as the people spoke in tongues.

The third account of the Holy Spirit baptism in Acts was the conversion of the apostle Paul (Acts 9:3–19). Luke did not record any accompanying phenomenon when the apostle received the Holy Spirit. However, an argument from silence does not prove that Paul did not speak with tongues. Paul's testimony is clear in his later writings that he was a prolific tongues-speaker. He wrote to the Christians at Corinth that he spoke with tongues more than all of them (1 Cor. 14:18). He also expressed his desire that all believers would both speak in tongues and prophesy (1 Cor. 14:5).

The story of the revival at Caesarea in Cornelius' house shows speaking in tongues was the evidence by which the apostle Peter and his ministry team knew these Gentiles had received the Holy Spirit.

> The circumcised believers who had come with Peter were astonished that the gift of the Holy Spirit had been poured out even on the Gentiles. For they heard them speaking in tongues and praising God.
> —Acts 10:45–46

The fifth account of people receiving the baptism with the Holy Spirit in the book of Acts occurred during Paul's final visit to Ephesus. The twelve disciples Paul met on the strand of the Aegean Sea received the Holy Spirit when "Paul placed his hands on them." The result was "they spoke in tongues and prophesied" (Acts 19:1–7).

Of these five occasions when believers received the baptism with the Holy Spirit in the early apostolic church, the stated initial evidence was specifically tongues in the Upper Room, Caesarea, and Ephesus. In the account of Paul's personal Pentecost, the Scriptures are silent, yet we know Paul spoke in tongues often and wanted all believers to have the experience (1 Cor. 14:5, 18). In the Samaritan revival, the context reasonably supports the conclusion that tongues-speaking was present. This evidence forms the biblical basis for the teaching that speaking in tongues is the believer's first or initial evidence he has received the baptism with the Holy Spirit.

This understanding of initial evidence does not presume that tongues will be the only verification that will follow in the life of a Spirit-filled believer. In fact, it is but the first of many. When the Holy Spirit indwells a believer, He makes Jesus Christ come alive in his life, and other evidences result. Among them are boldness and power for witnessing, as well as the demonstration of one or more of the gifts of the Spirit. In addition, the Spirit will grow to maturity the fruit of the Spirit and focus a Spirit-filled believer on the Lord's agenda for the nations.

N. The Continuing Need in Every Generation

Some teach that the Acts 2 experience of the baptism in the Holy Spirit with speaking in tongues was a special gift of God made available only to the disciples of the first century. This cessationist teaching maintains that first-century believers needed special powers to establish Christianity in the pagan Roman world. According to this view, after the Holy Spirit established the church in the Roman Empire, the Lord withdrew tongues from worship in His church because the phenomenon was no longer needed. The Scripture passage most often chosen to support this erroneous stance is 1 Corinthians 13:8: "Love never fails. But where there are prophecies, they will cease; where there are tongues, they will be stilled; where there is knowledge, it will pass away."

Are we to understand that prophecies failed too, and that knowledge vanished at the close of the apostolic age? If not, by what criteria can one reach the conclusion that only tongues ceased? Why, one might also ask, is the Acts 2 experience any less needed in our modern, pagan world than in the first century?

The conclusion is obvious. Believers need the indwelling power of the Holy Spirit just as much today as in the first century. An additional conclusion is also apparent: the indwelling Spirit, including speaking in tongues, is just as available to believers today as in the first century.

⊰ Leading New Believers Into Sanctification ⊱ and the Baptism With the Holy Spirit

"In the early years of my ministry," says Pastor Joel Downing, "the Sunday evening service was the special opportunity for people to pray through and experience God. When our congregation dropped Sunday night services, I knew we had to offer a creative alternative for the Sunday evening altar service."

Pastor Joel's model for leading people into the set-apart lifestyle and the baptism with the Holy Spirit is the Encounter Weekend. He views the Encounter Weekend concept (Friday evening through Sunday noon) as "the single most significant ministry tool" that he has "witnessed in nearly forty years of ministry."

"In these retreats," he says, "we have repeatedly watched young and spiritually immature believers, held by various bondages, take quantum leaps in their spiritual life. It happens through a series of encounters with God over the course of the weekend.

"The emphasis of the teaching on Friday evening is to lead the participants to a powerful, biblical assurance of personal salvation.

"Saturday is devoted primarily to dealing with the old self. New believers are encouraged to place their entire spirit, mind and body on the cross and receive the victory Christ bought for them with His blood. The cross and the path of death take on new meaning that is forever written in their hearts, as they release the old man with his wounds, bondages, habits, and strongholds, and experience cleansing from past hurts and unforgiveness. We have watched joy and inner peace blossom time-and-again, as young believers 'die' to their sinful nature.

"The ministry on Sunday morning begins with teaching on receiving the baptism with the Holy Spirit. Often there is an Upper Room atmosphere. We have found it normal for everyone to be filled with the Spirit with speaking in tongues. This spiritual impact has lasting effects on these God seekers.

"The Encounter experience ends Sunday morning with a call to the attendees to surrender their plans to God and develop a personal vision for His plans at home and abroad through their church. This call to surrender normally results in a deep and genuine commitment to be used by the Lord in the ministry of the church.

"The Encounter Weekend includes focused teaching, small group ministry, and special opportunities to experience God. No TV's, telephones and cell phones are permitted. The teaching makes use of various props that include a rustic cross, a crown of thorns, slides, and pictures that help participants identify in faith with the death and resurrection of Jesus. These include having each person hold a crown of thorns, as well as giving each participant a large spike-like nail. The goal is for these and other props to become points of contact that help people walk their own path of death. Identifying in faith with the suffering of Jesus at Calvary is vital to releasing the old self with all of his sinful baggage.

"I estimate that ninety percent of our leaders in Higher Ground Church have been deeply impacted by an Encounter. Our most devoted and generous financial supporters are people who were dramatically touched in an Encounter. Our greeters, ushers, children's leaders, youth workers, praise team and small group leaders are all men and women who have been through an Encounter Weekend. Every facet of ministry at Higher Ground Church is led by someone who has been through an Encounter."⁶

III. The Fruit of the Spirit

The Holy Spirit grows a lovely orchard of fruit in the lives of believers. These character traits are a marvelous portrait of the mind of Christ. Even pagans pass no laws against the fruit of the Spirit (Gal. 5:22–25; Phil. 2:5, KJV).

- **Love.** Paul is not talking here about self-centered love, parental love, or conjugal love. Rather, he speaks of *agape*, the divine love that motivated God to give His Son, Jesus, who volunteered to die for each of us (John 3:16). *Agape* is love that springs not from feelings but from decisions and choices. It has the power to issue commands and give direct orders, to compel and "hem in" (Matt. 28:19; John 13:34; 2 Cor. 5:14; Ps. 139:5). Love even disciplines (Heb. 12:5–11), but *agape* never forces anyone to do anything against his will. The parable of the good Samaritan reflects this love, and 1 Corinthians 13 marvelously sets it in poetry (Luke 10:30–37). Jesus clearly called for it when He gave the Great Command (John 13:34–35).
- **Joy.** The foundation of this fruit is the delight of a personal relationship with Jesus Christ. Serving Christ by walking in the Spirit epitomizes elation. This fruit, when anchored in Christ is "unspeakable and full of glory" (1 Pet. 1:8, KJV). Hence, joy is rooted in fellowship with the Lord, not outward circumstances (Phil. 4:4–8; John 16:22).
- **Peace.** The relaxed inner satisfaction that comes from knowing one's relationship with Christ is in order is the essence of peace. Rapport with Christ is its foundation, not one's environment or living conditions. Knowing one's sins are forgiven is its ultimate expression, with all enmity removed between a man and his God. Isaiah prophesied that Jesus would be the Prince of peace, and the Holy Spirit produces this wonderfully luscious fruit in Christ's followers (Isa. 9:6; John 14:27; Rom. 5:1).
- **Longsuffering.** This fruit of the Spirit is not quick-tempered or short-fused. Instead, it enables a person, as the Lord did, to stand up for right and truth with toleration and patience, but without compromise. A longsuffering person, like the Lord,

can also take heavy pressure over an extended period of time because he has learned to do it in the power of the Spirit (Luke 4:13; 2 Tim. 4:16–22; Num. 14:18; 2 Pet. 3:9).

- **Gentleness.** Evidence of this fruit of the Spirit is a man's ability to remain calm, kind, and tender amid great stress. It also includes being easily approachable. Even women and little children felt very comfortable in the gentle presence of Jesus (Zech. 9:9; Mark 10:14–15; 15:41; 1 Thess. 2:7; 2 Tim. 2:24; James 3:17; 1 Pet. 2:18). Nothing was flamboyant or bombastic in the Lord's servant demeanor, for example, when He rode the lowly donkey into Jerusalem on Palm Sunday (Zech. 9:9; Matt. 21:1–11).

- **Goodness.** Goodness expresses itself in life relationships as decency and honesty inspired by the Holy Spirit. Goodness is very akin to grace (the unmerited favor of God). Goodness asks, how can I be kind to you, whether or not you deserve it and whether or not you return the goodness to me? Jesus' premier story about goodness, a narrative that describes the Lord's own character, is the parable of the Good Samaritan (Luke 10:30–37).

- **Faith.** "Faith is the substance of things hoped for, the evidence of things not seen" (Heb. 11:1, KJV). It gives men the ability to believe God with fidelity and results in the new birth (John 3:3). A confident and trusting heart "sees" even when there is nothing tangible to see. One of history's greatest examples of the faith of God is surely the incarnation of Jesus (Luke 1:27, 34; Rom. 3:3, KJV). The bond between the Lord Jesus and His Father anchored implicitly in this trust, and the attachment proved during His ministry to be impregnable. The Holy Spirit matures men in this same acceptance and trust, teaching them to subscribe their complete loyalty and confidence for every situation to Jesus Christ as Savior and Lord. When such fidelity is given, it matures into an undying, loyal trust of Christ's divine capability and willingness to perform fully all He has promised. Herod intended to kill Peter the next day, but Peter trustingly slept (Acts 12:6). That is faith.

- **Meekness.** Meekness is the willful, disciplined exercise of power and authority to achieve a worthy goal. Meekness is not weakness. Instead, it is power restrained by gentleness, borne on the wings of compassion. Nor is it condescending, dictatorial, or egotistical. Meekness will cause a person to limit the

use of his power and even suffer being wronged in the greater
interest of helping a brother or of winning his lost soul (Gal.
6:1; 2 Tim. 2:25; Num. 12:1–3, KJV). Meekness always accepts
boundaries and restrictions for the greater good. Jesus Christ
is the supreme example, because He exercised His power with
such restraint (Zech. 9:9; Matt. 5:5; 11:29; 21:5, KJV; Phil. 4:5).

- **Self-control.** All of God's children need a divine ability to
  reflect temperance or moderation in their words and deeds.
  Jesus was always masterfully in control of Himself, and the
  Holy Spirit matures this self-discipline in Spirit-filled believers.
  As Paul preached, Felix trembled before the thought of self-
  control (Acts 24:25). King Solomon said, "A man who lacks
  self-control" is "like a city whose walls are broken down" (Prov.
  25:28). Moderation is a core value for those who walk in the
  Spirit (Matt. 23:25).

IV. The Sacraments

Jesus showed His sheer genius when He established water baptism and the
Lord's Supper as the sacraments of the church that were intended to help His
followers remember His death and resurrection.

A sacrament is a formal religious act that is sacred as a sign or a badge of
a spiritual reality. Sacraments serve as public pledges of a believer's fidelity to
the Lord, binding him to his commitment of loyalty and distinguishing him
from the world. They give powerful witness to unbelievers of the commitment
the children of God have made to Jesus Christ (Acts 4:13).

The sacraments are a primary reason for the ongoing success of the Lord's
church through the centuries. The Holy Spirit's role is to insure that believers
never forget the horribly bitter cross on which God's Son died. The sacraments
guarantee, in fact, that believers will remember the crucifixion and resurrection of Jesus.

A. The Lord's Supper

It was a solemn, sacred night—the night of the Lord's betrayal. Jesus
"eagerly desired" to eat His last Passover meal with His disciples. In fact, His
heart was set on it (Luke 22:15). At this final meal with the Twelve before His
crucifixion, Jesus launched the new covenant.

> While they were eating, Jesus took bread, gave thanks and broke it,
> and gave it to his disciples, saying, "Take and eat; this is my body."
> Then he took the cup, gave thanks and offered it to them, saying,

"Drink from it, all of you. This is my blood of the covenant, which is poured out for many for the forgiveness of sins."

—MATTHEW 26:26–28

The sacrament of the Lord's Supper has Old Testament roots in the first Passover Feast in Egypt. The Lord told Moses, "When I see the blood, I will pass over you" (Exod. 12:13). Jesus fulfilled in the Upper Room that night the rich meaning and history of the Passover meal. A few short hours later, He poured out His own blood as the final sacrifice for sin to make "perfect forever those who are being made holy" (Heb. 10:10–14; Titus 3:6).

The Passover was much more than a dinner. It included a two-part covenant: God would spare the Israelites from the wrath of the death angel and deliver them from Egypt, but the nation covered by the blood was responsible to follow the Lord wholeheartedly (Exod. 12:21–30).

Jesus' broken body and shed blood is the only covering for man's sins (Acts 4:12; Heb. 2:9, 17). The Passover banquet of the old covenant, therefore, merged the night of Jesus' betrayal into the Lord's Supper of the new covenant. The Messiah Himself came to the table, made the meal His own, and established the New Testament in His own blood (Matt. 26:28; Heb. 9:15). Publicans and sinners can freely come to the Paschal Lamb of Calvary, enjoying faith-inspiring fellowship with the risen Lord (Luke 15:2; Matt. 11:18–19).

Jesus' two phrases, "This is my body" and "this is my blood" have given rise in church history to three schools of interpretation.

1. Transubstantiation

Roman Catholic teachers interpret these statements in the most literal sense possible.[7] When the priest consecrates the elements, the bread and wine actually become the body and blood of Christ in all particulars except taste, hence the teaching that the meal actually imparts saving grace. In this view, Christ is as present in the bread and wine as He was in the earthly body of Jesus. Roman Catholics understand themselves, therefore, as actually adoring Christ Himself when receiving the Eucharist.

Transubstantiation is a fundamentally flawed teaching because it frustrates the cross of Christ. Should a believer trust for his salvation in a priest's re-enactment of the crucifixion? Or, does his confidence rest solely in the triumphant Lord of the empty tomb who personally intercedes at God's right hand for His church? In addition, when Jesus consecrated the elements at the Last Supper, are we to understand that the bread became His body and the wine became His blood, with Jesus standing there bodily holding the bread and wine in His hands?

Clearly, the Lord used figurative language when He said, "This is my body," and, "This is my blood."

2. Consubstantiation

An important cause for Martin Luther's revolt against papal Rome was his reaction against the extremes of transubstantiation. In doing so, Luther (1483–1543) framed a position akin to that of Roman Catholicism. *Consubstantiation* means the simultaneous coexistence of two substances: in this case the elements of the meal and the presence of Christ.[8] Luther taught that the bread and wine remain only bread and wine, yet Christ was present in, with, and under the symbols at the consecration of the elements.

Luther held that all who receive the elements actually receive Christ, although consecration of the elements does not change the elements themselves into the actual body and blood of Christ. Therefore, when a believer receives the Holy Communion in faith, he also receives saving grace. If he does not receive the elements in faith, then he partakes to his own condemnation (1 Cor. 11:27–31).

3. The Lord's Supper as a Memorial

The Swiss reformer Ulrich Zwingli (1484–1531)[9] was a contemporary of Luther. Zwingli taught that the two affirmations of the Lord ("This is my body" and "This is my blood") are only figures of speech.[10] To Zwingli there was no more of the actual presence of Christ in the bread and wine of the Lord's Supper after the consecration than there was before the consecration. Since Zwingli understood no objective presence was in the elements, the benefit of the communion feast to him was motivation to remember Calvary: "do this...in remembrance of me" (Luke 22:19; 1 Cor. 11:25). According to Zwingli, the elements of the communion functioned as symbols to inspire the believer, by the Holy Spirit, never to forget the broken body of Christ and His shed blood.

The apostle Paul explained how the church should understand the body and blood of Christ when he told the Corinthians: "The cup of blessing which we bless, is it not the communion of the blood of Christ? The bread which we break, is it not the communion of the body of Christ?" (1 Cor. 10:16, KJV). Paul did not interpret Jesus' teaching by saying "the cup which we bless" is the blood of Christ. Nor did he say "the bread which we break" is the body of Christ. Rather, he said the elements are the "communion of the blood" and the "communion of the body." The word here translated "communion" is *koinonia*. The root meaning of the term is "participation in fellowship," which refers to a relationship in which believers accept the Lord's invitation to come to His table and share together the rich companionship they enjoy in common.

The Lord loved sinful men enough to give His body and blood to save them. When a person receives Christ's forgiveness, he naturally returns to his Lord a deep and abiding love. In the Lord's Supper, the elements of bread and wine symbolize this holy, intimate communion. The function of the communion service, therefore, is to seal this fellowship publicly, before all men, angels, and even devils.

The purpose of the Lord's Supper was not a literal transformation of the bread and wine into the objective presence of Christ, subscribing saving merit to the elements themselves. Instead, the goal of the sacrament is for a believer to take his place at the Lord's table of spiritual intimacy. At this banquet, he enjoys the sweet communion that springs from Christ's great gift of His life at Golgotha. The meal is all about celebrating the Lord's achievement on the cross.

He has taken me to the banquet hall, and his banner over me is love.
—SONG OF SOLOMON 2:4

The dishes the Lord selected for the table are bread and the fruit of the vine. They symbolize Christ's body and blood, the believer's most needed spiritual nourishment. At this table, both the child of God and the Lord enjoy the company of each other. The result is that worshipers receive new strength from their Lord.

The exalted Savior is just as eager to share *koinonia* with His brethren today as He was to enjoy the Twelve at the last Passover meal. To this day His heart is set on this kind of fellowship (Luke 22:15). As for the believer, the meal is actually futuristic, because as oft as he comes to Jesus' table, he proclaims "the Lord's death until He comes" (1 Cor. 11:25–26).

The communion the believer enjoys with Jesus through the symbolism of the body and blood of Christ is a prototype of the *koinonia* that will exist between the Lord and His church at the Wedding Supper of the Lamb (Rev. 19:9). In the great day of the Lord's second advent, symbolism will fade away before the bright light of Christ's glorious, literal, and personal presence.

B. Water Baptism

John the Baptist practiced water baptism as a public testimony of repentance (Luke 3:3). The Lord honored the rite and commanded John to baptize Him, even though Jesus was "without sin" and had no personal need for repentance (Matt. 3:13–15; Heb. 4:15). In His own ministry, Jesus taught His disciples to practice the ordinance but did not baptize anyone Himself (John 4:1–2). The Lord commanded the practice in His Great Commission, wanting the practice of water baptism to spread worldwide (Matt. 28:19–20; Mark 16:16). In giving this mandate, Jesus also announced that the trinitarian baptismal formula to be pronounced worldwide is "in the name of the Father and of the Son and of the Holy Spirit" (Matt. 28:19).

The disciples obeyed, practicing the ordinance and teaching it to their followers (Acts 2:38, 41; 8:12–13, 36; 10:47; 16:15; 18:8; 19:5). The apostle Paul also submitted to the sacrament and taught it in His preaching and writings (Acts 9:18; 22:16).

Paul also viewed water baptism as a symbol and did not give it stature equal to repentance before God that imparts saving faith in Jesus Christ. The line of demarcation he drew stood out boldly in his ministry at Corinth. Paul reminded the Corinthians that during the time he preached there, he had baptized only Crispus and Gaius, and the household of Stephanus. Paul added that the Lord did not send him "to baptize but to preach the gospel" (1 Cor. 1:16–17).

Paul did not reject water baptism as a sacrament at Corinth; instead, he focused the ordinance so that it could fill its rightful place in the body of Christ. By not making water baptism a priority for salvation, Paul was teaching that the ordinance imparted no saving merit. Instead, it gave public testimony to an inward work of saving grace Jesus had already wrought through the Holy Spirit.

Later generations of the church misinterpreted such passages as John 3:5: "Jesus answered, 'I tell you the truth, no one can enter the kingdom of God unless he is born of water and the Spirit.'" The claim that developed, identified by the term *baptismal regeneration*, was that Jesus Himself made baptism essential for salvation, so that water baptism actually releases saving faith.

In the Lord's public ministry, the reason He did not baptize, but delegated that role to His disciples, may have focused on this very concern. Jesus foreknew that if He personally baptized, it would be easier for people to link water baptism with the new birth. However, the fact that Israel's Messiah did not personally baptize anyone distanced Himself from that incorrect conclusion (John 4:2). And, of course, the thief on the cross, who went that same day to Paradise with the Lord, was not baptized (Luke 23:43). If it truly was the Lord's intent for His apostles to teach baptismal regeneration, the apostle Paul failed to present the whole counsel of God to the believers at Corinth.

Water baptism has survived through the centuries as a vitally important and sacred ordinance that publicly symbolizes a person has by faith come to Christ, repented of his sins, and accepted Jesus as Savior and Lord. It is also presented in Scripture as a vivid illustration of sanctifying grace, and of the baptism with the Holy Spirit (Luke 3:16; Rom. 6:1–4; Col. 2:12). Jesus even described His suffering in His passion as a baptism, signifying His death and resurrection (Luke 12:50; Rom. 6:3–4).

In submitting to the sacrament, a believer pledges himself to a covenant relationship with Jesus, no matter the cost. "This water *symbolizes* baptism that now saves you," Peter said, "not the removal of dirt from the body but the pledge of a good conscience toward God. It saves you by the resurrection of Jesus Christ" (1 Pet. 3:21, emphasis added).

⚞ "She Brought Her Luggage" ⚟

When Texas pastor Jim Denison was in college, he served as a summer missionary in East Malaysia. While there, he attended a small church. At one of the worship services, a teenage girl came forward to announce her decision to follow Christ and to accept Christian baptism.

During the service, Denison noticed some worn-out luggage leaning against the wall of the church. He asked the pastor about it. The pastor pointed to the girl who was to be baptized. He told Denison, "Her father said that if she was baptized as a Christian she could never go home again. So she brought her luggage."[11]

The testimony of water baptism brings to mind a word picture in which a person, with his luggage in his hand, dies to the world. Because no one can live under water, the symbolism is that he dies to his sins and old way of life. Then, when the water flows downstream, the message is that his sins are washed away and now are gone. He comes up out of new water, portraying resurrection to a new life, based on the lifestyle of Jesus Christ.

As a seal of a notary on a legal document makes a deed official in the courts, so water baptism is the seal on the title deed of the new birth that renders it publicly official. While the seal inspires public confidence, it is not the document. The seal does give public credence; however, that the covenant is official. In submitting to water baptism, the believer is testifying that the Holy Spirit has buried him with Christ and raised him to a new life (Rom. 6:2–4). The witnesses who observe the baptism become the eyewitnesses to the public testimony (1 Pet. 3:21).

Immersion has always been the most desirable mode of water baptism because it shows the symbolism best, but it is not the only acceptable method. Sprinkling was also valid in the Old Testament ritual cleansings, for example (Num. 8:7; 19:13–20; Ezek. 36:25). Pouring, too, continues to be a valid mode of baptism in the church today.

❧ I Wrote As Tiny As I Could—"Abortion" ❧

I remember my fear. In fact, it was the most fear I remember in my life. I wrote as tiny as I could on that piece of paper the word abortion. I was so scared someone would open the paper and read it and find out it was me. I wanted to get up and walk out of the auditorium during the service, the guilt and fear were that strong.

When my turn came, I walked toward the cross and pinned the paper there. I was directed to a pastor to be baptized. He looked me straight in the eyes, and I thought for sure that he was going to read this terrible secret I kept from everybody for so long.

But instead, I felt like God was telling me: *I love you. It's okay. You've been forgiven.*

I felt so much love for me, a terrible sinner. It's the first time I ever really felt forgiveness and unconditional love. It was unbelievable, indescribable.[12]

We now continue this study of the Lord's church by seeking to discover just how passionately Jesus feels about His church.

Chapter Nine

THE CHURCH—
UNVEILING THE MYSTERY

I went down to the grove... to look at the new growth in the valley.

—SONG OF SOLOMON **6:11**

I will build my church.

—MATTHEW **16:18**

Christ loved the church and gave himself up for her.

—EPHESIANS **5:25**

I. The Church, the Secret Hid in God

A. The Prophetic Institution

God spoke to Abimelech in a dream while Abraham was living in the Negev and told him Abraham was a "prophet" (Gen. 20:7). The word *prophet* in Hebrew is *nabiy'*, and it means "an inspired man." When God revealed Himself to Moses in the Sinai desert, He told him, "Your brother Aaron will be your prophet [*nabiy'*]," meaning that Aaron would speak for Moses on God's behalf (Exod. 7:1).

The ministry of the prophet in the national life of Israel came into being at Sinai as part of God's ongoing plan to reveal Himself. When the Israelites "saw the thunder and lightning and heard the trumpet and saw the mountain in smoke" they actually trembled (Exod. 20:18). In their fear, they stayed at a distance and said to Moses: "Speak to us yourself and we will listen. But do not have God speak to us or we will die" (Exod. 20:19–20).

The Holy Spirit continues to commission prophets to this day because so many have the same tendency the Israelites showed when they were in the manifest presence of God:

> The people remained at a distance, while Moses approached the thick darkness where God was.
>
> —EXODUS 20:21–23

At the end of his life, Moses summarized this event. He also gave the people God's promise of the great Messianic prophet, who would speak on God's behalf.

> This is what you asked of the Lord your God at Horeb on the day of the assembly when you said, "Let us not hear the voice of the Lord our God nor see this great fire anymore, or we will die." The Lord said to me: "What they say is good. I will raise up for them a prophet [nabiy'] like you from among their brothers; I will put my words in his mouth, and he will tell them everything I command him."
> —DEUTERONOMY 18:16–18

The Hebrew term *nabiy'* in the Old Testament translates as *prophetes* in the Greek of the New Testament (Heb. 1:1–3). This term transliterated into English as *prophet*.[1]

B. The Church, Hidden From the Prophets

Herein rests a mystery that the apostle Paul addressed in his letter to the church at Ephesus. The Holy Spirit foretold many facts about the Messiah, including His conception and birth and especially His crucifixion and resurrection (Isa. 7:14; 53:1–12). The inspired writers also talked about His second coming (Zech. 14:4). But the Spirit gave no more than hints to the prophets about the mystery of the church, "that through the gospel the Gentiles are heirs together with Israel, members together of one body and sharers together in the promise in Christ Jesus" (Eph. 3:6). The word translated as *church* most often in the New Testament is *ekklesia*, which means "a called-out assembly."

Stephen in his Sanhedrin address referred to Israel as the "church in the wilderness" (Acts 7:38, KJV). Obviously, the Hebrew nation, called out of Egypt by the God of heaven and led out of Goshen by the cloud and pillar of fire, was a prototype of the church, but that understanding came to Stephen in the hindsight of the empty tomb.

King David, who was also a prophet, may have received a glimpse of the church when he wrote, "I will praise you among the nations, O LORD; I will sing praises to your name" (Ps. 18:49; Rom. 15:8–9).

Isaiah was arguably the prophet who came closest to seeing the church. In his first and second Servant Songs, for example, Isaiah perceived the Messiah would be a light to the Gentiles, that His message of salvation would go to the ends of the earth, and that the Messiah would lift His banner to all peoples (Isa. 42:4–9, KJV; 49:6).

The prophet Simeon was "moved by the Spirit" and "went into the temple courts" at the precise time when Mary and Joseph "brought in the child Jesus to do for him what the custom of the Law required" (Luke 2:25, 27). Simeon was a "righteous and devout man," who was "waiting for the consolation of Israel." He took baby Jesus "in his arms and started praising God" (Luke 2:25, 28). His prophesy recognized the suffering that was ahead and affirmed what Isaiah had written, that the child would be "a light for revelation to the Gentiles" (Isa. 42:6; Luke 2:31–32, 34–35). So, the Holy Spirit did give the prophets hints that God was up to something big, but none of them were able to figure it out.

Assimilating this should give a dynamic, new appreciation for just how passionately the Lord feels about His church. Jesus delights to go "down to the grove…to look at the new growth in the valley" (Song of Sol. 6:11). Little wonder the apostle Peter wrote that the prophets "searched intently and with the greatest care trying to find out the time and circumstances to which the Spirit of Christ in them was pointing when he predicted the sufferings of Christ and the glories that would follow" (1 Pet. 1:10–11).

God's relationships with Adam's seed in the Old Testament pointed step by step toward ushering-in the church. God dealt with:

- the entire human race in Noah (Gen. 6:8, 13)
- a selected, called-out family in Abraham (Gen. 12:1)
- a particular nation in Israel (Exod. 5:1)
- a special royal line in David (2 Sam. 7:8–17)
- a remnant of the nation in the returning exiles (Isa. 10:20–21; Ezra 9:8)
- a select family of Aaron's seed in Zachariah and Elizabeth (the tribe of Levi), and of David's royal line in Joseph and Mary (the tribe of Judah) (Luke 1:5–6; Matt. 1:16)
- the twelve disciples, one of whom was a devil (John 6:70).

But the Twelve all forsook Him and fled, leaving only the Christ Himself to personify the church (Mark 14:50). To birth the church, Jesus withstood alone the white flames of Golgotha. The promise that Christ can redeem sinful men, therefore, found fulfillment in only one Man, the Lord Himself, who paid the price singlehandedly on Calvary. As the scripture says, "*He* became the source of eternal salvation for all who obey him" (Heb. 5:9, emphasis added). Jesus Christ, in His own person, is the essence of the church.

C. The Announcement Reserved for "the Prophet"

The church was so special in the heart of God that the Father reserved the special privilege of announcing it for His only Son, the Messiah-Prophet.

Asaph was King David's worship leader on Mount Zion. He prophesied that the Messiah would "utter hidden things, things from of old" (Ps. 78:2). Matthew observed the Lord's use of parables and applied the statement to Jesus. He interpreted the great musician's expression, saying Messiah would "utter things hidden since the creation of the world" (Matt. 13:35).

The church was uniquely the idea of Jesus Christ. He came to serve His Father's plan and die for the salvation of all men (1 Pet. 2:24). His holy objective was to give His life to gather all who trust in Him into one body, the church (Eph. 5:25). In this context, it is understandable why Paul said the Lord actually "cherishes" His church (Eph. 5:29, KJV; see Acts 20:28).

This understanding of how deeply the Lord felt about the church made the trip all the more exceptional that Jesus took with His disciples to Caesarea Philippi. Ancient paganism was so very pronounced there that many Jews thought of it as the gates of hell. In that wicked setting, Peter confessed Jesus as "the Christ, the Son of the living God" (Matt. 16:16).

Jesus the Prophet responded to that confession by giving one of the greatest prophecies of His ministry. He unveiled to the disciples the secret that had been in the heart of God from eternity, held for that very special moment. Jesus' passionate feelings and His holy determination must have come through in His voice when He said, "Blessed are you, Simon son of Jonah, for this was not revealed to you by man, but by my Father in heaven. And I tell you that you are Peter, and on this rock I will build my church, and the gates of Hades will not overcome it" (Matt. 16:17–18).

At the time, not one church existed anywhere in the world; it was only an announcement, a prophecy. This new institution of the new covenant, the church, had to be constructed, but Jesus said, "I will build it!"

A follower of the Lord will never be able to comprehend how passionately Jesus feels about His church until he grasps the Lord's claim: *"My* church" (Matt. 16:18, emphasis added). The church belongs to Jesus. He gave His blood to establish it because He loves the church. He is its head and its protector (Eph. 5:23).

Only as the disciples looked through the lens of the Upper Room, stained by the royal blood of Calvary, could they comprehend the import of the announcement at Caesarea Philippi. Jesus had a marvelous strategy; He did not intend to leave His followers as urchins to fend for themselves (John 14:18). Jesus planned to form an invisible body that would also take on a visible form. The Holy Spirit would indwell them, and Jesus would meet with them wherever they assembled (John 14:17; Matt. 18:20).

Born again believers are the *ecclesia,* assemblies of faith called out of their communities, anywhere they gather in the world. In the strength of these gatherings, believers become the people of God, finding faith, family, fellowship, motivation, forgiveness, and restoration as they do so (Eph. 3:15; Matt. 16:18; Ps. 68:6).

⚜ Who Jesus Is and What He Did ⚜ —the Foundation

Jeremy Bowen, the presenter of a new British Broadcasting Corporation (BBC) documentary on Jesus stated, "The important thing is not what he was or what he wasn't—the important thing is what people believe him to have been. A massive world wide religion, numbering more than two billion people follows his memory—that's pretty remarkable, 2,000 years on."

Bowen couldn't be more wrong. Who Jesus is and what he did is the foundation of our faith.[2]

D. People—the Temples of the New Covenant

1. The Torn Veil

At the precise moment of Jesus' death on His cross, the curtain in the Jerusalem temple miraculously tore from the top to the bottom (Matt. 27:51). Throughout the fifteen hundred years since the dedication of the tabernacle in the wilderness, a veil had separated the holy place from the holy of holies. Only the high priest could enter the holy of holies, and he could do so but once yearly (Exod. 30:10; Heb. 9:25). The masses of the people could not even hope to enter this inner sanctum where God dwelt (Exod. 25:17–22; 1 Sam. 4:4).

The torn veil was a bold signal of the new covenant (Jer. 31:31; Heb. 12:24). The way was now open for anyone with a hungry heart to come boldly to the mercy seat of God (Matt. 27:51; Heb. 4:16; Lev. 16:2–14). All sons of Adam have "hope as an anchor for the soul, firm and secure. It enters the inner sanctuary behind the curtain, where Jesus, who went before us, has entered on our behalf. He has become a high priest forever, in the order of Melchizedek" (Heb. 6: 20, KJV; Eph. 2:14; Ps. 110:4).

2. The New Beginning

The gift of the Holy Spirit, therefore, ended the fifteen-hundred-year era in which Abraham's children had built their lives around first their tabernacle and then their temple. Pentecost marked a new beginning and birthed the church as the visible expression of the invisible body of Christ (1 Cor. 12:27;

1 Pet. 2:5). The temple of the new order is people who actually walk and talk, move about, and come and go.

In the Pentecostal revival launched at Azusa Street in Los Angeles in 1906, Spirit-filled believers received the same anointing that characterized the experience of the 120 in the Upper Room, which is also the same Spirit in the most holy place of the tabernacle (Heb. 9:25; Lev. 16:2; 2 Kings 19:14–16; Ps. 46:4). Spirit-filled people do not merely talk about the Father and His Word; instead, in their hearts they have a keen sense that Jesus is the living Word and that God is with them. The Holy Spirit in them continually shows Jesus to the world.

Central to Pentecostalism is the awareness that God is this near to His children. Jesus' journey to Calvary presupposes that each of His followers make the spiritual trip themselves. From the Hill of the Skull, the Lord's intention for every believer is that he then walk past the Empty Tomb and Mt. Olivet to the Upper Room.

3. A Personal Relationship With God

The genius of the Lord's Great Commission is that Spirit-filled people, in personal relationship with God, take the new spiritual temple to lost neighbors through their relationships in community (1 Pet. 2:4–5, NLT). In the new covenant, people no longer need to make annual pilgrimages over long distances to worship in the "house of the Lord" (Ps. 122:1–4; Jer. 31:31; Luke 22:20). "Where two or three are gathered together in my name," Jesus taught, "there am I in the midst of them" (Matt. 18:20, KJV). The "temple" went with these Spirit-filled followers of the Christ, because each of them had become a dwelling place of God.

Hence, the message of this personal relationship with God simply must go to the people in the next town and then to the next, and then to the next. One day it would encircle the earth. Isaiah said the Servant of the Lord will not tire until even the islands of the sea "put their hope" in Him (Isa. 42:4). Paul taught that Christ became a servant to the Jews, confirming "the promises to the patriarchs" so that the Gentiles could "glorify God for his mercy" (Rom. 15:8–9; Ps. 18:49).

Paul also said to the believers in Galatia:

> You are all sons of God through faith in Christ Jesus, for all of you who were baptized into Christ have clothed yourselves with Christ. There is neither Jew nor Greek, slave nor free, male nor female, for you are all one in Christ Jesus. If you belong to Christ, then you are Abraham's seed, and heirs according to the promise.
> —Galatians 3:26–29

4. *The Vision—Access to God*

The special vision that had been in the heart of Jesus from eternity was coming true. Both Jews and Gentiles "have access by one Spirit to the Father" (Eph. 2:18; 3:6). In Christ's church, there are no foreigners, only "fellow citizens with God's people and members of God's household" (Eph. 2:19).

What happened on Mount Calvary births unity and means a segregationist lifestyle has no place at the foot of the cross. Jesus prayed for all of His children to "be one," just as the Father was in Jesus and Jesus was in the Father (John 17:21). This harmony exists through the agency of the Spirit, who binds believers to Christ. Paul actually compared this spiritual accord in the church to the unity of the Trinity: "There is one body, and one Spirit, even as ye are called in one hope of your calling; One Lord, one faith, one baptism, One God and Father of all, who is above all, and through all, and in all" (Eph. 4:4–6, KJV).

I will build my church.

—MATTHEW 16:18

E. The Spiritual Essence of the Church

The church Jesus announced at Caesarea Philippi has a highly visible quality as the assembly of worshipers in community. The true essence of the church, however, is spiritual and invisible.

The church invisible includes all those of every nation and tongue, in every generation, anywhere in the world who confess Jesus as Savior and Lord. "I am the good shepherd," the Lord said. "I know my sheep" (John 10:14). It is within the unlimited capacity of the God who is Spirit to have intimate relationship with each of them individually and all of them simultaneously. Even though they, together, make up an innumerable host, He knows each of their names (Rev. 7:9; John 10:3). Even the hairs on their heads "are all numbered" (Luke 12:7).

When a person grasps the close, spiritual nature of Jesus' ongoing relationship with each of the millions of members of His spiritual body, he will begin to comprehend the amazing genius of the Lord's church. In each called-out assembly, every believer has opportunity to enter into an intensely personal, spiritual friendship with "the Son of God, who loved me and gave himself for me" (Gal. 2:20; Exod. 33:11). God's children respond to Jesus' loving care by:

- communicating with their Lord regularly in the closet of prayer (Matt. 6:6);
- enjoying fellowship at the Lord's table, savoring sweet communion (Luke 22:19);

- maturing in the attitude, character, and agenda of the Lord by avidly studying His Word (Ps. 119:11; 2 Pet. 3:15–16);
- worshiping the Lord with true devotion amid the fellowship of believers (John 4:24); and
- honoring the Lord's worldwide vision by faithfully fishing for men and then bringing them into the fellowship of the church (Matt. 4:19).

The Lord crafted His church as an invisible organism that would forever grow into the likeness of its Head (Eph. 5:23). The Good Shepherd did not bind His followers to a legal system or to a governmental polity. He bound them personally to Himself, the resurrected last Adam, the Christ of Calvary (John 10:11; 1 Cor. 15:45; Matt. 16:18). Jesus Himself is the curriculum and the energy, the foundation and the chief cornerstone of the building of God (1 Cor. 3:11; Eph. 2:20–22).

Jesus is also the sole keeper of the Lamb's Book of Life, in which the names of the redeemed are recorded (Luke 10:20; Rev. 3:5; 21:27). "I give them eternal life," Jesus said, "and they shall never perish; no one can snatch them out of my hand" (John 10:28).

A fisherman knows his catch. He sorts out the marketable fish and discards the remainder. A farmer sifts his wheat to remove the tares and the chaff. In the same way, the Lord Jesus keeps accurate records in the Lamb's Book of Life. He knows each person who is in His church (Matt. 13:30, 47–48; Rev. 21:27).

Since the nature of the invisible church is this personal, who can discern it? Obviously, only the Lord Himself ultimately identifies the redeemed of all centuries. At the same time, the Spirit bears witness with our spirit that we are sons of God. In fact, we receive "the Spirit of sonship. And by him we cry 'Abba, Father'" (Rom. 8:15). People who are walking in the Spirit will have good insight too, for the Holy Spirit will operate in them the manifestation gift of discerning of spirits (1 Cor. 12:7, 10, KJV). A vital part of this sensitivity comes by observing the fruit of the Spirit in a person's life (Gal. 5:22; Matt. 12:33). The Lord said, "By their fruit you will recognize them" (Matt. 7:16; Luke 6:44). Jesus also taught, "By this all men know that you are my disciples, if you love one another" (John 13:35).

F. The Church and the Kingdom

Jesus spoke often about His kingdom, using the terms *kingdom of God* and *kingdom of heaven* interchangeably (Mark 1:15; Matt. 4:17). By definition, the Lord's kingdom is the entire sphere of His rule and embraces the entire created order of God. The kingdom also includes the remnant of Israel that one day will look on Him whom they pierced and acknowledge His lordship (Zech. 12:10; 14:9; Jer. 3:16–18; Matt. 25:32–33; Rev. 20:4–7).

When Gabriel announced the birth of Jesus to Mary, he did so in kingly terms: "The Lord God will give him the throne of His father David, and he will reign over the house of Jacob forever; his kingdom will never end" (Luke 1:32–33). Jesus taught us to pray, "Your kingdom come" (Matt. 6:10). At Jesus' trial, Pilate asked the Lord, "So you are a king?" (John 18:37, rsv). Jesus answered him, "You are right in saying I am a king. In fact, for this reason I was born, and for this I came into the world, to testify to the truth. Everyone on the side of truth listens to me" (John 18:37).

The Lord taught that His kingdom "does not come with…careful observation, nor will people say, 'Here it is,' or 'There it is'" (Luke 17:20–21). It is not at all like the easily observable institutions of a national government. Instead, "the kingdom of God is within you" (Luke 17:21). The sphere of His reign is in the heart, and the door through which people enter Jesus' domain is the new birth.

As regards His rule in the hearts of His children, His kingdom has already come. In this sense, the dominion of Jesus Christ is in the earth even now. As regards His lordship over the nations, His kingdom is still future. The Scriptures promise that this coming kingdom of God will be literal and that people will begin to experience the ultimate meaning of the Lord's kingdom at His second coming (1 Cor. 15:24–27, 53–54; Rev. 1:7). At that time, all His enemies will be made His footstool (Heb. 10:13).

In the timetable of God, the current age is the era of the church. The Lord's church is an incubator for the kingdom; yet the kingdom is greater than the church. The ultimate destiny of the church is to become the bride of Christ in His kingdom (Rev. 19:6–9). The kingdom of God, therefore, has a "now" dimension. It is anywhere Jesus reigns. It also demonstrates a "not-now" aspect, in that "He waits for his enemies to be made his footstool" (Heb. 10:13). It is very important to discern the difference between the two. For example, Jesus said to Pilate when on trial for His life, "My kingdom is not of this world" (John 18:36). The mission of the people of God, therefore, is to grow the Lord's church by winning people to Christ.

The best way to hold tightly in this age of the church to the blessed hope of the coming literal reign of Christ is to adopt the Lord's twin passions. Jesus loves all people and died to see them saved (John 3:16). He also hung on the cross to establish His church (Eph. 5:25; Acts 20:28). Jesus wants all of His children to find family, faith, and fellowship in its ministries, maturing them in Christ (Ps. 68:6). The Lord was also very emphatic about His Great

Commission, passionately wanting the gospel story to advance to the ends of the earth in every generation (Matt. 28:16–20; Acts 1:1–8).

It is a mistake in the age of the church to go chasing after the Lord's kingdom, seeking to usher in Jesus' reign. The finest way to be a kingdom man in the church age and "speed his coming" is to commit heart and soul to expand the Lord's church (2 Pet. 3:12).

II. The Church Moves Out Into the Roman Empire

We now turn our attention to tracing the advance of the infant church in the first twenty years after Pentecost.

A. The Birth of the Church in Jerusalem

The heavenly Father honored Jesus' request and birthed the church in the Upper Room on the Day of Pentecost (John 14:16). The fact that God poured out the Holy Spirit with such a huge crowd of pilgrims in the city for the festivities showed the Lord's capacity to announce publicly the humble birth of His church. About 120 believers seated in the Upper Room received the Holy Spirit that spring morning and began to speak in tongues (Acts 1:15; 2:4). Visitors from some fifteen nations and people groups quickly congregated. They listened in amazement as the 120 fluently spoke "the wonderful works of God" in the travelers' languages they had not learned (Acts 2:5–12, KJV).

Following Peter's sermon, the Lord added three thousand people to the church. In Acts 4:4, the number of believers climbed to about five thousand men. Luke recorded in Acts 5:14 that "more and more men and women believed in the Lord and were added to the number." As "the word of God increased, the number of the disciples multiplied in Jerusalem greatly; and a great company of the priests were obedient to the faith" (Acts 6:7, KJV). As God gave to Adam and Eve the mandate to "be fruitful and multiply and replenish the earth," so in the age of the church all believers are to reproduce themselves (Gen. 1:28). In this way God's promise to Abraham will be fulfilled (Gen. 15:5; Matt. 28:16–20; Acts 1:8).

B. The Revival in Samaria

From Jerusalem and Judea, the forward march of the church moved northward. This resulted from "a great persecution" that erupted in Jerusalem, dispersing the believers but not the apostles (Acts 8:1–3).

> Those who had been scattered preached the word wherever they went. Philip [one of the first deacons] went down to a city in Samaria and

proclaimed the Christ there. When the crowds heard Philip and saw the miraculous signs he did, they all paid close attention to what he said. With shrieks, evil spirits came out of many, and many paralytics and cripples were healed. So there was great joy in that city.

—Acts 8:4–8

After the apostles heard about the work of the Spirit in Samaria, they sent Peter and John to give the revival guidance.

When they arrived, they prayed that they might receive the Holy Spirit, because the Spirit had not yet come upon any of them; they had been baptized only in the name of the Lord Jesus. Then Peter and John placed their hands on them, and they received the Holy Spirit.

—Acts 8:15–17

C. The Gentile Pentecost

The first recorded time Gentiles received the baptism with the Holy Spirit occurred in Caesarea, the beautiful Middle Eastern seaport capitol of the Roman world. Among the many soldiers garrisoned there was a centurion who commanded the Italian regiment. He and his family were devout and God-fearing. This centurion "gave generously to those in need and prayed to God regularly" (Acts 10:1–2). One day at about three in the afternoon, this Roman commander had a vision.

When the angel who spoke to him departed, Cornelius called two of his servants and a devout soldier who was one of his attendants. He told them everything that had happened and sent them to Joppa.

—Acts 10:7–8

The same Holy Spirit who spoke to Cornelius also prepared Peter through a trance, motivating him, a Jew, to be willing to visit this Gentile's home and preach the gospel to him and his family. Following the trance, the Holy Spirit gave Peter explicit instructions: "Three men are looking for you. So get up and go downstairs. Do not hesitate to go with them, for I have sent them" (Acts 10:19–20).

Simon Peter obeyed the Spirit and went. The apostle to the Jews used in Cornelius' house the keys to the kingdom and opened the way for ministry to the Gentile world (Matt. 16:19; Gal. 2:7–8). He proclaimed there, "God anointed Jesus of Nazareth with the Holy Spirit and power and...he went about doing good and healing all who were under the power of the devil, because God was with him" (Acts 10:38). So much meaning for the future of the church rested on that little word, *all*. The ministry of Jesus can never be bound by any ethnic or national limits (Matt. 8:5–13).

While Peter was preaching this message in Cornelius' house, he and his entourage watched as the Holy Spirit came on this Roman military officer and "all who heard the message." They began to speak in tongues as the apostles did in the Upper Room (Acts 10:44–46; 11:15, 17). Cornelius and his household were the first Gentiles to receive the Holy Spirit, making Caesarea the Gentile "Upper Room."

D. The Revival in Antioch

As the administrator of the Lord's church, the Holy Spirit moved next from Caesarea northward, up the Mediterranean coast to Antioch, a city in Syria. Syrians had been among the first Gentiles to respond to Jesus in the early months of His ministry. In fact, "His fame went throughout all Syria" (Matt. 4:24, KJV).

The apostles did not start the revival in Antioch. Instead, it was a spontaneous work of the Spirit.

> Those who had been scattered by the persecution in connection with Stephen traveled as far as Phoenicia, Cyprus and Antioch, sharing the message only with Jews. Some of them, however, men from Cyprus and Cyrene, went to Antioch and began to speak to Greeks also, telling them the good news about the Lord Jesus. The Lord's hand was with them, and a great number of people believed and turned to the Lord.
>
> —ACTS 11:19–21

1. The Ministry of Barnabas and Saul

When the apostles in Jerusalem learned of the revival, they sent Barnabas, the son of encouragement, to Antioch (Acts 11:22). Barnabas was a Levite landowner from Cyprus who "was a good man, full of the Holy Spirit and faith" (Acts 4:36–37; 11:24). The apostles chose Barnabas, no doubt, because he could relate better to the Greeks living in Antioch. His assignment was to give the revival stability and direction.

Barnabas made a trip on further north into Asia Minor to the city of Tarsus and located a man named Saul. Barnabas had befriended Saul when he first came to Christ, after Saul's Damascus Road conversion (Acts 9:27–30). Saul accepted Barnabas' invitation and returned south with him to participate in the work of God in Antioch: "For a whole year Barnabas and Saul met with the church and taught great numbers of people" (Acts 11:26). Antioch was the first Gentile city to receive the message of Jesus Christ, preached in the power of the Holy Spirit.

2. Christians, People of the Anointing

"The disciples were called Christians first in Antioch" (Acts 11:26). Believers in Jesus ever since have carried the Lord's Greek Messianic name—*Christos*, which is translated into the name "Christ." It is from this word that the term *Christian* is derived. This term recognized the anointing of the Holy Spirit on Jesus Christ, an unction that transferred to His followers. Christians are people whose lives manifest that same anointing.

The Greeks who came to Christ in such large numbers in Antioch saw something special in the lives of the Lord's servants who taught them: they observed their anointing. Some of them no doubt had journeyed south to Israel at the beginning of Jesus' ministry (Matt. 4:24). They surely recognized that the anointing on the believers in Antioch was the same presence that had caught their attention in the life of Jesus, so the followers of the Way were themselves people of the anointing (Acts 9:2). Jesus commissions each of His followers, as an extension of the Messiah's anointing, to reproduce themselves by reaching out to others.

3. The Simultaneous Principle

The simultaneous principle of apostolic ministry has always been the paradigm of the Holy Spirit. It focuses on *while*, not *after*—*while* winning your city and your nation for Christ, take the gospel to the ends of the earth, doing both *at the same time.* The Lord stated this principle just before His ascension: "You will receive power when the Holy Spirit comes on you, and you will be my witnesses both in Jerusalem, and in all Judea, and Samaria, and to the ends of the earth" (Acts 1:8, KJV). The principle says that as you are winning your city for God, go to the nations simultaneously. Do "both" at the same time. The way apostolic ministry developed in Acts of the Apostles illustrates this principle in action.

The Lord used this paradigm to grow His church in the apostolic era, with Jerusalem as its launching pad. The simultaneous principle notes that while revival was continuing in the young Jerusalem church, the Good News also spread across Judea. While the church was getting started in Judea, the good news then spread to Samaria. While simultaneous efforts were underway to win Jerusalem, Judea, and Samaria, the Holy Spirit birthed the Lord's church in Caesarea. While the church was simultaneously growing in Jerusalem, Judea, Samaria, and Caesarea, a spontaneous revival sprang up in Antioch in Syria. Many Greeks started coming to the Lord.

On day while the ministry team in Antioch was "worshiping the Lord and fasting, the Holy Spirit said, 'Set apart for me Barnabas and Saul for the work to which I have called them.' So after they had fasted and prayed, they placed their hands on them and sent them off" (Acts 13:2–3). The church in Antioch was probably no more than two years old.

This new church in Antioch was far from winning its city, yet the Holy Spirit chose to take the best and brightest servants out of the growing Antioch church and send them on the first missionary journey of the apostolic era. That trip made them the first missionaries of the Christian church. So the simultaneous principle says that as you are winning your city for God, go to the nations concurrently, doing both at the same time.

The way apostolic ministry developed in Acts of the Apostles illustrates this simultaneous principle in action. The church at Antioch obeyed the Lord's Great Commission as expressed by the voice of the Holy Spirit, and doing so did not hurt the development of the church at Antioch. Instead, the congregation emerged as the epicenter of the early post-apostolic church. Antioch's Bishop Ignatius, who was martyred in Rome in A.D. 107 is arguably the most remembered early post-apostolic leader.[3]

If a church embraces *after–then* thinking, it will make a major mistake. The mindset that says, "*After* reaching our city and developing a mature church, *then* we will start thinking about the regions beyond," will miss the heart of Jesus Christ and the high standard of ministry that characterizes a congregation as apostolic. A congregation with apostolic faith today does not have the option to wait until after it reaches maturity to embrace the Lord's Great Commission.

While, not *after* is the apostolic model.

E. The Macedonian Call

Another red-letter moment in the forward advance of the Lord's church occurred while Paul was on his second missionary journey. His plan was to turn eastward and preach the gospel in Asia, but the Holy Spirit stopped him. In that swirl of events, Paul ended up in Troas. One night he had a vision of a man from Macedonia standing and begging, saying to him, "Come over to Macedonia and help us" (Acts 16:9). Instead of going eastward, the Holy Spirit sent him westward. That revelation set the course of the Lord's church in the western hemisphere, which characterized its advance for the next two millennia.

The time span from Pentecost to Paul's great vision at Troas was about twenty years. The international vision of Jesus Christ was coming true as the gospel moved out to the nations. "You will receive power when the Holy Spirit comes on you," Jesus promised, "and you will be my witnesses in Jerusalem, and in all Judea and Samaria, and to the ends of the earth" (Acts 1:8).

F. Two Revelations Helped Launch the Church

As Paul pondered the cross of Jesus, the Holy Spirit gave him two biblical concepts that he included in Galatians, his first epistle (written around A.D. 48). Both had been implicit in the teaching of Jesus (John 8:31–44; Matt. 3:9; Luke 3:8). The first related to the meaning of Abraham's seed. The revelation clearly unfolded to Abraham after he had been willing to offer his only son, Isaac, as a sacrifice on Moriah (Gen. 22:1–13).

> "By myself have I sworn," saith the LORD, "for because thou hast done this thing, and hast not withheld thy son, thine only son: that in blessing I will bless thee, and in multiplying I will multiply thy seed as the stars of the heaven, and as the sand which is upon the sea shore; and thy seed shall possess the gate of his enemies; and in thy seed shall all the nations of the earth be blessed; because thou hast obeyed my voice."
> —GENESIS 22:15–18, KJV

The full import of that disclosure lay dormant for 1,800 years, until the apostle Paul comprehended it by looking at it through the lens of Jesus' death and resurrection. He wrote to the Galatians "that the blessing of Abraham" had come upon "the Gentiles through Jesus Christ, that we might receive the promise of the Spirit through faith" (Gal. 3:14, KJV). It took Golgotha to perceive the meaning that had rested in Abraham's story for almost two millennia: "Now to Abraham and his Seed were the promises made. He does not say, 'And to seeds,' as of many, but as of one, 'And to your seed,' who is Christ" (Gal. 3:16; Gen. 12:7; 13:15; 22:18; 24:7, KJV).

This apostolic revelation unveiled the secret of the church as an international force. Jesus Christ as Israel's Messiah is the Seed who brings redemption to all—Jews and Gentiles alike. The Christ who voluntarily poured out His blood on the cross loves everyone (Titus 3:6). His death makes no distinctions and includes no favorites (John 3:16; Rom. 2:11; Eph. 6:9).

This awesome exercise of apostolic authority—to say what the term "seed" had always meant in the heart of God (but was misunderstood for centuries)—opened up a big superhighway for the gospel to go to the peoples of all ethnicities.

A second and related insight recorded in Galatians was Paul's teaching that anyone, Jew or Gentile, who has Abraham's faith is a son of Abraham and an heir of the promise (Gal. 3:29). Many people at the time saw it as a radical construal of Scripture that Abraham's faith and not his bloodline is what defined his true heirs.

These two explanations obviously angered many Jews. They also demonstrated the sovereign guidance the Holy Spirit gave to Jesus' infant church. Both of these revelations came to Paul with perfect timing, fitting them into the first letter he wrote. They swung the door wide open for the faith of Abraham to find a completely new seedbed in the Gentile world (Gen. 15:6).

G. Gallio's Ruling

Gallio was the Roman governor of Achaia in southern Greece. During Gallio's tenure (A.D. 51–52), while Paul was establishing the church in Corinth, the Jews made a united attack against Paul, hauling him into the governor's pagan court. Judaism was a recognized religion under Roman law, which meant Romans viewed Christians as an offshoot of Judaism. The goal of Paul's enemies was to get a ruling in Gallio's court that Christianity was not a branch of Judaism (Acts 18:12–16). They alleged to Gallio that Paul was "persuading the people to worship God in ways contrary to the law" [of both Judaism and Rome]; therefore, Roman law should not protect these Christians as a wing of Judaism. Herod had tried to kill baby Jesus in the cradle, and now the strategy was to use Roman law to stop the infant church (Matt. 2:13–18). But Gallio refused to get involved in what he perceived as an internal Jewish dispute.

> Just as Paul was about to speak, Gallio said to the Jews, "If you Jews were making a complaint about some misdemeanor or serious crime, it would be reasonable for me to listen to you. But since it involves questions about words and names and your own law—settle the matter yourselves. I will not be a judge of such things." So he had them ejected from the court.
>
> —ACTS 18:14–17

Gallio's ruling was pivotal. It meant in the eyes of Roman law the New Testament church remained under the wing of Judaism, and it allowed valuable time for the church to strengthen and continue to spread. Without question, a Jewish cradle rocked Christianity, even though it was destined to become a worldwide religion in its own right.

H. Embracing the Lord's Vision

Jesus trusted His Father implicitly and was the faithful servant to His plan, and the Lord's early followers delighted to adopt His attitude (Phil. 2:5; Heb. 10:7–9). They served by developing ministries that grew the church and changed people's lives. These believers went to every area of the Roman world, proclaiming Jesus Christ as the urgent message the people needed to hear. In doing so, they won men and women to Christ and developed active, growing churches. These Spirit-filled believers became ambassadors who brought reconciliation between God and men, and did it joyfully, even at the risk of horrible beatings, jail, and death (2 Cor. 5:20; Acts 16:16–24). Everywhere the good news went, the anointing of the Holy Spirit in the life of Jesus, which descended in the Upper Room, characterized these evangels.

The global strategy of Jesus Christ was underway to redeem all people everywhere, thereby destroying "the devil's work" (1 John 3:8). Jesus also wanted to mature His children in His own character in the "called out assemblies" or churches His disciples established. Fundamental to achieving this was folding them into the Lord's spiritual body in the invisible church (1 Pet. 2:5; Eph. 1:3–7).

These new converts realized that in Christ they could make a difference; Jesus' vision gave their lives new meaning. God wanted them. He had called them, commissioned them, and filled them with the Holy Spirit to serve their generation. They knew they had something invaluable to give to the world (2 Cor. 4:7).

These Christians went up against the might and power of Rome, the intellectual skill of the Greeks, and the religious pride and arrogance of the Jews (1 Cor. 1:22). To do it required absolute confidence God was with them. It also presupposed certainty that the gospel accurately identified the human problem—all people everywhere are in rebellion against God and will be lost forever if they do not accept Jesus Christ as Savior and Lord (John 8:24, 34; Rom. 3:23; 6:23).

These evangels felt a firm commitment to convince Romans, Greeks, and Jews of their deepest need, even when their hearers did not think they had a problem. They trusted absolutely in the unparalleled superiority of the crucified Christ over all rivals.

The book of Acts opens with a reaffirmation of the Great Commission and records the gift of the Holy Spirit and the birth of the church on the Day of Pentecost (Acts 1–2). It ends with Paul in Rome, in a rented house, spreading the gospel in the capitol of the Roman Empire. "Boldly and without hindrance" for two whole years, "he preached the kingdom of God and taught about the Lord Jesus Christ" (Acts 28:30–31). Those two years of ministry helped to make the church in Rome pivotal in the conversion of the empire over the next two centuries.

III. Walking in the Spirit

The gift of the Holy Spirit in the Upper Room unveiled a fresh dynamic of walking in the Spirit (Acts 2:1–4; Gal. 5:16, 25). To walk in the Spirit is to walk with Jesus, because the Holy Spirit always delights to reveal Jesus (John 14:26). The apostles who walked with the Lord in the flesh learned what walking in the Spirit meant from their master Teacher. Jesus always kept pace with the Spirit, who guided His life (Acts 10:38; Gal. 5:25). After Pentecost, even the most ordinary among Spirit-filled believers discovered they, too, could walk in the Spirit, all the while manifesting spiritual gifts with servant hearts.

The apostle John recorded Jesus had a sensitive capability to see what the Father was doing and saying and then to act on what He saw and heard (John 5:19–21, 30; Isa. 50:4). The Lord also applied that same principle to the ministry of the Holy Spirit. "He will not speak on his own," Jesus said. Instead, "He will speak only what he hears" (John 16:3).

Walking in the Spirit is all about adopting the Lord's attitude and following His example (Phil. 2:1–5). Jesus anchored His life in the Old Testament Scriptures, with a very active prayer life. He trained His spiritual eyes to see what His Father was doing and schooled His spiritual ears to hear what His Father was saying. Walking in the Spirit assumes these servant qualities, flowing from the lives of set-apart believers who are filled with the Spirit.

Moses had such a keen spiritual sensitivity to the voice of God that the Spirit actually gave him whole sections of the Law verbatim. The Great Emancipator's account of how God talked to him when he received the Ten Commandments is just one example. "God spoke all these words," Moses recorded (Exod. 20:1–17; Deut. 5–6).

Peter quoted David's testimony in his Upper Room sermon: "'I saw the Lord always before me. Because he is at my right hand, I will not be shaken'" (Acts 2:25; Ps. 16:8–11). King David's life, therefore, had been characterized by his willingness to see and hear what the Father was doing and saying, and then acting on it. The same dynamic was at work when Peter healed the lame man at the Beautiful Gate of the temple. It happened in the moment Peter and John "looked straight at him." As a result of that knowing look, the apostle said to him, "Look at us!" (Acts 3:4–5). The lame man was healed immediately, and went into the temple jumping and leaping and praising God (Acts 3:6–8, KJV).

In Lystra, a crippled man who had never walked listened to Paul. "Paul looked directly at him" and "saw that he had faith to be healed" (Acts 14:9). "Stand up on your feet!" Paul said to him (Acts 14:10). After that, "the man jumped up and began to walk."

Lydia was a member of a women's prayer group that met on the bank of the Gangitis River at Philippi. While Paul was preaching, "the Lord opened her heart to respond" (Acts 16:14). She became a pillar in this church that sprang up in northern Greece and a great friend and supporter of Paul's ministry.

Because the Holy Spirit is indeed spirit, God's children perceive Him, of necessity, with spiritual eyes and ears (John 10:1–6; Acts 16:13–18). Walking in the Spirit inherently embraces this dynamic, with:

- adherence to the primacy of the scriptures for all matters of faith and practice (Matt. 7:15; 2 Tim. 3:16; 2 Pet. 1:21; 1 John 4:1).
- a deep yearning to mature in the mindset of Jesus Christ, who so completely trusted His Father (Phil. 2:5–8);
- an active prayer life (Luke 9:28); and
- an understanding that the Holy Spirit does speak to Christ's followers, giving them specific guidance that can be tested by the Word of God (Acts 8:29; 13:2; Isa. 50:4–5).

Maturing in Jesus' attitude is at the heart of Christian living. To that end, Paul admonished his readers at Philippi, "Work out your own salvation with fear and trembling" (Phil. 2:12–13). The caution, "with fear and trembling," certainly embraces how one deals with disputable matters, like the modes of water baptism. More importantly, it takes into account the new birth and set-apart living, and it involves a personal visit to the Upper Room. It also assumes discovering how the Holy Spirit has gifted each of Christ's followers for service so that the Spirit can show Jesus to the world.

When the Lord goes "down to the grove" He looks for "the new growth in the valley" (Song of Sol. 6:11). Jesus wants to know "if the vines [have] budded or the pomegranates [are] in bloom," and it delights Him when the fruit is ripening on the trees.

IV. The Tithe

The Lord's church must have a financial plan. God's design is for His children to tithe on all of their sources of income (Lev. 27:30; 2 Chron. 31:2–5; Luke 11:42; 18:9–14). The practice of giving a tenth to the Lord dates to the time of Abraham, who gave tithes to Melchizedek of all the plunder from war (Gen. 14:20; Heb. 7:2–9). The custom was also well established in the Mosaic Law, which affirmed the tithe belonged to the Lord (Lev. 27:30–33; Num. 18:21–32). Malachi went so far as to say the nation had robbed God because the people had not kept the practice of bringing tithes and offerings into the storehouse—so "there may be food in my house" (Mal. 3:10; 2 Chron. 31:5; Neh. 10:37; 12:44; 13:5, 12). In robbing God, they were bringing a curse on themselves and on God's house, because lack of adequate funding stymied the work of God in the new temple Zerubbabel built (Mal. 3:8).

Jesus rebuked the Pharisees for their legalisms in tithing, while at the same time He made a clear affirmation of the tithing principle. "You should have practiced the latter [judgment, mercy, and faith]" He told the Pharisees, "without leaving the former [the tithe] undone" (Luke 11:42; 18:9–14). Jesus addressed the same theme when He taught, "Give, and it will be given to you. A good measure, pressed down, shaken together and running over will be poured into your lap. For with the measure you use, it will be measured to you" (Luke 6:38).

Jesus also demonstrated His keen interest in the grace of giving by actually watching what people gave into the temple treasury. As He did so, He commended the sacrifice of the poor widow who out of her poverty gave all she had. Since the Lord observed the giving habits of both the rich and the poor in the temple, it follows that He knows our giving habits today (Luke 21:1–4).

Jesus loves people, and He loves His church. For this reason, giving tithes and offerings generously to the Lord's church becomes the believer's delight. A child of God is a steward; all that he has rightly belongs to God (Luke 12:42). Good managers of the Lord's possessions will make it their primary interest to help fulfill the Great Commission, because doing so is one of Jesus' primary interests (Matt. 28:16–20).

The apostle Paul called for happy generosity and wrote letters to the churches encouraging people to give freely. "God loves it when the giver delights in the giving," he said (2 Cor. 9:7, THE MESSAGE; 1 Cor. 16:1; 2 Cor. 8–9). Paul went on to say believers would experience blessing to such an extent they could "be generous on every occasion" (2 Cor. 9:11).

"Remember the Lord your God," Moses admonished the nation in the last month of his life. His goal was to teach the people that God "gives you the ability to produce wealth and so confirms his covenant" (Deut. 8:18). God told Malachi that special blessings come to people who practice tithing, and that the principle can actually be proven:

> Test me in this, says the Lord Almighty, and see if I will not throw open the floodgates of heaven and pour out so much blessing you will not have room enough for it.
>
> —MALACHI 3:10

V. The Church and the Secular State

Children of God in the church have the responsibility to be salt and light in community. To do so, the church must respect civil authority. Jesus taught His followers to "give to Caesar what is Caesar's" (Matt. 22:21). The apostle Paul wrote a letter to the believers in Rome before he visited the capitol of the

Empire that taught the believers there to "submit…to the governing authorities" (Rom. 13:1). Paul viewed all established authority as coming from God and went so far as to say that anyone who rebelled against the authority was rebelling "against what God has instituted" (Rom. 13:2).

Paul saw even pagan governmental officers as "God's servants to do you good" (Rom. 13:4). The believers in Rome were to submit to their civil authorities to avoid punishment and keep a clear conscience. A servant of the Lord whose life is manifesting the gifts and fruit of the Spirit will choose to be a model citizen in the secular state.

A Christian's dedication to do his part to fulfill the Great Commission takes into account that the primary focus of the Great Commission is to win people to Christ. A secondary benefit of the gospel is that Christian moral and ethical principles bless nations. Therefore, it makes good sense for the state to permit the church to function unhindered. This is true because the spiritual kingdom of Jesus Christ redeems people. It cleans up their habits and bondages and makes them good citizens of the state.

The Lord's kingdom is not of this world. If it were, Jesus would have permitted His followers to arm themselves and fight with the swords and spears of the nations (Matt. 26:52; John 18:36). His is a spiritual kingdom that exists amid all governments, and the weapons of its warfare are spiritual (2 Cor. 10:4).

The biblical doctrine of being subject to the higher powers is not saying the church must endorse all actions of the secular state. To the contrary, Spirit-filled Christians who are committed to fulfilling the Great Commission will bring judgment on this world by pointing out its sins (John 9:39). The church must always remember as it does so, "God did not send his Son into the world to condemn the world, but to save the world through him" (John 3:17).

Occasions do come when members of the body of Christ must disobey the authority of the state. This would surely be true when the civil authority calls on believers to deny the eternal lordship and ultimate authority of Jesus Christ. Both Daniel and the three Hebrew children were willing to disobey Babylonian law when it specifically conflicted with the law of God (Dan. 1:8; 3:1–30; 6:4–28). Peter and the other apostles, when they were on trial, answered the Jewish Sanhedrin, "We must obey God rather than men" (Acts 5:29). The history of the church is resplendent with martyrs who have given their lives for Jesus Christ rather than give an idolatrous allegiance to the secular state.

The Scriptures teach that men of God should involve themselves in civil service and seek positions of political leadership. David, the shepherd boy of Bethlehem, became a king and a man after God's own heart. Daniel became prime minister of Babylon. The three Hebrew children taken into captivity with him became governors of Babylonian provinces (Dan. 3:30; 5:29; Acts 13:22; 1 Sam. 13:14). It is certainly biblical, therefore, for Spirit-filled men and women to enter the political arena, as they take seriously their responsibility to fulfill the Lord's international vision.

Since God has established the authorities that exist, it naturally follows there is a rightful place for contemporary "Daniels" in the political spheres of government (Rom. 13:1).

It is now appropriate to turn our attention to how the Lord structured and gifted His church so that it duplicates His ministry and thrives amid all civil governments and cultures.

Chapter Ten

THE CHURCH—DUPLICATING JESUS' MINISTRY WORLDWIDE

Awake, north wind, and come, south wind! Blow on my garden,
that its fragrance may spread abroad.
—SONG OF SOLOMON 4:16

The gates of Hades will not overcome it.
—MATTHEW 16:18

He…gave some to be apostles; some to be prophets; some to be
evangelists; and some to be pastors and teachers.
—EPHESIANS 4:11

THE HOLY SPIRIT birthed the church with Jesus Christ as its head (Col. 1:18). The objective of the Spirit as the administrator of the church was to duplicate the ministry of Jesus in every ethnic group in the Empire and in the regions beyond Rome's influence. That motivation is unchanged to this day. When people come to Christ, they:

- immediately become part of Jesus' spiritual and invisible body,
- join assemblies or churches where they grow and mature in the attitude and vision of Jesus Christ and choose to commit to His plan for the nations,
- are filled with the Holy Spirit, and
- are gifted and empowered by the Spirit to reproduce themselves and their churches, both at home and abroad.

Roman government, Greek culture, and the Jewish religious system all vigorously opposed the development of Jesus' vision, but did not prevail. The church actually thrived amid all of the hostility it faced. The genius of Jesus' strategy made the difference and goes to the heart of the survivability of the church through the centuries. Jesus emphatically said, "I will build my church" (Matt. 16:18).

This study will seek to discover how the Lord did it so successfully that His church has survived for two thousand years and shows no signs of decline worldwide. The role of the Trinity in gifting the church will also receive consideration, and the function of the gifts of the Spirit in duplicating the ministry of Jesus will receive special attention.

⚜ Cellmates Hungry for the Gospel ⚜

"I was attending a training course for my house church network's council members and youth leaders," said Chinese Christian leader, Brother Zhong. "The Public Security Bureau (PSB) raided us the first day. All the leaders were arrested. The prison authorities shaved our heads and interrogated us. We were warned that the hardened inmates would beat us. So with much trepidation, another brother and I entered our cell.

"We were greeted by the sight of 16 other inmates, lined up in two rows and thumping their fists. My heart beat rapidly as I sent prayers up to God.

"The leader of the gang asked, 'Why are you here?'

"'Because we are Christians,' I replied.

"'You don't beat people up?'

"'No,' I assured him.

"'Do you sing?'

"'Yes,' I answered.

"The leader ordered me to sing a song. I wept as I sang. The Holy Spirit moved in our midst, and by the time I finished singing, every prisoner was also in tears. To my shock, the gang leader then asked to hear the gospel. After that, my cellmates hungered to hear the gospel every day.

"One Sunday, we held a worship service. The prison guard demanded to know who was behind it. He threatened to punish everyone if no one spoke up. I stood up and confessed.

"I was forced to remove my clothes and stand at an inclined angle to the wall. The gang leader couldn't bear it anymore. He asked to be punished with me. All the others volunteered to do the same. The infuriated guard stormed out.

"I was moved by my cellmates' act. One of them, who had been there for three years, became a believer that day."[1]

I. The Body of Christ

A. His Invisible Body

The heavenly Father appointed Jesus as the "supreme Head of the church" (Eph. 1:22, TLB). It is part of the Lord's genius that His church thrives even amid persecution (Matt. 5:11–12). Jesus stated before His crucifixion that the

Holy Spirit would serve as the administrator of His church, and the Spirit can go anywhere to exalt Christ's name, even to jail (John 14:16; 15:26; 16:7–11; Acts 1:8; 16:22–34; Eph. 1:13–14).

When the Holy Spirit brings a person to Christ in the new birth, he immediately becomes part of the universal and invisible body of Christ (Eph. 5:30). At the same time, he joins the family of the church visible (Rom. 1:7; 1 Cor. 1:2).

The church universal and the church visible are each distinctive, but they are also interlinked. So a dual membership is part of the strategy of Jesus for the growth of His church. Coming to Christ takes place in community, among brothers and sisters.

> How, then, can they call on the one they have not believed in? And how can they believe in the one of whom they have not heard? And how can they hear without someone preaching to them? And how can they preach unless they are sent? As it is written, "How beautiful are the feet of those who bring good news!"
>
> —ROMANS 10:14–15

The writer of Hebrews said the people in the spiritual body of Christ come to:

> Mount Zion, to the city of the living God, to the heavenly Jerusalem. You have come to tens of thousands of angels joyfully gathered together and to the assembly of God's firstborn children (whose names are written in heaven). You have come to a judge (the God of all people) and to the spirits of people who have God's approval and have gained eternal life. You have come to Jesus, who brings the new promise from God.
>
> —HEBREWS 12:22–23, GW

The blessings of the New Birth are just that exalted (Eph. 3:10, 21; 5:23–32; and Col. 1:24). Yet, God's children also live on this earth and must grow and mature in Christlikeness in a fallen world. Giving focus to the invisible body of Christ is essential, but not to the exclusion of its earthly manifestation as the church visible. To make that mistake is to become so heavenly minded a person is no earthly good at helping to fulfill the Great Commission.

The truth is that both dimensions, the heavenly and the earthly, must exist in balance. To that end, Jesus asked His Father not to take His followers "out of the world" but for them to have the Father's protection "from the evil one" while in the world. He also prayed for His disciples to be set apart or sanctified "by the truth" and affirmed the Word of the Father as "truth" (John 17:15–17).

B. The Visible Body of Christ

The strategy of the Lord, therefore, includes bringing His children into visible groups of believers. They become the *ecclesia*, or assemblies called out of the culture. These communities stand on the historical foundation of the death and resurrection of Jesus Christ. In Jesus' mind, the *ecclesia* could be as simple as house churches: "Where two or three come together in my name, there am I with them" (Matt. 18:20).

C. Jesus: Both Dogmatic and Flexible

Jesus revealed a striking capacity to be firmly dogmatic about the things that are basic to the well-being of His followers. He told Nicodemus, "You must be born again" (John 3:3, 7). Jesus taught His disciples, "I am the way and the truth and the life. No one comes to the Father except through me" (John 14:6). He was equally firm about the demands of discipleship: "Anyone who comes to me but refuses to let go of father, mother, spouse, children, brothers, sisters—yes, even one's own self!—can't be my disciple. Anyone who won't shoulder his own cross and follow behind me can't be my disciple" (Luke 14:26–27, THE MESSAGE; see also John 8:24).

Jesus was specific about giving His disciples a new commandment: "As I have loved you, so you must love one another" (John 13:34). This mandate is the ethical bedrock by which Jesus duplicates Himself worldwide. By this singular standard, people recognize the Lord's disciples wherever they gather in community (John 13:35). Regarding His commitment to grow the church worldwide, Jesus was equally emphatic: "I will build my church" (Matt. 16:18). Jesus also made very clear to the rich ruler that entrance into the kingdom of God cannot be bought with silver and gold (Luke 18:18–27; Isa. 55:1).

⋙ Is This "a Great Way"? ⋘

In June of 2006, Warren Buffet, the world's second-richest man at the time, announced that he would donate 85 percent of his $44 billion fortune to five charitable foundations.

Commenting on this extreme level of generosity, Buffet said, "There is more than one way to get to heaven, but this is a great way."[2]

Concerning the matter of how the Lord wanted His church governed as a visible institution in society, Jesus' omniscience expressed itself in striking flexibility. He did not prescribe any kind of organizational system for His church. In fact, He did not even address the subject of church government. Instead, He designed His church so that it could adapt to the customs of any culture.

In His eternal wisdom, Jesus understood how to communicate both by what He said and did. Nothing in His life happened by chance. For example, the Lord knew well the flexibility He wanted people to pick up from His actions when He avoided announcing any plans for the administrative polity of His church.

The principle of flexible government in the visible church, therefore, is foundational to the Lord's strategy. The fact that His church has been so very adaptable in its governmental forms is a major reason for its international success.

II. The Purpose of Spiritual Gifts

A. Setting the Agenda

The highest priority of the church is to conform to the primary passions of the Lord. Jesus dragged His cross up Golgotha and poured out His blood to redeem people (John 3:16). Jesus also "loved the church and gave himself up for her," purchasing the church "with His own blood" (Eph. 5:25; Acts 20:28). These two passions—loving people and loving His church—frame the strategy for all congregations of believers in their places of worship.

The Lord's plan to fulfill this agenda always includes a personal Upper Room experience for each of His followers. "If any man thirsts, let him come to me and drink," is the ongoing cry of Jesus' heart. John interpreted the statement saying, "By this he meant the Spirit, whom those who believed in him were later to receive" (John 7:37, 39). His plan is for each child of God to receive this infilling, empowering him to reproduce the Lord's ministry. Jesus placed strong emphasis on calling, positioning, and gifting followers who were full of the Holy Spirit and set apart to His attitude and character, that so undergird His international vision (Rom. 1:1).

B. Revealing the Heart of Jesus

The special abilities the Lord demonstrated in His own ministry became the spiritual gifts the Holy Spirit released after Pentecost in the lives of His followers. Just the gift list Jesus gave to Paul in Ephesians 4:11–13 will make the point.

- Jesus is the *Apostle* and High Priest of our profession, sent by His Father into the world to provide redemption for all people (Heb. 3:1; John 3:16).
- Jesus is the *Prophet* of God, whose astounding prophecies have changed the world. Two of the most striking are His prophecy announcing the church and the promise of the gift of the Holy Spirit (Matt. 16:18; John 14:16).
- Jesus is the faithful *Evangelist*. His ability to seek and to save the lost is classic, as in the story of the woman at Jacob's well (John 4:4–42; Matt. 18:11).
- Jesus is the ideal *Pastor*, the great Shepherd of our souls (John 10:11; 1 Pet. 5:4).
- Jesus is also the master *Teacher*. The Sermon on the Mount is just one example of His amazing teaching ability (Matt. 5; John 11:28).

The gifts of the Spirit, therefore, show people their need for Christ, and each in its own way reflects a dimension of the heart of Jesus. All of them in their composite exhibit His full-orbed ministry in action, demonstrating what it was like watching Him in the flesh as He served people. These gifts duplicate the mindset and ministry of Jesus generation after generation (Rom. 12:6–8; 1 Cor. 12:4–11, 28–31; Eph. 4:11–13; 1 Pet. 4:9–11).

The most essential nature of the church is an invisible kingdom. Only secondarily is it a visible institution in society. This takes on special meaning in the arena of the gifts of the Spirit. They are clearly spiritual gifts that have tangible expression. This means a child of God cannot hold them in his hand, but he certainly can cherish them in his heart and see them demonstrated in His life. Hence, the gifts of the Spirit reveal how the heart of Jesus beats to bless people.

Many local churches, however, do not focus on the priorities of Jesus Christ, loving the things Jesus loves. The result is their members do not share the Lord's mindset—His attitude of implicit trust toward His Father, as well as His values and international vision. These congregations direly need prophets who will teach them to function as spiritual incubators that birth and mature people in Christlikeness (Rev. 3:14–22).

Jesus was a servant, first of His Father and then of people (John 5:19, 30; Heb. 2:17; Isa. 42:1). To this day, the Holy Spirit produces servants like the lowly Nazarene (1 Pet. 5:3). Even a casual reading of the gift lists demonstrates how focused the gifts of the Spirit are on serving people's needs.

C. Opening Blinded Eyes

Everywhere Jesus went He unlocked the hearts of people. His ability to do it was awe-inspiring to witness. Jesus' disciples saw it time after time. One classic illustration is the story of the Samaritan woman at Jacob's well (John 4). She had lived with five husbands and was not married to the man she was living with. The conversion she experienced while talking with the Lord opened her eyes and gave her a new life, making her a chaste lady again. The miracle she experienced also opened the hearts of many people in her community.

The first great example in Acts of the Apostles that demonstrates the marvelous capability of the Holy Spirit to open spiritual eyes is what happened to the God-fearing Jews visiting in Jerusalem for the celebration of Pentecost. A large crowd converged on the site in utter amazement when they heard the sound coming from the Upper Room (Acts 2:6).

"What does this mean?" they sincerely asked (Acts 2:12).

Right in the middle of the miracle of Pentecost, their eyes opened, and before noon that day, three thousand people from some fifteen countries became part of the Lord's church (Acts 2:5–41). From its beginning, therefore, the church has had a decidedly international flavor. The three primary spiritual gifts at work that morning were the gift of prophecy, expressed in Peter's preaching; the gift of tongues, as manifested by the 120 who were praising God; and the gift of evangelism, as expressed in the harvest of 3,000 souls (Luke 10:2; John 4:35). The result was the Holy Spirit birthed the church that Jesus prophesied He would build (Matt. 16:16–18).

The conversion of Saul of Tarsus, a proudly religious Pharisee, is another case in point. To get his full attention and open his spiritual eyes, the Lord knocked him to the ground with a bright light, temporarily blinding him. While lying in the dust, his spiritual eyes opened and he asked, "Who are you, Lord?" "I am Jesus, whom you are persecuting," the Lord answered (Acts 9:5). Three days later, Ananias went to pray for Saul's sight to return and for the Holy Spirit to fill him (Acts 9:10–18).

Paul, as a Spirit-filled apostle, perceived correctly that "the god of this age has blinded the minds of unbelievers, so that they cannot see the light of the gospel of the glory of Christ, who is the image of God" (2 Cor. 4:4).

Paul quickly perceived that both Jews and Gentiles lived in spiritual blindness, just as had been true of him. He also comprehended a host of Gentiles would turn to Jesus if the eyes of their hearts could be unlocked (Isa. 6:10; 2 Cor. 4:4; 1 John 2:11). So releasing blinded eyes was a special function of the gifts of the Spirit in the apostolic church, a blessing that continues to this day. The gifts are amazingly effective at doing it (Acts 3:1–10; 5:1–16).

Toward the end of his ministry, Paul summarized this understanding by quoting the assignment the Lord gave him at his conversion: "I am sending you to them to open their eyes and turn them from darkness to light, and from the power of Satan to God, so that they may receive forgiveness of sins and a place among those who are sanctified by faith in me" (Acts 26:17–18).

Awake, north wind, and come, south wind! Blow on my garden, that its fragrance may spread abroad.
—Song of Solomon 4:16

The Holy Spirit is this wind, the breath of God (Gen. 2:7; John 20:22).

D. Developing Government in the Visible Church

As the number of believers grew in the invisible church, a companion reality was the explosive growth of the church visible. This heightened the need for organization in the institutional church. Paul wrote, "God has appointed…gifts of administration" (niv) or "governments" (kjv) to give leadership to the church (1 Cor. 12:28). [See also Matthew 22:17–22 for the Lord's attitude toward civil government and Romans 13:1–7 for Paul's teaching.]

Since Jesus neither said nor did anything to structure the government of the church He was so determined to build, His successors had to develop church polity. The Holy Spirit permitted the apostles and those who have followed them through the centuries to construct the governmental frameworks needed to manage the harvest. Local practices and ethnic patterns have influenced the church's government everywhere it has blossomed. Because the Lord allowed flexibility regarding polity, the church has become a mosaic that expresses the rich variety of the ethnic customs where it has spread (1 Cor. 9:20, 22).

The institutional church has always existed with a dynamic tension between emphasis on governmental polity and desire for ministry to the invisible body of Christ. All too often, however, the pendulum has swung to the side of structure, organization, and church buildings. At times in church history, more and more ornate construction projects have indeed substituted for the leadership of the Spirit.

When believers walk in the Spirit, however, they are able to announce with authority the Lord's diagnosis of the human problem, no matter the risk to themselves. They also share the cross of Jesus Christ as the only cure (Mark 7:20–23; John 3:3; 14:6; Acts 4:12). In doing this, they manifest Christ to the world. The result has been that blinded eyes have opened to new appreciation of the lovely face of Jesus (Mark 9:8; Luke 8:54–55).

The great lesson from the life of the Lord is that people are living in the darkness of rebellion against God, with its accompanying depression and gloom. Day after day they sit by the roadside of life, begging for help (Matt. 9:27–30). What a tragedy that many churches give them primarily programs instead of a vision of the "altogether lovely" Savior who is of the Seed of David and the Son of God (Song of Sol. 5:6, 16; Matt. 20:31–34; Luke 1:35). Jesus is both their lover and friend. He not only can open their eyes; He does it with delight (Matt. 8:2; Mark 10:51–52).

⚜ Seeing the Defects ⚜

"Cliff Barrows and I were in Atlantic City many years ago with our wives," wrote Billy Graham. "We had had a service, and we were walking down the boardwalk. A man was auctioning diamonds and other jewelry. We decided to go in.

"When we got married, I had given my wife a diamond that was so small, you couldn't see it with a microscope. So I decided to get her a better diamond. I had $65 in my pocket. I eventually bid it all and bought the diamond. It was a perfect diamond, I thought.

"The next day, I went to a jeweler, and I said, 'Can you look at this diamond and tell me how much it is worth?'

"He looked at it through his glass and said, 'Oh, maybe $35 or $40.'

"'What?' I said. 'This is supposed to be two carats!'

"'Look at it,' he said and gave the glass to me. I looked at it, and even I could see it was full of defects."[3]

Spiritual gifts serve as the jeweler's magnifying glass to help people see the sin in their hearts. When viewed in the sunlight of the Word of God, the many flaws in their souls become evident. Without that magnifying glass, people so easily succumb to the delusion they can save themselves.

The gifts of the Spirit are indicative of what God desires to do through His children to bring them into His spiritual body and mature them in His likeness. "God's solid foundation stands firm," wrote Paul, "sealed with this inscription: 'The Lord knows those who are his,' and, 'Everyone who confesses the name of the Lord must turn away from wickedness'" (2 Tim. 2:19).

Believers can easily develop spiritual pride and begin to exalt themselves as they minister in the gifts. The great balancer is the fruit of the Spirit, because the fruit expresses the character of Jesus in His followers (Gal. 5:22–26), and the Holy Spirit always produces servant hearts (Deut. 15:17; Rom. 1:1).

E. The Gift Lists

The apostle Paul used four Greek words to describe the gifts God places in the Lord's spiritual body. In Ephesians 4:8, Paul chose *doma* to describe the gifted people the Lord Jesus gives to the church: "He…gave gifts [*doma*] to men." Paul used the term *charismata* in 1 Corinthians 12:4, 31 and Romans 12:6, emphasizing spiritual endowments that equip for miraculous ministry. The apostle Peter also used *charisma* in 1 Peter 4:10. The English word *charismatic* is a transliteration of that term. Paul selected *phanerosis* to identify the list in 1 Corinthians 12:7. The term focuses manifestations of the Spirit in believers that exhibit outshining aspects of the Lord's ministry. In 1 Corinthians 12:28 and in Acts 20:28 he used *etheto* (from *tithemi*, meaning "to set in place"), which speaks to placing or setting the gifts in the body.

Paul taught his readers at Corinth that the Holy Spirit gave him the list, identified by the term *manifestation gifts*.

> Now to each one the manifestation [phanerosis] of the Spirit is given for the common good. To one there is given through the Spirit the message of wisdom, to another the message of knowledge by means of the same Spirit, to another faith by the same Spirit, to another gifts of healing by that one Spirit, to another miraculous powers, to another prophecy, to another distinguishing between spirits, to another speaking in different kinds of tongues, and to still another the interpretation of tongues. All these are the work of one and the same Spirit, and he gives them to each one, just as he determines.
> —1 CORINTHIANS 12:7–11, EMPHASIS ADDED

Paul also wrote to the Corinthians:

> In the church God has appointed [etheto] first of all apostles, second prophets, third teachers, then workers of miracles, also those having gifts of healing, those able to help others, those with gifts of administration, and those speaking in different kinds of tongues. Are all apostles? Are all prophets? Are all teachers? Do all work miracles? Do all have gifts of healing? Do all speak in tongues? Do all interpret? But eagerly desire the greater gifts.
> —1 CORINTHIANS 12:28–31, EMPHASIS ADDED

Paul commanded the Ephesian elders who met with him on the strand of the Aegean Sea, "Keep watch over yourselves and all the flock of which the *Holy Spirit* has made [*tithemi*] you overseers [*episkopos*, or bishops]. Be shepherds of the church of God, which he bought with his own blood" (Acts 20:28, emphasis added).

To the believers in Rome, Paul said:

> In Christ, we who are many form one body, and each member belongs to all the others. We have different gifts [*charismata*], according to the grace given us. If a man's gift is prophesying, let him use it in proportion to his faith. If it is serving, let him serve; if it is teaching, let him teach; if it is encouraging, let him encourage; if it is contributing to the needs of others, let him give generously; if it is leadership, let him govern diligently; if it is showing mercy, let him do it cheerfully.
>
> —ROMANS 12:5–8, EMPHASIS ADDED

Paul told the believers at Ephesus, Jesus "gave [*doma*] some to be apostles, some to be prophets, some to be evangelists, and some to be pastors and teachers, to prepare God's people for works of service, so that the body of Christ may be built up" (Eph. 4:11–12).

It is evident from these lists that the Godhead (the Father, the Son, and the Holy Spirit) has always been actively involved in the impartation of the manifold spiritual gifts intended to reveal Christ to the world. The Father's strategy from eternity has been to give the Holy Spirit to all of Christ's followers, making them His living temples. He endows each of them with one or more of these special gifts, designed to reproduce the ministry of His Son and opening the eyes of spiritually blind people (Acts 16:13–15; 28:26–28).

III. Duplicating the Ministry of Jesus Through Spiritual Gifts

With this in mind, we now begin to explore the giftings that have been so important in Jesus' strategy to duplicate His own ministry and open blinded eyes to His triumph at Calvary. His plan of action has never changed.

A. Jesus, the Foremost Apostle

The strategy begins with Jesus Himself, the foremost apostle. (The term derives from the Greek word *apostolos*, which transliterates into English as *apostle* and means "sent.") An apostle by definition is one whom God sends on a specific mission. The heavenly Father sent His only begotten Son into the world (John 3:34; Gal. 4:4). Therefore, the ministry of apostles in the new covenant begins first with Jesus (Heb. 3:1–2). The Lord repeatedly stated His Father sent Him (John 7:29; 8:42; 10:36). "Christ Jesus himself" is "the chief cornerstone" of the church (Eph. 2:20). Therefore, the church of the Lord Jesus Christ is built on the premise, "As the Father has sent me, I am sending you" (John 20:21). The writer of Hebrews challenged his readers to "fix [their] thoughts on Jesus, the apostle and high priest whom we confess. He was faithful" (Heb. 3:1–2).

B. The Ephesians 4 List

When Jesus "ascended on high," He had a specific strategy to open up the pagan world to the sunlight of the gospel. He gave His own ability to minister to people as "gifts to men" (Eph. 4:8; Heb. 2:4).

1. "It Was He Who Gave Some to Be Apostles"

a) Foundational Apostles

The wisdom of the Lord's plan becomes clear when one observes the people He pulled around Him. Among the Lord's greatest gifts to His church were the twelve men He chose and matured as His disciples. They lived with Him in His ministry as He permitted them to hear, see, touch, and taste the good Word of life (1 John 1:1; Heb. 6:5). They followed Him and learned from Him how to serve people as He did. In time, He transitioned them into apostles, or sent ones, and entrusted the destiny of His church to them (Mark 3:14; John 20:21–22).

When Jesus commissioned the Seventy for a preaching tour, He "sent [*apostello*] them two by two" (Luke 10:1, KJV). These apostles set out to do what they had seen Jesus do. When they completed their preaching tour, "The seventy disciples came back very happy. They said, 'Lord, even demons obey us when we use the power and authority of your name!'" (Luke 10:17, GW). Jesus was not surprised. Instead, He told them, "I saw Satan fall like lightning from heaven" (Luke 10:18; Isa. 14:12–15; Ezek. 28:11–17). The Lord proceeded to give His disciples a word of caution intended to keep them in balance, and it has the same effect today. "Do not rejoice that the spirits submit to you," Jesus said, "but rejoice that your names are written in heaven" (Luke 10:20).

Their report filled Jesus with joy "through the Holy Spirit" and motivated Him to give thanks to His Father for their success. Their accomplishment was also the Father's "good pleasure" (Luke 10:21). The success of His servants even today is His special delight.

Under Jesus' headship, the apostles after Pentecost became the recognized servant leaders of the infant church (1 Cor. 3:10). They had been specifically chosen, trained, and gifted by the Lord and personally sent by Him. Their mission was to open closed hearts to Jesus Christ and as they did it, lay the foundation for the church (John 15:27; Eph. 2:20).

Jesus has a singular ability to win people to Himself; He is the Head of the church (Eph. 1:10, 22; 4:15). It is so easy for the institutional church to believe winning people to the visible church equals winning them to Christ. Such a conclusion surely grieves the heart of God. The goal of the church must always be to bring people to a new birth in Christ. The apostle John actually saw Jesus standing outside knocking on the door, trying to get into the Laodicean church (Rev. 3:20).

It must have been quite a contrast to the proud Roman leaders and the intellectual Greek scholars when an apostle of Jesus Christ came to town. True apostles were meek and lowly of heart like their Lord and not at all haughty, demanding, greedy, or arrogant (Matt. 11:29, kjv). These humble servants rode no proud stallions and owned no chariots. They commanded no retinue of servants, held the deed to no palatial homes, and commanded no soldiers. Their authority rested solely in who sent them. They were ambassadors of the resurrected Christ (2 Cor. 5:20).

They had been with the Lord and understood they had a foundation-laying ministry (Acts 1:21–22; 4:13; Eph. 2:20; 1 John 1:1–2). They exercised authority to interpret the Old Testament Scriptures through the lens of the Cross so that their interpretations became part of the New Testament books they wrote (Rom. 4:16–25).

The apostles discovered by watching their Lord what would penetrate the pagan veneer of Greece and Rome. For example, Paul was in jail when he wrote his letter to the Ephesians and underscored the character traits that did the job: "As a prisoner for the Lord, then, I urge you to live a life worthy of the calling you have received. Be completely humble and gentle; be patient, bearing with one another in love. Make every effort to keep the unity of the Spirit through the bond of peace" (Eph. 4:1–3).

Neither the Romans' quest for power nor the Greeks' quest for learning could withstand servant hearts willing to go to prison for the Lord, showing humility, gentleness, patience, forbearing love, and unity in the Spirit as they walked into the smelly and stale dungeons of the Empire. These traits in the apostles' lives yielded great compassion for people and birthed enormous spiritual power for ministry, but not one apostle could offer silver and gold (Acts 3:6).

Apostolic duties included preaching and teaching the gospel in such a way that it revealed the character and concern of Jesus for people (Acts 2:40; 2:42; 6:3–6; 17:3). They also pioneered new churches and administered the affairs of the growing church (Acts 13; 14:23).

Miracles regularly occurred when Jesus walked into town (Luke 4:31–37). Miraculous things, including signs and wonders, were routine when an apostle came to town, too. The believers in Lydda, for example, heard Peter was in the area. They took him to pray for a woman named Dorcas who had died (Acts 9:36–43). After interceding in the name of Jesus, Peter commanded Dorcas to get up, and she did! Her marvelous story "became known all over Joppa, and many people believed in the Lord" (Acts 9:42).

The apostle Paul served at this foundational level as the apostle to the Gentiles. He said the Lord appeared personally to him and commissioned him as an apostle through revelation (1 Cor. 1:1; Acts 9:11–16; 26:19–23). Paul considered himself "as…one born out of due time" (1 Cor. 15:8, KJV; Gal. 2:8). Paul did many miraculous things in his ministry, including raising the dead (Acts 20:9–10). He also taught that apostles have a four-fold identification: "The things that mark an apostle—*signs, wonders* and *miracles*—were done among you with *great perseverance*" (2 Cor. 12:12, emphasis added; Acts 5:12). Paul specifically defended his claim in Galatians 1 and 2 that he was equal to the other apostles.

Apostolic authority expressed itself in two problem areas in the early church: settling the dispute that arose among the Grecian widows by establishing the role of deacons (Acts 6:3), and working out the doctrinal differences regarding loyalty to the Law of Moses that prompted the Jerusalem Council (Acts 15).

Foundational apostles and their close associates also wrote or were responsible for writing the New Testament (Eph. 2:20–22). As the apostles did so, they fulfilled a vital function in the young New Testament church by interpreting Old Testament Scripture through the lens of Jesus' cross and empty tomb.

It really was an exercise of awesome authority when Peter said on the Day of Pentecost "this is that," specifying what the Holy Spirit intended through the pen of Joel, an Old Testament prophet who had spoken some seven hundred years earlier (Acts 2:16, KJV; Joel 2:28–32). Peter specifically equated the writings of Paul with the Old Testament Scriptures (2 Pet. 3:16).

The apostle Paul, who served as a foundational apostle, penned more than half of the New Testament. He and the other apostles won people to Christ wherever they went and established house churches as places for them to assemble throughout the Roman world. Apostles led in worship, memorialized the Lord's Supper, maintained a proper discipline in the congregations, and manifested spiritual gifts, including exorcising demons and healing the sick (Acts 3:6–8; 5:1–11; 16:16–18; 19:11). In addition, people received the Holy Spirit when the apostles prayed (Acts 8:15). Planting new churches in the Roman Empire, with accompanying signs, wonders, and miracles amid great perseverance, was a specific apostolic assignment (2 Cor. 12:12).

b) Functional Apostles

The New Testament establishes no order of apostolic succession. When the foundational apostles deceased, the remaining apostles did not appoint their successors, other than in the case of Judas, who fell by transgression (Acts 1:15–26). However, the New Testament does identify an additional level of apostolic ministry. They are termed here "functional" apostles because of the nature of their ministry. The Holy Spirit commissioned Barnabas, for example, who went on to become the first missionary of the Christian era (Acts 13:2; 14:14). Paul probably meant that same title for Timothy and Silas, among others (1 Thess. 1:1; 2:6).

Many missionaries in church history have filled this role and continue to do so in the contemporary church. An evidence of this is how missionary apostles have gone into pagan countries, won people to Christ, and established new churches. Apostolic ministry also finds expression in going to an ethnic or cultural group in one's own nation that is unreached with the gospel. Signs, wonders, and miracles, wrapped in great perseverance, characterize these ministries and result in folding new believers into the churches they establish.

It is important to note the foundational apostles had a diminished but very important role in comparison to "*the* apostle and high priest"—our Lord Jesus Christ (Heb. 3:1). To Him alone belongs the preeminence. The ministry of the functional apostles in the New Testament was certainly important in helping win the Roman world, but their function diminished in comparison to foundational apostles. Their specific task was not the same at all.

In four key areas, functional apostles could not duplicate the most basic duties of the foundational apostles.

- *Having seen the Lord.* The biblical record gives no indication that any functional apostles actually saw the Lord in His ministry or after His resurrection. Functional apostles can have a revelation of the Lord as Paul did, that was at least similar to having seen the Lord serving in the flesh.
- *Building on the foundation already laid by the foundational apostles.* Functional apostles could not add to the underpinning of the gospel established by the foundational apostles. Paul wrote, "God's household [is] built on the foundation of the apostles and prophets, with Christ Jesus himself as the chief cornerstone. In him, the whole building is joined together and rises to become a holy temple in the Lord. And in him you too are being built together to become a dwelling in which God lives by his Spirit" (Eph. 2:19–22).

The biblical text portrays functional apostles as serving along-side the foundational apostles. Barnabas and Saul launched the first missionary journey in Acts as a team, although Saul emerged as the leader at the first stop of their ministry on Cyprus (Acts 13:2, 9, 13). He also took the Greek name *Paul*. Silas and Timothy worked closely under Paul's oversight. After Barnabas and Paul separated, Barnabas took John Mark and returned to Cyprus (Acts 15:39). Later, in the confrontation between Paul and Peter at Antioch, Barnabas joined with Peter in the hypoc-risy regarding circumcision (Gal. 2:11–13).

- Interpreting Old Testament Scripture with the result that the interpretation itself became part of the New Testament canon. This authority did not extend to the functional apostles, either. Instead, they had to submit to the interpretations of the founda-tional apostles. Paul, for example, spoke a very bold anathema on anyone, including even an angel from heaven, who preached a gospel other than what he preached (Gal. 1:8–9).

The great revivals of modern church history, such as the Lutheran Reformation of justification by grace through faith (sixteenth century), Wesley's revival of holiness and perfect love (eighteenth century), and the Azusa Street Pentecostal revival (twentieth century), plowed no new biblical ground in the sense of new revelation added to the canon. Instead, each revival sprang out of the illumination the Spirit brought to the revela-tion the foundational apostles had already recorded in the New Testament.

- Writing New Testament books. No biblical evidence indicates that a functional apostle wrote a New Testament book.

All apostles today are functional apostles. Although they never rise to the level of the foundational apostles, functional apostles can serve with equal anointing, gifting, and power for ministry. No one should minimize or depre-ciate this marvelous reality. "Anyone who has faith in me," Jesus said, "will do what I have been doing. He will do even greater things than these, because I am going to the Father" (John 14:12).

In addition, functional apostles continue to have a compelling foundation-laying ministry, establishing the faith in the new areas they open up for the gospel. However, the base they build must always square with the historic faith, as laid by the foundational apostles who wrote the New Testament (Gal. 1:8).

As they blaze new trails, functional apostles serve humbly like their Lord. Most of them willingly labor outside the spotlight. They open up new ministries and reach new ethnic groups that most in the body of Christ have not thought about or perceived as possible.

c) Closing the New Testament Canon

The Council of Jamnia was a gathering of Jewish scholars who met in A.D. 90 in the Philistine town identified by the name Jabneh in 2 Chronicles 26:6. This council officially affirmed the thirty-nine books of the Old Testament as the Jewish Bible, effectively closing the Old Testament canon.

In the second and third centuries of the church, the Holy Spirit brought the twenty-seven books of the New Testament into the commonly accepted usage of the church. The third Council of Carthage in A.D. 397 recognized the Spirit's work in compiling these books as the New Testament, effectively closing the New Testament canon.[4]

The understanding of a closed canon has shut the door since then to adding more books to the New Testament. It also assumes that canonical revelation ceased. The sixty-six books of the Bible, therefore, are the believer's sourcebook for all matters of faith and practice, and no modern-day apostle or prophet can give proclamations equal to God's word as revealed in the Holy Bible. We join with our fathers across the centuries and rest our eternal souls to this day on both the authority of Holy Scripture and the sufficiency of the Word of God.

d) Recognizing True and False Apostles

In addition to the foundational and functional apostles, the Scriptures identify a category of false apostles. God did not appoint these people. Instead, carnal men usurped the role for their own glory. Paul labeled them as "false apostles, deceitful workmen, masquerading as apostles of Christ. And no wonder, for Satan himself masquerades as an angel of light. It is not surprising, then, if Satan's followers masquerade as servants of righteousness. Their end will be what their actions deserve" (2 Cor. 11:13–15; see Matt. 24:5; Rev. 2:2).

The most accurate way to discern a false apostle is to understand the character and ministry of a true apostle. The following is a list of characteristics possessed by true apostles.

1. They hear from God, whom they implicitly trust, and receive their appointment from God (Acts 13:2).
2. True apostles serve with humility, gentleness, patience, forbearing love, and unity in the Spirit, like Jesus (Eph. 4:1–6). They never lord it over others (1 Pet. 5:3, KJV; Matt. 5:3).

3. They accept personal responsibility to motivate the churches to obey the Lord's Great Commission and duplicate their churches, even at great cost to themselves (Matt. 28:16–20). They give themselves to their calling (2 Tim. 4:5).

4. They look through the eyes of the Holy Spirit and see needs in a society that, for the most part, others do not perceive. Led by the Spirit, they develop new spheres of ministry to meet those needs (which normally include church planting). They do this even when it includes stepping across cultural, racial, or language barriers to achieve what the Holy Spirit has assigned them to do (Rom. 15:20; 1 Cor. 3:10).

5. True apostles minister with complete faithfulness to the writings and teachings of the foundational apostles. They never lay a new foundation (Gal. 1:8–9).

6. They never proclaim new revelation, claiming equality with the twenty-seven books of the New Testament and the thirty-nine books of the Old Testament. They respect that the canon is closed (Matt. 5:18; 1 Cor. 3:11; Rev. 22:18–19).

7. They labor for the Lord in ministry accompanied by signs, wonders, and miracles, showing great perseverance (2 Cor. 12:12).

8. True apostles continue to serve, even when no one confers on them a title or recognizes their role (Gal. 1:11–12; 1 Cor. 4:1–4).

9. They equip the saints for the work of the ministry (Eph. 4:12).

10. They bring unity to the body of Christ (John 17:23; Eph. 4:3, 7–16). In this sense they are ecumenical, with a universal interest and authority in the whole body of Christ (Gal. 2:8).

11. They speak the truth in love (Eph. 4:15).

12. They live free from the love of money (Luke 9:58; 12:15; 1 Tim. 6:10; Heb. 13:5).

13. True apostles are authoritative teachers of the truths in the Word of God (Acts 20:20).

While the New Testament actually records no names of false apostles, examples certainly exist in church history. To give one, Joseph Smith (1805–1844) claimed to be an apostle. Smith wrote books that he asserted were superior to the Bible. He also organized the Mormon Church with twelve last-day apostles as leaders of his new movement and created a line of apostolic succession among these twelve apostles.

2. *"Some to Be Prophets"*

a. Their Role

The same Holy Spirit who anointed the prophets of the first covenant also blessed and empowered the life of the Messiah–Prophet in His incarnation. Hence, prophetic ministry continued in the New Testament church (Deut. 18:15–22; John 1:21; 5:45–47).

As was true with an apostle, when a prophet came to town, the whole city was soon astir. This was no doubt true because the prophet's role has always been to represent Jesus Christ, the living Word. They do it in the power of the Spirit in order to correct and exhort believers and sometimes to foretell the future. Both unbelievers and believers alike have always been drawn to the ministry of prophets. Many hope the prophet will be the voice of God to them in their decision making. Others are simply curious, hoping to hear predictive prophecy.

Prophets had a vital part in laying the foundation of the infant church (Eph. 2:20). The eyes of the spiritually blind always start opening to the gospel when a prophet of God is in the congregation.

The ministry of Jesus in His incarnation was resplendent with prophetic expressions that included both fore-telling (predictive prophecy) and forthtelling (the ministry of exhortation). Jesus knew the life story of the woman at Jacob's well, for example. He spoke directly to her needs in a conversation characterized by striking prophetic exhortation: "If you knew the gift of God and who it is that asks you for a drink, you would have asked him and he would have given you living water" (John 4:10). This woman was totally caught off guard when Jesus stated that she had been married to five men, and at the time was living with a man who was not her husband (John 4:18). Her response to Jesus was, "Sir, I can see that you are a prophet" (John 4:19). Her spiritual vision so opened that, "leaving her water jar," she went back into the city saying, "Come, see a man, who told me all things I ever did: could this be the Christ?" (John 4:28–29).

Jesus also freely spoke predictive prophecy. When the Lord wanted the meal prepared for His last supper with His disciples, He said to Peter and John:

> As you enter the city, a man carrying a jar of water will meet you. Follow him to the house that he enters, and say to the owner of the house, "The Teacher asks: Where is the guest room, where I may eat the Passover with my disciples? He will show you a large upper room,

all furnished. Make preparations there." They left and found things just
as Jesus had told them. So they prepared the Passover.

—Luke 22:10–13

A Spirit-gifted person in the church today who gives one or two measurable
facts in predictive prophecy that actually come true will stir a sense of awe in
people, and unbelievers will open their eyes. In preparation for His last Passover
celebration with His disciples, Jesus gave an extended series of such facts, each of
which fitted into a time-specific sequence, as recorded in Luke 22:10–13.

> As you enter the city [you must walk into the city] a man [not a
> woman or a child] carrying [he will be holding something] a jar
> [not a leather flask, for example] of water [not wine or some other
> liquid] will meet you [the man will walk up to you]. Follow him
> to the house [he will not lead you to the marketplace, for example,
> but to a house] that he enters [he will go into the house, and not
> merely stand at the door] and say to the owner [the homeowner
> will be present], "The Teacher asks: Where is the guest room where
> I may eat the Passover with my disciples?" [You are to assume he
> has a guest room, and ask him in my name for permission to use
> it.] He will show you a large upper room [it will be large enough for
> Jesus' full group, and it will be an upstairs room and not a ground
> level room], all furnished. Make preparations there [the room will
> already have everything needed for the Passover celebration].

The probability would be mind-boggling that a person by mere chance
could get all of these facts correct and in precisely this order, so that they
would be fulfilled in probably less than an hour's time. Peter and John no
doubt never forgot how their own eyes opened because of this experience with
Jesus, the prophet. When John was imprisoned on Patmos, an angel told him,
"The testimony of Jesus is the spirit of prophecy" (Rev. 19:10).

After the church was born on the Day of Pentecost, the ministry of
prophecy continued. Agabus foretold a coming famine (Acts 11:28; 21:10).
Judas and Silas were prophets who were highly respected by the apostles. They
trusted these brethren to carry to the church at Antioch the decisions at the
Jerusalem Council (Acts 15:29–32). Phillip "had four unmarried daughters
who prophesied" (Acts 21:9).

While the New Testament establishes the ministry of prophets, the Lord
was clear that His followers needed to "watch out for false prophets." The
reason for alertness was because "they come to you in sheep's clothing, but

inwardly they are ferocious wolves" (Matt. 7:15; 24:11, 24; Luke 6:26; 2 Pet. 2:1; 1 John 4:1).

b. Judging False Prophets

It is a basic value of the Pentecostal revival that believers in Christ can have a warm, personal, and intimate relationship with Jesus Christ. In that ongoing walk with God, they receive the baptism with the Holy Spirit and enjoy specific guidance as they walk in the Spirit (Acts 8:29).

Precisely because Scripture establishes this kind of direct illumination from God, situations develop from time to time when prophecies require judgment. The Lord Himself taught this and gave the formula, "By their fruit you will recognize them" (Matt. 7:16). Judgments must be made, however, in the loving spirit of the great command and in such a way as not to discourage ongoing, prophetic ministry (John 13:34; 1 Cor. 14:39; 1 Thess. 5:20).

Without seeking to be exhaustive, four principles offer guidance for judging fruit.

- *First, does the prophecy conflict with Holy Scripture?* The primacy of the written Word of God over all inner personal guidance is a firm anchor of the church. The sixty-six books of the Old and New Testaments are the final revelation of God for all matters of faith and practice. The doctrine of the closed canon is also instructive. No prophecy can be elevated to equality with Holy Scripture. When prophetic proclamations take away from or add to Holy Scripture, they must be judged as false prophecy (Matt. 7:15–17; 2 Pet. 2:1; 1 John 4:1; Ps. 33:4).
- *Second is the test of "taste,"* because prophetic pronouncements from God ultimately yield sweet fruit and maintain "the unity of the Spirit through the bond of peace" (Eph. 4:3; Ps. 133:1). Does the Holy Spirit witness to the prophecy? Does it promote harmony in the body of Christ, or is it divisive and calculated to sow dissension and discord among brethren? Is its tone angry, bitter, or vindictive? Is it rebellious or insubordinate? Is there a sour flavor in the prophecy that creates a check in one's spirit? If the fruit has this kind of taste, then it is probably false prophecy (See Gal. 5:19–21; Rom. 1:29–32; 16:17–19, reading each passage in the KJV and the NIV).
- *Third, does the prophecy result in sidetracking believers from the primary emphases of gospel ministry, and in that process elevate secondary issues into the position of primary gospel issues?* If the

prophecy yields this kind of fruit, majoring in minors, it is an indicator of false prophecy (1 Tim. 1:20; 2 Tim. 2:17–19; 4:10; 1 Kings 13:11–24).

- *Fourth, does the prophet have a potential for a personal, vested interest in the outcome?* If the prophecy calls in the name of God for something to be done that turns out to be in the personal self-interest of the prophet, it is a strong indication that manipulation is at work and not the spirit of prophecy (2 Kings 5:20–27).

3. "Some to Be Evangelists"

Phillip's ministry is an excellent portrayal of the evangelist's role. Luke introduced him in Acts as one of the seven deacons who served in the distribution of food to widows (Acts 6:1–5). His spiritual gift as an evangelist soon blossomed. This godly evangelist was a servant who was full of the Holy Spirit and wisdom (Acts 6:3). Philip evangelized Samaria and "proclaimed the Christ there" (Acts 8:5–13). He welcomed Peter and John, who brought apostolic wisdom and anointing to the revival. These apostles introduced the Samaritans to the baptism with the Holy Spirit and led them into the experience.

Philip was also content to leave the revival in the apostles' good hands when the Spirit spoke to him to depart from Samaria. On the way, he accepted the guidance of an angel who told him to go down to the desert road that went to Gaza. When he arrived, he obeyed the Holy Spirit and led the Ethiopian eunuch to the Lord. Phillip baptized him and sent him "on his way rejoicing" (Acts 8:26–39). The Spirit then snatched Philip away to Azotus, where he preached "the gospel in all the towns until he reached Caesarea" (Acts 8:40, KJV).

Holy Spirit-filled evangelists often manifest a prophetic gift as well. They have a marvelous capacity to preach Jesus Christ with such spiritual authority people begin to see their Lord clearly for the very first time. Jesus was the evangelist who won the blind man at the pool of Siloam. The man then confessed Jesus as a prophet and said to the Pharisees, "One thing I do know. I was blind but now I see" (John 9:17, 25).

Luke referred to some additional unnamed evangelists in Acts, like the "men from Cyprus and Cyrene" who went to Antioch and began talking to the Greeks there, preaching "the good news about the Lord Jesus" (Acts 11:20). Their soul-winning ministry was fruitful, for "a great number of people believed and turned to the Lord." The church that sprang up in Antioch went on to become one of the strongest and most enduring churches in the Roman Empire (Acts 11:21).

4. "Some to Be Pastors"

The word rendered "pastors" in Ephesians 4:11, *poimenas*, can best be translated "shepherds," persons who tend to flocks or herds (Matt. 9:36; 25:32). The term also included responsibility to serve as a guardian or a ruler (Matt. 2:6; John 10:11; Rev. 2:27). Jesus described Himself as "the good shepherd" who "lays down his life for the sheep" (John 10:11–12). The apostle Peter described the Lord as the "Chief Shepherd" (1 Pet. 5:4).

A pastor accepts responsibility to care for Jesus' flock, never forgetting they are the Lord's sheep and not his. The shepherding demeanor of pastors has turned so many to Christ over the centuries. Pastors serve to win the lost, nurture believers, administer the sacraments of the church, and conduct its administrative affairs. Like their Lord, the pastor (or under-shepherd) gives of himself, even his own life, if necessary. Pastors are not hirelings who run when wolves spring out of hiding to devour the flock (John 10:12–13). Instead, theirs is the high office of a servant whom the Holy Spirit trusts to feed and protect both the sheep and the lambs who come into the family of God (John 21:15–17). The faithful servant hearts of pastors in every generation have shown the true spirit of Jesus to multitudes of people.

5. "And Teachers"

It is of great benefit to a pastor's ministry if he is also an evangelist. However, a pastor must always be a teacher. Teachers are responsible to establish Jesus' flock in the Word of God and teach them to obey the instruction of the Lord (Matt. 28:20).

A teacher is a servant who makes his contribution through personal study and devotion and then shares what he learns with hungry believers. Teachers help to explain the Scriptures to believers in the church and motivate them to adopt the Lord's attitude, values, and vision for the nations.

The ministry of a teacher is serious business. James wrote that those "who teach will be judged more strictly" (James 3:1). Paul taught Timothy that the persons who filled the roles of preaching and teaching were "worthy of double honor" (1 Tim. 5:17).

Paul described the purpose of these five ministry gifts in the Book of Ephesians:

> To prepare God's people for works of service, so that the body of Christ may be built up, until we all reach unity in the faith and in the knowledge of the Son of God and become mature, attaining to the whole measure of the fullness of Christ. Then we will no longer be infants, tossed back and forth by the waves, and blown here and there by every wind of teaching and by the cunning and craftiness

of men in their deceitful scheming. Instead, speaking the truth in love, we will in all things grow up into him who is the Head, that is, Christ.

—EPHESIANS 4:12–16

C. The Catalog in Romans 12

Paul wrote that the Holy Spirit gave him an additional listing of seven gifts. These are the *charismata*, or spiritual endowments for miraculous ministry:

In Christ, we who are many form one body, and each member belongs to all the others. We have different gifts [charismata], according to the grace given us. If a man's gift is prophesying, let him use it in proportion to his faith. If it is serving, let him serve; if it is teaching, let him teach; if it is encouraging, let him encourage; if it is contributing to the needs of others, let him give generously; if it is leadership, let him govern diligently; if it is showing mercy, let him do it cheerfully.

—ROMANS 12:5–8, EMPHASIS ADDED

1. Serving. Rendering assistance is a primary value of being a Christian. Jesus taught by His own example that a life of service, based on the ethic of love, is the superior lifestyle. All who want to mature in Christlikeness will choose to adopt the mantle of the lowly Nazarene who became the servant of all. So many thousands of people over the centuries have opened their eyes to Christ after watching believers faithfully live out the servant lifestyle of Jesus.

    The gift of service includes the miraculous ability the Holy Spirit imparts to believers to bless the body of Christ in dependable, supporting roles, often behind the scenes. One biblical example is the ministry of deacons, who became servants of the apostles' agenda (Acts 6:1–6). The word *deacon* comes from the Greek term *diakonein,* which means "to wait on" or "to serve."

2. Encouraging. Jesus certainly manifested this quality. In fact, He was the greatest encourager of all time. When Mary poured the precious perfume worth a year's wage on Jesus' feet, a chorus of criticism followed. The Lord strongly defended her, telling her critics, "Leave her alone! [It was intended] that she should save this perfume for the day of my burial" (John 12:7). Mary must have felt vindicated and encouraged by this strong defense.

So many people have come to Christ because a Spirit-gifted encourager blessed them with hope and strength. Joseph, the Levite from Cyprus, was a son of encouragement in the early church. Over time he earned the name Barnabas, meaning "one who encourages" (Acts 4:36).

Encouragers know how to reassure the wavering, add strength to those who are faltering, and bring peace to the troubled in a mixed-up world. The gift in operation manifests a vital dimension of the Lord's character. It has opened many blinded eyes to the beauty of Christ and kept countless others stable in the faith.

3. Giving. History's greatest example of generosity springs from the Tri-unity of God: "God so loved the world that he gave his only begotten Son" (John 3:16 KJV). All of God's children who grow in His character, therefore, will be faithful givers like Him. In addition, certain people in the church have a special gift from the Holy Spirit to do much more than give the tithe. They delight to do so because they want to provide material resources for the church. Giving is a joy to them and has a miraculous quality about it (2 Cor. 9:7). This gift, too, has Holy Spirit power to open people's eyes to the giving heart of Jesus Christ.

4. Leadership. The spiritual gift of leadership is the special ability that some people have to organize the church and direct it toward God-given objectives. Paul said everything should be done "in a fitting and orderly way" (1 Cor. 14:40; Rom. 13:1–6). The apostle Peter spoke forcefully against self-willed people who "despise government" and "are not afraid to speak evil of dignities" (2 Pet. 2:10, KJV). A well-organized church encourages people and gives them a sense of stability.

    Jesus was certainly the greatest of leaders. When He called Peter and Andrew as His disciples, He told them, "Follow me, and I will make you fishers of men" (Matt. 4:19). He also showed His character as a determined leader at Caesarea Philippi when He said, "I will build my church" (Matt. 16:18).

5. Mercy. Jesus Christ is our "merciful and faithful High Priest in service to God" (Heb. 2:17). Mercy, in fact, is one of the most attractive elements of His character. When Jesus took His disciples north into the region of Tyre, a Canaanite woman cried out to Him, "Lord, Son of David, have mercy

on me! My daughter is suffering terribly from demon-posses-sion" (Matt. 15:22–28). Jesus mercifully granted her request.

Every congregation needs believers whom the Holy Spirit gifts to show the miraculous compassion and love of Jesus, which restores and cheers hurting people. These Spirit-gifted people feel empathy and bring healing to distressed brothers and sisters amid their mental, emotional, and physical issues. Onesiphorus showed great mercy toward Paul while the apostle was in jail, "and was not ashamed of [his] chains" (2 Tim. 1:16–18). The gift in action powerfully manifests the character of Jesus to people.

In addition to these gifts, Paul included prophecy and teaching in the Romans 12 list. The prophetic gift is also listed in the catalogs in 1 Corinthians 14 and Ephesians 4. The ministry of teaching is also listed in Ephesians 4 and 1 Corinthians 12.

The fact that prophets and teachers are repeated in this list reflects their broad importance in the New Testament church, as well as in any healthy contemporary church. The faithful ministries of prophecy and teaching are vitally important for opening blind eyes to the truth of the gospel and for encouraging believers. Whatever else are the strengths of a local congregation of believers, it will be anemic spiritually without prophetic and teaching ministries.

D. The Manifestation Gifts of the Spirit

The apostle Paul identified nine gifts the Holy Spirit manifests in 1 Corinthians 12.

> To each one the manifestation of the Spirit is given for the common good.
>
> —1 CORINTHIANS 12:7

The word translated "manifestation" in this passage is *phanerosis*, which means "outshinings." By using this word, Paul meant the Spirit shines out of believers' hearts at times and places of the Spirit's choosing. The person does not own these gifts. Instead, they are manifestations or outshinings of the Spirit. They enable Spirit-filled believers to serve the worldwide agenda of Jesus Christ more effectively by opening people's eyes to the power of the gospel. Spirit-filled sons of God enjoy the high privilege of expressing them from time to time "for the common good" at the Spirit's discretion (1 Cor. 12:7). A heightened ability to see and perceive in the realm of the Spirit, which was diminished in Adam's fall, is to this day one of the grand benefits of the baptism with the Holy Spirit.

1. The *word of wisdom* relates to a situation when the Holy Spirit manifests in a person a special ability to comprehend and understand the mind of the Lord to meet a need. A child of God perceives this wisdom quite apart from human reasoning. It results from an outshining of the Holy Spirit from a person's spirit and through his faculties. The Spirit told the ministry team of the church at Antioch, for example, what God already knew was the wisest use of the abilities of Barnabas and Saul (Acts 13:2; Rom. 11:33). The result was that the church released them to become the first missionaries of the Christian era.

2. The *word of knowledge* is akin to the word of wisdom but relates more to the divine impartation of facts and/or information for the need of the hour. Peter, by the Spirit, perceived exact knowledge about what Ananias and his wife had contrived (Acts 5:1–11).

3. *Prophecy* may be of two types. Forth-telling embraces edification, exhortation, and comfort (1 Cor. 14:3) and is the most common form of prophecy seen in Acts and the Epistles of the New Testament. Foretelling is predictive prophecy that writes tomorrow's news today. The prophet Agabus, for example, predicted a severe famine (Acts 11:28). Paul said a prophetic manifestation of the Spirit was typically for the benefit of believers, not unbelievers (1 Cor. 14:22).

    When Peter preached on the Day of Pentecost, he exercised the prophetic function of exhortation, proclaiming the Word of God (Acts 2:40). Stephen also preached under the same anointing, giving an exhortation to the Sanhedrin that the leaders rejected (Acts 7). Obviously, Peter and Stephen's sermons came from a power greater than either of them. The Holy Spirit prophetically shined out the Word of God through them as yielded vessels.

4. The gift of *different kinds of tongues* is a divine enabling of a believer to speak an utterance in an unknown language that the Holy Spirit wants an individual or the whole body of Christ to hear. Tongues are a sign, not for believers but for unbelievers. The message spoken can be in a living language

or a tongue not known to the human family. Messages given in different kinds of tongues have a unique place in worship.

So if the whole church comes together and everyone speaks in tongues, and some who do not understand or some unbelievers come in, will they not say that you are out of your mind? But if an unbeliever or someone who does not understand comes in while everybody is prophesying, he will be convinced by all that he is a sinner and will be judged by all, and the secrets of his heart will be laid bare. So he will fall down and worship God, exclaiming, "God is really among you!"

—1 CORINTHIANS 14:23–25

Tongues have a distinctive ministry in a worship service, therefore, convincing unbelievers to open their hearts to the gospel. Paul also taught the validity of praying in the Spirit (known as one's prayer language), as well as singing in the Spirit (1 Cor. 14:15; Rom. 8:26; Jude 1:20). Such experiences may be viewed as devotional tongues.

5. The *interpretation of tongues* is a supernatural enabling of a believer to share with the congregation what has been said in an utterance in tongues. Paul also gave regulations for these verbal gifts so that all things can be done "in a fitting and orderly way" (1 Cor. 14:26–33, 39–40).

6. The manifestation of the gift of *faith* enables a Christian to believe God for the answer to a pressing need. This is not the ordinary faith God has given to all men in a measure, nor is this saving faith (Rom. 12:3). Rather, an example is the extraordinary confidence Paul reflected in the Euroclydon on the stormy Mediterranean when he said, "Sirs, be of good cheer, for I believe God that it shall be even as it was told me" (Acts 27:25, KJV).

7. *Discerning of spirits* is a manifestation (a "shining out") of the Holy Spirit that enables a believer to know a person's attitude, disposition, or mindset. Jesus had that ability perfectly. He knew what was in man and needed no one to testify to Him about man (John 2:25). The Holy Spirit had that same divine capability to know the deepest core motivation in a person that was determining his actions. Peter discerned exactly the plot that Ananias and his wife had schemed. Paul exercised the gift as well during the Philippian revival when he cast the

spirit of divination (fortune-telling) out of a slave girl (Acts 16:19).

8. *Gifts of healings* enable Spirit-filled believers to become vessels through whom the virtue of Christ flows for restoration and recovery of the human body. Praying for the sick has always been vital to Pentecostal worship. Jesus Christ is the healer. He is Jehovah-Rapha. The Lord has never met an illness that intimidated Him, a sickness He could not stop. Gifts of healings are outshinings of the ability that was in Jesus to restore health, both physical and emotional. Peter and John exercised the gift when they healed the lame man at the gate called Beautiful, giving back to him the priceless use of his limbs (Acts 3:1–9).

9. *Working of miracles* is a manifestation of the Spirit that refers to the unusual signs and wonders that take place from time to time in the body of Christ. The judgment pronounced on Ananias and Sapphira in Acts 5:1–11 is an example. Luke recorded that many "miraculous signs and wonders" were wrought among the people by the hands of the apostles (Acts 5:12).

E. The Catalog in 1 Corinthians 12:28–31

In the church, God has appointed [or set in place] first of all apostles, second prophets, third teachers, then workers of miracles, also those having gifts of healing, those able to help others, those with gifts of administration, and those speaking in different kinds of tongues.
—1 CORINTHIANS 12:28, EMPHASIS ADDED

Each of the gifts in this list is in other catalogs. The important emphasis here focuses on the fact that God appoints or sets these gifts in His body. These "set gifts" include apostles, prophets and teachers, as well as those who work miracles, bring healing to the sick, and speak with tongues (Eph. 4:11; 1 Cor. 12:7–11). In addition to these giftings, the Holy Spirit sets in place helpers and those who serve His church as administrators (Rom. 12:5–8).

The word in 1 Corinthians 12:28 translated as "helps" (KJV) is used only this once in the New Testament. It is probably analogous to the serving gift in Romans 12:7, referring to the role of deacons.

The Gospels are clear that the Lord was a great helper of people. Peter's mother-in-law, for example, was bed-ridden with fever. "They asked Jesus to help her," and He did (Luke 4:38). Her cure was so immediate, "she got up and prepared a meal for them" (Luke 4:38–39).

God set this gift in the body. It certainly addresses the needs of the poor and often is out of the spotlight. While the person with the gift of helps may well serve tables, he can also blossom into a "Stephen" in the body of Christ, and a "Phillip." With both of these deacons, their gift to help became miraculous, much larger than serving tables (Acts 6:8; 8:5). The gift of helps will surely open blinded hearts to the message of the gospel.

F. The Apostle Peter's List

Peter identified hospitality, speaking (exhortation or encouraging), and service as three gifts of the Spirit.

> Above all, love [agapa] each other deeply, because love covers over a multitude of sins. Offer hospitality to one another without grumbling. Each one should use whatever gift [charisma] he has received to serve others, faithfully administering God's grace in its various forms. If anyone speaks, he should do it as one speaking the very words of God. If anyone serves, he should do it with the strength God provides, so that in all things God can be praised through Jesus Christ. To him be the glory and the power for ever and ever.
> —1 PETER 4:8–11, EMPHASIS ADDED

The earlier lists in this study, given by the apostle Paul, identified speaking (exhortation) and serving. However, only Peter adds the spiritual gift of hospitality. Many Spirit-filled people show pleasant and agreeable traits that delight visitors and guests, including welcoming and refreshing them in their homes. The gift of hospitality, however, includes a special grace from the Holy Spirit to love people so much they make visitors feel welcome, comfortable, and "at home" in the presence of the demonstrated power of the Holy Spirit. The Spirit endows just that kind of hospitality in the body of Christ, putting new people at ease in the presence of the holy. The Lord certainly showed the gift to His disciples when He prepared the meal on the bank of the Sea of Galilee and invited them to come and dine.

While Paul and Peter recorded these lists of spiritual gifts, the church should not conclude they exhaust the subject in the sacred canon. For example, when the time came to construct the tabernacle in the wilderness, the Lord told Moses, "I have chosen Bezalel son of Uri, of the tribe of Judah, and I have filled him with the Spirit of God, with skill, ability and knowledge…to engage in all kinds of crafts" (Exod. 31:1–5). The Lord also said, "I have appointed Oholiab…of the tribe of Dan, to help him" (Exod. 31:6).

G. Perceiving the Focus of the Spirit

It is obvious from the wide-ranging variety in these lists, including the participation of the Trinity in giving them, that the Holy Spirit places focus on humble servants whom He gifts to duplicate aspects of Jesus' own ministry. Precisely because they are gifts of the Spirit, they should not be confused with offices and officers in the church visible. It is tragic when people try to take the gifts away from the Holy Spirit and make them gifts of the institutional church. When that happens, the gifts become little more than administrative scaffolding.

In Paul's list in 1 Corinthians 12:27–31, for example, teachers, workers of miracles, those having gifts of healing, helpers, administrators, and those who speak in different tongues are placed or set in the body of Christ by the Spirit, just like apostles and prophets. It is interesting that in the Ephesians 4 gift list, Jesus gave to Paul a five-fold identification: apostles, prophets, evangelists, pastors, and teachers. If these should be understood as *the* five ministry gifts the ascended Christ gave to the visible church, then why did the Holy Spirit list only three of them (apostles, prophets, and teachers) in the catalog of the "set" gifts (*etheto*) in 1 Corinthians 12:28?

When a student of the Word understands the gifts of the Spirit as the domain of the Holy Spirit to set or place in the Lord's spiritual body according to His sovereign choosing, the need to form neat packages disappears. The result is that the gifts bless the body of Christ by showing various aspects of the Lord's ministry. They open blinded eyes to the hope expressed in the crucifixion and resurrection of the Christ and help mature believers in the attitude and worldwide agenda of Jesus.

It is important to reaffirm that Jesus manifested all of these spiritual gifts in His ministry as "the apostle and high priest whom we confess" (Heb. 3:1). The writer of Hebrews made clear that "God...testified" to the plan of salvation "by signs, wonders and various miracles, and gifts of the Holy Spirit distributed according to his will" (Heb. 2:3–4).

How exciting to participate in an assembly of believers that in the overall structure of its ministry has organized itself to give the Holy Spirit freedom to portray all of the gifts. One can only imagine how many people would turn to Christ as the gifts operate in the lives of Spirit-filled people. In a congregation's routine service to its community:

- miracles would regularly happen.
- the sick would be healed.
- prophecy would be the norm.
- evangelists would win people to Christ.

- helpers would joyfully serve the needs of people, both physically and spiritually.
- administrators would pick up the load of managing the institutional church.
- children would grow up hearing the gift of tongues in operation and unbelievers would be drawn to Christ because of the gift.
- apostles would dream in the Spirit about opening up new ministries at home and abroad that no one has yet even thought about, and then go blaze the trail.
- prophets would exhort believers to "continue in the faith," even as from time to time they predict the future, writing tomorrow's newspaper today (Acts 14:22).
- teachers would be filling believers with the Word of God so they can be "established and firm, not moved from the hope held out in the gospel" (Col. 1:23).

Worship in such a congregation would be dynamic, and ministry would flow powerfully in the anointing of the Spirit through Spirit-gifted people.

H. Picking up the Challenge

A group of Greeks visiting in Jerusalem shortly before the Lord's crucifixion appealed to Phillip, saying, "'Sir…we would like to see Jesus'" (John 12:21). Spiritual gifts in action answer that yearning in the hearts of people in every generation, introducing them to the Lord.

The two cardinal sins of postmodernism are intolerance (questioning the validity of any aspect of another's religion) and claiming objective, universal truth. However, God revealed Himself in history in Jesus Christ and gave an objective record of Himself in the Bible. In the name of having no universals, therefore, postmodernism advances its own universal as "toleration of all." Interestingly, the tolerance of postmodernism has an escape clause. It advocates tolerance of all who do not challenge its mantra of toleration. Intolerance against Bible-believing Christians is appropriate in postmodernism because Christians believe the absolutes taught by Jesus Christ.

Is there a key to reach postmoderns? We answer that the gifts of the Spirit in operation will open blinded eyes in the twenty-first century, just as they did in the Roman Empire. Humankind suffers, not from seeing too much of Jesus, but too little. A watered-down Jesus is not Jesus. Hence, there is no reason to fear that the historical death and resurrection of Jesus are "found wanting" up against the questions raised by postmodern thinking (Dan. 5:27). To this day the cross of Jesus and His empty tomb remain "the power of God and the wisdom of God" (1 Cor. 1:24). With this in mind, the Lord's church must never lose the genius of Paul's strategy as he evangelized pagan Corinth: "I resolved to know nothing while I was with you except Jesus Christ and him crucified." Paul went on to add, "My message and my preaching were not with wise and persuasive words, but with a demonstration of the Spirit's power, so that your faith might not rest on men's wisdom, but on God's power (1 Cor. 2:2–5).

Let the challenge from postmodernism be picked up by those who implicitly trust the heavenly Father as Jesus did and are confident of Jesus' superiority over all rivals. "But I, when I am lifted up from the earth," Jesus said, "will draw all men to myself" (John 12:32).

I. The Ministry of Bishops

The apostle Paul commanded the Ephesian elders on the strand of the Aegean Sea, "Keep watch over yourselves and all the flock of which the Holy Spirit has made [*etheto*] you overseers [*episkopous*, or "bishops"]. Be shepherds of the church of God which [Jesus] bought with his own blood" (Acts 20:28).

This use of *etheto*, which means "to set in place," is the same word Paul chose in 1 Corinthians 12:28 when He wrote, "God has appointed..." and then proceeded to name eight gift areas God set in the church. The gift to the church of overseers or bishops, also flows from the work of the Holy Spirit. He sets this servant ministry in the body of Christ. It is in this sense that we understand Paul's statement, "Here is a trustworthy saying: If anyone sets his heart on being an overseer [or bishop], he desires a noble task" (1 Tim. 3:1).

By comparison, Paul, Peter, and James had much more to say about the reputation and moral fiber of bishops than about functional apostles (1 Tim. 3:2–5; Titus 1:7–9; 1 Pet. 5:2; James 5:14–15).

a. A Bishop's Character

1. The bishop is to live "above reproach" (1 Tim. 3:2; Titus 2:7). To serve in this role a bishop must not participate in unchristian activity.

2. He is required to be the "husband of but one wife" (1 Tim. 3:2; Titus 1:6). In the pagan Roman Empire where immorality was commonplace, Paul established a strict marital policy for bishops. In addition, the bishop was expected to "rule well his house, having his children in subjection with all gravity" (1 Tim. 3:4, KJV; Titus 1:6). To Paul, the point was obvious: if a person "does not know how to manage his own family, how can he take care

of God's church?" (1 Tim. 3:5). A bishop, therefore, needs to be a dedicated family man.

3. The bishop is to be "temperate" and "self controlled," a manager of his own person (1 Tim. 3:2; Titus 1:8). He must have the mastery over the desires of his own flesh.

4. The bishop is to be a "sober" man who lives wisely, possessing foresight in the management of practical affairs. He must be sensible (Titus 1:8; 1 Tim. 3:2, KJV).

5. The bishop is required to be a man "of good behavior" (or "orderly" TLB. The term *orderly* is a translation of the word *kosmion*, from which comes the English term *cosmos*, or "universe." As God placed order in His universe, so the bishop must be an orderly man who brings stability into the lives of people (1 Tim. 3:2, TLB).

6. The bishop is to be "a lover of hospitality," whose social graces enable him to enjoy guests and treat them with cordiality and generosity (Titus 1:8, KJV; 1 Tim. 3:2). The bishop must also be willing to share unselfishly with others.

7. He must be ready to teach sound doctrine and refute false doctrine (Titus 1:9). He is also required to be gentle and not given to argumentation (2 Tim. 2:24–26).

8. The bishop must not be "given to drunkenness" (1 Tim. 3:3; Titus 1:7, KJV).

9. He cannot be a "striker" (Titus 1:7; 1 Tim. 3:3, KJV). The word in the Greek carries the meaning of both physical and verbal violence. The bishop must be a servant like His Lord and not a violent, quarrelsome man (1 Pet. 2:23). Instead, he is to be forbearing and patient (1 Tim. 3:3). He should possess the ability and wisdom to know when not to enforce something that is due, recognizing that there will be times to act with leniency and patience.

10. The bishop must not be a brawler, given to being contentious (1 Tim. 3:3, KJV).

11. He cannot be a man who is "a lover of money" (1 Tim. 3:3; 1 Pet. 5:2; Titus 1:7). Rather, he should be able to teach people how to handle capital assets. Nor can he be covetous, desiring money or possessions that are not and could not be his own. Instead, the bishop should be liberal and generous and not self-seeking.

12. The bishop could not be a recent convert who is a novice or neophyte in the faith (1 Tim. 3:6). Rather, he is to be a seasoned man of mature wisdom and experience.

13. The bishop must not be conceited in his own self-estimate of his worth (1 Tim. 3:6). This kind of pride will cause him to fall into the condemnation of the devil.

14. A bishop is required to be a man of good reputation among those from outside the household of faith who know him. Otherwise, Satan will use someone acquainted with the weakness of his character to set a snare for him, making him "fall into disgrace and into the devil's trap" (1 Tim. 3:7).

15. The bishop cannot be "self-willed," loving his own thinking to the point that he stubbornly wants only his own way regardless, nor can he be overbearing or insensitive to the feelings of others. (Titus 1:7, GW). He must not try like a dictator to force his own views on others.

16. Nor can he be "quick-tempered" (Titus 1:7). The personality of the bishop must not be impulsive, given to wrath that seeks to punish with vengeance.

17. The bishop must be a "lover of good men" (Titus 1:8, KJV). He is expected to assemble around himself people who are holy and honorable like himself, men who delight to think about and do good things.

18. The bishop is required to be a just man, capable of rendering fair and impartial decisions based on the facts. His rulings must be made on principle and his life sanctioned by sober piety (Titus 1:8). This stature is gained because of his ongoing lifestyle of observing all duties toward God, which is the essence of piety.

19. The bishop is required to be a man who practices holding "firmly to the trustworthy message as it has been taught" (Titus 1:9). How can he teach sound doctrine and convince the gainsayers if he himself vacillates in the doctrine?

b. A Bishop's Ministry

On his way to Jerusalem, the apostle Paul held a brief meeting on the strand of the Aegean Sea with the leaders of the church at Ephesus. At that time, he said to them, "Keep watch over yourselves and all the flock of which the Holy Spirit has made [*etheto,* from the word *tithemi,* which means "set in place"] you overseers [*episkopous,* or "bishops"]. Be shepherds of the church of God, which he bought with his own blood" (Acts 20:28).

Since the Holy Spirit set in place the Ephesian brethren as "overseers," it follows that they received their commission from God, too (Acts 20:28). The passage explicitly demonstrates that the Holy Spirit, as the great Administrator of the church, chooses, equips, and commissions bishops. These God-appointed servants of the Lord were responsible to keep watch over themselves and the flock so effectively that they actually fed and cared for the people of God. As they did so, Paul charged them never to forget that Jesus "bought" the church "with his own blood" (Acts 20:28; 1 Tim. 3:1–5; 1 Pet. 5:2). Their shepherding role also included watching out for "savage wolves" that would arise from both inside and outside the church to devour the flock by drawing people away from the gospel and creating their own following (Acts 20:29).

Titus may have served in a functional apostolic role under the spiritual leadership of the apostle Paul (1 Thess. 1:1; 2:6). His ministry on the island of Crete, however, seems to have been in the role of an elder (or bishop), doing follow-up ministry after Paul departed the island. Paul specifically directed him to "appoint elders in every town" (Titus 1:5).

Paul wrote to the believers in Rome that He had started the church in Illyricum, the Balkan region of southern Europe (Rom. 15:19). Titus went to this area, Dalmatia, as well after Paul had blazed the trail and departed (2 Tim. 4:10). Titus is a New Testament example, therefore, of a bishop or elder with an administrative role who also served as a missionary with a Great Commission focus.

Bishops are to be servants like the Lord. They:

- give themselves to care for the flock with shepherds' hearts. Jesus humbled Himself and became the servant of all, and bishops are to serve like Him (Mark 9:35).
- teach the doctrine with a Great Commission focus, always looking for ways to multiply believers and plant new churches (Matt. 16:18; 28:16–20; 2 Tim. 4:3).
- protect the people from false teachers by refuting false doctrines (Acts 20:28–30; Titus 1:9).
- manage God's church (1 Tim. 3:5).
- direct the affairs of the church, including its teaching ministries, which makes them worthy of double honor (1 Tim. 5:17).
- lead without becoming dictators or acting as "lords over those entrusted to [them]" (1 Pet. 5:3).
- pray the prayer of faith for the sick, anointing them with oil (James 5:14–15).
- direct the congregation in worship and administer the sacraments of the church.

These qualifications speak only minimally to administrative experience, or in modern thought, management expertise. The Lord searches primarily for character in choosing His ministers. God said to Samuel, "Man looks on the outward appearance but the Lord looks at the heart" (1 Sam. 16:7).

The apostle Peter was a foundational apostle who was in the inner circle of the Lord's disciples (Matt. 17:1). Yet, Peter described himself as a co-elder or a "fellow elder" with the elders (or bishops) in Pontus, Galatia, Cappadocia, Asia, and Bithynia, to whom he addressed his first epistle (1 Pet. 5:1). The apostles intimated this dynamic when they chose a successor for Judas Iscariot, who betrayed Jesus. In that discussion, Peter actually used the term translated elsewhere in the New Testament as "bishop" to refer to apostolic ministry: "It is written in the book of Psalms, 'Let his habitation be desolate, and let no man dwell therein: and his bishoprick [*episkopain*] let another take'" (Acts 1:20, KJV; Ps. 69:25). At a minimum, this statement is a hint of the close relationship between bishops and functional apostles that did in fact emerge in the post-apostolic church.

When one studies carefully the character qualities and ministry duties of bishops and compares them to the role of functional apostles as presented in the New Testament, it becomes apparent that a striking similarity and close identification exists between the ministry of functional apostles and bishops.

J. Spiritual Gifts and Natural Talents

Natural talents and the gifts of the Holy Spirit are fundamentally different. Native abilities can develop great corporations, even great "corporate" churches, but natural talents will never produce a church that opens spiritually blinded eyes to the gospel, or break open Satan's grip on the minds and hearts of people, or open physically blinded eyes to the beauty of the sunlight. Gifts of the Spirit are essential to do these things.

> No one knows the thoughts of God except the Spirit of God. We have not received the spirit of the world but the Spirit who is from God, that we may understand what God has freely given us. This is what we speak, not in words taught us by human wisdom but in words taught by the Spirit, expressing spiritual truths in spiritual words. The man without the Spirit does not accept the things that come from the Spirit of God, for they are foolishness to him, and he cannot understand them, because they are spiritually discerned..."For who has known the mind of the Lord that he may instruct him?" But we have the mind of Christ.
> —1 Corinthians 2:11–14, 16

For a church to mirror Jesus in its culture, it must have in its ranks the broad range of Spirit-filled people operating in the gifts of the Spirit. Without them, the church will not even come close to fulfilling the job description Isaiah the prophet wrote for Jesus Christ: "The Spirit of the Lord is on me, because he has anointed me to preach good news to the poor. He has sent me to proclaim freedom for the prisoners and recovery of sight for the blind, to release the oppressed, to proclaim the year of the Lord's favor" (Luke 4:18–19; see Isa. 61:1–2).

What a blessing, however, when the gifts of the Spirit are in operation. They bring wonderful news to the poor and scales fall from the blinded eyes of the unconverted. Spiritual gifts in operation have the power to open up the vision of people for the first time to see the beautiful character of Jesus. All of them in action become a full-canvas portrait of the ministry of Christ and constitute a key explanation for the survivability of the church, century after century.

- *1 Corinthians 12:7–11*—the word of wisdom, the word of knowledge, faith, gifts of healing, miraculous powers, prophecy, distinguishing between spirits, different kinds of tongues, and the interpretation of tongues
- *1 Corinthians 12:28–31*—first, apostles; second, prophets; third, teachers; then workers of miracles, also those having gifts of healing, those able to help others, those with gifts of administration, and those speaking in different kinds of tongues
- *Romans 12:6–8*—prophesying, serving, teaching, encouraging, contributing to the needs of others, leadership, and showing mercy
- *Ephesians 4:11*—apostles, prophets, evangelists, pastors, and teachers
- *1 Peter 4:8–11*—"faithfully administering God's grace" through hospitality, exhortation (encouraging), and service
- *Acts 20:28*—the office of overseers (bishops or elders)

Natural talents alone will never fulfill the Great Commission. As John 3:6 points out, "Flesh can [only] give birth to flesh, but the Spirit gives birth to spirit." Only the Holy Spirit will mature believers in Christ to the point they begin to work miracles themselves, including miraculous healings.

The Spirit will also gift and mature apostles, prophets, evangelists, pastors, and teachers. Natural talents cannot do that job. Nor will natural talents call and mature the next generation of apostles, prophets, evangelists, pastors, teachers, encouragers, those with the gift of mercy, or bishops, and continue the cycle until Jesus comes.

It is essential, therefore, that all of the gifts of the Holy Spirit work "in a fitting and orderly way" (1 Cor. 14:40). After all, "except the Lord build the house, they labor in vain that build it" (Ps. 127:1, kjv).

To the extent all of the spiritual gifts are at work in the church, the congregation will be strong and vibrant, portraying Jesus Christ in its community. Without these impartations, it will be anemic and lethargic. Such congregations desperately need prophetic voices to call them back to the purity and power of the gospel. Only Holy Spirit-called and gifted believers who implicitly trust their heavenly Father can perpetuate the Lord's church, generation after generation, until Jesus comes.

And He will return! (John 14:3).

K. Gift Mixes

Spiritual leaders in the early church manifested gift mixes, or combinations of gifts, in their ministries. For example:

- The ministry of the foundational apostles probably demonstrated all of the gifts.
- Phillip was a deacon whom the Spirit gifted as an evangelist (Acts 6:5; 8:5, 29).
- Stephen was a deacon whom the Spirit gifted as a prophet (Acts 6 and 7).
- Peter wrote to the elders, instructing them also to serve as "overseers" (bishops) and "shepherds" (pastors) (1 Pet. 5:1–2).
- Peter himself served both as an apostle and as a "fellow elder" (or bishop) (1 Pet. 5:1).
- Two foundational apostles, Paul and John, served as apostolic pastors of the great church in Ephesus, the church Paul pioneered; John was serving as the apostolic pastor at Ephesus when banished to Patmos.
- Titus may have carried the title of a functional apostle (1 Thess. 1:1; 2:6). However, Paul's letter to Titus portrays a foundational apostle who trusts a promising son in the faith to do the work of a bishop or an elder on the island of Crete.

The range of gift mixes, therefore, is multiple. It is reasonable to assume that pastors can serve as apostolic pastors, prophetic pastors, evangelistic pastors, or pastor-teachers. The gift mixes can even be as broad as a combination of apostolic, prophetic, evangelistic pastor-teachers, who also serve with the gift of governments and work miracles, etc. The same principle follows for all of the other gifts.

The important factor to underscore is that the Holy Spirit imparts gifts "to each one just as He determines" to build up the spiritual body of Christ (1 Cor. 12:11). A church whose members are operating in the rich variety of the gifts of the Spirit will be attractive to the culture. The price of time, energy, and resources the wise men were willing to invest to find baby Jesus is an illustration of the deep yearning for God in the hearts of people. It is often true that the person one might least expect to want to enjoy the fellowship of the Lord may be the one who yearns secretly for a new life (Matt. 2:1–12; John 4:4–42; Acts 9:1–19). It takes the gifts of the Holy Spirit to get through to them, showing God to hurting people.

L. Apostolic Governance and Spiritual Gifts

The New Testament presents no one governmental form as *the* model of leadership for the Lord's church. What is unmistakable is that when the apostle Paul won people to Christ (the church invisible), he also organized them into bodies of believers (the visible church). Paul then "appointed elders...in each church" that he planted, "and with prayer and fasting, committed them to the Lord, in whom they had put their trust" (Acts 14:23). These elders became the spiritual and administrative servants of the earliest New Testament churches.

When people in a church are regularly receiving the baptism with the Holy Spirit, the gifts of the Spirit will naturally manifest, thereby unveiling Christ to a community. In fact, for a church to demonstrate a complete painting of the ministry of Jesus Christ presupposes all of the gifts of the Spirit in operation outside the four walls of the church (Eph. 4:11–12; Rom. 12:5–8; 1 Cor. 12:6–11; 27–31; 1 Pet. 4:8–11; Acts 20:28; Exod. 31:1–5).

M. Evaluation

The big temptation has always been to try to define and organize the gifts so that they fit into a preconceived ecclesiastical structure. But the New Testament portrays them as gifts of the Holy Spirit, and not gifts conferred by the organized church. The key is for the visible church to develop governmental forms that complement and release the gifts of the Spirit in their rich variety. There must be no effort to force the gifts into a governmental mold that establishes offices, officers, and authority figures in the organized church.

In the early church, the gifts were unique to the needs of a servant church whose members lived on the cutting edge of evangelism (Luke 10:2; 12:2;

John 18:36; Acts 1:8). Through the gifts in operation in the marketplace, the Spirit forced hardened religious leaders and even pagans to acknowledge the Lord (Acts 4:13; 26:28).

The Mediterranean world had never seen anything like these Spirit-filled Christians. To be around them and watch the gifts in action compelled Gentiles to open their eyes and see Jesus. It was routine, in fact, when they talked about Jesus for people actually to sense the Lord was present—and indeed, He was, because they were His temple. The goal of a Christian servant is to become more and more invisible so that Jesus becomes more and more visible. The gifts in operation always make that happen.

The gifts of the Spirit continue today to speak convincingly to unbelievers everywhere that Jesus Christ is King. They also help to mature new generations of Spirit-gifted people, preparing "God's people for works of service so that the body of Christ may be built up" (Eph. 4:12).

It is very important to underscore that nothing is elitist about how the Holy Spirit imparts the gifts. His distribution has always sprung from His grace and has never created a hierarchy or a special class. There is no room for spiritual pride regarding the gifts of the Spirit, which always mature servants and only servants.

This ongoing ministry model of spiritual gifts is the Father's singular plan.

> Until all of us are united in our faith and in our knowledge about God's Son, until we become mature, until we measure up to Christ, who is the standard. Then we will no longer be little children, tossed and carried about by all kinds of teachings that change like the wind. We will no longer be influenced by people who use cunning and clever strategies to lead us astray. Instead, as we lovingly speak the truth, we will grow up completely in our relationship to Christ, who is the head. He makes the whole body fit together and unites it through the support of every joint. As each and every part does its job, he makes the body grow so that it builds itself up in love.
> —Ephesians 4:13–16, GW

When Syrians, Greeks, Egyptians, Romans, or Medes looked at the church of Jesus Christ, they did not at all see emperors, governors, tetrarchs, prefects, magistrates, or tax collectors. Instead, the giftings in these gatherings of dedicated Christians, graced by the fruit of the Spirit, were light-years away from how the governmental systems of the nations operated (Gal. 5:22).

Because of these faithful and humble servants of Jesus, the Lord has delighted through the centuries to awaken the wind to blow on His "garden, that its fragrance may spread abroad" (Song of Sol. 4:16).

What a gifted Savior!
What an awesome gospel!
What an equipped church!

IV. The Church's Organizational Forms

A. Scaffolding

Administrative gifts and physical structures have always been necessary complements to grow the fruit of the Spirit in the spiritual body of Christ. Even grapevines must have arbors and trellises to hold up their fruit. In the same way that these supports never produce a single grape, however, "church scaffolding" is not the raw material that builds the body of Christ. Governmental structures and facilities, at their best, are only trellises. The Lord's great delight is to develop believers, not grape arbors. He is interested in trellises to the extent that they help believers learn to grow and harvest grapes (Matt. 9:37; John 15:5–6).

An assembly of believers that does not enjoy the vibrant presence of the Holy Spirit will usually keep trying to expand the church by adding more arbors. They can professionally paint and decorate them, illuminate them with bright lights, and cover the floors with palatial hardwoods, carpets, and rare stones, all the while thinking they are growing the church. But they actually are growing only first-class trellises that yield no harvest—no grapes, none at all.

⤳ When the Church Becomes a Sham ⤳

The church of God apart from the person of Christ is a useless structure. However ornate it may be in its organization, however perfect in all its arrangements, however rich and increased with goods—if the church is not revealing the Person, lifting Him to the height where all men can see Him, then the church becomes an impertinence and a sham, a blasphemy and a fraud, and the sooner the world is rid of it, the better.[5]

The Lord never envisioned that His church would constitute a rival nation-state, because Jesus' kingdom is not of this world (John 18:36). The church anchors uniquely in God's love. It has no need for a police force, a military, or tax collectors. Jesus' followers are givers, not because they fear a governmental tax audit, but because the love of Christ compels them (2 Cor. 5:14). Precisely because Jesus' realm is this unique, He imparted special spiritual gifts to find the sheep that are lost (Luke 15:6–7).

The Lord's people who are walking in the Spirit understand the church has always been about rescuing the perishing (Matt. 18:12–14). One soul is more important than any governmental scaffolding. Jesus did not die to establish Episcopal, Presbyterian, congregational, independent, or apostolic government, but He did give His life to seek and save the lost (Luke 19:10). It follows that the Lord equips each of His followers to win others as they walk in the Spirit. Church government is necessary and is at its best when it provides an open superhighway for Christ's followers to commit to the attitude and mindset of Jesus.

In achieving this goal, the church must first comprehend itself as an organism (the spiritual body of Christ) and only second as an organization (the visible church), without ever reversing the two. Then it can understand scaffolding exists to complement its nature as an organism uniquely designed for search-and-rescue.

B. Social Responsibility and the Ministry of Completion

The account of the ministry of deacons in Acts 6 demonstrated that from its earliest days, the church felt responsible to care for the needy, including prisoners. The Lord certainly taught the practice.

> I was hungry and you gave me something to eat, I was thirsty and you gave me something to drink, I was a stranger and you invited me in, I needed clothes and you clothed me, I was sick and you looked after me, I was in prison and you came to visit me.
> —Matthew 25:35–36

Jesus demonstrated this principle while hanging on His cross. In His hour of greatest suffering, He actually established a ministry of completion. As Mary's firstborn son, Jesus was accountable for her livelihood and welfare.

The Lord fulfilled His role by assigning His mother to the apostle John, whom He knew would love her and provide for her. Jesus said to John, "Here is your mother" (John 19:27). To Mary He said, "Dear woman, here is your son" (John 19:26). From that time, the disciple "took her into his home" (John 19:27). John's assignment was to complete what Jesus would not be able to finish in caring for His mother.

Three examples illustrate the ministry of completion:

- grandparents who must rear grandchildren
- a Christian father or mother in a blended family who must finish rearing children not their own

- a brother or sister, because of some life tragedy, who must take in nephews or nieces and complete rearing them

When a person, by choice or misfortune, is no longer fulfilling his responsibility to a child or a sick or aging parent, it is very "Christian" for someone to accept the task to complete the job. "Though my father and mother forsake me," wrote David, "the Lord will receive me" (Ps. 27:10).

The apostle James expressed it by saying, "Religion that God our Father accepts as pure and faultless is this: to look after orphans and widows in their distress and to keep oneself from being polluted by the world" (James 1:27). The apostle Paul reflected this same point of view when he received a special love offering from the Gentile churches in Macedonia and Achaia to give to the poor saints in Jerusalem (Rom. 15:26).

C. Church Government and Denominationalism

"God has set in the church…governments" because people in the visible church need structure (1 Cor. 12:28, kjv). However, the Lord did not specify the details of the church's constitution. The lesson of church history is that church government develops as the need grows for better scaffolding, without which it would not be possible to keep expanding the Lord's vineyard. In the decades following the ministry of the Lord's foundational apostles, improved administrative oversight in the apostolic church became essential, in view of its exponential growth, particularly in the face of intense persecutions. One of the fundamental purposes of the church visible is to provide a place where the Holy Spirit can "set the lonely in families" (Ps. 68:6). In these assemblies, people find structure, discipline, and training in the attitude of Jesus Christ, including His character and His plan to reach the world.

As Israel had her twelve tribes, local congregations quickly recognize the need for connection in the greater body of Christ. Denominations are at their best, therefore, when they serve as this visible family of God. In the combined strength of many local congregations, they develop colleges, universities, and youth camps, grow worldwide missions and evangelism programs, strengthen benevolence ministries, and provide a host of additional opportunities designed to benefit local congregations as well as the society at large.

Congregations, and the denominations they form, should rejoice in the benefits of the governmental structures they have chosen, never forgetting it is no more than a trellis, a facilitating framework that yields no fruit. Then they will be better able to keep in focus that the primary objective of government in the visible church is to complement the spiritual mission of the invisible church.

The prophet Daniel saw several astounding visions during his lifetime, including the revelation of Messiah as a stone cut out of a mountain, but not by the work of men (Dan. 2:34). Daniel comprehended that the Messiah would set up a kingdom that would never be destroyed, a kingdom that would ultimately conquer all rivals (Dan. 2:44). Daniel also saw visions that were "closed up and sealed until the time of the end" (Dan. 12:9).

Daniel even glimpsed the coming resurrection and was told, "Multitudes who sleep in the dust of the earth will awake: some to everlasting life, others to everlasting shame and contempt" (Dan. 12:2). As for Daniel himself, the angel said, "Go your way till the end. You will rest, and then at the end of the days you will rise to receive your allotted inheritance" (Dan. 12:13).

We now add the final strokes of this tribute to our awesome Lord. What is lacking is the grand story of Jesus' second appearing, when all His enemies will come under His feet (Heb. 2:8).

It is important that the reader gazes on the remaining hues, the ultimate destiny of the Lord's church. Paul said the inheritance of the faithful includes "a crown of righteousness" (2 Tim. 4:8). Peter identified a "crown of glory" (1 Pet. 5:4). James and John wrote about a "crown of life" (James 1:12; Rev. 2:10). John the Revelator painted Jesus as "the son of man" who was wearing "a crown of gold" (Rev. 14:14).

Oh, that blessed day.

Chapter Eleven

THE TRIUMPH OF THE SERVANT

Father, I want those you have given me to be with me where I
am, and to see my glory.
—John 17:24

Do not seal up the words of the prophecy of this book.
—Revelation 22:10

Place me like a seal over your heart, like a seal on your arm.
—Song of Solomon 8:6

∽꒰ I Know Who I Am, ꒱∾ and Where I'm Going!

In January 2000, leaders in Charlotte, North Carolina, invited their
favorite son, Billy Graham, to a luncheon in his honor.

Mr. Graham initially hesitated to accept the invitation because he was
beginning to struggle with Parkinson's disease. But the Charlotte leaders
said, "We don't expect a major address; just come and let us honor you."

So he agreed. After wonderful things were said about him, Dr. Graham
stepped to the rostrum, looked at the crowd, and said, "I'm reminded
today of Albert Einstein, the great physicist who this month has been
honored by *Time* magazine as the Man of the Century. Einstein was once
traveling from Princeton on a train when the conductor came down the
aisle, punching the tickets of every passenger. When he came to Einstein,
Einstein reached in his vest pocket. He couldn't find his ticket, so he
reached in his trouser pockets. It wasn't there, so he looked in his brief-
case but couldn't find it. Then he looked in the seat beside him. He still
couldn't find it.

The conductor said, "Dr. Einstein, I know who you are. We all know
who you are. I'm sure you bought a ticket. Don't worry about it."

Einstein nodded appreciatively. The conductor continued down the
aisle punching tickets. As he was ready to move to the next car, he turned
around and saw the great physicist down on his hands and knees looking
under his seat for his ticket.

The conductor rushed back and said, "Dr. Einstein! Dr. Einstein! Don't worry, I know who you are. No problem. You don't need a ticket. I'm sure you bought one." Einstein looked at him and said, "Young man, I too, know who I am. What I don't know is where I'm going.'"

Having said that Billy Graham continued, "See the suit I'm wearing? It's a brand new suit. My wife, my children, and my grandchildren are telling me I've gotten a little slovenly in my old age. I used to be a bit more fastidious. So I went out and bought a new suit for this luncheon and one more occasion. You know what that occasion is? This is the suit in which I'll be buried. But when you hear I'm dead, I don't want you to immediately remember the suit I'm wearing. I want you to remember this: I not only know who I am; I also know where I'm going."[1]

I. The Introduction: John the Apostle on Patmos (Rev. 1)

The Revelation is the final volume in the sacred canon and the primary New Testament book that tells how God will roll up the scroll of Father Time. Christ the Servant, who sits with the highest honor at the right hand of God, will one day complete His Father's plan (Acts 2:34–35). To do so, He will leave His throne to return to this earth, and so will launch the final consummation of all things. "I will come back," Jesus promised His disciples before His crucifixion, "and take you to be with me that you also may be where I am" (John 14:3). "Do not be afraid," Jesus spoke to John on Patmos. "I am the First and the Last" (Rev. 1:17).

John the Revelator portrayed Christ, the Redeemer, as fully remembering the part of the tapestry of redemption that lacked His finishing strokes. This awesome Lord of all holds in His own person the total authority for the consummation of all things, including the redemption of nature. "I am...the ending," He said (Rev. 1:8, KJV).

Such sweeping, universal claims of eternal authority would be the grossest examples of egotism if anyone spoke them other than Jesus Christ. The Messiah was not content merely to make these claims, however; He also gave John His credentials to prove them: "I am the living one; I was dead and behold I am alive for ever and ever! And I hold the keys of death and Hades" (Rev. 1:18).

The apostle Paul summed up the significance of the glorification of Jesus Christ and the ultimate adulation He will receive on that great day: "God exalted [Jesus] to the highest place and gave him the name that is above every name, that at the name of Jesus every knee should bow, in heaven and on earth and under the earth, and every tongue confess that Jesus Christ is Lord, to the glory of God the Father" (Phil. 2:9–11; Rom. 14:11; Isa. 45:23).

The story of our awesome Lord reaches its climax in this grand hope of the ages. The prophets of the centuries have foretold it, and the saints of all time have longed for it. One day, angels will rejoice to help make it happen. The Lord Himself will come. He will not tarry (Hab. 2:3; Heb. 10:37–38). Righteousness will ultimately prevail. "The earth will be filled with the knowledge of the glory of the Lord, as the waters cover the sea" (Hab. 2:14; Isa. 11:9). Jesus Christ has, in fact, placed us like a seal over His heart, like a seal on His arm (Song of Sol. 8:6; Eph. 1:13). Because of His "great love for us," He will fulfill all righteousness (Eph. 2:4; Matt. 3:15; Rom. 1:17).

No serious student of the Bible would wish to neglect such sacred terrain (Rev. 1:3). The Lord's coming is imminent. The cry is about to go out to announce, "Here's the bridegroom. Come out to meet him" (Matt. 25:6). Just the thought of David's greatest Son reigning from Mount Zion is enough to set the soul to dancing (Rom. 1:3; Jer. 31:4; Matt. 21:9, 14).

The book of Revelation embraces three major themes.

- The seven letters Jesus sent by the apostle John to the seven churches in Asia.
- The worship Jesus Christ will receive in heaven. John also contrasts the heavenly worship of God's Son with the reverence evil men on the earth will give to Satan and the Antichrist.
- The events that will unfold both on the earth and in heaven in the last days, marking the consummation of all things.

Patmos is a rocky island four by eight miles in size, located off the coast of Turkey in the Aegean Sea. It is about fifty miles southwest of ancient Ephesus. Because of his witness to the "word of God and the testimony of Jesus," a Roman court tried and convicted the apostle John, who was the apostolic pastor of the great church in Ephesus (Rev. 1:9). His sentence was banishment on Patmos.

Although isolated from the people He loved, John was in the Spirit on the Lord's day and received a magnificent vision from the ascended Savior (Rev. 1:10–16). It began with his hearing behind him a loud voice, like a trumpet.

"I am the Alpha and the Omega," says the Lord God, "who is, and who was, and who is to come, the Almighty.... Write on a scroll what you see and send it to the seven churches: to Ephesus, Smyrna, Pergamum, Thyatira, Sardis, Philadelphia and Laodicea."
—Revelation 1:8, 11

The book John wrote on Patmos came from "Jesus Christ... the faithful witness, the firstborn from the dead and the ruler over the kings of the earth" (Rev. 1:5). He is the One who "loves us and has freed us from our sins by his blood and made us to be a kingdom and priests to serve his God and Father" (Rev. 1:5–6).

At the beginning of the Revelation, John spoke a special benediction on all who read the words of this prophecy. "Blessed are those who hear it," he said, "and take to heart what is written in it, because the time is near" (Rev. 1:3). Then in the grand finale at the end of the volume, the Lord Jesus spoke the benediction, "Behold, I am coming soon! Blessed is he who keeps the words of the prophecy in this book" (Rev. 22:7).

After the first blessing, John's heart began to overflow with exhilarating thoughts of the grand conclusion of all things. He wrote, "Look, he is coming with the clouds, and every eye will see him, even those who pierced him; and all the peoples of the earth will mourn because of him. So shall it be! Amen" (Rev. 1:7).

The view of Jesus Christ that John received on rocky Patmos was very different in its grandeur from the last time John observed Jesus at His ascension from the Mount of Olives.

> I turned around to see the voice that was speaking to me. And when I turned I saw seven golden lamp stands, and among the lamp stands was someone like a son of man, dressed in a robe reaching down to his feet and with a golden sash around his chest. His head and hair were white like wool, as white as snow, and his eyes were like blazing fire. His feet were like bronze glowing in a furnace, and his voice was like the sound of rushing waters. In his right hand he held seven stars, and out of his mouth came a sharp double-edged sword. His face was like the sun shining in all its brilliance.
>
> —REVELATION 1:12–16

John said when he saw the Lord, he "fell at his feet as though dead," but the Lord revived him and reassured him (Rev. 1:17).

> I am the Living One; I was dead, and behold I am alive for ever and ever! And I hold the keys of death and Hades. Write, therefore, what you have seen, what is now and what will take place later. The mystery of the seven stars that you saw in my right hand and of the seven golden lamp stands is this: The seven stars are the angels of the seven churches, and the seven lamp stands are the seven churches.
>
> —REVELATION 1:18–20

II. Letters to the Seven Churches of Asia (Rev. 2-3)

The epistles sent by John to the seven churches in Asia, located in Asia Minor, which is modern Turkey, came from the exalted Savior. He addressed them to the "angel," or pastor, of each church. The sins the Lord identified in these seven congregations illustrate the basic shortcomings that have confronted the church through the centuries since then. These letters portray the exalted Savior as a tender but firm shepherd, passionately concerned about the welfare of His flocks. Each of the letters has similar traits: a word of commendation, a word of correction, a blessing for faithfully making the modification, and a concluding word of caution.

In His incarnation, the Lord restricted the voluntary exercise of His attributes and submitted in His ministry to the word of His Father in the Old Testament, as empowered by the Holy Spirit. He labored with a commitment of steel, serving His Father's agenda in all things. Achieving that goal called for Him to see and repeat what the Father was doing and saying (John 5:17–20; 10:4–5). By that standard, He triumphed as the Son of man and the last Adam—another "Adam" will never be needed (Matt. 24:17–44; 1 Cor. 15:45).

As Jesus in the *kenosis* listened to His Father and then did what His Father said, so believers are to develop the same quality. "He who has an ear," Jesus said to each of the congregations, "let him hear what the Spirit says to the churches" (Rev. 2:7). In each of these letters, the Lord called for precisely the *kenosis* quality that characterized His own life.

A. Ephesus, a Church Missing Its First Love (Rev. 2:1–7)

The letter to Ephesus must have been especially poignant to John, because he had been the pastor there. Jesus commended the congregation for its ability to work with patience and perseverance without becoming weary. This church had even developed a system for judging if a person were an apostle and found some false pretenders to be liars. However, the Lord corrected the church for losing its first love and called on the believers there to "remember the height from which [they had] fallen." He also admonished them to "repent and do the things you did at first." Otherwise, "If you do not repent I will come to you and remove your lamp stand from its place" (Rev. 2:5). The Lord then blessed the congregation at Ephesus, saying to them, "He who has an ear, let him hear what the Spirit says to the churches. To him who overcomes I will give the right to eat from the tree of life, which is in the paradise of God" (Rev. 2:7).

B. Smyrna, a Persecuted Church (Rev. 2:8–11)

Smyrna was a suffering church. The Lord commended the believers there who served amid great tribulation and poverty and encouraged them to remain steadfast, even when it meant going to jail. Jesus spoke no word of correction to these believers. Instead, the Lord pled with them to "be faithful, even to the point of death," and He would give them "the crown of life" (Rev. 2:10). He also promised that those who overcome "will not be hurt at all by the second death" (Rev. 2:11).

He who has an ear, let him hear what the Spirit says to the churches.
—Revelation 2:11

❧ Curse the Christ and Live! ❧

Polycarp was Smyrna's most noted martyr. He was a student of the apostle John, and became bishop of the congregation at Smyrna in A.D. 96. When his life ended in A.D. 155, he had emerged as one of the most famous Christian leaders among the post-apostolic church fathers.

The Roman proconsul of Smyrna, swept up in the persecution fever in the Empire, put out an order that Polycarp, Bishop of Smyrna, was to be found, arrested, and brought to the public arena for execution.

Thousands of spectators screamed for his blood. But the proconsul had compassion because Polycarp was approaching a hundred years old. The proconsul signaled the crowd to silence. To Polycarp he said, "Curse the Christ and live!"

The crowd waited for the old man to answer. In an amazingly strong voice, he did: "Eighty and six years have I served him, and he has done me no wrong. How dare I blaspheme the name of my God and King!"

His dying words have lived through the centuries since, and continue to inspire millions.[2]

C. Pergamum, a Compromising Church (Rev. 2:12–17)

Jesus commended Pergamum for holding fast in the face of martyrdom. He also rebuked them because they had allowed the compromising spirit of Baalam to get into the church. Baalam was a seer who was willing to prophesy for money, leading Israel into gross immorality and idolatry (Num. 22–24). The doctrine of the Nicolaitans also infested Pergamum. Their doctrine may have sprung from the teaching of Nicolas of Antioch, one of the first deacons (Acts 6:5). Nicolaitans believed their liberty in Christ gave them leeway to practice sexual immorality and idolatry.

The Lord called on the people of Pergamum to listen to what the Spirit was saying to the churches and repent of these evils. If they did, Jesus promised them "hidden manna" and "a white stone with a new name written on it, known only to him who receives it" (Rev. 2:17).

In ancient Greek culture, stones served as tokens. White and black stones registered the verdicts of juries, for example; black for condemnation, and white for acquittal. For the Lord to promise these believers a white stone could suggest blessing them with great affirmation, not only for admission into His kingdom but also for entrance into the heavenly banquet at the Marriage Supper of the Lamb.[3]

D. Thyatira, a Corrupted Church (Rev. 2:18–29)

The Lord commended this church for its works, love, service, and faith, and especially its patience. A so-called prophetess with the spirit of Jezebel, however, had polluted the church at Thyatira. Like her Old Testament name-sake, she was leading the people into immorality (1 Kings 21:25–26). She also taught them to blend corruptly into the pagan culture of Asia Minor by eating things sacrificed to idols. Jesus pledged to judge this Jezebel spirit very harshly. To the faithful in Thyatira, He promised to give power over the nations, and the morning star.

He who has an ear, let him hear what the Spirit says to the churches.
—Revelation 2:29

E. Sardis, a Dead Church (Rev. 3:1–6)

Sardis had a few worthy people in the congregation who had not defiled their garments, but it was functionally a dead church. The Lord boldly called on them to repent. He also promised that those who were overcomers would be clothed in white garments and that He would not blot their names from the Book of Life.

He who has an ear, let him hear what the Spirit says to the churches.
—Revelation 3:6

F. Philadelphia, a Faithful Church (Rev. 3:7–13)

The Lord described Philadelphia as a church to whom He had given an open door for ministry that no one could shut. (*Philadelphia* means "brotherly love.") These brethren had faithfully kept the Lord's word. Even when battered by the synagogue of Satan, they had not denied Jesus' name. The Lord promised to judge those who professed they were Jews but were not, and to make each overcomer a pillar in His temple. He also pledged that He would return quickly. For each person "who overcomes," the Lord said, "I will write on him the name of my God, and the name of the city of my God, the new Jerusalem, which is coming down out of heaven from my God; and I will also write on him my new name" (Rev. 3:12).

> He who has an ear, let him hear what the Spirit says to the churches.
> —REVELATION 3:13

G. Laodicea, a Lukewarm Church (Rev. 3:14–22)

The problem with the Laodiceans was their spiritual fervor was tepid and halfhearted, neither cold nor hot. The Lord found nothing to commend in this congregation. Because they were lukewarm, Jesus was about to vomit them out of His mouth.

> You say, "I am rich; I have acquired wealth and do not need a thing." But you do not realize that you are wretched, pitiful, poor, blind and naked. I counsel you to buy from me gold refined in the fire, so you can become rich; and white clothes to wear, so you can cover your shameful nakedness; and salve to put on your eyes, so you can see. Those whom I love I rebuke and discipline. So be earnest, and repent.
> —REVELATION 3:17–19

The Lord describes Himself as being outside this church, not inside it. He is standing at the door knocking, trying to get inside His own church. "If anyone hears my voice and opens the door," the Lord pleads, "I will come in and eat with him, and he with me" (Rev. 3:20). It is a heart-rending appeal, graced with a truly glorious reward: "To him who overcomes, I will give the right to sit with me on my throne, just as I overcame and sat down with my Father on his throne. He who has an ear to hear, let him hear what the Spirit says to the churches" (Rev. 3:21–22).

These seven letters demonstrate that Jesus' passionate feelings for His church are ongoing. He did not return to His Father and then forget about His church. In every generation since the Lord's bold prophecy of the church at Caesarea Philippi, Jesus' concern has been personal and intimate and His knowledge detailed. He will never leave or forsake His church (Heb. 13:5).

In these seven letters, John witnessed this commitment in action. The Lord was engaged and passionately involved in growing, maturing and motivating believers. Even in His lofty position at the Father's right hand, Jesus has continued throughout the Church Age to have the most personal knowledge and the most ardent feelings for the welfare of each of His congregations. In fact, "He always lives to intercede for them" (Heb. 7:25).

III. Revelation, a Great Book About Worship (Rev. 4–19)

This study will focus on nine worship scenes in Revelation 4–19, each of them centered on the triumphant Savior. They take place in heaven. Woven around these panoramas are the major phases of the last days' judgments on the earth. In stark contrast, they also show evil men stubbornly giving worship to the devil and refusing to adore the triumphant Lord of the empty tomb. John's descriptions portray heavenly worship as spontaneous and enthusiastic, and at times, the adulation is loud.

A. Worship Honoring God as Creator (Rev. 4)

After receiving the Lord's letters to the seven churches of Asia, John looked upward and saw a door "standing open in heaven." The first voice he heard was like a trumpet speaking to him, saying, "Come up here, and I will show you what must take place after this" (Rev. 4:1).

1. The Setting

On the calendar of God, this trumpet blast is the summons for the Rapture of the church. The Greek term *arapagasometha* carries the meaning of "caught up" or "snatched away" (1 Thess. 4:17). This term translated into Latin as *rapio*; hence, the English transliteration, "rapture."[4] The people of God have a glorious destiny in the Lord's eternal reign. The Rapture will mark the end of the church age and begin to usher in the kingdom of Jesus Christ.

God the Father will make good on the seal of the Spirit in the hearts of His children, "guaranteeing what is to come" (2 Cor. 1:22). To that end, Jesus prayed, "Father, I want those you have given me to be with me where I am, and to see my glory, the glory you have given me because you loved me before the creation of the world" (John 17:24).

The Lord's first visit to the earth in flesh and blood spanned many events over thirty-three years. His second appearing will represent a span of time as well, beginning with the Rapture of the church. Jesus taught this catching away will happen as quickly as a flash of lightning (Matt. 24:27). Paul said the Rapture would happen in "the twinkling of an eye" (1 Cor. 15:52).

Some thirty years before John's experience on Patmos, the Holy Spirit gave the apostle Paul a revelation of the beginning moments of these end-time events, marking the grand hope of the body of Christ.

> According to the Lord's own word, we tell you that we who are still alive, who are left till the coming of the Lord, will certainly not precede those who have fallen asleep. For the Lord himself will

come down from heaven, with a loud command, with the voice of the archangel and with the trumpet call of God, and the dead in Christ will rise first. After that, we who are still alive and are left will be caught up together with them in the clouds to meet the Lord in the air. And so we will be with the Lord forever. Therefore encourage each other with these words.

—1 Thessalonians 4:15–18

This wonderful episode marks the beginning of the first resurrection, of which Jesus is the firstfruits (1 Cor. 15:20). Paul described it as unveiling a secret.

Listen, I tell you a mystery: We will not all sleep, but we will all be changed—in a flash, in the twinkling of an eye, at the last trumpet. For the trumpet will sound, the dead will be raised imperishable, and we will be changed. For the perishable must clothe itself with the imperishable, and the mortal with immortality. When the perishable has been clothed with the imperishable, and the mortal with immortality, then the saying that is written will come true: "Death has been swallowed up in victory." "Where, O death, is your victory? Where, O death, is your sting?" The sting of death is sin, and the power of sin is the law. But thanks be to God! He gives us the victory through our Lord Jesus Christ.

—1 Corinthians 15:51–57

Doctor, What Lies on the Other Side?

A terminally sick man turned to his doctor, as he was preparing to leave the examination room and said, "Doctor, I am afraid to die. Tell me what lies on the other side."

Very quietly, the doctor said, "I don't know."

"You don't know? You, a Christian man, do not know what is on the other side?"

The doctor was holding the handle of the door; on the other side of which came a sound of scratching and whining, and as he opened the door, a dog sprang into the room and leaped on him with an eager show of gladness.

Turning to the patient, the doctor said, "Did you notice my dog? He's never been in this room before. He didn't know what was inside. He knew nothing except that his master was here, and when the door opened, he sprang in without fear. I know little of what is on the other side of death, but I do know one thing…I know my Master is there and that is enough."[5]

Jesus has lovingly given us many insights into the eternal tomorrow. One day He will stand in splendor on the clouds and give His angels orders to gather His elect from "the ends of the earth to the ends of the heavens" (Mark 13:27). Every believer in the spiritual body of Christ from every generation will then be given a glorified body like that of the Lord (1 John 3:2–3). Such is the destiny that awaits the Lord's church.

Regarding when the Lord will appear, "No one knows about that day or hour, not even the angels in heaven, nor the Son" (Matt. 24:36). Only the Father has that knowledge. Therefore, this blessed hope defines a great motivation to faithful service in the body of Christ. What the Lord says to one, He says to all. His message is to "be on guard! Be alert! You do not know when that time will come" (Mark 13:33, 37; see also 1 Thess. 5:6; Matt. 24:44). The apostle John said, "Everyone who has this hope in him purifies himself, just as [Christ] is pure" (1 John 3:3; see also 2 Pet. 3:11; Matt. 25:6–7). The verb rendered "purifies" (*hagnizei* in the Greek) is in the present tense, meaning the ongoing practice of keeping oneself pure or set apart unto the Lord's character, attitude, and vision to save all people. This motivation inspires continuing alertness and holy living, and helps keep the spiritual body of Christ ready for the Lord's second advent (Luke 12:39; Matt. 25:5–6).

Apostolic Christianity finds its purest incentive in this blessed hope. Surely anyone who loves and waits for Jesus' appearing will yearn to mature in Jesus' attitude of implicit trust in His Father and will not be slovenly in loving the things the Lord loves (John 14:15; Phil. 2:5; 2 Tim. 4:7–8).

Believers who love His appearing choose to adopt the supreme passions of the Lord, embracing the two reasons Jesus gave His life. Jesus died to save lost people, and He died to establish His church as a place for His children to grow in Christlikeness (Luke 2:52; Phil. 2:12–13; 1 John 4:17). Such committed disciples have their "citizenship...in heaven," from which they "eagerly await a Savior...the Lord Jesus Christ" (Phil. 3:20–21). Peter spoke poignantly to the matter when he said, "Prepare your minds for action; be self-controlled; set your hope fully on the grace to be given you when Jesus Christ is revealed" (1 Pet. 1:13). Believers who "love His appearing" also choose to develop servant hearts like His (Matt. 20:26; John 13:4–17; 2 Tim. 4:8, KJV).

2. The Worship (Rev. 4)

"At once I was in the Spirit," John said, "and there before me was a throne in heaven" (Rev. 4:1–2). John witnessed the Lord sitting on the throne, with a "rainbow around the throne, in sight like unto an emerald" (Rev. 4:3, KJV). The twenty-four elders seated around the throne were wearing crowns of gold, representing the redeemed of all the ages. The volume of the worship was high and included "flashes of lightning, rumblings and peals of thunder" (Rev. 4:5).

In this first worship experience in heaven, John witnessed four living creatures leading the adoration around the throne. He wrote that "day and night they never stop saying: "Holy, holy, holy is the Lord God Almighty, who was, and is, and is to come" (Rev. 4:8).

Whenever the living creatures "give glory and honor and thanks to Him who sits on the throne, who lives forever and ever," the twenty-four elders fall down before Him and "lay their crowns before the throne" (Rev. 4:9–10). Their desire is to adore God as the maker of the heavens and the earth, so they say, "You are worthy, our Lord and God, to receive glory and honor and power, for you created all things, and by your will they were created and have their being" (Rev. 4:11).

The love of God brought the creation into being. All that God made in the first five creative days, He "saw that it was good" (Gen. 1:24). Then regarding man, formed on the sixth day, God said His work was "very good" (Gen. 1:31). In this majestic scene in heaven, the redeemed of the millennia enjoy the ultimate experience of worship, thanking God for His creative fiat.

B. Worship Honoring the Lamb as Redeemer (Rev. 5)

John participated in a second worship experience around the throne of God. "In the right hand of him who sat on the throne" was a "scroll with writing on both sides and sealed with seven seals" (Rev. 5:1). John heard the loud voice of a strong angel saying, "Who is worthy to break the seals and open the scroll?" (Rev. 5:2).

John's gaze was transfixed, waiting to see who would answer the summons. He quickly realized no one was stepping up to open the book of redemption or even to look at it, so John began to weep profusely. One of the twenty-four elders then told John to stop crying, because "the Lion of the tribe of Judah, the Root of David, had triumphed. He is able to open the scroll and its seven seals" (Rev. 5:5).

John said he saw "a Lamb, looking as if it had been slain" (Rev. 5:6). The Lamb took the scroll to open it, and when He did, heaven erupted in spontaneous worship. This time, the four living creatures, who had been the worship leaders in the first scene, fell down before the throne with the twenty-four elders. Each had a harp and golden bowls of incense, which are the prayers of the saints. They began to sing a new song, honoring the Lamb as Redeemer.

You are worthy to take the scroll and to open its seals, because you were slain, and with your blood you purchased men for God from every tribe and language and people and nation. You have made them to be a kingdom and priests to serve our God, and they will reign on the earth.

—REVELATION 5:9–10

The angels numbering in the millions joined in the worship. "They encircled the throne" and sang "in a loud voice" about what angels know well—the inestimable value of the Lamb.

Worthy is the Lamb who was slain to receive power and wealth and wisdom, and strength and honor and glory and praise!

—REVELATION 5:12

John then "heard every creature in heaven and on earth and under the earth and on the sea, and all that is in them, singing: 'To him who sits on the throne and to the Lamb be praise and honor and glory and power, for ever and ever!'" (Rev. 5:13). The four living creatures responded with a bold affirmation, saying, "Amen!" The twenty-four elders also joined the refrain and "fell down and worshiped him who lives forever and ever" (Rev. 5:14, KJV).

The elder at the throne of God had told John, "The Lion of the Tribe of Judah, the root of David," would open the book of redemption (Rev. 5:5). But when the scene unfolded, John saw a Lamb that looked like it had been slain actually step up to do the job (Rev. 5:6–7).

Jesus in His incarnation did not win the throne of the universe by the qualities of the roaring and ferocious king of the jungle. Instead, the Lord triumphed as the meek and lowly servant of all. Jesus is God's Lamb, and in the heart of His Father, He was slain from the foundation of the world (1 Pet. 1:20; Rev. 13:8).

A marvelous truth about the ways of God is that the Lamb is also God's lion. The motif of the lamb, in fact, is a dominant theme in the whole of Scripture. The storyline of the life and ministry of Jesus Christ is that the only lion God needed for His conquests was His Lamb, "led to the slaughter" (Isa. 53:7; John 1:29, 35–36). The helpless, defenseless Lamb, anointed by the Holy Spirit and holding resurrection power in His hands, proved far more than a match for any weapon in Satan's arsenal.

This exhilarating scene of heavenly worship also marks on Earth the beginning of the era the Lord gave the name "the Great Tribulation" (Matt. 24:21). Daniel described its catalyst as "the abomination that causes desolation" (Dan. 9:27). Jeremiah referred to it as the period of "trouble for Jacob" (Jer. 30:7). John the Revelator heard it described as the great day of "the wrath of the Lamb" (Rev. 6:16–17).

Daniel received prophetic insight in his vision of seventy weeks that give a timeline of God's dealings with Israel (Dan. 9:20–27). Each of these weeks have seven years' duration. Sixty-nine of the weeks, from "the decree to restore and rebuild Jerusalem" (483 years), accurately dated the span of years from Daniel's prophecies to the ministry of Messiah, "the anointed One" (Dan. 9:25). Since the Holy Spirit did not give Daniel a vision of the church, the church age is a gap between the sixty-ninth and the seventieth weeks. The seventieth week will follow the Rapture of the church as the seven years of the wrath of the Lamb, known as the Great Tribulation.

C. Worship Honoring the Plan of Salvation (Rev. 7:9–17)

1. The Setting

John saw the Lamb take the book of redemption and begin to open its seals. As he did, each seal represented divine wrath poured out on the earth, because the hour of judgment had arrived (Rom. 2:5–6; 2 Thess. 2:3–4; Rev. 6:17).

The call John heard to "come up here" also frames the phasing in of the Great Tribulation (Rev. 4:1). After God removes the church from the earth, the primary hindrance to the reign of Satan will be "taken out of the way" (2 Thess. 2:7–8, KJV). The devil as the "son of perdition" then will have a free hand to "exalt himself above all that is called God, or that is worshipped; so that he as God" will actually sit "in the temple of God, showing himself that he is God" (2 Thess. 2:3–4, KJV). Satan will require worship from everyone. The fact that many people will give him the adoration he seeks is an important sub-theme of the Revelation. The nation of Israel, hoping for his protection, will actually make a peace treaty with him (Dan. 9:27, TLB).

As John continued to witness the opening of the seals, he observed great earthquakes, the sun turning black like sackcloth of hair, the moon turning red like blood, the stars falling out of heaven, and the sky receding like a scroll. John realized the basic geography of the earth was being revamped as "every mountain and island...moved out of their places" (Rev. 6:12–14, KJV). Even though these cataclysmic events were taking place, many people refused to repent.

> And then pandemonium, everyone and his dog running for cover—kings, princes, generals, rich and strong, along with every commoner, slave or free. They hid in mountain caves and rocky dens, calling out to mountains and rocks, "Refuge! Hide us from the One Seated on the Throne and the wrath of the Lamb! The great Day of their wrath has come—who can stand it?"
>
> —REVELATION 6:15–17, THE MESSAGE

Although the Holy Spirit will catch the church up to heaven, the Spirit will continue to draw a great multitude on earth. Many who missed the Rapture will turn to God and even lay down their lives as a testimony during the reign of Antichrist. Then will unfold an act of God that seals 144,000 Jews. John heard the command go out in heaven, "Don't hurt the earth! Don't hurt the sea! Don't so much as hurt a tree until I've sealed the servants of our God on their foreheads!" (Rev. 7:3, THE MESSAGE).

2. The Worship

A worship experience then unfolded in heaven, having two parts. It involved the hosts of the redeemed and the hosts of the angels, and it reveals the promise of God to Abraham has been fully achieved (Gen. 15:5; 22:18; Gal. 3:16, KJV). John observed the redeemed as "a huge crowd, too huge to count. Everyone was there—all nations and tribes, all races and languages. And they were standing, dressed in white robes and waving palm branches, standing before the Throne and the Lamb" (Rev. 7:9, THE MESSAGE). John listened as this multitude cried out with a loud voice, worshiping and honoring God for the plan of redemption (Gen. 15:6; Eph. 2:1–9). They were "heartily singing: 'Salvation to our God on his Throne! Salvation to the Lamb!'" (Rev. 7:10, THE MESSAGE).

One of the elders then identified this multitude to John as those who had come "out of great tribulation" and had "washed their robes and made them white in the blood of the Lamb" (Rev. 7:14, KJV). The elder explaining this scene to John proceeded to unveil the eternal benefits that flow from the plan of salvation.

> They are before the throne of God, and serve Him day and night in His temple. And He who sits on the throne will dwell among them. They shall neither hunger anymore nor thirst anymore; the sun shall not strike them, nor any heat; for the Lamb who is in the midst of the throne will shepherd them and lead them to living fountains of waters. And God will wipe away every tear from their eyes.
> —REVELATION 7:15–17

Amid this grand adulation, the second phase of adoration unfolds: "all of the angels...around the throne...fell down on their faces before the throne and worshiped God, saying: 'Amen! Praise and glory and wisdom and thanks and honor and power and strength, be to our God for ever and ever. Amen!'" (Rev. 7:10–12).

God's holy angels cannot sing the song of redemption because they did not rebel in heaven with Lucifer (Isa. 14:9–15). For this reason, they have no need to experience the redemption of Jesus Christ (Matt. 26:53; Jude 6). They do, however, worship God, subscribing to Him "blessing, and glory and wisdom, and thanksgiving, and honor, and power, and might...forever and ever" (Rev. 7:12, KJV). They cannot celebrate the redeeming blood of the Lamb, but they can exult in the wisdom of the plan of salvation.

D. Worship Honoring King Jesus' Triumphant Reign (Rev. 11:15–18)

1. The Setting

Fierce judgments resulted on the earth when the Lamb broke each of the seven seals on the book of redemption (Rev. 6:1–8:5). Then the seven trumpet judgments followed (Rev. 8:6–11:19). "During those days men will seek death but will not find it. They will long to die, but death will elude them" (Rev. 9:6).

God raises up two witnesses during this season of judgment who prophesy for 1260 days, or three and one-half years (Rev. 11:3). These witnesses may be Enoch and Elijah, who went to heaven without tasting death (Gen. 5:24; 2 Kings 2:11; Heb. 11:5; Jude 1:7). They will be empowered with unusual anointing. Elijah called fire from heaven, and the witnesses will be able to defend themselves against their enemies with fire that will proceed out of their mouths (1 Kings 18:36). They will also have the authority of Elijah to stop rain from heaven, and like Moses, they will be able to turn water into blood and smite the earth with plagues "as often as they want" (1 Kings 17:1; Exod. 9:13; Rev. 11:6).

When the ministry of the two witnesses ends, Satan will raise up the Beast out of the bottomless pit to make war against them (Rev. 11:7–10). This Antichrist will overcome the two witnesses and kill them. For three and one-half days they will lie in the streets of Jerusalem, the city where evil men crucified Jesus. The people of the nations will see their dead bodies but do nothing to bury them. Wicked men will actually rejoice and make merry because of their deaths. They will even send gifts to one another, because the two witnesses' message of repentance and salvation will have been the cause of tormenting conviction to them (Rev. 11:7–10).

John observed as the Holy Spirit resurrected the two witnesses on the third day. In the vision, he actually saw the men stand up and noted the great fear that came on their enemies. The Holy Spirit then took the two witnesses into heaven and a massive earthquake destroyed one-tenth of Jerusalem (Rev. 11:11–14).

2. The Worship Scene

After the two witnesses had completed their ministry, John saw an angel sound a trumpet and heaven erupted in worship. This time the celebration was about the triumphant reign of Jesus Christ. The apostle John heard "loud voices in heaven which said, 'The kingdom of the world has become the kingdom of our Lord and of his Christ; and he will reign for ever and ever'" (Rev. 11:15).[6]

Again, the twenty-four elders who sat before God fell on their faces and worshiped Him, saying:

> We give thanks to you, Lord God Almighty, the One who is and who was, because you have taken your great power and have begun to reign. The nations were angry; and your wrath has come. The time has come for judging the dead, and for rewarding your servants the prophets and your saints and those who reverence your name, both small and great—and for destroying those who destroy the earth.
>
> —REVELATION 11:17–18

At His crucifixion, the Lord explained His kingdom to Pilate.

> Jesus said, "My kingdom is not of this world. If it were, my servants would fight to prevent my arrest by the Jews. But now my kingdom is from another place." "You are a king, then!" said Pilate. Jesus answered, "You are right in saying I am a king. In fact, for this reason I was born, and for this I came into the world, to testify to the truth. Everyone on the side of truth listens to me."
>
> —JOHN 18:36–37

Jesus decisively won the victory at Calvary, but the beginning of His royal dominion over all was still in the future. This explains why, when the Lord went back to heaven, His Father told him, "Sit at my right hand until I make your enemies a footstool for your feet" (Ps. 110:1; Luke 20:42–43).

This panorama showed the arrival of the time when Jesus' enemies have become His footstool. "Everyone on the side of truth listens to me," Jesus said to Pilate at His trial (John 18:37). Pilate was not one of those who listened to Jesus, but the worship in heaven demonstrates that millions through the centuries have hung on His every word, and now they are rewarded.

What an anthem!

> The kingdom of this world has become the kingdom of our Lord and of his Christ, and he will reign forever and ever.
>
> —REVELATION 11:15

E. Worship Honoring Jesus' Triumph Over Satan (Rev. 12:10–12)

1. *The Setting*

The apostle John witnessed "a great and wondrous sign" that appeared in heaven (Rev. 12:1). The woman and the dragon in this scene are a snapshot of Satan's struggle for supremacy that began with Lucifer's rebellion in heaven. In that battle, the archangel Michael and his angels prevailed against the dragon. Michael cast out of heaven that ancient serpent, Satan, who landed on the earth (Rev. 12:7–9; Isa. 14:9–15; Ezek. 28:17). Jesus gave testimony that He watched "Satan fall like lightning from heaven" (Luke 10:18). As the accuser of the brethren "before God day and night," Satan has been at war ever since (Rev. 12:10). The primary battlefields have not been the mountains, the plains, or the high seas, but the hearts of men (Eph. 6:12; Jer. 31:33).

Mary gave birth to the baby, the Messiah that "will rule all the nations with an iron scepter" (Rev. 12:5). The dragon opposed the male child and tried to destroy Him, but God protected and preserved His Son (Rev. 12:13–17). The result was the pregnant woman and her baby prevailed. The red dragon did not devour the infant (Matt. 2:1–18).

Moses used vivid language to record the first messianic promise in the Bible, wording that indicates the intensity of the struggle: "I will put enmity between you and the woman, and between your offspring and hers; he will crush your head, and you will strike his heel" (Gen. 3:15). The colossal struggle continued throughout Jesus' ministry. At His crucifixion, the accuser surely thought Jesus would come down from the cross because of the horrendous pain and suffering and hand him the victory, but Satan was soundly defeated at Calvary. Then, Jesus "made a public spectacle" of the devil when He arose from the dead (Col. 2:15).

2. *The Worship Scene*

This understanding serves as the backdrop for the loud voice in heaven that the apostle John heard exulting thunderously the triumph of Jesus Christ over Satan.

> Now have come the salvation and the power and the kingdom of our God, and the authority of his Christ. For the accuser of our brothers, who accuses them before our God day and night, has been hurled down. They overcame him by the blood of the Lamb and by the word of their testimony; they did not love their lives so much as to shrink from death. Therefore rejoice, you heavens and you who dwell in them!

But woe to the earth and the sea, because the devil has gone down to you! He is filled with fury, because he knows that his time is short.

—REVELATION 12:10–12

F. Worship of the 144,000, Singing the New Song (Rev. 14:1–5)

1. The Setting

The Antichrist, at the midpoint of the seven years of the Great Tribulation, will break his peace treaty with Israel (Dan. 9:24–27; Rev. 13:7–8). He will try to destroy the Jews and anyone else refusing to give him worship. Antichrist's control will be total, and he will institute the mark of the Beast. His sign ("666") will be stamped in the hand or forehead of every person on Earth (Rev. 13:16–18). Without that mark, no one will be able to buy or sell. The Antichrist will demonstrate great but deceptive signs, like calling fire from heaven in full view of all men. He will even install the image of the Beast in the rebuilt temple in Jerusalem and have the power to give life to the image so that it will speak (Rev. 13:11–18).

2. The Worship Scene

"Then I looked," John said, "and there before me was the Lamb, standing on Mount Zion, and with him the 144,000 who had His name and his Father's name written in their foreheads" (Rev. 14:1; see also 7:1–8). These are Jewish "servants of God," twelve thousand from each tribe. These 144,000 witnesses worshiped God to the accompaniment of harps. John heard:

> …a sound from heaven like the roar of rushing waters and like a loud peal of thunder. The sound I heard was like that of harpists playing their harps. And they sang a new song before the throne and before the four living creatures and the elders. No one could learn the song except the 144,000 who had been redeemed from the earth. These are those who did not defile themselves with women, for they kept themselves pure. They follow the Lamb wherever he goes. They were purchased from among men and offered as firstfruits to God and the Lamb. No lie was found in their mouths; they are blameless.
>
> —REVELATION 14:2–5

Then John witnessed a marvelous demonstration of the grace of God, extended to the people living on the earth.

> I saw another angel flying in midair, and he had the eternal gospel to proclaim to those who live on the earth—to every nation, tribe, language and people. He said in a loud voice, "Fear God and give

him glory, because the hour of his judgment has come. Worship him
who made the heavens, the earth, the sea and the springs of water."

—REVELATION 14:6–7

G. Worship Honoring the Song of Moses and the Lamb (Rev. 15:1–8)

1. *The Setting*

"I saw in heaven another great wonder and marvelous sign," said the apostle
John (Rev. 15:1). In this scene, he observed seven angels with the seven last
plagues that complete the wrath of God.

2. *The Worship*

John witnessed what appeared to him as a crystal sea mixed with fire.
Standing beside the sea of glass were all who "had been victorious over the
beast and his image and over the number of his name" (Rev. 15:2). They had
harps given to them by God, and they sang "the song of Moses the servant of
God and the song of the Lamb: 'Great and marvelous are your deeds, Lord
God Almighty. Just and true are your ways, King of the ages. Who will not
fear you, O Lord, and bring glory to your name? For you alone are holy. All
nations will come and worship before you, for your righteous acts have been
revealed'" (Rev. 15:3–4).

Moses was the great emancipator and lawgiver who overcame everything
the Egyptian pharaoh threw at the budding Hebrew nation. When the exodus
had just begun, for example, the Egyptian commanders surely thought Israel
was easy prey. Pharaoh had equipped his military with fast chariots and
trained horsemen, supported by foot soldiers. The great lesson of history is
that Pharaoh woefully miscalculated "the Lord as a warrior" (Exod. 15:3–4).

The Song of Moses on the victory side of the Red Sea is an Old Testament
epic, among the grandest in all literature.

> I will sing to the LORD, for he is highly exalted. The horse and its
> rider he has hurled into the sea. The LORD is my strength and my
> song; he has become my salvation. He is my God, and I will praise
> him, my father's God, and I will exalt him. The LORD is a warrior;
> the LORD is his name. Pharaoh's chariots and his army he has hurled
> into the sea. The best of Pharaoh's officers are drowned in the Red
> Sea. The deep waters have covered them; they sank to the depths
> like a stone.
>
> —EXODUS 15:1–5

They also sang "the song of the Lamb" (Rev. 15:3). When Moses and Elijah
talked with Jesus at His transfiguration, their topic was Jesus' "departure

which he was about to bring to fulfillment in Jerusalem" (Luke 9:31). The Greek term for "departure" is *exodon,* transliterated into English as *exodus.* Jesus, Moses, and Elijah talked about the exodus, the mass departure of the people of God from Earth to heaven that would result from Jesus' atonement at the cross.

This study has already noted that Satan threw everything in his arsenal at Jesus to break His bond of implicit trust in His Father. The devil fully intended to stop the exodus Jesus planned to lead from Mount Calvary. Moses prevailed in a great victory at the Red Sea, and Jesus' triumph was far greater at "the Place of the Skull" (Mark 15:22). The song of Moses and the Lamb in heaven honors both of these epic triumphs.

H. The Song of the Angel, Defending the Judgments of God (Rev. 16:1–7)

1. The Setting

As the revelation has unfolded, the Lord has poured out the full cup of His wrath on the earth in the judgments of the seals, the trumpets, and "the seven last plagues" (Rev. 6:1; 8:6; 15:1). Then the bowls of His wrath followed (Rev. 16:1).

Revelation is indeed a great book about worship that also offers insight into the character of God, which requires Him to judge the earth. The mighty acts of God associated with pouring out the seven bowls sharply focus the point.

> The first angel went and poured out his bowl on the land, and ugly and painful sores broke out on the people who had the mark of the beast and worshiped his image. The second angel poured out his bowl on the sea, and it turned into blood like that of a dead man, and every living thing in the sea died. The third angel poured out his bowl on the rivers and springs of water, and they became blood.
> —Revelation 16:2–4

The judgments of God raise a penetrating question about the character of God: is God fair? Thinking people will inevitably ask the question amid all of these fearsome judgments. Has the Lord been too hard on evil men and on the earth where they live? Can the fairness of His acts of judgment and the justice He metes out be called into question?

2. The Worship Scene

The angel of the third bowl, in charge of the waters hit so hard by the mighty acts of God, offered worship to God by actually defending God's fairness and justice. (See Romans 3:4; Psalm 51:4; and Ezekiel 18 for more study on the fairness of God.)

John said he "heard the angel in charge of the waters" say in powerful worship:

> You are just in these judgments, you who are and who were, the Holy One, because you have so judged; for they have shed the blood of your saints and prophets, and you have given them blood to drink as they deserve." And I heard the altar respond: "Yes, Lord God Almighty, true and just are your judgments."
> —REVELATION 16:5–7

I. Worship at the Wedding of the Lamb and His Bride (Rev. 19:1–10)

1. The Setting

The Bible, from Genesis to Revelation, is the story of a courtship. As Eliezar accepted Abraham's commission and went searching for a bride for his lord Isaac, so the Holy Spirit is on a mission (Gen. 24:1–4; John 14:26). He is looking for a bride for God's dear Son, Jesus Christ (Eph. 5:27). Holy matrimony on Earth points to the mystical union between Christ and His bride. Paul spoke of it as a profound mystery.

> Husbands, love your wives, just as Christ loved the church and gave himself up for her to make her holy, cleansing her by the washing with water through the word, and to present her to himself as a radiant church, without stain or wrinkle or any other blemish, but holy and blameless. After all, no one ever hated his own body, but he feeds and cares for it, just as Christ does the church—for we are members of his body. 'For this reason a man will leave his father and mother and be united to his wife, and the two will become one flesh.' This is a profound mystery—but I am talking about Christ and the church.
> —EPHESIANS 5:25–32

King Solomon penned the Song of Solomon to describe a maiden's pure, spontaneous love in response to Solomon's courtship. The Song of Solomon is indeed a majestic, poetic drama. However, the Song is much more than beautiful poetry between young lovers. It is also an allegory that speaks to the deep heartthrob of the children of God to spend eternity with the Lord Jesus Christ.

> Listen! My lover! Look! Here he comes, leaping across the mountains, bounding over the hills. My lover is like a gazelle or a young stag. Look! There he stands behind our wall, gazing through the windows, peering through the lattice. My lover spoke and said to me, "Arise, my darling, my beautiful one, and come with me. . . . The fig tree

forms its early fruit; the blossoming vines spread their fragrance. Arise, come, my darling; my beautiful one, come with me."
—SONG OF SOLOMON 2:8–10, 13

The message of the gospel is that sin has paralyzed all men, and everyone desperately needs the love of God. Jesus came to our rescue, pouring bountiful adoration on us and capturing our hearts (Ps. 139:5; Song of Sol. 4:9; Eph. 1:7–8; 1 John 3:1). The good news is all about how Jesus lifted us out of the wheelchair that bound us. He then placed us "like a seal over [His] heart, like a seal on [His] arm" (Song of Sol. 8:6). Our response to His abundant love must be to welcome His redeeming and sanctifying grace. Then we can accept that we truly are His beloved and make our choice to position Him as a seal over our hearts.

～ The Bright Eyes of a Bridegroom's Love ～

"I felt awkward as my girlfriends strained to shift my paralyzed body into a cumbersome wedding gown," said Joni Eareckson Tada, who is a paralyzed quadriplegic. "No amount of corseting and binding my body gave me a perfect shape. The dress just didn't fit well.

"Then, as I was wheeling into the church, I glanced down and noticed that I'd accidentally run over the hem of my dress, leaving a greasy tire mark.

"My paralyzed hands couldn't hold the bouquet of daisies that lay off-center on my lap. And my chair, though decorated for the wedding, was still a big, clunky gray machine with belts, gears, and ball bearings. I certainly didn't feel like the picture-perfect bride in a bridal magazine.

"I inched my chair closer to the last pew to catch a glimpse of Ken in front. There he was, standing tall and stately in his formal attire. I saw him looking for me, craning his neck to look up the aisle. My face flushed, and I suddenly couldn't wait to be with him. I had seen my beloved. The love in Ken's face had washed away all my feelings of unworthiness. I was his pure and perfect bride.

"How easy it is for us to think that we're utterly unlovely, especially to someone as lovely as Christ. But he loves us with the bright eyes of a Bridegroom's love and cannot wait for the day we are united with him forever."[7]

---

2. The Worship Scene

The scene in heaven John the Revelator saw next was not merely a poetic allegory of a beautiful wedding. John is writing about the real thing. He witnessed the panorama change to an exuberant and festive wedding. John watched in awe as a magnificent vista unveiled before him, painting a breathtaking portrait of the eternal reward of the Lord's church.

In the ancient counsels of the Godhead, the Trinity decided that in Jesus' kingdom the church would be His bride. He would redeem her with His own blood and transform her into the children of God. Jesus really did prove His great love for His church when He "gave Himself up for her" (Eph. 5:25; Acts 20:28). Even before He dragged His cross up Calvary, He told His disciples He was leaving this world to build her a house and promised, "I will come back and take you to be with me" (John 14:2–3).

The Lord Jesus has also granted her the status of co-heir with Himself (Rom. 8:17). His ultimate plan has always been to present her to himself as "a glorious church, not having spot, or wrinkle, or any such thing," a bride who is "holy and blameless" (Eph. 5:27, KJV).

In this setting, the consummation of her grand destiny is at hand.

> After this I heard what sounded like the roar of a great multitude in heaven shouting: "Hallelujah! Salvation and glory and power belong to our God, for true and just are his judgments. He has condemned the great prostitute who corrupted the earth by her adulteries. He has avenged on her the blood of his servants." And again they shouted: "Hallelujah! The smoke from her goes up for ever and ever." The twenty-four elders and the four living creatures fell down and worshiped God, who was seated on the throne. And they cried: "Amen, Hallelujah!" Then a voice came from the throne, saying: "Praise our God, all you his servants, you who fear him, both small and great!" Then I heard what sounded like a great multitude, like the roar of rushing waters and like loud peals of thunder, shouting: "Hallelujah! For our Lord God Almighty reigns. Let us rejoice and be glad and give him glory! For the wedding of the Lamb has come, and his bride has made herself ready. Fine linen, bright and clean, was given her to wear." (Fine linen stands for the righteous acts of the saints.) Then the angel said to me, "Write: Blessed are those who are invited to the wedding supper of the Lamb!" And he added, "These are the true words of God."
> —REVELATION 19:1–9

The Wedding of the Lamb and His bride totally captivated John, as did the Marriage Supper of the Lamb that followed. John was so overwhelmed he actually fell at the feet of the messenger who showed him the grand landscape and offered him worship.

"Do not do it!" his instructor responded. "I am a fellow servant with you and with your brothers who hold to the testimony of Jesus. Worship God! For the testimony of Jesus is the spirit of prophecy" (Rev. 19:10).

J. Summary

These nine majestic and triumphant worship scenes began with the great host of the raptured saints singing around the throne of God, giving honor to the Lord, who is the creator and sustainer of all. They conclude with the Wedding of the Lamb, followed by the Marriage Supper of the Lamb.

The grand destiny of the Lord's church has arrived. She is the altogether lovely bride of Jesus Christ, the ruling monarch of the ages. Little wonder Paul said, "Christ loved the church and gave himself for her" (Eph. 5:25; Acts 20:28).

These vistas have been enthusiastic, heartfelt, exhilarating, loud, and colored with spontaneity. And, as these panoramas have unfolded, Jesus has remained the Servant of His Father's plan, "because of his great love for us" (Eph. 2:4).

IV. The Battle of Armageddon (Rev. 19:11–20:10)

John saw the fourth angel pour out his bowl on the sun, and it received power to scorch men with fire. The fifth angel emptied his wrath on the throne of the Beast, and the Antichrist's kingdom plunged into darkness. "Men gnawed their tongues in agony and cursed the God of heaven because of their pain and their sores, but they refused to repent of what they had done" (Rev. 16:10–12). The sixth angel emptied his bowl on the great river Euphrates, and the river dried up to prepare the way for the kings from the East.

Then John witnessed three evil spirits that were demons performing miraculous signs. They went out to the kings of the whole world and gathered them for battle "to the place that in Hebrew is called Armageddon" (Rev. 16:13–16).

In this battle, God will use as His weapons of war flashes of lightning, rumblings, peals of thunder, the most severe earthquake in all history, and huge hailstones "of about a hundred pounds" (Rev. 16:17–21). Armageddon will result in so much loss of life, the blood will flow several feet deep, rising up to the horses bridles, for about 180 miles (Rev. 14:20, NLT).

Zechariah is the Old Testament prophet who spoke with the most specificity about this conflagration. He comprehended the part it will play as the grand design of God moves toward a new heaven and a new earth.

I will gather all the nations to Jerusalem to fight against it; the city will be captured, the houses ransacked, and the women raped. Half of the city will go into exile, but the rest of the people will not be taken from the city. Then the LORD will go out and fight against those nations, as he fights in the day of battle. On that day his feet will stand on the Mount of Olives, east of Jerusalem, and the Mount of Olives will be split in two from east to west, forming a great valley, with half of the mountain moving north and half moving south. You will flee by my mountain valley, for it will extend to Azel. You will flee as you fled from the earthquake in the days of Uzziah king of Judah. Then the LORD my God will come, and all the holy ones with him. On that day there will be no light, no cold or frost. It will be a unique day, without daytime or nighttime—a day known to the LORD. When evening comes, there will be light. On that day living water will flow out from Jerusalem, half to the eastern sea and half to the western sea, in summer and in winter. The LORD will be king over the whole earth. On that day there will be one LORD, and his name the only name.

—ZECHARIAH 14:2–9

This manifestation of the Lord's sovereign power will actually alter the geography of Israel. A river will open up that will stream from Jerusalem in two directions—to the Mediterranean and to the Dead Sea, so that "living water will flow out from Jerusalem" (Zech. 14:8).

The apostle John also gave his own description:

I saw heaven standing open and there before me was a white horse, whose rider is called Faithful and True. With justice he judges and makes war. His eyes are like blazing fire, and on his head are many crowns. He has a name written on him that no one knows but he himself. He is dressed in a robe dipped in blood, and his name is the Word of God. The armies of heaven were following him, riding on white horses and dressed in fine linen, white and clean. Out of his mouth comes a sharp sword with which to strike down the nations. "He will rule them with an iron scepter." He treads the winepress of the fury of the wrath of God Almighty. On his robe and on his thigh he has this name written: KING OF KINGS AND LORD OF LORDS. And I saw an angel standing in the sun, who cried in a loud voice to all the birds flying in midair, "Come, gather together for the great supper of God, so that you may eat the flesh of kings, generals, and mighty men, of horses and their riders, and the flesh of all people, free and slave, small and great." Then I saw the beast and the kings of the earth and their armies gathered together to make war against the rider on the horse and his army. But the beast was captured, and with him the false prophet who had performed the miraculous signs on his behalf. With these signs he had deluded those who had received the mark of the beast and worshiped his image. The two of them were thrown alive into the fiery lake of burning sulfur. The rest of them were killed with the sword that came out of the mouth of the rider on the horse, and all the birds gorged themselves on their flesh.

—Revelation 19:11–21

V. The Millennial Reign of Christ

Phase one of the Lord's second coming began with Jesus' personal appearance in the sky as a thief in the night to Rapture the church (1 Thess. 4:17). The final segment will be the Battle of Armageddon that will consummate the second coming of Jesus Christ to the earth. At the time of this great battle, Jesus will appear "with the clouds, and every eye will see him, even those who pierced him; and all the peoples of the earth will mourn because of him" (Rev. 1:7). At Jesus' first appearing, He will snatch away His bride, which is the church. At His second manifestation, He will set His feet again "on the Mount of Olives, east of Jerusalem" (Zech. 14:4). The hosts of the saints will accompany Him as He defeats the Antichrist and his armies. Then, as the kingdom of Jesus Christ continues to unfold, the Lord Jesus will launch His millennial reign, ruling from Jerusalem (Rev. 20:1–3).

Jesus Christ truly is "the ending" (Rev. 1:8, kjv).

A. A Literal Government

The millennial reign will be a literal government on the earth, led by King Jesus for one thousand years. The nation of Israel will fully turn to the Lord at that time, accepting Him as the legitimate ruler on David's throne. This is when the Jews will ask Jesus, "What are these wounds in your hands?" He will answer that His scars came from "the house of [his] friends" (Zech. 13:6). In that grand day, the Promised Land will belong to Israel as an eternal inheritance (Ezek. 20:33–38; Amos 9:14–15; Jer. 23:3–8; Isa. 66:8–10). What a revival it will be when Israel, with sincerity, says, "Surely this is our God. We trusted in him and he saved us. This is the Lord, we trusted in him; let us rejoice and be glad in his salvation" (Isa. 25:9).

It will also be the time of the "regeneration when the Son of Man shall sit in the throne of his glory." His apostles will be positioned with Him "on twelve thrones, judging the twelve tribes of Israel" (Matt. 19:28, kjv). His reign of righteousness will be a government in which Jews and Gentiles will combine to worship the Lamb. All nations will flow into His kingdom.

B. A Time of Great Peace

In the early part of His reign, the Lord will order the armaments from Antichrist's armies melted down and converted to peaceful uses. "They shall beat their swords into plowshares and their spears into pruning hooks: nation shall not lift up sword against nation, neither shall they learn war any more" (Isa. 2:4, KJV). In Christ's government, the delight of all men will be to go to the house of the Lord to learn the ways of Him who rules from Mount Zion.

C. The Redemption of Nature

In the Fall of man in Eden, God told Adam the ground would be cursed for man's sake (Gen. 3:17). The sacrifice of Jesus at Calvary, dripping His blood to the ground, made provision for the ultimate redemption of the earth. This lifting of the curse of sin from nature will take place at the beginning of Christ's millennial reign. The vicious brutality in the natural order will then end. "The creation itself," Paul said, "will be liberated from its bondage to decay and brought into the glorious freedom of the children of God" (Rom. 8:21–23).

> The wolf will live with the lamb, the leopard will lie down with the goat, the calf and the lion and the yearling together; and a little child will lead them. The cow will feed with the bear, their young will lie down together, and the lion will eat straw like the ox. The infant will play near the hole of the cobra, and the young child put his hand into the viper's nest. They will neither harm nor destroy on all my holy mountain, for the earth will be full of the knowledge of the LORD as the waters cover the sea.
>
> —ISAIAH 11:6–9

D. A Time of Expanded Lifespans

The age of the mortals in that glorious day will increase.

> Never again will there be in it an infant who lives but a few days, or an old man who does not live out his years; he who dies at a hundred will be thought a mere youth; he who fails to reach a hundred will be considered accursed.
>
> —ISAIAH 65:20

E. An Era of Honest Commerce

It will be a time of booming, but honest, business transactions.

They will build houses and dwell in them; they will plant vineyards and eat their fruit. No longer will they build houses and others live in them, or plant and others eat. For as the days of a tree, so will be the days of my people; my chosen ones will long enjoy the works of their hands. They will not toil in vain or bear children doomed to misfortune; for they will be a people blessed by the LORD, they and their descendants with them. Before they call I will answer; while they are still speaking I will hear.

—ISAIAH 65:21–24

Agriculture will flourish to the point "the reaper will be overtaken by the plowman and the planter by the one treading grapes. New wine will drip from the mountains and flow from all the hills" (Amos 9:13).

F. The Ethical Morality of Christ's Reign

The Holy Spirit also gave Zechariah the privilege to pen a vivid description of the morality that will characterize the millennial reign of Christ.

In that day shall there be upon the bells of the horses, HOLINESS UNTO THE LORD; and the pots in the LORD's house shall be like the bowls before the altar: Yes, every pot in Jerusalem and in Judah shall be holiness unto the LORD of hosts.

—ZECHARIAH 14:20–21, KJV

This reign of ethical spotlessness will emanate from the attributes of the Godhead. The Lord's holiness will penetrate economics and politics, as well as the religious and social orders. The Antichrist cursed the earth with condemnation, sickness, disease, and death. David's greater Son cures the curse with regeneration, peace, and prosperity, as proven by His resurrection from the dead (John 10:10; Acts 17:31).

Oh, to live and "reign with [Christ] for a thousand years" (Rev. 20:6).

VI. Rolling Up the Scroll of Father Time

A. The Battle of Gog and Magog (Rev. 20:7–10)

By Revelation 20 in the account of the End Times, God and the Lamb have almost rolled up the scroll of Father Time.

Almost.

When the thousand years of Christ's millennial reign are over, the Lord will loose the devil from the Abyss and he will go out one more time to deceive the nations. Satan will be successful for the last time at gathering a multi-national army, like "the sand of the seashore" (Rev. 20:7–8). This military force will march against the people of God, headquartered at Jerusalem. It will be the last battle in the era of time, before God ushers in the eternal ages. This invasion of Israel and the battle that follows have the name Gog and Magog.

In the table of nations in Genesis 10, Magog was the second of the seven sons of Japheth (Gen. 10:2.) The chief combatants in this confederation appear to be "Gog and Magog" (Russia) and "Persia" (Iran), joined by a large number of other nations (Rev. 20:8; Ezek. 38:2, 5–6). Ezekiel described them as "a great hoard, a mighty army" from "many nations" that will come from "their place in the far north" (Ezek. 38:15).

The Lord will wage this last of all battles "as He fights" with fire that will fall out of heaven, as well as torrents of rain, hailstones, and burning sulfur (Zech. 14:3; Ezek. 38:22; Rev. 20:9). This time God will arrest Satan and throw him into the lake of fire, where the Beast and the false prophet were cast after the battle of Armageddon (Rev. 20:10).

Then will follow the Great White Throne Judgment, which is the final judgment of the persistently wicked.

> I saw the dead, great and small, standing before the throne, and books were opened. Another book was opened, which is the book of life. The dead were judged according to what they had done as recorded in the books. The sea gave up the dead that were in it, and death and Hades gave up the dead that were in them, and each person was judged according to what he had done. Then death and Hades were thrown into the lake of fire. The lake of fire is the second death. If anyone's name was not found written in the book of life, he was thrown into the lake of fire.
> —Revelation 20:12–15

The Lord blessed John the Revelator to see what both Isaiah and Paul had prophesied. "As surely as I live," says the Lord, "every knee will bow before me; every tongue will confess to God" (Rom. 14:11–12; Isa. 45:23; Phil. 2:10–11).

⤚ There Must Be Some Mistake! ⤙

Several years ago, a man of wealth invited professional singer Ruthanna Metzgar to perform at his wedding. According to the invitation, the reception would follow on the top two floors of Seattle's Columbia Tower, the Northwest's tallest skyscraper.

After the wedding she and her husband went over to the reception. Waiters in tuxedos offered luscious hors d'oeuvres and exotic beverages.

The bride and groom approached a beautiful glass and grass staircase that led to the top floor, followed by their guests.

At the top of the stairs, a maitre d' with a bound book greeted the guests outside the doors.

"May I have your name, please?"

"I am Ruthanna Metzgar and this is my husband, Roy."

He searched the M's. "I'm not finding it. Would you spell it please?"

Ruthanna spelled her name slowly. After searching the book, the maitre d' looked up and said, "I'm sorry, but your name isn't here."

"There must be some mistake," Ruthanna replied. "I'm the singer. I sang for this wedding!"

"It doesn't matter who you are or what you did. Without your name in the book you cannot attend the banquet." With that he motioned to a waiter and said, "Show these people to the service elevator, please."

The Metzgars followed the waiter past beautifully decorated tables laden with shrimp, whole smoked salmon, and magnificent carved ice sculptures. Adjacent to the banquet area, an orchestra was preparing to perform, the musicians all dressed in dazzling white tuxedos.

The waiter ushered Ruthanna and Roy into the service elevator, and pushed "G" for the parking garage.

After locating their car and driving several miles in silence, Roy reached over and put his hand on Ruthanna's arm. "Sweetheart, what happened?"

"When the invitation arrived, I was busy. I never bothered to RSVP. Besides, I was the singer. Surely I could go to the reception without returning the RSVP!"[8]

B. Jesus, the Eternal Champion

This study of our awesome Lord has shown that Jesus' triumph happened because He emptied Himself of the voluntary and independent exercise of the prerogatives of His deity and submitted to His Father. Jesus served His Father's agenda with implicit trust, as superintended by the Holy Spirit. The apostle Peter summarized the plan of action in this way: "God anointed Jesus of Nazareth with the Holy Spirit and power…He went around doing good and healing all who were under the power of the devil, because God was with him" (Acts 10:38). The reward for such faithful service was "God exalted him to the highest place and gave him the name that is above every name" (Phil. 2:9).

Jesus' accomplishments, as outlined in the Sacred Canon, are indeed stunning. Every step of the way, He has moved from victory to victory, time after time. He is the captain of the Lord's hosts who has never known defeat (Josh. 5:14–15). Even His death on Mount Calvary, which looked like such utter failure, turned out to be His most spectacular success. He clearly deserves the title King of kings and Lord of lords (Rev. 19:16; 1 Tim. 6:11–16).

Jesus' success was not His alone, however. His triumph also belonged to His Father. In the interrelationships of the Tri-unity of God, the Father, the Son, and the Spirit work in the harmony of mutual interdependence to complete the plan of salvation. Even today, that concord continues as we long for His appearing, which will embrace the consummation of all things (2 Tim. 4:1, 8; 2 Pet. 3:13; Rev. 21:1).

The apostle Paul, in his great Christological statement in Philippians 2, made the profound statement that the honor for all that Jesus accomplished actually goes to His Father.

> At the name of Jesus every knee should bow, in heaven and on earth and under the earth, and every tongue confess that Jesus Christ is Lord, to the glory of God the Father.
>
> —PHILIPPIANS 2:10–11

In this context, John 3:16 becomes the greatest statement of love in relationship of all time: "God so loved the world that he gave his one and only Son, that whoever believes in him shall not perish but have eternal life." No student should miss how active and involved and how totally supportive and engaged God the Father and the Holy Spirit have always been in the ministry of Jesus Christ, God's Son.

Without question, the revelation in the Bible unveils much about the God who is One (Deut. 6:4). The Trinitarian nature of this one God is a biblical revelation, too, yet it remains wrapped in the mystery of unrevealed truth. We do know, for example, Christ Jesus would not have been able to achieve the Incarnation, which climaxed with His crucifixion and resurrection, apart from the complete backing He enjoyed in His unity with His Father (John 10:30; 17:11; 17:22; 1 Cor. 15:21). The Son of man was very careful throughout His ministry, in fact, not to grasp even one time for His deity and act independently of His Father and of the Holy Spirit.

The implications of this truth apply to all God's children. The God who is One is fully engaged on our side, too, encouraging us to go forward in implicit trust, until we gain the crown of life (Luke 12:32; John 14:16; 2 Tim. 4:7–8; Jude 1:24–25; Rev. 2:10).

The apostle Paul made a great affirmation about the relationship between the Father and His Son in his first letter to the church at Corinth that can now begin to come into focus (Ephesians 1:22 and Hebrews 2:8).

Then the end will come, when he hands over the kingdom to God the Father after he has destroyed all dominion, authority and power. For he must reign until he has put all his enemies under his feet. The last enemy to be destroyed is death. For he "has put everything under his feet." Now when it says that "everything" has been put under him, it is clear that this does not include God himself, who put everything under Christ.

—1 CORINTHIANS. 15:24–27

This statement is encased in the mystery of undisclosed revelation. The heavenly classroom in the ages to come will be required to fathom the depths of the relationships and roles of the three persons in the Tri-unity of the God who is One (Matt. 28:19; Eph. 2:7; Deut. 6:4). Yet, while we see through a glass darkly, this passage helps to comprehend why Paul told his Philippian readers the glory for Jesus' achievements really does belong "to…God the Father" (Phil. 2:11; 1 Cor. 13:12).

C. A New Heaven and Earth (Rev. 21–22)

1. The Passing Away of the Present Order

"Heaven and earth will pass away," Jesus taught, "but my words will never pass away" (Luke 21:33). Such will be the radical change in the very nature of the cosmos that John saw "a new heaven and a new earth: for the first heaven and the first earth had passed away; and there was no longer any sea" (Rev. 21:1).

By Revelation 21, the Rapture is past and the exhilarating scenes of worship in heaven have unfolded. The Great Tribulation is over and the Marriage Supper of the Lamb has consummated the wedding of the heavenly bridegroom and His bride. The church, about which Jesus feels so passionately, has achieved her destiny. The Lamb has won at Calvary, at Armageddon, and at Gog and Magog. The Lord has judged Satan, the Beast, and the false prophet—the devil's counterfeit trinity—and all of the persistently wicked, and cast them into hell.

God has finished rolling up the scroll of Father Time. As the Servant of His Father's plan for the salvation of all people, Jesus has completed the agenda given to Him in the eternal councils of the Trinity. God's Son has achieved it all without changing the plan one time or even fine-tuning it. Jesus has truly been the faithful Servant. He perfectly watched and listened to the Father, doing what He heard and saw. He never broke faith with His Father, not even one time (Isa. 50:4–9; John 8:28).

What a Savior!

2. The New Jerusalem

The scene that unfolds next reveals a new heaven and new Earth.

John saw "the holy city, the new Jerusalem, coming down out of heaven from God, prepared as a bride beautifully dressed for her husband" (Rev. 21:2). Death, sorrow, crying, and pain are in the past.

"I am making everything new," John heard God say. This Lion-Lamb is the beginning and the ending, who gives to the thirsty "the fountain of the water of life freely" (Rev. 21:5–6, KJV).

The city is fifteen hundred miles foursquare with twelve gates, each gate a solid pearl. The walls are of jasper; and streets of pure gold. It is a city with foundations of precious stones. The splendor of the nations will flow into it, and its gates never shut. Nothing will ever defile that city, and only those whose names "are written in the Lamb's book of life" will populate it (Rev. 21). The pure river of the water of life, clear as crystal, flows out from the throne of God and of the Lamb. The tree of life also grows beside the river, bearing twelve different fruits, with one of the twelve ripening every month. The leaves of the tree will heal the nations. The Lamb and His servants will live together in love, face to face, and His name will be in their foreheads throughout eternity (Rev. 22:4).

Hence, the qualities of the Lamb will ultimately emerge as the values of the New Jerusalem. This is so true John used two word pictures, *temple* and *sunlight*, to focus the triumphant glory deserved by the virtues of the Lamb. "I saw no *temple* in it," John wrote, "for the Lord God the Almighty and the Lamb are its temple. And the city has no need of the *sun* or of the moon to shine on it, for the glory of God has illumined it, and its lamp is the Lamb" (Rev. 21:22–24, NAS, emphasis added).

What a picture! The lowly servant qualities that redeemed the world will be glorified throughout eternity, to the point that their glow will be the sunlight in the New Jerusalem and frame the worship in that celestial "city which has foundations, whose builder and maker is God" (Heb. 11:10). Included in the portrait are:

- The humble birth of the God–man from the womb of the Virgin Mary (Matt. 1:18–22; Phil. 2:7–8)
- The kenosis strategy by which the Lord emptied Himself of the independent exercise of His divine attributes in His true manhood, surrendering them to His Father and to the Holy Spirit (Phil. 2:7)
- His attitude or mindset of implicit trust in His Father, by which He became His Father's servant, living as the Lamb of God that takes away the sins of the world (Phil. 2:5–8)

- His refusal to grasp for the independent exercise of His divine attributes, even one time, although He suffered the torture of Golgotha's bloody cross (Phil. 2:6)
- His determination to remain faithful to the blueprint of redemption, without changing it even one iota, no matter how tough the pressure became (Phil. 2:8; Luke 22:42), and
- The march to the Upper Room, where His followers received the gift of the Holy Spirit, experienced the birth of the church, and went out as living temples to the nations to accomplish the Lord's worldwide agenda (Acts 1:4, 8; 2:1–4; Matt. 16:18; 28:18–20; 1 Cor. 3:16–17).

These are qualities that will be glorified in Jesus Christ throughout eternity, to the point that their glow will be the sunlight in the New Jerusalem. They will also frame the worship in the celestial "city which has foundations, whose builder and maker is God" (Heb. 11:10). Abraham's search for just this city has ended.

Until the redeemed arrive at the city that is built foursquare (Rev. 21:16), the Spirit teaches through the apostle Paul what the mindset of believers must be.

> Your attitude should be the same as that of Christ Jesus: Who, being in very nature God, did not consider equality with God something to be grasped, but made himself nothing, taking the very nature of a servant, being made in human likeness. And being found in appearance as a man, he humbled himself and became obedient to death—even death on a cross!
>
> —Philippians 2:5–8

What that mindset, what Jesus Christ accomplished is truly glorious.

> Therefore God exalted him to the highest place and gave him the name that is above every name, that at the name of Jesus every knee should bow, in heaven and on earth and under the earth, and every tongue confess that Jesus Christ is Lord, to the glory of God the Father.
>
> —Philippians 2:9–11

The Servant of all is the eternal victor over all. The Lamb has triumphed "to the glory of God the Father," bringing His bride with Him (Phil. 2:11; Eph. 5:25–32; Rev. 19:7–9).

It is surely worth repeating that in anticipation of the Lord's ultimate triumph, all of God's children are to work out their "salvation with fear and trembling," knowing that God is working in them "to will and to act according to His good purpose" (Phil. 2:12–13).

No one should think laziness and indulgence will characterize life in heaven. Instead, the Holy Spirit revealed through the apostle Paul that eternal life with God will be meaningful, purposeful, and pure—a marvelous and ongoing learning experience. "In the coming ages [God will] show the incomparable riches of his grace expressed in his kindness to us in Christ Jesus" (Eph. 2:7). In the present church age, the Holy Spirit is the teacher (John 14:26). In that eternal tomorrow, the Father will invite the redeemed of the ages into His own heavenly classroom.

John heard the Lord conclude the grand apocalypse with a final blessing, a wonderful invitation, and an admonition, each of them springing from the heart of God. This exultation, too, is Trinitarian.

> "See, I am coming soon, and my reward is with me, to repay everyone according to the deeds he has done. I am the A and the Z, the Beginning and the End, the First and Last. Blessed forever are all who are washing their robes, to have the right to enter in through the gates of the city and to eat the fruit from the Tree of Life.
>
> Outside the city are those who have strayed away from God, and the sorcerers and the immoral and murderers and idolaters, and all who love to lie, and do so. I, Jesus, have sent my angel to you to tell the churches all these things.
>
> I am both David's Root and his Descendant. I am the bright Morning Star.
>
> The Spirit and the bride say, "Come." Let each one who hears them say the same, "Come." Let the thirsty one come—anyone who wants to; let him come and drink the Water of Life without charge.
>
> And I solemnly declare to everyone who reads this book: If anyone adds anything to what is written here, God shall add to him the plagues described in this book. And if anyone subtracts any part of these prophecies, God shall take away his share in the Tree of Life, and in the Holy City just described.
>
> He who has said all these things declares: Yes, I am coming soon!" Amen! Come, Lord Jesus! The grace of our Lord Jesus Christ be with you all. Amen!
>
> —Revelation 22:12–21, TLB

❧ TO CONTACT THE AUTHOR

franktunstall@cox.net

❧ NOTES

Chapter One
The Incarnation Strategy

1. Philip Schaff and Henry Wace, *Nicene and Post-Nicene Fathers of the Christian Church, Vol. 6, St. Athanasius: Select Works and Letters* (Grand Rapids, MI: Wm. B. Eerdmans Publishing Company, 1980), 36–72.

2. Ravi Zacharias, *Leadership*, accessed at www.preachingtoday.com.

3. Earl E. Cairns, *Christianity Through the Centuries* (Grand Rapids, MI: Zondervan Publishing House, 1996), 231.

4. Robert Payne, from *"Christian History"* (Issue 73), accessed at www .preachingtoday.com.

5. Henry Bettenson, ed., *Documents of the Christian Church* (London: Oxford University Press, 1963), s.v. "The Nicene Creed," 26.

6. Ibid., s.v. "The Chalcedonian Creed," 51–52.

7. Ibid., s.v. "The Nicene Creed," 26.

8. Schaff and Wace, 36–72. (For a concise study of Athanasius in his historical and cultural milieu, see Cairns, 125–130.)

9. James Malone, "From Horror to Healing," *Courier Journal* (December 17, 2004), www.preachingtoday.org.

10. Ralph Earle, *Word Meanings in the New Testament* (Kansas City, MO: Beacon Hill Press, 1986).

11. Marvin R Vincent, *Word Studies in the New Testament* (Grand Rapids, MI: Wm. B. Eerdmans Publishing Co., 1983).

12. Mark Twain, *A Connecticut Yankee in King Arthur's Court*, chapter xxix, accessed at www.preachingtoday.com.

Chapter Two
Jesus, the Servant, Living Out the Plan

1. *New York Times* (October 24, 1999), article accessed at www.preachingtoday.com.

2. Source unknown.

3. Dietrich Bonhoeffer, *Meditating on the Word*, David Mel Gracie, trans. and ed. (Lanham, MA: Cowley Publications, 1986), quoted material accessed at www .preaching today.com.

4. *Luther*, accessed at www.preachingtoday.com.

5. Terry Fisher, *Leadership*, Vol. 12, No. 2, accessed at www.preachingtoday.com.

6. Source unknown.

Chapter Three
The Colossal Effort to Break the Servant

1. C. S. Lewis, accessed at www.preachingtoday.com.

2. Dwayne K. Buhler, "The Upper Room Devotional Guide" (January–February 2008), General Board of Discipleship, 32.

3. "Lioness in Zoo Kills Man Who Invoked God," *Yahoo! News* (June 5, 2006), article accessed at www.preachingtoday.com.

4. Adapted from the Oklahoma City National Memorial and Museum.

5. C. S. Lewis, accessed at www.preachingtoday.com.

6. Mark Buchanan, "Singing in the Chains," *Christianity Today* (February 2008), 33, accessed at www.preachingtoday.com.

7. Timothy George, "Unseen Footprints," *Preaching Today* Audio (Issue 290), accessed at www.preachingtoday.com.

8. Billy Graham, *Decision* (March 2006), accessed at www.preachingtoday.com.

9. Fisher, *Leadership*, Vol. 6, No. 4, accessed at www.preachingtoday.com.

Chapter Four
Jesus—What a Savior

1. Fisher, *Leadership*, Vol. 8, No. 2, accessed at www.preachingtoday.com.

2. Johnny V. Miller, "The Great Rescue," accessed at www.preachingtoday.com.

3. Max Lucado, *3:16 Stories of Hope* (Lionsgate 2007), accessed at www.preachingtoday.com.

4. Wayne Cordeiro, "A Personal Relationship," *Preaching Today* Audio (No. 225), accessed at www.preachingtoday.com.

5. "Good Week for...All Humanity," The Week (December 8, 2006), 4, accessed at www.preachingtoday.com.

6. *Webster's New World Dictionary*, (New York City: Simon and Schuster, 1994).

7. Everett H. Harrison, *Baker's Dictionary of Theology* (Grand Rapids, MI: Baker Book House, 1960).

8. Luis Palau, "Experiencing God's Forgiveness," *Christianity Today* (Vol. 34, No. 1), article accessed at www.preachingtoday.com.

9. H. A. Ironside, *Illustrations of Bible Truth* (Chicago: Moody Press, 1945), 104–106, accessed at www.preachingtoday.com.

10. Harrison, *Baker's Dictionary of Theology*, s.v. "dikaioo."

11. Cairns, 282.

12. Ron Hutchcraft, www.hutchcraft.com (accessed January 18, 2007).

13. Lorne Sanny, "The Right Way to Respond to Authority," *Discipleship Journal* (March/April 1982), accessed at www.preachingtoday.com.

14. Anne Lamott, "Sincere Meditations," article accessed at www.preachingtoday .com.

15. Bill Bright, accessed at www.preachingtoday.com.

16. W. Wiersbe, *The Wycliffe Handbook of Preaching and Preachers*, 202, accessed at www.sermonillustrations.com.

17. William M. Greathouse, *Romans: Beacon Bible Expositions* (Kansas City, MO: Beacon Hill Press, 1975), 103, accessed at www.preachingtoday.com.

18. Rob Bell, *Velvet Elvis* (Grand Rapids, MI: Zondervan Publishing House, 2005), 151–152, accessed at www.preachingtoday.com.

Chapter Five
Jesus, What a Sanctifier

1. Raymond V. Edman, *They Found the Secret* (Grand Rapids, MI: Zondervan Publishing Company, 1984), 18–20.

2. Ed Rowell, accessed at www.preachingtoday.com.

3. Ron Jenson, "When Did 'Servant' Become a Dirty Word?" accessed at www .familylife.com.

Chapter Six
Illustrations of Set-Apart Living

1. Cordeiro, "A Personal Relationship," Preaching Today audio #25, accessed at www.preachingtoday.com.

2. "Killing the Spider," accessed at www.elbourne.org.

3. "Dr. Godbey Has It," accessed at www.sermonillustrations.com.

4. Dietrich Bonhoeffer, *The Cost of Discipleship* (New York: Simon and Schuster, 1959), 89.

5. Henri J. M. Nouwen, *Christianity Today* (Vol. 32, No. 15), accessed at www. preachingtoday.com.

6. Source unknown.

7. Bill White, accessed at www.preachingtoday.com.

8. Bonhoeffer, 89.

9. C. S. Lewis, "Building a Palace," excerpt from *Mere Christianity*, accessed at www.preachingtoday.com.

10. *The Treasure of the Sierra Madre*, Warner Brothers, 1948, accessed at www .preachingtoday.com.

11. Leonard Sweet, *Agua Church*, accessed at www.preachingtoday.com.

Chapter Seven
Forty Days with the Master-Teacher

1. Helen Keller, *The Story of My Life*, accessed at www.preachingtoday.com.

2. Luis Palau, "Brother, Your Sins Are Forgiven," *Discipleship Journal* (July/August 1983), accessed at www.preachingtoday.com.

3. Van Morris, *Beyond the Gates of Splendor*, accessed at www.preachingtoday.com.

4. Tom Tripp, *Colusa, California*, accessed at www.preachingtoday.com.

Chapter Eight
The Gift of the Holy Spirit Births the Church

1. Frank Bartleman, *The Apostolic Faith* (Vol. 1, No. 1), September 1906. The center of gravity for the outpouring of the Holy Spirit that began in 1906 was the Apostolic Faith Mission at 312 Azusa Street in Los Angeles, California. Continuous meetings were held there every day for three and one-half years, beginning in mid-April, 1906. The great work of God at Azusa Street launched the worldwide Pentecostal movement that has continued into the twenty-first century.

2. A. W. Tozer, "Power for Living," *Christianity Today* Vol. 33, no. 13 (October 16, 1977), article accessed at www.preachingtoday.com.

3. Ignatius died a martyr's death in Rome in A.D. 107. "Church History and Biography Newsletter" (January 12, 2008), accessed at www.preachingtoday.com.

4. Alan Redpath, *Christian Life* magazine, vol. 29, no. 18, accessed at www .preachingtoday.com.

5. Becky Tirabassi, *Marriage Partnership* (Vol. 11, No. 2), from *Wild Things Happen When I Pray*, accessed at www.preachingtoday.com.

6. Pastor Joel's testimony used by permission.

7. Cairns, 111, 163, 193, 209.

8. Guy P. Duffield and N. M Van Cleave, *Foundations of Pentecostal Theology* (Los Angeles, CA: L.I.F.E. Bible College, 1983), 438.

9. Cairns, 293–297.

10. Duffield and Van Cleave, 438.

11. Raymond McHenry, *Stories for the Soul* (Peabody, MA: Hendrickson Publishers, 2001), 48, accessed at www.preachingtoday.com.

12. Lee Strobel, "Meet the Jesus I Know," *Preaching Today* Audio (No. 211), accessed at www.preachingtoday.com.

Chapter Nine
The Church—Unveiling the Mystery

1. Harrison, *Baker's Dictionary of Theology*.

2. Alex Webb, "Looking for the Historical Jesus," accessed at www.preachingtoday .com.

3. Cairns, 76.

Chapter Ten
The Church—Duplicating Jesus' Ministry

1. "Where God Is Behind Bars," *Today's Christian* (September/October 2004), article accessed at www.preachingtoday.com.

2. Van Morris, accessed at www.preachingtoday.com.

3. Billy Graham, accessed at www.preachingtoday.com.

4. Duffield and Van Cleave, 9–15.

5. G. Campbell Morgan, "Giant Steps," *Christianity Today* (Vol. 40, No. 6), article accessed at www.preachingtoday.com.

Chapter Eleven
The Triumph of the Servant

1. John Huffman, "Who Are You and Where Are You Going?" Preaching Conference, 2002, accessed at www.preachingtoday.com.

2. Leith Anderson, "Can Jesus Trust Us?" *Preaching Today* Audio (No. 126), accessed at www.preachingtoday.com. Also, Cairns, 76–77, tells Polycarp's story in its historical context.

3. G. B. Caird, *A Commentary on the Revelation of St. John the Divine* (Peabody, MA: Hendrickson Publishers, 1993), 42.

4. Harrison, *Baker's Dictionary of Theology*.

5. Source unknown.

6. This magnificent moment in the Revelation became the inspiration for George Frederic Handel (1685–1759) to write the "Hallelujah Chorus" as part of *The Messiah*, his most famous oratorio, published in 1741.

7. *This We Believe: The Good News of Jesus Christ for the World*, accessed at www .preachingtoday.com.

8. Randy Alcorn, *Heaven*, www.preachingtoday.com.

Alcorn, Randy. *Heaven*. Carol Stream, IL: Tyndale House Publishers, 2004.

Arrington, French L. *Christian Doctrine: A Pentecostal Perspective*, Vol. 1–3. Cleveland, TN: Pathway Press.

Barclay, William. *Jesus as They Saw Him*. Grand Rapids, MI: Eerdmans Publishers, 1978.

Beacham, Paul F. *Questions and Answers on the Scriptures and Related Subjects*. Franklin Springs, GA: Advocate Press, 1950.

Bell, Rob. *Velvet Elvis*. Grand Rapids, MI: Zondervan Publishing House, 2005.

Bettenson, Henry, ed. *Documents of the Christian Church*. London: Oxford University Press, 1962.

Brooks, Noel. *Let There Be Life*. Franklin Springs, GA: Advocate Press, 1975.

_____. *Scriptural Holiness*. Franklin Springs, GA: Advocate Press, 1967.

Bonhoeffer, Dietrich. *The Cost of Discipleship*. New York City: Simon and Schuster. 1959.

_____. *Meditating on the Word*, translated and edited by David Mel Gracie. Lanham, MA: Cowley Publications, 1986.

Borland, James A. *Christ in the Old Testament (A Comprehensive Study of Old Testament Appearances of Christ in Human Form)*. Chicago, IL: Moody Press, 1978.

Caird, G. B. *A Commentary of the Revelation of St. John the Divine*. Peabody, MA: Hendrickson Publishers, 1993.

Cairns, Earle E. *Christianity Through the Centuries*, 3rd ed., Revised and Expanded. Grand Rapids, MI: Zondervan Publishing House, 1996.

Chadwick, W.E. *Pastoral Teaching of Paul*. Grand Rapids, MI: Kregel Publishing Company, 1984.

Duffield, Guy P., and N. M Van Cleave. *Foundations of Pentecostal Theology*. Los Angeles, CA: L.I.F.E. Bible College, 1983.

Dunn, D. G. *Jesus Remembered, Christianity in the Making*, Vol. 1. Grand Rapids, MI: William B. Eerdmans Publishing Company, 2003.

Earle, Ralph. *Word Meanings in the New Testament*. Kansas City, MO: Beacon Hill Press, 1986.

Edman, Raymond V. *They Found the Secret*. Grand Rapids, MI: Zondervan Publishing Company, 1974.

Gromacki, Robert. *The Virgin Birth: A Biblical Study of the Deity of Jesus Christ*. Grand Rapids, MI: Kregel Publishing Company, 1974.

Hardy, Edward R. *Christology of the Later Fathers*. Philadelphia: Fortress Press, 1954.

Harrison, Everett H., et. al. *Baker's Dictionary of Theology*, Grand Rapids, MI: Baker Book House, 1960.

Hendriksen, William. *Exposition of Paul's Epistle to the Romans*. Grand Rapids, MI: Baker Academic, 1981.

Hershborger, Ervin N. *Seeing Christ in the Old Testament*. Manassas, VI: Choice Books of Northern Virginia, 1999.

Hobermas, Gary R. *The Verdict of History*. Nashville, TN: Thomas Nelson Publishers, 1988.

Holmes, Rev. N. J. *The Baptism By the Spirit, the Baptism by Christ and Other Topics*, 3rd ed. Greenville, SC: Holmes Theological Seminary, 1971.

_____. *God's Provision for Holiness*, 3rd ed. Greenville, SC: Holmes Theological Seminary, 1969.

Johnston, Graham. *Preaching to a Postmodern World: A Guide to Reaching Twenty-First Century Listeners*. Grand Rapids, MI: Baker Books, 2001.

Keller, Helen. *The Story of My Life*. New York City: Doubleday Publishing Company, 1954.

King, Joseph Hillary. *Christ: God's Love Gift*. Franklin Springs, GA: Advocate Press, 1969.

_____. *From Passover to Pentecost*, 4th ed. Franklin Springs, GA: Advocate Press, 1976.

Kingsburg, Jack Dean. *Matthew: Structure, Christology, Kingdom*. Minneapolis, MN: Fortress Press, 1975.

Lahaye, Tim. *Understanding Biblical Prophecy*. Eugene, OR: Harvest House Publishers, 1998.

_____. *Rapture Under Attack*. Minneapolis, MN: Multnomah Publishers, 1998.

_____. *Revelation Unveiled*. Grand Rapids, MI: Zondervan Publishing House, 1999.

Lockyer, Herbert. *All the Messianic Prophecies of the Bible*. Grand Rapids, MI: Zondervan Publishing House, 1954.

McDowell, Josh. *The New Evidence That Demands a Verdict*. Nashville, TN: Thomas Nelson Publishing, 1999.

McHenry, Raymond. *Stories for the Soul*. Peabody, MA: Hendrickson Publishers, 2001.

Erickson, Millard J. *The Word Became Flesh*. Grand Rapids, MI: Baker Book House, 1996.

More, T.V. *The Last Days of Jesus: The Forty Days Between the Resurrection and Ascension*. Edinburg: Banner of Truth, 1981.

Muse, Dan T. *The Song of Songs*. Franklin Springs, GA: Advocate Press, 1947.

Nee, Watchman. *Normal Christian Life*. Carol Stream, IL: Tyndale House Publishers, 1977.

_____. *The Renewing of the Mind*. Anaheim, CA: Living Stream Ministry, 1998.

Nickolson, William R. *The Six Miracles of Calvary*. Chicago, IL: Moody Press, 1928.

Parrott, Les and Leslie. *Relationships*. Grand Rapids, MI: Zondervan Publishing House, 1998.

Payne, J. Barton. *A Biblical Prophecy*. Grand Rapids, MI: Baker Book House, 1973.

Pentecost, J. Dwight. *Things to Come: A Study in Biblical Eschatology*. Grand Rapids, MI: Zondervan Publishing House, 1958.

Robinson, H. Padgett. *Redemption Conceived and Revealed*. Franklin Springs, GA: Advocate Press, 1965.

Ross, Jerry L. *The Teenage Years of Jesus Christ*. Muffreesboro, TN: The Sword of the Lord Publishers, 2000.

Ryken, Philip. *The Message of Salvation*. Downers Grove, IL: InterVarsity Press, 2001.

Schaff, Philip, and Henry Wace. Nicene and Post-Nicene Fathers of the *Christian Church. St. Athanasius: Select Works and Letters*, Vol. 4. Grand Rapids, MI: Wm. B. Eerdmans Publishing Company, 1980.

Schnackenburg, Rudolf. *Jesus in the Gospels: A Biblical Christology*. Louisville, KY: Westminister John Knox Press, 2005.

Seiss, J. A. *The Apocalypse: Lectures on the Book of Revelation*. Grand Rapids, MI: Zondervan Publishing House, 1957.

Strong, James. *The Exhaustive Concordance of the Bible*. New York: Abingdon Press, 1890.

Swails, John W. *The Holy Spirit in the Messianic Age*. Franklin Springs, GA: Advocate Press, 1975.

Synan, J. A. *Christian Life in Depth*. Franklin Springs, GA: Advocate Press, n.d.

Thiessen, Henry Clarence. Revised by Vernon D. Doerksen. *Lectures in Systematic Theology*. Grand Rapids, MI: William B. Eerdmans Publishing Company, 1979.

Underwood, B. E. *The Gifts of the Spirit*. Franklin Springs, GA: Advocate Press, 1967.

_____. *Spiritual Gifts: Ministries and Manifestations*. Franklin Springs, GA: Advocate Press 1984.

Vincent, Marvin R. *Word Studies in the New Testament*. Grand Rapids, MI: Wm. B. Eerdmans Publishing Co., 1983.

Walvoord, John F. *The Rapture Question*. Grand Rapids, MI: Academie Books, 1979.

Webster's Seventh New Collegiate Dictionary. Springfield, MA: G & C Merriam Company, 1971.

Wesley, John. *A Plain Account of Christian Perfection*. London: Epworth Press, 2007.

Wiersbe, Warren. *The Wycliffe Handbook of Preaching and Preachers*. Chicago, IL: Moody Press, 1984.

Wiley, H. Orton. *Christian Theology*, Vol. 1–3. Kansas City, MO: Beacon Hill Press, 1940.

Williams, J. Floyd. *Christ Jesus—The God-Man*. Franklin Springs, GA: Advocate Press, 1975.

_____. *The Church*. Franklin Springs, GA: Advocate Press, 1973.

Witherington, Ben, III. *The Christology of Jesus*. Minneapolis, MN: Fortress Press, 1990.

Wood, Rev. J. A. *Perfect Love*. Chicago, IL: The Christian Witness Company, 1880.

Yancey, Phillip. *The Bible Jesus Read*. Grand Rapids, MI: Zondervan Publishing House, 1999.

_____. *The Jesus I Never Knew*. Grand Rapids, MI: Zondervan Publishing House, 1999.

www.Elbourne.org

www.PreachingToday.com, a division of Christianity Today, Inc.

www.SermonIllustrations.com